Forms Manual for the CPA

For Audit, Review, and Compilation of Financial Statements

Forms Manual for the CPA

For Audit, Review, and Compilation of Financial Statements

BENJAMIN NEWMAN

Adjunct Professor of Accounting
Pace University

Professor Emeritus of Accounting
New York University

A Ronald Press Publication

JOHN WILEY & SONS
New York · Chichester · Brisbane · Toronto

A RONALD PRESS PUBLICATION
Copyright © 1980 by John Wiley & Sons, Inc.

This publication is designed to provide accurate and
authoritative information in regard to the subject
matter covered. It is sold with the understanding that
the publisher is not engaged in rendering legal, accounting,
or other professional service. If legal advice or other
expert assistance is required, the services of a competent
professional person should be sought. *From a Declaration
of Principles jointly adopted by a Committee of the
American Bar Association and a Committee of Publishers.*

Library of Congress Cataloging in Publication Data:

Newman, Benjamin.
  Forms manual for the CPA: For audit, review, and
compilation of financial statements.

  "A Ronald Press publication."
  Includes index.
  1. Financial statements—Forms. 2. Accounting—
Forms. I. Title.

HF5681.B2N43   657'.3   80-17271
ISBN 0-471-05762-2

Printed in the United States of America

10 9 8 7 6 5 4 3 2 1

Preface

This book has been designed as a comprehensive reference work for use by certified public accountants in their professional practice as it relates to the audit, review, and compilation of financial statements. The individual practitioner and the small and medium-size accounting firms should find this volume especially helpful, but it is also my expectation that national and international CPA firms will find much to choose from and to use in various ways. Among those who should find much of value in this work I would also include corporate executive officers, controllers and accountants, internal auditors, and members of corporate audit committees. They have a direct and vital interest, and obviously so, in the professional engagement, the standards followed, the procedures employed, the system of internal accounting control, the financial statements, and the reports thereon.

In devising the forms to be included in this manual, I have interpreted the term broadly so as to permit me to provide a compendium of checklists, planning guides, audit program guides, internal accounting control guides, review guides, questionnaires, engagement letters, confirmation forms and letters, illustrative reports, and other forms. So that the forms presented may be perceived and their use understood in the proper professional context, I have provided explanatory and analytical commentary throughout the book. Presented either as an introduction to, or as an integral part of, a form or series of forms, the commentaries cover a wide scope that takes in authoritative references, selective summaries of official pronouncements, clarification of professional standards and responsibilities, caveats, and other analytical comments. Whether the focus of the reader will be on the forms or commentary or both will depend on the research needs at a given time.

Forms and commentary have been systematically presented in a logical framework in which topics are treated in an order corresponding, to the extent practicable, to the progression of the major stages of a professional engagement, beginning with the initial planning and ending with the review procedures and other responsibilities associated with the completion phase.

My endeavor has been to provide the reader with an original and richly detailed sourcebook that reflects a solid integration of authoritative theoretical principles and quality professional practice.

The Statements on Auditing Standards, the Statements on Standards for Accounting and Review Services, and other such officially promulgated pronouncements are referred to throughout the book. When illustrative reports or other forms are drawn from such sources, appropriate credit has been given, and I wish to express my appreciation to the AICPA for permission to use them. I have not hesitated, however, to elucidate, interpret, or expand upon these pronouncements. In doing so I have sought, with the utmost scrupulousness, to adhere to and avoid conflict with the letter and spirit of the standards, requirements, and recommendations incorporated in them. AICPA pronouncements are referred to by the code designation used in the AICPA *Professional Standards* volumes: AU, Statements on Auditing Standards; AR, Statements on Standards for Accounting and Review Services; AC, Official Accounting Pronouncements. Some of the more recent SAS and SSARS statements are also referred to by statement number.

To ensure that this book is thoroughly anchored in professional practice of the highest order, I examined the forms and related materials in current audit manuals and practice files made available to me by a number of representative CPA firms of varying size. My objective was to note the best features of the materials examined and also to use them as a kind of broad checklist so that, in the writing of the book, I would not overlook any details in program guides or other forms that a number of CPA firms may have found to be significant. In this connection, however, it is essential to stress that, except for selected AICPA items of an official nature, all forms and other materials in this book are original in design, language, and content.

This is a reference book and, as such, can be used in a variety of ways. Many sections of the volume may be read in their entirety by those researching particular topics, say, on planning, analytical review procedures, audit committees, or compilation and review of financial statements. For others, the interest may be in a specific confirmation form, an audit program, an internal control questionnaire, or an illustrative report. Some accountants may wish to note the techniques used in certain guides to document the accountant's findings and conclusions. There is much in the manual that can be easily adapted by CPA firms developing or revising their audit manuals. It can be a sourcebook, too, for staff educational and training programs.

There are also caveats to be expressed. The CPA practitioner should not use this book as a substitute for reading the official pronouncements pertinent to the matter being researched. The book does not purport to provide a complete and exhaustive coverage of a given subject through either the forms presented or the associated commentary. Interpretation of fact or principle may often be necessary. The book and its contents should be used only as a guide that must necessarily be adapted by the reader in accordance with individual judgment and circumstances and the requirements of a given engagement.

I owe a great debt to all the accounting firms that cooperated with me in my undertaking. It is with pleasure and appreciation that I list the names of these firms: Arthur Andersen & Co.; Arthur Young & Company; Alexander Grant & Company; CPA Associates (an organization of independent firms); Grayson & Bock; Main Hurdman and Cranstoun; Mason & Company; Paneth, Haber & Zimmerman; Peat, Marwick, Mitchell & Co.; Richard A. Eisner & Company; Seidman & Seidman; and Touche Ross & Co.

My indebtedness also extends to the accounting firms that have provided the AICPA special EDMAX (Educational Materials Exchange) library with copies of their in-house educational and training materials derived from their professional practice. My review of this literature was similarly helpful to me and I am grateful to the AICPA for permission to use the EDMAX library.

BENJAMIN NEWMAN

Rockville Centre, New York
August 1980

Contents

List of Forms

CHAPTER 3   INTERNAL ACCOUNTING CONTROL GUIDE

CHAPTER 4   AUDIT PROGRAM GUIDE

CHAPTER 5   CONFIRMATION FORMS AND LETTERS

CHAPTER 6   AUDITORS' REPORTS

UNQUALIFIED OPINION REPORTS

REPORTS ON UNAUDITED FINANCIAL STATEMENTS OF PUBLIC ENTITIES

Forms Manual for the CPA

**For Audit, Review, and Compilation
of Financial Statements**

CHAPTER **1**

Audit Planning

AUDITING STANDARDS, AUDITING PROCEDURES, AND ENGAGEMENT PLANNING

The first standard of field work states that "the work is to be adequately planned and assistants, if any, are to be properly supervised." The concept of planning, however, enters into all ten of the auditing standards and the related auditing concepts and procedures. The auditing standards, which are incorporated in both the Statements on Auditing Standards (AU 150) and the AICPA's Code of Professional Ethics (Rule 2-02) are presented in Figure 1-1.

Auditing standards are measures or gauges by which the quality and adequacy of the auditor's examination can be judged. They represent the underlying principles of auditing and the criteria which: (a) govern the competence and integrity of the auditor; (b) relate to the quality of the examination and of the judgment exercised by the auditor; (c) control the nature and extent of the evidence obtained by auditing procedures; and (d) ensure compliance with acceptable reporting practices.

While the auditing standards are expressed in broad terms, auditing procedures are usually more specific and represent acts to be performed by the auditor in application of the standards. The procedures entail the gathering of sufficient competent evidential matter as a basis for the expression by the auditor of an opinion on the fairness of the financial statements.

The discussion of the first standard of field work in AU 311 makes it clear that planning takes place throughout the examination. The concept embraces the development of strategies and guides for and during the various stages of an engagement—pre-engagement stage; orientation and initial planning stage following the acceptance of an engagement; study and evaluation of the system of internal accounting control; performance of auditing procedures in the various areas of audit concern; preparation of the report; audit review procedures and controls: and the final engagement completion stage.

The materials presented in this chapter are related especially to matters of audit concern in pre-engagement planning and in the early period following acceptance of an engagement. But it should be emphasized that many of the areas considered in this chapter and the procedures associated with them will be of concern throughout the engagement. Thus the guide covering related party transactions should be referred to throughout the engagement, and certain of the procedures will be performed while carrying out regular auditing procedures in other areas. Guides of this type may be categorized as Audit Planning and Control Guides to differentiate them from the Audit Program Guides. Some accountants, however, may prefer to regard the planning and control guides presented in this chapter as simply additional sections of the audit program, or perhaps even as individual and uncategorized areas of audit responsibility.

Figure 1-1
The Generally Accepted Auditing Standards

General Standards

1. The examination is to be performed by a person or persons having adequate technical training and proficiency as an auditor.
2. In all matters relating to the assignment an independence in mental attitude is to be maintained by the auditor or auditors.
3. Due professional care is to be exercised in the performance of the examination and the preparation of the report.

Standards of Field Work

1. The work is to be adequately planned and assistants, if any, are to be properly supervised.
2. There is to be a proper study and evaluation of the existing internal control as a basis for reliance thereon and for the determination of the resultant extent of the tests to which auditing procedures are to be restricted.
3. Sufficient competent evidential matter is to be obtained through inspection, observation, inquiries, and confirmations to afford a reasonable basis for an opinion regarding the financial statements under examination.

Standards of Reporting

1. The report shall state whether the financial statements are presented in accordance with generally accepted accounting principles.
2. The report shall state whether such principles have been consistently observed in the current period in relation to the preceding period.
3. Informative disclosures in the financial statements are to be regarded as reasonably adequate unless otherwise stated in the report.
4. The report shall either contain an expression of opinion regarding the financial statements, taken as a whole, or an assertion to the effect that an opinion cannot be expressed. When an overall opinion cannot be expressed, the reasons therefor should be stated. In all cases where an auditor's name is associated with financial statements, the report should contain a clear-cut indication of the character of the auditor's examination, if any, and the degree of responsibility he is taking.

PRE-ENGAGEMENT PLANNING

A pre-engagement planning and control guide is presented in Figure 1-2. Some of the procedures undertaken during the pre-engagement stage, such as identifying major trouble or risk areas or obtaining knowledge of the company's business, will be performed on a preliminary basis appropriate for that stage but should be followed through in greater depth subsequent to acceptance of the engagement. Certain of the procedures, such as the communication with predecessor auditors, will not be applicable in subsequent consecutive engagements for the same client.

Figure 1-2
Pre-Engagement Planning and Control Guide

(Entity)	(Prepared by) (Date)
(Period of financial statements)	(Reviewed by) (Date)
(Type of Engagement)	(Reviewed by) (Date)

INSTRUCTIONS

1. Each item should be initialed in the columns captioned *Performed by* or "NA" (not applicable), as appropriate.
2. If an item has been initialed as NA, an explanation should be given in the comment section appearing at the end of the Guide.
3. Working paper code numbers should be recorded, where applicable, in the "WP/ref" column.
4. Any problems, questions and clarifications, as well as the resolution of such problems and questions, should be set forth in the comment section and keyed to the specific item.

PROCEDURES

	Performed by	NA	WP ref
1. Ascertain the dimensions of the engagement and type of report and examination expected by the entity.			
2. Explain to management the relationship between the character of the examination and the type of report and opinion to be submitted, as well as the requirements of generally accepted auditing standards.			
3. Inquire as to the reasons the entity is changing auditors, obtain an overview of the nature of its relationships with predecessor auditors, and review			

prior reports taking note of the character of the examination and opinion expressed.

4. Communicate with predecessor auditors. (See Figure 1-5.)

5. Obtain business, professional, and banking references from the client and check these references as well as credit reports and other sources of information for enlightenment regarding the honesty, integrity, reputation, and general character of the company and its senior officials.

6. On a preliminary and tentative basis during the pre-engagement period of inquiry:

(a) Gain some insight as to the condition of the records and the adequacy of the system of internal accounting control.

(b) Obtain some preliminary knowledge of the company's business, its organization and characteristics. (See Figure 1-7.)

(c) Identify major trouble or risk areas requiring special attention and alertness. (See Figure 1-8.)

(d) Inquire regarding irregularities, errors, or frauds that may have occurred. (See Figure 1-10.)

(e) Make general inquiries regarding any illegal acts. (See Figure 1-11.)

(f) Determine whether the company engages in related party transactions. (See Figure 1-12.)

7. Before accepting the engagement make a judgment as to whether:

(a) We are capable of handling the engagement competently and efficiently, taking into account such matters as: time constraints; staffing requirements; our knowledge of an industry with highly specialized operating and accounting practices.

(b) We wish to accept the client, taking into account such matters as: the integrity of the client; condition and auditability of the records; inability to satisfy ourselves sufficiently regarding risk areas or other matters of potential vulnerability to us; adequacy of fees; ability to undertake major auditing procedures, such as inventory observation, on a timely basis; degree of expected client cooperation.

8. Obtain a signed engagement letter incorporating mutual understandings and obligations. (See Figures 1-3 and 1-4.)

9. Prepare a memorandum setting forth the basis for the conclusions on acceptance or rejection of the engagement and, if it is accepted, a description of any unusual or noteworthy matters.

COMMENTS

(Use this section of the Guide to comment on and clarify any problems or questions that may have arisen. The manner in which matters

Figure 1-3
Usual Content of Engagement Letters for an
Audit Engagement—A Checklist Guide

1.   Name and address of the client. The individual addressed should be the official given the authority by the company to retain the auditor— chairman of the board of directors, audit committee chairman, or chief executive.

2.   Specification as to the financial statements to be examined, period covered, and fiscal closing dates.

3.   Scope of examination and any limitations or restrictions imposed by the client.

4.   Type of report and opinion to be rendered—short-form or long-form; unqualified, qualified, or disclaimer; and circumstances that might preclude an unqualified opinion or that might call for an adverse opinion.

5.   Assertion that the examination provides no assurance that illegal acts of the company or its personnel will be detected.

6.   A statement that the examination may not in fact uncover material errors or irregularities although their detection would be one of the objectives of the examination.

7.   A statement that the ordinary examination is not designed to uncover minor errors, irregularities, or fraudulent acts.

8.   An indication that the financial statements and the underlying records and supporting documents are the representations of management, that the company assumes full responsibility for their integrity and fairness, and that representation letters will be requested.

9.   The cooperation to be afforded by the client in the preparation of working papers, availability of its staff, and so on.

10.   The fact that significant matters will be called to the attention of the company, such as material weaknesses in internal accounting control, condition of the records, and indications of irregularity.

11.   Tax, management consulting, and other services to be rendered by the auditors.

12.   Provisions as to fees and billing arrangements.

Figure 1-4
Engagement Letter for an Audit Engagement

(Accountant's Letterhead)

(Date)

(Appropriate Salutation)

It is a source of satisfaction to us that you have engaged our firm to perform certain professional services for the Client Corporation whose headquarters are at the address noted above. This letter will confirm our mutual understanding of the terms of the engagement and the nature of the services to be provided.

We will examine the consolidated balance sheet of the Client Corporation and its subsidiaries, Subsidiary A Corporation, Subsidiary B Co., Inc., and Subsidiary C Corporation, as of June 30, 19.., and the related consolidated statements of income, retained earnings, and changes in financial position for the year then ended. Our examination will be conducted in accordance with generally accepted auditing standards and will include such tests of the accounting records and such other auditing procedures as we consider necessary in the circumstances.

A short-form report will be submitted following the completion of our examination, in which we express our opinion regarding the fairness of the financial statements taken as a whole. Circumstances may arise that may preclude an unqualified opinion and, in accordance with the requirements of generally accepted auditing standards, may call for a qualified opinion, an adverse opinion, or a disclaimer. Such circumstances will be discussed with you as soon as they become evident.

An examination of financial statements in accordance with generally accepted auditing standards includes a review of the system of internal accounting control and is conducted by testing and sampling the records and supporting data. A detailed examination of the data and transactions, therefore, is not contemplated. Thus, while our examination will take into account the possibility that errors and irregularities may exist that can materially affect the financial statements, it must be understood that the examination carries the basic limitation that such material errors and irregularities may not in fact be detected. This basic limitation is especially applicable to errors, fraud, defalcations, and similar irregularities that do not materially affect the financial statements, as well as to illegal acts, inasmuch as the examination conducted in accordance with generally accepted auditing standards is not designed to provide assurance that they will be detected. You will be informed, however, of any abnormal or questionable matters that may come to our attention. Similarly, we will communicate to you information regarding material weaknesses in internal accounting control that we become aware of during our examination.

As required by generally accepted auditing standards, during the examination we will request, and you will submit to us, signed written representations containing a variety of assertions relating to the fairness of the financial statements, including the basic acknowledgment of the company's responsibility for the fairness of those financial statements in conformity with generally accepted accounting principles.

You have assured us of your cooperation in facilitating the progress of our examination and, more specifically, in furnishing us upon request with schedules, analyses, reconciliations and other such working papers, a tentative listing of which is included in an accompanying letter.

Our services also include a review of the Federal income tax returns and of the income tax returns for the following states: . . . .

Our fees for these services are based on our regular standard hourly (or per diem) rates, as follows . . . . Our invoices, which will also include out-of-pocket costs, will be submitted for payment on a monthly basis as the engagement progresses.

If the terms of this letter meet with your approval, please sign one copy in the space provided and return it for our files. We look forward to a pleasant association and the opportunity to render the services contemplated by this engagement.

Sincerely,

John A. Accountant & Co.

_____

Partner, Walter P. Brown

_____

Date_____

We are in agreement with the terms of this letter.

Client Corporation

_____

William E. Smith, President

PREDECESSOR AND SUCCESSOR AUDITORS

Before accepting an engagement, the auditor should undertake the very necessary procedure of communicating with the predecessor auditor to obtain information regarding the reason for the change in accountants. Such information may disclose disagreements between auditor and client involving accounting treatment, auditing restrictions, and even matters that reflect on the client's integrity. AU 315, "Communications Between Predecessor and Successor Auditors" provides authoritative guidance on the subject. Figure 1-5 is a checklist of the procedures to be followed and of matters for the successor auditor to be aware of.

Figure 1-5
Communicating With Predecessor Auditor—
A Checklist Guide

	Peformed BY	NA	WP ref

1. Obtain from the client an explanation of the reason for the change in auditors. During the discussion, inquire specifically as to any disagreements and request permission to contact former auditor. Such contact and inquiry is a necessary procedure. If permission is refused or limited, determine the reasons and consider whether the engagement should be accepted.

2. Make general and specific inquiries of the predecessor auditor regarding the reasons for the change in auditors and any circumstances that might affect acceptance of the engagement. These could relate to management's integrity; disagreements as to accounting principles, audit scope, or other important matters; or misunderstandings.

3. The former auditor should normally be expected to respond promptly. But if, for reasons of litigation or otherwise, his response is not complete, he is expected to indicate that it is limited. Evaluate his explanations, including, if applicable, any limitation in response, and consider whether the engagement should not be accepted.

4. Request the client's authorization for the former accountant to permit a review of the working papers and to provide copies if necessary. Such a request and review will usually take place after acceptance of the engagement. It is understood that the working papers are the property of the predecessor auditor who may, for valid reasons, not permit such a review.

5.   Consider the impact of any such refusal on our auditing procedures relating to opening balances and transactions in prior periods.

6.   Make inquiries (either before or after accepting engagement, as appropriate) of the former auditor regarding any matters that may facilitate or affect the examination, including character and integrity of the client, audit problems, critical audit areas, special accounting problems, and industry or business peculiarities.

7.   If it is later determined that the financial statements included in the prior auditor's report require revision, the client should be asked to arrange a three-party meeting to discuss and resolve the matter. Our attorneys should be consulted in the event the client refuses to make the arrangement or the results of the discussion are not satisfactory.

8.   Prepare a memorandum covering the contacts with predecessor auditors, any significant information obtained, and relevant conclusions.

AUDIT PLANNING

Following consummation of the agreement with the client that the engagement is to be undertaken, the auditor should make appropriate preparations for the examination. This audit planning phase will encompass updating and expanding the information obtained on a preliminary basis during pre-engagement planning, undertaking procedures of a broad nature designed to provide evidential matter as well as additional information regarding the corporate environment, and developing an overall strategy for the expected conduct and scope of the audit, taking into account the client's individual circumstances. An audit planning and control guide is presented in Figure 1-6.

Figure 1-6
Audit Planning and Control Guide

(Note: For illustrative prefatory material, including identification of client, preparer, reviewer, and use of comment section appended to Guide, see Figure 1-2.)

	Performed by	NA	W/P ref
1. Review provisions of signed engagement letter. Review Pre-Engagement Planning and Control Guide (Figure 1-2) and related memorandum.			
2. Review working papers reporting results of communication with predecessor auditor (Figure 1-5).			
3. Review correspondence and tax files in our office, noting significant matters covered in all correspondence pertaining to the client accumulated since the last examination.			
4. Review permanent file and last year's working papers and financial statements and take note especially of such matters as material or unusual adjusting entries, risk or trouble areas, internal control deficiencies and recommendations, and auditing procedures and results.			
5. Arrange audit planning conferences with client's officers and personnel. A number of items listed below will also be covered at these conferences, including updating essential information, obtaining important documents and other materials, and audit scope and arrangements.			
6. Meet with the audit committee of the board of directors for a discussion of the scope and character of the examination and of any special problems.			
7. Update information (and ascertain whether significant changes have taken			

place since the last examination) with respect to the client's business (Figure 1-7), risk areas (Figure 1-8), related party transactions (Figure 1-12), and so on, and consider the impact of such data on the scope and character of the examination.

8. Consider the effect on the examination and report of accounting and auditing pronouncements issued during the past year.

9. Review with management changes that have occurred in the system of internal accounting control since the last examination and the disposition of recommendations and comments made in prior year's report on material weaknesses in internal accounting control.

10. Obtain and review copies of basic documents and materials, including:

(a) Copies of financial statements forming the subject of the current examination.

(b) Minutes of meetings of stockholders, board of directors, and executive or operating committees.

(c) Documents relating to corporate organization.

(d) Interim reports.

(e) Reports of internal audit department.

(f) Accounting, systems, organization and other such manuals, charts, flowcharts, and similar descriptive materials covering accounting policies and procedures, flow of transactions, information systems, and system of internal accounting control.

(g) Updated listing of office and plant locations.

(h) Copies of significant contracts, agreements, and pension and other plans.

11. Prepare a timetable for the audit work in general, incorporating the dates when certain actions or procedures are expected to be undertaken, like observation of inventory count, confirmations, or surprise inspections or counts, and taking into account target date for submission of the report.

12. Establish criteria for gauging materiality with respect to both audit tests and accounting matters including informative disclosures.

13. Arrange a conference with appropriate personnel regarding the inventory count to discuss preparatory arrangements, controls, and coordination with the auditor's observation and test-count procedures.

14. Obtain, in a designated format, copies of completed trial balances, schedules, analyses, reconciliations, and other working papers previously requested either in a letter accompanying the engagement letter or in a subsequent planning conference. (See Figures 1-13, 1-14, and 1-15.)

15. Assign assistants, meet with them, and provide them with a full understanding of the client and its environment and of the problems or trouble areas that exist or are likely to be encountered during the engagement.

16.   Consider whether the services of specialists—within our own firm, on the client's staff, or outside consultants—will be required during the examination.

17.   Undertake the procedures described in Figure 1-9, designed to provide an orientation-type review and preliminary assessment relating to the following and their interrelationships: accounting books and records and supporting files and documents; transaction flow and cycles and supporting systems; and internal accounting control environment.

18.   Make a tentative judgment regarding the auditability of the financial statements.

19.   Consider whether the findings of the orientation-type review of the system of internal accounting control warrant undertaking a fuller study of the system. Such a study would include acquiring a more detailed knowledge of the system and undertaking auditing procedures (compliance testing) for assurance that the system is actually functioning as intended.

20.   Prepare audit plan (subject to modification as circumstances warrant during the progress of the examination), including objectives, procedures and audit scope relating to both compliance and substantive testing.

21.   Prepare a detailed budget for the engagement.

22.   Meet with our own partners and other personnel as appropriate: partner in charge for consultation approvals, industry or other specialists as necessary, former partner and manager on engagement to ensure meaningful continuity.

KNOWLEDGE OF THE ENTITY'S BUSINESS

A knowledge of the entity's business should be obtained by the auditor as a prerequisite for the planning and conduct of an examination. Presented in Figure 1-7 are the objectives in gaining such knowledge, selected matters to be covered, and sources of information. An informative memorandum on the subject should be prepared and retained for reference during the examination. It should be updated for use on subsequent engagements.

Figure 1-7
Understanding the Client's Business—
A Checklist Guide

Objectives in Gaining Such Knowledge

1. To identify questionable or risk areas.
2. To gain an understanding of the internal control environment and thus facilitate the review of internal accounting control.
3. To utilize a knowledge of the business and economic environment, including trends and types of business transactions and arrangements, as a basis for understanding and evaluating evidential matter and for undertaking appropriate auditing procedures.
4. To assess the accounting systems, conditions, and controls under which business transactions and events are reflected in the production and recording of accounting data.
5. To better understand company accounting policies and practices when making necessary audit judgments, as in evaluating the reasonableness of estimates such as for doubtful accounts, depreciation, inventory valuation, and contingencies.
6. To permit a more informed judgment as to the reasonableness of the client's explanations and representations and their consistency with the realities of the business and its economic environment.

Sources of Information

1. Industry and trade association publications.
2. Security investment services, credit reports, and magazine and newspaper articles.
3. Industry audit guides and other such publications of the AICPA and other professional societies.
4. Prior experience with the entity or other companies in the industry.
5. Audit working papers of prior years of an ongoing client or those of predecessor auditors.
6. Financial statements of companies in the industry.
7. Inquiries of company officers and personnel.
8. Observations and inspections undertaken during the examination.
9. Review of company's annual and interim financial statements for current and prior years.
10. Actual review of the company's systems and procedures, the system of internal accounting control, and associated company charts, manuals, minutes, and so on.

Matters to be Covered

1. *Industry.* Economic conditions; government regulations; financial trends and ratios; relative standing in the industry; changes in technology, products, marketing, and so on.

2. *Corporate and financial structure and policies.* Capital stock, and whether publicly or closely held; long-term debt; ownership of stock by officers and employees; changes in ownership; major stockholders; dividend policy; earnings and cash flow; ability to meet short- and long-term obligatoins; banking relationships; investment policies.

3. *Corporate divisions.* Subsidiary companies and operating divisions and departments and their locations.

4. *Organization and personnel.* Directors, officers and key management personnel; executive committees; compensation, pension and other plans; union contracts; numbers of personnel in various categories.

5. *Corporate goals.* Long- and short-term plans for meeting corporate goals as to products, sales, diversification, profits, and so on; formalization of plans; capability of achieving goals; past successes and failures.

6. *Production and facilities.* Products and services; plant capacities and actual production; warehousing; types of production problems; processing techniques; obsolescence and perishability of products; new product development and research and development policies; age and condition of equipment and degree of automation; capital budgets; insurance coverage; ownership versus leasing of properties and equipment; volume and type of materials produced; major suppliers; availability of materials.

7. *Sales and marketing.* Methods of selling (salesmen, consignments, franchised dealers, brokers, direct mail, wholesalers, retailers, etc.); commission arrangements; freight; size and geographical location of markets; numbers and types of customers; dependence on small number of major customers; recent gains or losses of important customers; sales trends in products, volume, and prices; profit margins by product lines; intercompany sales; credit, collection, discount, and sales return policies; bad debt experience; warranties and customer services.

8. *Accounting policies and controls.* Accounting principles, methods and practices followed, especially in specialized matters; methods

of promulgating company policies; type and condition of records; information systems; cost accounting; documentation of policies and controls (minutes, budgets, forecasts, manuals, charts, memoranda, and, in general, written documentation); periodic reporting; detailed subsidiary records for assets and other accounts; system of authorization and approval; monitoring techniques; internal auditing.

9. *Other matters.* Related party transactions; adequacy of insurance; specialized income tax problems; results of revenue agents' examinations; lawsuits and other contingencies; involvement with regulatory agencies; names of attorneys for the company.

IDENTIFYING MAJOR TROUBLE OR RISK AREAS

The task of identifying the entity's critical areas that require an additional measure of due care and alertness by the auditor begins, although on a preliminary basis, during the pre-engagement planning stage. That effort must be expanded during the later audit planning stage and, in fact, carried on throughout the engagement. A failure to exercise vigilance in identifying trouble areas can adversely affect the scope and proper focus of the examination and can result in considerable professional risk for the auditor. Once the problem areas are identified, they must be evaluated within a wide range of options, including rejection or modification of the original engagement, or simply the exercise of greater vigilance along with appropriate adjustments in the scope of the examination.

A questionnaire checklist of major risk conditions is presented in Figure 1-8 under several classifications, but these categories are often interrelated.

Figure 1-8
Risk Areas Questionnaire Guide

INSTRUCTIONS

1. The auditor's initials should be recorded in either the "yes" or "no" column.

2. All "yes" responses should be explained in the comment section appended to the Guide.

3. Support for the conclusions reached should be recorded in the working papers to which appropriate reference should be made in the "W/P ref" column.

4. A memorandum should be prepared summarizing the findings and specifying the nature of their impact on the scope of the examination.

QUESTIONNAIRE

	Yes	No	W/P ref

Solvency, Profitability, and Asset Realization

1. Are working capital and liquid assets insufficient to enable the company to meet its obligations and carry on its regular operations?

2. Is the company having difficulty in increasing lines of credit or raising capital through stock issuances or long-term borrowing?

3. Is the industry in general experiencing a severe decline in sales volume and profits?

4. Has the company been experiencing substantial declines in actual or expected volume or profits?

5. Does the company have high or excessive fixed costs?

6. Is unused plant capacity excessive?

7. Have major developments taken

place that are new to the client or are speculative in nature—products, ventures, acquisitions, and so on?

8. Has there been a notably rapid expansion of the business—sales volume, product lines, plant acquisitons, and so on?

9. Are there substantial past-due receivable accounts?

10. Is the bad debt history of the client unfavorable?

11. Are uncollectible accounts being carried on the books?

12. Do inventories require material write-downs because of obsolescence, shortages, or market declines?

Contingencies and Commitments

13. Is present or expected litigation material in amount or otherwise significant?

14. Is the company burdened with unfavorable commitments, material or unusual in nature, relating to such matters as long-term leases, merchandise purchases or sales, and warranties and guarantees?

15. Is there undue dependence on a single or few products and are these products vulnerable because of government regulation or shifts in style or demand?

16. Do a few customers account for a large percentage of sales volume?

17. Are the operations of the company likely to be seriously impaired by such occurrences as actions by foreign governments, government regulation, loss of present sources of raw material and other inventories, and air pollution and other environmental controls?

18. Are the company's products unprotected by patents or otherwise as appropriate in the circumstances?

19. Is a material proportion of sales volume attributable to consignment sales?

Management and Personnel

20. Are there any indications that management may lack integrity?

21. Does management seem to be oriented in the direction of overstating asset values, profits, and financial condition? Or a comparable understatement for tax purposes or other reasons?

22. Has there been considerable turnover in senior management positions?

23. Does management have a good reputation in the industry for competence and integrity?

24. Is the company or its personnel engaged in related party transactions?

25. Have any fraud situations or illegal acts been uncovered or investigated by the company?

Accounting and Auditing

26. Are there any problems affecting the auditability of the financial statements, such as deficient or missing records or documents or serious weaknesses in the internal accounting control system?

27. Has management failed to correct material weaknesses in internal accounting controls that can in fact be corrected?

28. Is the client's accounting function seriously understaffed or in a state of constant crisis?

29. Does it appear that the management may place restrictions on the scope or conduct of the auditor's examination?

30. Are there signs that management may not be giving the auditors their fullest cooperation?

31. Does the company fail to maintain well-kept perpetual inventory records?

32. Do major or unusual accounting, valuation, or going-concern problems exist regarding long-term construction type contracts, allowance for doubtful accounts, inventory pricing, timing of revenue realization, other accounts, or the company as a whole?

33. Do any obstacles exist to the timely undertaking of auditing procedures, including observation of inventory count and confirmation with customers and others?

34. Are specialist services required by the auditor as an aid in the conduct of the examination, and in what areas?

35. Is the internal audit function either nonexistent or inadequate?

36. Is the auditor's report to be used as a basis for seeking or reviewing a loan, sale of the business, or other special or immediate purpose?

INITIAL REVIEW OF ACCOUNTING RECORDS
AND INTERNAL ACCOUNTING CONTROLS

Before accepting an engagement, the auditor will have acquired, as part of the pre-engagement planning process, some insight on a very preliminary, limited, and tentative basis, into the condition of the accounting records and the adequacy of the system of internal accounting control. This insight will have been gained mainly by general inquiries and a relatively cursory scanning of some of the company's records and documents.

Following the acceptance of the engagement and before an audit plan can be prepared on an informed basis, the auditor must become more familiar with, and gain greater understanding of, the accounting records maintained by the client, their tie-in with the transaction cycles, the sources used as a basis for entry in the accounts, and the nature and quality of the internal accounting controls. The audit plan can then be devised and will reflect at least an initial determination of whether the audit programs are to provide for a further study of the system of internal accounting control and for compliance testing of the system, or whether substantive testing is to be employed exclusively in the absence of any reliance on the internal control system.

The procedures to be undertaken in an orientation-type review of accounting records and internal accounting controls are listed in Figure 1-9. The relative place of this type of review within the total framework of the auditor's general responsibilities for a review of the system of internal control under Auditing Standard of Field Work No. 2 is shown in Figure 2-14. But see the explanatory section relating to Figure 2-15 in which caution is expressed that the various stages of review of the internal accounting control system do not necessarily conform to a rigid sequence. Many auditors, for example, will have undertaken an orientation-type review before accepting an engagement. Moreover, such a review is not usually necesary on a repeat engagement inasmuch as the auditor is already familiar with the system, at least as it prevailed during the prior engagement, and will be undertaking a follow-up study for the current engagement with the focus on changes in the system.

The orientation-type review presented in Figure 1-9 can appropriately be considered as an introductory section of any one of the following master guides: Audit Planning and Control Guide, Internal Accounting Control Guide or Audit Program Guide. The choice of guide with which it would be associated would depend on the type of guides used by the accountant in his audit practice and his judgment as to the most convenient and practical placement.

Figure 1-9
Orientation Review of Accounting Records and Internal Accounting Controls—A Program Guide

AUDIT OBJECTIVES

1. To learn precisely what books and records are maintained by the client, and to identify the documentary support for accounting entries.

2. To identify transaction cycles and to relate those cycles to the accounting records.

3. To gain sufficient knowledge and understanding of the internal accounting control system to form at least a preliminary judgment of whether or not a more detailed study of the system is to be undertaken.

AUDITING PROCEDURES

	Performed by	NA	W/P ref
1. Review memorandum prepared on the client's business (See Figure 1-7.)			
2. Obtain from the client a complete listing of all accounting books and records, including general, subsidiary and special ledgers, and books of original entry. The listing should show: name of book or record; location; person responsible for selecting input and/or recording entries; and supervisor.			
3. Scan the books and records to gain familiarity with them and note sources of book entry, types of transactions recorded, and character of supporting evidence.			
4. Ascertain where the various correspondence, voucher, and other files are located.			
5. Obtain and review copies of all written materials pertinent to a review of internal accounting control, such as organization charts, systems and ac-			

counting manuals, chart of accounts, selected job descriptions, policy statements, and written instructions.

6. Take a tour (with assistants) through the client's offices, departments, and plant for appropriate introductions to key personnel and to gain some initial familiarity with the productive process, flow and storage of inventories, departmental structure, visible internal control features like time clocks and guards, and other such pertinent matters.

7. Determine the best approach to the study of the internal accounting control system—transaction cycle (revenue cycle, expenditure cycle, etc.), function, or department, or any meaningful combination. The choice of approach will depend on how management itself conceived of and designed the control system, the nature of the business, the actual operations of the company, and other such factors.

8. Obtain basic information regarding the broad general internal accounting control environment of the company by inquiries, observation, review of charts, manuals, and so on, received from the client and by undertaking the other procedures mentioned, and complete the general segment of the internal control questionnaire (see Figure 3-3.) (The general internal accounting control environment takes in such features as the presence of an audit committee and an internal audit function, clear statements of policy, emphasis upon authorization and approval of transactions, sound organizational structure, and periodic monitoring of prescribed policies and controls.)

9. For each of the transaction cycles, select several transactions and trace the documentary evidence through the various stages from their origin (such as a requisition form) to the final processing (such as paid and approved voucher), and then to their recording in the accounting records. At each point, take note of the existence of controls or their absence, as well as of the quality of supporting evidence. At the conclusion of this audit step, some contact should have been made with all books of original entry to ensure that all have been accounted for.

10. Prepare descriptions of the client's accounting and control systems and related transaction flows, using any appropriate or convenient method such as flow charts, narrative descriptions, annotated questionnaires, or any combination of them.

11. Prepare a memorandum setting forth the findings of the orientation-type review and preliminary assessments and conclusions regarding the adequacy of the system of internal accounting control. The memorandum should take in the general internal accounting control environment as well as specific accounting control areas, and should include comments as to both strengths and weaknesses. A conclusion should be expressed as to whether sufficient tentative reliance can be placed on the internal accounting controls in designated areas to warrant undertaking a more detailed study of the controls, including compliance testing.

RESPONSIBILITY FOR DETECTION OF
ERRORS OR IRREGULARITIES

Guidance on the subject of the independent auditor's responsibility for the detection of errors or irregularities in an examination made in accordance with generally accepted auditing standards is provided in AU 327.

It is management's responsibility to establish and monitor effective internal accounting controls to provide reasonable assurance that the financial statements are not materially misstated because of errors or irregularities. In expressing his opinion on the financial statements, the auditor recognizes that errors or irregularities may have a material effect on the financial statements. Consequently, he has the responsibility to be alert to this possibility in employing the usual auditing procedures. The focus and concern of the audit, however, is not directed to uncovering minor errors or irregularities, although if they do come to the auditor's attention while undertaking the usual auditing procedures—which may sometimes bring them to light—they should be reported to the appropriate level of management.

It must be recognized that there are basic limitations relating to both the auditor's examination and the client that create the inherent risk that material errors or irregularities may not in fact be detected by the auditor. Among the limitations are: the use of testing and sampling and the impracticability of undertaking a detailed examination; difficulty in detecting unrecorded transactions, especially those involving unexpected or unknown parties or sources; management override of internal accounting controls; collusion within the client's organization or between client personnel and third parties; falsified documents; and forgery.

Definitions of terms and audit objectives and audit procedures for the detection of errors or irregularities are presented in Figure 1-10.

Figure 1-10
Detection of Errors or Irregularities—
A Planning and Control Guide

DEFINITIONS

Errors are unintentional mistakes in the financial statements and underlying records due to mathematical or clerical lapses, misinterpretation of facts, lack of knowledge, oversights, and unwitting misapplications of accounting principles.

Irregularities are improper acts deliberately perpetrated. When they involve intentional distortions of the financial statements by management, the term *management fraud* is sometimes used. The term *defalcation* is used in referring to misappropriation of assets.

AUDIT OBJECTIVES

1. To plan the examination to search for errors or irregularities that may have a material effect on the financial statements. However, the search does not ordinarily require extended procedures beyond those customarily employed in the conduct of the usual examination.

2. To be alert during the regular examination to the possibility that minor errors or irregularities may nevertheless have material significance for other aspects of the examination.

3. To evaluate the internal accounting controls in terms of effectiveness in preventing or detecting errors and irregularities.

AUDITING PROCEDURES

	Performed by	NA	W/P ref
1. In conducting the usual examination, maintain an attitude of vigilance and skepticism. However, recognize that this is a very delicate area calling for utmost discretion and caution and requiring that approval for any special procedures or contacts be obtained from the engagement partner.			
2. Make inquiries of management and also of the audit committee about			

their knowledge or suspicions regarding the commission of errors or irregularities.

3. Include a provision on the subject in the representation letter.

4. In reviewing the system of internal accounting control, evaluate its effectiveness in the various areas in preventing or uncovering errors or irregularities.

5. Scrutinize transactions relating to major trouble or risk areas.

6. Review internal audit reports that may have a bearing on the subject.

7. If the examination leads to the belief that material errors or irregularities may exist, discuss the matter and the question of extended investigation with an appropriate level of management that is at least one level above that of the people involved.

8. Obtain sufficient evidential matter to determine if in fact material errors or irregularities have taken place, the amounts involved and other important data, and the impact on the financial statements and report.

9. Consult periodically with the board of directors or audit committee and, at the appropriate time, communicate findings in writing.

10. Consider the implications for the examination and report that the existence of any material irregularities may have for reliance on the books, records and supporting evidence, internal control system, and management's integrity and representations.

11. If the financial statements have not been properly adjusted or disclosures made, where required, in connection with material errors or irregularities, issue a qualified or adverse opinion.

12. If there is indication of the existence of errors or irregularities but uncertainty about whether they may materially affect the financial statements, then, depending on the circumstance, qualify or disclaim an opinion or consider withdrawing from the engagement.

13. If the uncertainty regarding existence or impact of errors or irregularities results from management's restrictions on the scope of examination, disclaim an opinion and consider withdrawing from the engagement.

14. In the event that irregularities or errors do not materially affect the financial statements, refer such matters to the appropriate personnel at least one management level above those involved, with the recommendation that the circumstances be adequately investigated. Review subsequent findings for additional assurance that the matters in question are in fact insignificant in nature and impact.

ILLEGAL ACTS BY CLIENTS

Guidelines for the correct conduct of an auditor when he becomes aware of illegal acts committed by the client are provided in AU 328. For this purpose, the term *illegal acts* encompasses illegal political contributions, bribes, and other violations of laws and regulations.

The caution is expressed in AU 328 that the auditor's examination cannot be expected to provide assurance that illegal acts will be uncovered. The inherent limitations of an audit that account for this inability to provide such assurance are similar to those that account for the risk that material errors or irregularities may not be detected. In addition, the determination of whether an act is or may be illegal is beyond the professional competence of an auditor. Moreover, the difficulties in detection and identification of an illegal act increase the farther away it is from transactions and events reflected in the financial statements. The burden of responsibility for the noncommission, prevention, and detection of illegal acts rests with the client, whose internal control system should be designed to reflect that responsibility. The auditor's responsibilities and procedures relating to illegal acts by the client company and its personnel are described in Figure 1-11.

Figure 1-11
Illegal Acts: Identification, Auditing Procedures, and Reporting— A Planning and Control Guide

	Performed by	NA	W/P ref
Identification of Illegal Acts			
1. Be aware during regular review of internal control and the usual audit tests that illegal acts may have occurred that might have a material impact on the financial statements.			
2. Make inquiries of management about its own involvement or suspicions regarding the commission of illegal acts. Bear in mind that illegal acts may have been unwittingly committed.			
3. Include a provision on the subject in the representation letter.			
4. In reviewing the system of internal accounting control, inquire specifically regarding controls established by the company for the prevention or detection of illegal acts, and review those controls for effectiveness. Such controls might include promulgating a clear policy on the subject and obtaining periodic representations from officers and key personnel.			
5. Scrutinize the following types of transactions, actions, or events that may raise questions regarding illegal acts: unauthorized, improperly recorded, omitted from the records, not recorded in a timely manner, or whose business purpose is unusual, unreasonable, or otherwise questionable.			
6. In taking note of laws and regulations that directly affect the financial statements, like tax laws or those relating to revenue accrued under government contracts, consider the possibility of violations.			

7. When reviewing the area of contingencies and past and current litigation, and in making appropriate inquiries of client and client's attorneys, consider also any implications pertaining to illegal acts.

8. Consider the susceptibility of the company, because of its industry, products, location, and so on, to government laws, regulations, investigations, or enforcement proceedings in matters such as occupational safety and health, food and drugs, environmental standards, antitrust, pricing regulations, and international trade. Make appropriate inquiries and ascertain whether government investigations or other actions have occurred or are pending.

9. Review newspaper reports or other literature publicly available relating to the company or its senior officers.

10. Review internal audit reports that may have a bearing on the subject.

11. Include the subject of illegal acts among the matters to be discussed with the audit committee of the board of directors.

Procedures Following Identification

12. If the fact that an illegal act has been committed comes to our attention, report the circumstances and discuss the situation with a senior officer or, if indicated, with the audit committee or board of directors. Discussion should deal with financial impact (fines, penalties, damages, and the like), remedial actions, financial statement adjustments and disclosures, reporting to other authorities, and effect on auditor's report.

13. Obtain sufficient documentation and other evidential matter and make inquiries of client's legal counsel or other professionals or specialists to obtain an adequate understanding of the situation and its financial impact.

14. Consider the impact on the credibility and integrity of management and its representations and on reliance on the system of internal accounting control.

15. Communicate with the company's attorneys for information clarifying or confirming the question of illegality and the legal and financial dimensions of the problem.

16. Determine if loss contingencies in addition to fines and penalties have arisen as a consequence of the commission of such acts. These might include threat of expropriation of assets or discontinuance of operations in a foreign country, lawsuits, unfavorable changes in important business relationships, and cutoff of revenue sources.

Impact on Report and Opinion

17. If we are unable to obtain sufficient competent evidential matter (e.g., lack of documentation or refusal of client's attorney to advise on

whether an act of apparently material consequence is illegal) to corroborate a reasonable belief that an illegal act of significant import has been committed, or to ascertain the financial dimensions of an illegal act, qualify or disclaim an opinion because of scope limitation.

18.   If the loss contingency associated with illegal acts, alone or in the aggregate, is material in amount and has not been properly accounted for or disclosed in the financial statements, express either a qualified opinion or an adverse opinion because of the departure from generally accepted accounting principles.

19.   If the effects of an illegal act on the financial statements cannot be reasonably estimated and the situation falls under the reporting rules relating to material uncertainties, consider issuing a qualified opinion ("subject to") or a disclaimer.

20.   If the client refuses to accept our report and opinion as modified in accordance with these principles, we should withdraw from the engagement, consult with our legal counsel, and send a written communication to the board of directors explaining the reasons for the withdrawal.

Other Actions

21.   If management or the board of directors or its audit committee, with respect to illegal acts that are material or immaterial in nature, do not take appropriate action (e.g., adjustments or disclosures in the statements, remedial steps, disclosures in documents such as proxy statements, etc.), we should consider, after consulting with counsel, withdrawing from the current engagement and disassociating ourselves from any future relationship with the client.

22.   Although notification, where indicated, to outside parties regarding the illegal acts is management's responsibility, and we are under no obligation to notify such parties, we should consult with legal counsel regarding additional actions to be taken by us apart from withdrawal from the engagement.

23.   If illegal acts have come to our attention during the engagement, prepare an informative memorandum for our working papers.

RELATED PARTY TRANSACTIONS

The auditor must be aware of the possibility that related trans-actions may have taken place that can have a material bearing on the financial statements and on disclosure requirements. However, an examination conducted in accordance with generally accepted auditing standards does not provide assurance that such transac-tions will be uncovered. Some of the procedures undertaken should be specifically directed to discovering and verifying the nature and significance of related party transactions, but many other proce-dures employed in other areas are also pertinent to that objective. The auditing procedures that may be employed in this area as well as other related considerations are presented in Figure 1-12. They are based on AU 335. Much of the information and the guidance and procedures reflected in Figure 1-12 may also be applied during the engagement to the examination of unusual transactions in gen-eral, even though many related party transactions may not at all be unusual in character.

Figure 1-12
Related Party Transactions—
A Planning and Control Guide

DEFINITIONS

1. The term *related parties* as defined in AU 335 refers to: the reporting entity; its affiliates; principal owners, management, and members of their immediate families; entities for which investments are accounted for by the equity method; and any other party dealing with the entity when either one or any other entity can significantly adversely influence the management or policies of the transacting parties.

2. An *affiliate* is a party that directly or indirectly, through one or more intermediaries, controls, is controlled by, or is under common control with, another party. "Control" means basically the power to influence management and policies of another party.

3. A *principal owner* is the actual or beneficial owner of more than 10% of the voting interests of the reporting entity.

4. The term *management* in this context means any person having the authority to establish policies and make decisions to achieve the entity's objectives. Normally included are members of boards of directors, the president and other senior officers including officers in charge of major business functions, and any individuals having simlar policy-making responsibilities.

5. The term *immediate family* is interpreted (AU 9335) to include spouse, parents, children, brothers and sisters and their spouses, and any other persons in the household as well as other relatives who can significantly influence or be influenced by management.

6. Related party transactions can be said to exist even if specific transactions have not taken place or do not receive accounting recognition. For example, a party may have the power to control the volume of business undertaken by a related party with unrelated companies; or an entity may not charge a related entity for services performed.

7. Parties that are dependent on a single or few customers, suppliers, debtors, creditors, and so on, are not considered related parties because of economic dependency if they are otherwise unrelated, unless significant management influence exists. Financial statement disclosure of such dependency, however, may be necessary. Appropriate auditing procedures similar to those for related party transactions can be undertaken in such circumstances.

AUDITING PROCEDURES

	Performed by	NA	W/P ref

Determining Existence of Related Parties

1. After first providing them with a comprehensive definition of *related parties,* obtain a list from officers and other management personnel of all related parties with whom the client or its personnel have had or are contemplating any dealings.

2. Make inquiries of senior officers and others about whether such transactions have in fact taken place or are contemplated, and obtain details of the circumstances.

3. Determine if the company has any internal control procedures for identifying, authorizing, and monitoring related party transactions.

4. Inquire of predecessor auditors as well as auditors of related companies regarding the existence of related parties and the extent and nature of dealings with them.

5. Obtain credit reports on known or suspected related parties and on major suppliers and customers for possible disclosure of multiple affiliations.

6. Review stockholder listings of related closely held companies.

7. Review SEC or other governmental agency reports filed by the client containing names of related parties or of other companies in which the client's officers and directors may have similar positions.

8. Obtain basic data regarding employee pension and other trusts and the names of their officers and trustees.

9. Review prior years' working papers for relevant data acquired on previous engagements for the client.

10. As investments are made by the company, add to the listing of related parties the names of investee companies and their officers and directors.

Identifying Transactions With Related Parties

11. In testing transactions during the conduct of the audit generally, compare the names of parties involved with the listing of known related parties. Copies of the listing should be distributed to the audit team.

12. Make inquiries of management about whether transactions with related parties have taken place.

13. Include in a representation letter a reference to the subject of related party transactions as well as to "conflict of interests."

14. Examine the minutes of the board of directors and executive and other management committees for data regarding material transactions that may involve related parties.

15. Review SEC or other governmental filings by the client.

16. Scrutinize transactions in which the form of the transactions differs markedly from their economic substance for indications that they may reflect dealings with related parties. Some examples are: borrowing or lending without interest or at low interest rates, selling properties at prices varying considerably from appraisal or market values, nonmonetary exchanges, rendition of gratuitous services, clearly unreasonable charges by professional parties (attorneys, consultants, etc.).

17. Consider the impact of the existence of major risk and trouble areas (such as material earnings decline and cash flow problems) in motivating management to engage in related party transactions.

18. Appraise the business arrangements with major customers, suppliers, and others for any peculiarities indicative of special relationships.

19. Examine invoices from law firms and other professional parties for indications that transactions with related parties may have occurred.

20. Scrutinize unusual or nonrecurring transactions as well as those recorded close to the year-end.

21. Where guaranties have been granted to or received by the client in connection with loan agreements, determine if a related party situation exists.

22. Review reports of the internal auditors.

Examining Related Party Transactions

23. Obtain a clear understanding of the nature and business purpose of the transaction by inquiry of and discussion with management and by examination of supporting evidence.

24. Examine documentary evidential matter such as invoices, agreements and contracts, and receiving and shipping reports.

25. Judge the reasonableness of the transaction; if necessary, obtain specialist advice.

26. Ascertain whether written authorization and approval have been given by the board of directors and appropriate officials. If such authorization and approval are lacking, obtain specific approval.

27. Inspect or confirm collateral and verify its transferability and value.

28. Review and reconcile intercompany account balances as of the same date.

29. Communicate with auditors of related or affiliated companies.

(Note: It is suggested in AU 335.15 that the following procedures may be considered in order to fully understand a transaction even though they might otherwise not be necessary to comply with auditing standards. However, it would seem that some of the following procedures might be routinely undertaken.)

30. Confirm with related parties details of transactions, agreements, guaranties, collateral, and the like.

31. Inspect supporting evidence in possession of other parties.

32. Confirm (or discuss) significant information with intermediaries such as banks, guarantors, agents, or attorneys.

33. Review credit reports and other financial reporting sources for information regarding related parties in the event that transactions with unfamiliar parties lack economic substance.

34. In the case of material uncollected balances, guaranties, and other obligations, obtain information regarding financial capability of the parties by review of audited and unaudited financial statements, income tax returns, and reports of regulatory agencies, tax authorities, financial publications, or credit agencies.

Disclosures

35. Determine if the related party transaction has been recorded in accordance with its substance.

36. Note whether appropriate disclosures and classifications have been made in the financial statements with respect to related party transactions that are material individually or in the aggregate, including:

(a) The nature of the relationships.

(b) Description of the transactions and dollar amounts.

(c) Effect of any change in method of establishing terms of the arrangements from that of the preceding period.

(d) Receivables or payables to related parties and terms of payment.

Impact on Opinion

37. In accordance with AU 335.18, express a qualified opinion or disclaim an opinion if the financial statements contain a representation that a material related party transaction was arranged on terms no less favorable than with an unrelated party, and if the auditor cannot substantiate this claim.

38. Express a qualified opinion or an adverse opinion if it is believed that the representation is misleading.

WORKING PAPERS

Broad guidelines on the form and content of working papers are contained in AU 338. Figure 1-13 is a checklist of broad guidelines and specific requirements for the preparation by the auditor of acceptable working papers. All personnel on the audit team should be thoroughly acquainted with these principles. They must understand too that while the working papers are the property of the auditor, he is under obligation to provide the client with copies of certain papers, such as adjusting journal entries, that are needed by the client for recordkeeping. Moreover, the affairs of the client must be held in strictest confidence by the auditor who must safeguard the working papers and refrain from any disclosures regarding them or the affairs of the company, even to successor auditors, unless so authorized by the client.

Figure 1-14 illustrates the type of form that may be used in listing the working papers to be prepared by the client. The form may also be used as a control checklist.

A schema for indexing working papers should connect the working papers (and the specific account it deals with) with the financial statements. If lead schedules are used to tie in to the statements, a subindexing scheme should be adopted to relate the supporting papers to the lead schedule. Schemes take a variety of forms. Some auditors use a letter system for financial statement accounts and numbers for supporting papers. For example, the symbol $(A - 1)/1$ might mean that A stands for *Cash*, the number 1 in the numerator might refer to a specific bank account (and perhaps a reconciliation) and the number 1 in the denominator to a secondary working paper (perhaps a list of outstanding checks) relating to working paper A-1. Other auditors may not use letters at all. Thus a number like 2000 might represent the lead schedule for *Cash*, while in the number 2002.1, the 2002 refers to a specific bank account while the .1 signifies a supporting paper such as a list of outstanding checks or perhaps a bank confirmation form.

Figure 1-15 presents an illustrative indexing scheme. Actually, any convenient system may be used that can easily be expanded to meet the requirements of a specific engagement.

Indexing for the permanent file can be a simple matter, the number assigned being preceded by the letter P. It can be tied in, where applicable, to the related symbol used in indexing current year's working papers. Thus excerpts from the bond indenture could be assigned the code P-3000; description of the entity's business, P-G110; and so on. Any convenient scheme may be used.

Upon the conclusion of the examination, many accountants prefer to gather their separate audit programs for the various accounts or areas of audit interest, and attach and file them in the working papers as a single unit making up the master Audit Program Guide. A similar procedure may be followed by them for the separate sections of the Internal Accounting Control Guide. The theory is that interrelationships as well as an overall perspective are thereby more easily discerned, especially on review by the audit manager and engagement partner. However, if an accountant prefers to file audit programs in the section of the working papers that covers the specific account, he can give all such programs a number ending with, say, 90 or 01. Thus the audit program for Cash would be assigned the number 190 (or 101). The separate sections of the internal accounting control guide can be similarly provided for.

Figure 1-13
Working Paper Preparation—
A Checklist Guide

Purposes of Working Papers

1. Working papers contain important documentation in support of the character and adequacy of the examination and of the opinion to be expressed regarding the fairness of the financial statements.

2. They are an aid in conducting the audit, permitting the work to be better organized and allocated among the assistants in the engagement.

3. They provide a basis for proper supervision and review of assistant's work and findings.

4. In addition, they contain materials that are needed for preparation of the report, for discussions with client personnel, and for tax and other governmental filings.

Basic Requirements

1. There should be sufficient data to show clearly that the financial statements are in agreement with the general ledger and underlying records after adjusting entries have been approved and recorded.

2. Schedules, analyses, and other working papers of the type whose balances tie in with the financial statements should as a general rule also show balances per the books before adjustments.

3. The working papers should provide clear support for the auditor's opinion and show clearly that sufficient competent evidential matter was examined consistent with the opinion expressed.

4. The papers should contain adequate evidence showing that the auditing standards relating to engagement planning, supervision of assistants, review and evaluation of internal control system, and the audit tests and procedures, have been complied with.

5. The way in which the evaluation of the system of internal accounting control affected the audit tests should be indicated.

6. Conclusions should be expressed regarding significant aspects of the examination.

7. The initials or signatures of both the preparer and reviewer should be recorded as well as dates of such preparation and review.

8. The working papers should be legible and clearly understandable and include, where necessary, legends or commentaries to explain tick marks or other symbols.

9. If the papers have been prepared by the client, all additions and other arithmetical features must be verified by independent calculation.

10. The papers should be clearly identified as to client, title and purpose, and date or period, and appropriately indexed.

11. Working papers should provide a clear explanation of the nature of unusual or questionable matters encountered during the examination, indicate the nature of the evidence examined, and specify how such matters were satisfactorily resolved or treated.

Figure 1-14
Listing of Working Papers to be
Prepared by Client—
Illustrative Form

Client _____

Period of financial statements _____

Your cooperation in preparing working papers for the items checked below will be greatly appreciated. The working papers should be prepared in pencil on the type of accounting paper and in the form corresponding to the samples attached. Unless otherwise indicated, papers should be prepared as of the statement date or for the period of the financial statements, as appropriate.

	Items to be prepared— check ( )	Date submitted to auditor
Cash: Bank reconciliations		
Receivables: Aged schedule		
Schedule of miscellaneous receivables Analysis of allowance for doubtful accounts		
Other _____		
Merchandise inventories: Priced copy		
Other _____		

Figure 1-15
Indexing Scheme for Working Papers

ILLUSTRATION OF BASIC SCHEME

Financial statement general category (lead schedule)—Cash	100
Specific working paper for bank account included in lead schedule	101
Paper supporting specific cash account, say, bank confirmation form	101A
Paper commenting on above bank confirmation form	101A1
Paper for another specific cash account	102
Assume three papers relating to item 102	102A
	102B
	102C
Assume two working papers relating to item 102C	102C1
	102C2
Assume two working papers relating to cash in general (say, list of exceptions and their disposition, and internal control comments)	100A
	100B

INDEX SYMBOLS

General Matters

G100	Audit planning and control guide
G200	Internal accounting control guide
G300	Audit program guide
G400	Review guides
G500	_____

Balance Sheet

100	Cash
200	Marketable securities
300	Receivables
400	Inventories
500	Other current assets
1100	Investments in and receivable from related companies
1200	Other investments
1300	Receivables—noncurrent

1400 Property, plant and equipment
1500 Deferred charges
1600 Intangible assets
1700 Other noncurrent assets
2100 Notes payable
2200 Accounts payable
2300 Dividends payable
2400 Employees' payroll withholdings
2500 Accrued expenses
2600 Income taxes payable
2700 Other taxes payable
2800 Other current liabilities
3000 Long-term debt
3100 Deferred credits
3200 Other noncurrent liabilities
3900 Contingent liabilities and commitments
4000 Capital stock
4500 Additional paid-in capital
4600 Retained earnings

Income Statement

5000 Revenue
5500 Cost of sales
6000 Selling expense
6500 General and administrative expense
7000 Other income
7100 Other deductions
7500 Income taxes
7600 Extraordinary items
7700 Disposal of segment

CHAPTER **2**

Sundry Areas Of General Audit Responsibility

CLIENTS' WRITTEN REPRESENTATIONS

The requirement is established in AU 333 that certain written representations by management be obtained by the auditor as part of any examination conducted in accordance with generally accepted auditing standards. The financial statements and the underlying books and records are in fact the representations of the client entity and its management who assume the full responsibility for their accuracy and fairness. In addition to impressing upon management the fact that it does have this responsibility as distinguished from the auditor's responsibility for his *opinion*, written representations serve to avoid misunderstanding, confirm oral statements, clarify important matters, and bring to light transactions, conditions, or events that might not otherwise have come to the auditor's attention.

The written representations are obtained in the form of one or more representation letters (sometimes referred to as representation certificates) addressed to the auditor and are signed by the chief executive of the company, the chief financial officer, and, in addition, for any letters that may separately deal with special areas like inventories, by a key official with related responsibility.

The representation letter does not relieve the auditor of his responsibility to perform the examination with due care and cannot be used as a substitute for procedures that should normally or necessarily be employed. While oral or written client representations are themselves evidential matter and correspond to the "independent inquiries" aspect of the third standard of field work, any such assertions of the client must in turn be corroborated by the auditor by other auditing procedures that are reasonable and practicable.

A comprehensive illustrative representation letter appears in Figure 2-1. It is a modified and expanded version of the illustrative representation letter presented in AU 333A. The italicized captions would not normally be used and they are shown simply to highlight the areas that may be covered, depending on the circumstances of the engagement. If the auditor requires a detailed representation for a given area, he may find it more practicable to obtain a separate letter on that subject. An example would be Figure 2-2 covering the completeness of the minutes, or an inventory letter as shown in Figure 2-3.

Obtaining written representations is a major procedure and should not be undertaken perfunctorily. The details should be discussed with those signing it, and a clear understanding reached regarding their significance and the materiality criteria to be used. In some instances, as in the reference to irregularities, a quantitative materiality criterion would be inappropriate because of the potential impact of such a circumstance on the examination in general.

The letter should be dated as of the date of the auditor's report so that the representations, especially as to subsequent events, may be up-to-date. If the representation letter is submitted or signed earlier, or if there is a time lag between the report and issuance dates or the report date has been changed, it would be desirable to obtain a supplementary updated letter similar to that shown in Figure 2-4.

AU 333 states that a refusal by management to give the auditor a representation letter deemed essential to the examination would preclude the expression of an unqualified opinion. Presumably, the situation would call for either a qualified opinion or a disclaimer of opinion.

Representation letters for compilation and for review of financial statements are presented as Figures 8-4 and 8-20, respectively, in Chapter. 8.

Figure 2-1
Comprehensive Representation Letter

(Client Letterhead)

(Date of auditor's report)

(Addressed to independent auditor)

Gentlemen:

In connection with your examination of the (identification of finan-cial statements) of (name of client) as of (date) and for the (period of examination) for the purpose of expressing an opinion as to whether the (consolidated) financial statements present fairly the financial position, results of operations, and changes in financial position of (name of client) in conformity with generally accepted accounting principles (other comprehensive basis of accounting), we confirm, to the best of our knowledge and belief, the representations recorded below made to you during your examination. Exceptions or supple-mentary comments, if any, will be stated at the end of this letter in the section captioned *Exceptions* and will be appropriately numbered to correspond with the related item.

1. *Fairness of Statements.* We are responsible for the fair presen-tation in the (consolidated) financial statements of financial position, results of operations, and changes in financial position in conformity with generally accepted accounting principles (other comprehensive basis of accounting). The statements are fairly presented in conformity with generally accepted accounting principles applied on a basis con-sistent with that of the preceding (period). Informative disclosures have been made in the statements including footnotes of all material matters whose disclosure is necessary to make the statements fair and not misleading.

2. *Availability of records and minutes.* We have made available to you all:
    (a) Financial records and related data.
    (b) Minutes of the meetings of stockholders, directors, committees of directors, and executive committees, or summaries of actions of recent meetings for which minutes have not yet been prepared. A com-

plete listing of meetings by dates is included in a supplementary representation letter.

3. *Irregularities.* There have been no:

(a) Irregularities involving management or employees who have significant roles in the system of internal accounting control.

(b) Irregularities involving other employees that could have a material effect on the financial statements.

(c) Communications from regulatory agencies concerning noncompliance with, or deficiencies in, financial reporting practices that could have a material effect on the financial statements.

4. *Illegal acts.* There have been no illegal acts (such as alleged political contributions, bribes, or other violations of laws and regulations) involving the company or its officers or key personnel and there have been no violations or possible violations of laws or regulations whose effects should be considered for disclosure in the financial statements or as a basis for recording a loss contingency.

5. *Related parties.* Related party transactions and related amounts receivable or payable, including sales, purchases, loans, transfers, leasing arrangements, and guarantees have been properly recorded or disclosed in the financial statements. For this purpose, the term *related parties* is defined as stated in Statements on Auditing Standards, AU 335.

6. *Plans affecting carrying values.* We have no plans or intentions that may materially affect the carrying value or classification of assets and liabilities.

7. *Options and warrants.* Capital stock repurchase options or agreements or capital stock reserved for options, warrants, conversions or other requirements have been properly recorded or disclosed in the financial statements.

8. *Compensating balances.* Arrangements with financial institutions involving compensating balances or other arrangements involving restrictions on cash balances and line-of-credit or similar arrangements have been properly recorded or disclosed in the financial statements.

9. *Repurchase of assets.* Agreements to repurchase assets previously sold have been properly recorded or disclosed in the financial statements.

10. Unasserted claims. There are no unasserted claims or assessments that our attorneys have advised us are probable of assertion and must be disclosed in accordance with Statement of Financial Accounting Standards No. 5 (AC 4311).

11. *Liabilities and contingencies.* All material liabilities or gain or loss contingencies have been properly recorded (accrued) or disclosed in the financial statements as required by Statement of Financial Accounting Standards No. 5 (AC 4311). Examples of loss contingencies include, among others: pending or threatened litigation, claims and assessments; obligations relating to product warranties and product defects; unusual risk of loss or damage of enterprise property by fire, explosion, or other hazards; threat of expropriation of assets; guarantees of indebtedness of others; receivables sold with recourse; notes discounted; receivables doubtful of collection.

12. *Complete recording.* There are no material transactions that have not been properly recorded in the accounting records underlying the financial statements.

13. *Obsolete merchandise.* Provision has been made to reduce excess or obsolete inventories to their estimated net realizable value.

14. *Title and pledging of assets.* The company has satisfactory title to all owned assets, and there are no liens or encumbrances on such assets nor has any asset been pledged.

15. *Sales commitments.* Provision has been made for any material loss to be sustained in the fulfillment of, or from inability to fulfill, any sales commitments.

16. *Purchase commitments.* Provision has been made for any material loss to be sustained as a result of purchase commitments for inventory quantities in excess of normal requirements or at prices in excess of the prevailing market prices.

17. *Contractual agreements.* We have complied with all aspects of contractual agreements that would have a material effect on the financial statements in the event of noncompliance. With respect to any issue of securities or bonds or loan agreements, there were no defaults in principal, interest, sinking fund or redemption provisions nor any breach of covenant of indenture or agreement.

18. *Subsequent events.* No events have occurred subsequent to the balance sheet date that would require adjustment to, or disclosure in, the financial statements. (Example of such events are: loss of major customers; casualty losses; bond or capital stock issuances; material plant or business acquisitions or disposals; bad debt losses; litigation or settlement of lawsuits or other claims; tax assessments; material or unusual sales returns and allowances.)

19. *Tax assessments.* Federal income tax returns have been examined by the IRS through the year ended (date) and all assessments through the year ended (date) have been paid or accrued.

20. *Adjusting entries.* Adjusting journal entries that have been proposed during your examination are accepted and approved by us, are reflected in the financial statements as of (date) and for the (period of examination), and will be recorded on the books of the company.

21. *Worthless assets.* No worthless assets (such as uncollectible receivables, valueless investments, abandoned or retired equipment) are carried in the accounts, whether or not covered by reserves or allowance accounts.

22. *Adequate insurance.* The company carries adequate liability, fire and other casualty insurance.

23. *Replacement cost.* (Where applicable.) Replacement cost information provided in note (identify) to the financial statements has been prepared and presented in accordance with the requirements of Regulation S-X.

24. *Interim period information.* (Where applicable.) Interim period financial information provided in note (identify) to the financial statements has been prepared in conformity with generally accepted accounting principles consistently applied.

EXCEPTIONS (*Note*: Exceptions to any of the foregoing representations are recorded below and are keyed by number to the specific item. For convenience, appropriate information may be conveyed by reference to specific notes to the financial statements or to supplementary attachments to this letter.)

_____

_____

_____

_____

Very truly yours,

_____   _____

(Signature of chief   (Date)
exccutive officer
and title)

_____   _____

(Signature of chief   (Date)
financial officer
and title)

Figure 2-2
Representation Letter Covering Minutes

(Client letterhead)

(Date of auditor's report)

(Addressed to independent auditor)

Gentlemen:

    This letter relates to the corporate minutes and is an integral part of the general representation letter dated (date) furnished to you in connection with your examination of the financial statements of (name of client) as of (date) and for the (period of examination).

    We have made available to you all minutes covering all meetings of stockholders, board of directors, committees of directors, and executive committees. These minutes constitute a full and complete record of those meetings. The following is a complete listing of such meetings held during the period from _____ to _____.

Type of meeting	Date	Remarks

Very truly yours,

_____   _____
(Signature of chief   (Date)
executive officer
and title)

_____   _____
(Signature of corporate   (Date)
secretary and title)

Figure 2-3
Inventory Representation Letter

(Client letterhead)

(Date of auditor's report)

(Addressed to independent auditor)

Gentlemen:

This letter is an integral part of the general representation letter dated (date) furnished to you in connection with your examination of the financial statements of (name of client) as of (date) and for the (period of examination). We make the following representations to you in connection with inventories as of (date). Any exceptions or supplementary comments, if any, will be stated at the end of this letter in the Exceptions section.

1. Inventories totaled (dollar amount) and consisted of:
    Finished goods $
    Work in process
    Raw materials   _____
    Total $_____

2. Quantities for inventories on owned premises were determined by (specify method: complete actual count, weight or measurement; perpetual inventory records; etc.)

3. Quantities for inventories held by others were determined by (specify method).

4. The physical count was started on (date and time) and completed on (date and time).

5. Satisfactory reconciliation of changes in inventory quantities between the count date and balance sheet date was made by (specify method).

6. All owned merchandise on hand, in transit or held by others at the closing date was included in inventory and all related liabilities were recorded and reflected in the financial statements.

7. The inventories are all owned by the company and no merchandise held on consignment or for the account of other parties or billed to customers is included.

8. The inventories are valued on a (specify principle) basis in conformity with generally accepted accounting principles.

9. Cost was determined by (method), market by (method), and lower of cost or market by (method).

10. Provision has been made to reduce excess or obsolete inventories to their estimated net realizable value.

11. Inventories have been valued on a basis consistent with the preceding period.

12. Purchase and sales commitments are not abnormal or unfavorable in any respect.

13. No material market declines or other significant events affecting the inventories have taken place subsequent to the balance sheet date.

14. Appropriate adjustments have been made to eliminate in the consolidated financial statements intercompany purchases and sales and intercompany profit in the inventories.

15. Inventories have not been hypothecated, pledged or otherwise encumbered.

EXCEPTIONS: _____

_____

_____

_____

_____

Very truly yours,

_____   _____
(Signature of chief   Date
executive officer
and title)

_____   _____
(Signature of chief   Date
financial officer
and title)

_____   _____
(Signature of official   Date
in charge of the physical
count and title)

Figure 2-4
Updated Representation Letter

(Client letterhead)

(Date)

(Addressed to independent auditor)

Gentlemen:

In connection with your examination of the (identification of financial statements) of (name of client) as of (date) and for the (period of examination) we furnished you with a general representation letter dated   (date) and supplementary representation letters dealing with (specify) and similarly dated (date).

We represent to the best of our knowledge and belief that the representations previously made in those letters continue to be correct and there have been no material changes since the dates of those letters. (Exceptions, if any, are to be stated here.)

Very truly yours,

_____   _____

(Same signatures as in   (Date)
previous representation
letters)

USE OF SPECIALISTS

The auditor may sometimes find it necessary to engage an outside specialist whose findings can provide additional competent evidential matter so that material items in the financial statements reflecting highly technical considerations may be properly corroborated. Technical areas may relate to, for example, valuation problems involving works of art, diamonds, etc., quantity determinations as in the case of mineral reserves, actuarial calculations, and interpretation of technical regulations or documents.

The auditor is not expected to have the expertise of specialists like actuaries, appraisers, attorneys, engineers, and geologists qualified to practice another occupation or profession. General guidance for the auditor who finds it necessary to use the services of a specialist is provided in AU 336 and applies to an outside specialist rather than one who is an employee of either the auditor or the client. AU 336 permits the auditor to use the work of a specialist unless he believes the findings are unreasonable. The use of a specialist related to the client is not precluded, providing that additional audit procedures are employed and the findings are not unreasonable.

Documented understanding should exist among the auditor, client, and specialist regarding the specialist engagement. A letter of understanding addressed to the auditor by the specialist and agreed to by the client is illustrated in Figure 2-6.

The audit objectives and procedures to be employed where circumstances warrant using the work of a specialist are presented in Figure 2-5. The guide can be incorporated as one of the sections in the regular audit program guide.

Figure 2-5
Audit Program Guide
Using the Work of a Specialist

(Note: See Chapter 4 for documentation requirements applicable to all sections of the Audit Program Guide.)

AUDIT OBJECTIVES

1. To acquire additional corroborative evidence regarding (identify area or accounts in question): _____

_____

_____

2. To gain satisfaction regarding the qualifications and independence of the specialist.

AUDITING PROCEDURES

	Performed by	NA
1. Obtain from client and review working papers and related documentation describing and substantiating the methods, assumptions, and calculations employed relative to the specialized matter.		
2. Make inquiries of client and consult with appropriate specialists on client's staff to gain additional understanding, and obtain supporting evidence where indicated.		
3. Consult with personnel on our own staff who may be knowledgeable in the area.		
4. If a decision is made to engage an outside specialist, discuss with client and obtain approval of the arrangement.		
5. Obtain satisfaction regarding the		

qualifications and independence of the specialist by inquiry, reference to directories of specialists, contact with professional societies, and checking of references.

6. Send engagement confirmation letter to specialist (see Figure 2-6) with provision for appended signatures of specialist and client as indications of their approval of the understanding regarding the scope of services, methods or assumptions used, and independence of the specialist.

7. Review the specialist's report and consider whether the findings are reasonable and support the corresponding representation in the financial statements.

8. If there is a material difference between the client's figures and data as reflected in the financial statements and those of the specialist, or if the findings of the specialist appear unreasonable, undertake the following procedures:

(a) Consult with client and client's specialist in order to clarify any differences or obscurities.

(b) Arrange a conference between the various internal and out-side specialists.

(c) Review any pertinent evidence that may be available.

(d) Relate the current year's situation and problems to those of the prior year.

(e) Consider using another independent specialist unless it is believed that the matter would not thereby be resolved.

Effect on Report

9. If the matter cannot or has not been resolved, consider the necessity of issuing a qualified opinion or a disclaimer because of the scope limitation due to inability to obtain sufficient evidential matter regarding material representations in the financial statements.

10. If it is determined that the representations in question do not conform with generally accepted accounting principles, express a qualified opinion or an adverse opinion.

11. If other than an unqualified opinion is expressed for the foregoing reasons, reference to the specialist may be made if considered necessary when giving the reasons for the qualifications. But in the case of an unqualified opinion, no such reference should be made. It could be misinterpreted by the reader of the report as a qualification or as a division of responsibility.

Figure 2-6
Confirmation Letter Covering
Understanding With Specialist

(Auditor's letterhead)

(Date)

(addressed to specialist firm)

Gentlemen:

This letter will serve to confirm our mutual understanding with respect to the services you are to provide as an independent specialist in connection with our audit engagement for (client's name). Our client's signature of agreement appears below and we would appreciate your similarly signing this letter at the specified place as indication of your agreement with the following understanding.

1. You recognize that your findings will be used by us as corroborative evidence in connection with our examination of the (identification of financial statements) of (name of client) as of (date) and for the period of examination), for the purpose of expressing an opinion as to whether the statements are fairly presented in conformity with generally accepted accounting principles applied on a consistent basis.

2. The objectives and scope of your work are as follows: (to be described).

3. You will be using methods or assumptions as follows: (to be described).

4. The foregoing methods or assumptions are to be compared by you with those used by the company in the preceding period (specify period).

5. Your report is to be submitted directly to us with a copy to (name of client) no later than (date). The report is to include your opinion as to the accuracy of the company's figures and data appearing in the financial statements regarding (specify items) and the consistency of methods used with those of the prior period; as well as an account of the scope of your work, methods or assumptions used, and findings, in sufficient detail to permit an appropriate review.

6. You represent to us that you are completely independent of (name of client) or any of its officers or key personnel and that neither you nor anyone closely associated with you has (or has had) any relationship with them.

7. Fees for your services are set forth in an accompanying letter.

Very truly yours,

_____

(Signature of partner)

Approved:

_____

(Client's name)

_____   _____

(Signature and title)   (Date)

Approved:

_____   _____

(Signature of specialist)   (Date)

USING AND EVALUATING THE WORK OF INTERNAL AUDITORS

AU 322 deals with "The Effect of an Internal Audit Function on the Scope of the Independent Auditor's Examination." The internal audit function is both one of the strongest elements in an internal accounting control system and one of the effective means available to a company of evaluating and strengthening the system. The work of the internal auditors and their competence and objectivity are of considerable interest to the independent auditor in his study and evaluation of the system of internal accounting control. The auditing objectives and procedures pertinent to the evaluation of the work of internal auditors are presented in Figure 2-7, which may be incorporated in the regular audit program guide as a distinct section.

The statement is made in AU 322 that internal auditors "may assist in performing substantive tests or tests of compliance" but the independent auditor "should consider their competence and objectivity and supervise and test their work to the extent appropriate in the circumstances." Needless to say, there is a risk involved in thus utilizing internal auditors as, in effect, assistants to the independent auditor. The internal audit function, however strong an element it may be in the system of internal accounting control, is a creature of management and part of its organizational structure, and any assistance rendered by the internal auditors should be sought by the independent accountant on a highly selective basis and the work done should be closely overseen and critically appraised.

Figure 2-7
Audit Program Guide
Evaluating the Work of Internal Auditors

(*Note*: See Chapter 4 for documentation requirements applicable to all sections of the Audit Program Guide.)

AUDIT OBJECTIVES

1. To determine competence and independence of the internal auditors.

2. To ascertain the effectiveness of their work for the bearing that it will have on the nature, timing, and extent of our audit procedures relating to both compliance testing and substantive testing.

AUDITING PROCEDURES

	Performed by	NA
1. Meet with internal auditors to: (a) develop background information regarding their activities: (b) obtain a list of their reports and working papers that may be needed: (c) consult regarding forthcoming internal audit programs of interest to us as independent auditors.		
2. Inquire about the qualifications of the internal auditors and the hiring, training, and supervision practices of the department.		
3. Ascertain whether they report to the audit committee of the board of directors or to senior officers of the company.		
4. Review their reports to judge whether the type of comments and recommendations made provide evidence of the internal auditor's independence.		
5. Inspect and evaluate manuals, audit programs, working papers, and reports prepared by the internal audit function and take note of:		

(a)   Thoroughness and adequacy of materials and work performed.

(b)   Indication of sound supervision and review procedures.

(c)   Reference to supporting evidential matter.

(d)   Appropriateness of report, conclusions, and recommendations.

6.   Test some of the work of the internal auditors by examining transactions or balances (the same or similar to those tested by the internal auditors) and compare results.

LAWYERS' LETTERS COVERING LITIGATION, CLAIMS, AND ASSESSMENTS

The subject of auditing procedures and letters of inquiry to a client's outside attorneys concerning litigation, claims, and assessments is discussed in AU 337. The accounting considerations in this area are part of the broader subject of loss contingencies, which is dealt with in FASB Statement of Financial Accounting Standards No. 5, as amended, entitled "Accounting for Contingencies" (AC 4311). A brief summary of the pertinent accounting principles and the criteria for accrual or disclosure of loss contingencies, as well as the the audit objectives and procedures with respect to identification and disclosure of litigation, claims, and assessments, are presented in Figure 2-8. This figure can be used as a section of the Audit Program Guide and would ordinarily have been included in Chapter 4 and placed in the part of the Guide dealing with liabilities. However, it was considered more practicable to associate Figure 2-8 more closely with the illustrative lawyer confirmation letters and thus present the entire subject as one of the general areas of audit responsibility.

The lawyer confirmation letters shown in Figure 2-9 (in which management lists the items in question) and Figure 2-10 (in which the attorney is requested to provide the listing) reflect the requirements for content of such letters specified in AU 337 and are modified versions of the illustrative letter appearing in AU section 337A. An updated letter to the client's attorney is presented in Figure 2-11. It may be used to obtain information regarding any changes in matters previously reported on in the attorney's letter of response, or any new developments arising subsequent to that date and prior to the issuance of the auditor's report.

Figure 2-8
Audit Program Guide
Litigation, Claims, and Assessments

(*Note*: See Chapter 4 for description of documentation requirements applicable to all sections of the Audit Program Guide.)

ACCOUNTING CONSIDERATIONS

1. An estimated loss from a loss contingency (including litigation, claims and assessments) should be accrued by a charge to income if *both* of the following conditions are met:

(a) It is *probable*, based on information received before the issuance of the financial statements, that a loss will be incurred in connection with conditions or situations existing as of the balance sheet date.

(b) The amount of the loss can be reasonably estimated.

2. A contingency loss should be disclosed in the financial statements (but not accrued) in any of the following circumstances:

(a) A loss has been accrued as of the statement date but there is a *reasonable possibility* (as distinguished from a *remote possibility*) that an additional loss relating to the matter may be incurred.

(b) One or both conditions for accrual of a loss have not been met but there is at least a *reasonable possibility* that a loss will be incurred.

(c) It is *reasonably possible* that a loss will be incurred in connection with a contingency loss relating to the post balance sheet period.

(d) With respect to unasserted litigation, claims, and assessments, it is considered *probable* that a claim will be asserted *and* there is a *reasonable possibility* that the outcome will be unfavorable.

3. Disclosures should indicate the nature of the contingency and provide an estimate of the possible loss or range of loss or state that an estimate cannot be made.

4. Materiality applies here as it does in all accounting matters but a lower threshold should probably apply in the case of loss contingencies because of the inherent uncertainties.

AUDIT OBJECTIVES

1. To ascertain whether contingency losses exist.

2. To obtain competent evidential matter in verification of the nature of the contingency, the applicable period (i.e., before or after

statement date), degree of probability of unfavorable outcome, and amount or range of loss.

3. To determine whether the contingency loss has been properly accrued or disclosed in the financial statements.

AUDITING PROCEDURES

	Performed by	NA

1. Obtain from management a full description and evaluation of all litigation, claims, and assessments existing at the balance sheet date as well as in the subsequent period.

2. Include in the client's written representation letter appropriate reference to pending, threatened, or unasserted litigation, claims, and assessments.

3. Evaluate the policies and procedures adopted by the client for identifying, evaluating, and accounting for loss contingencies.

4. Examine documents and other evidential matter such as: correspondence from governmental agencies and attorneys; invoices from attorneys; contracts, loan agreements, and leases.

5. Inspect evidential matter for possible indication of guarantees.

6. When confirming account balances and other matters with client's banks or other credit-grantors, inquire about possible guarantee arrangements.

7. Obtain relevant documentation and make inquiries of client's in-house counsel.

8. Send confirmation letter to client's lawyers.

9. Where necessary, for additional clarification or other reasons, arrange a joint meeting with in-house counsel, management, and outside attorney.

10. If the client's lawyer has resigned

or been replaced, make appropriate inquiries as to the reasons. Such inquiries may lead to important disclosures.

11. Utilize other customary auditing procedures that are also applicable in this area, such as review of the minutes and of subsequent events.

12. On the basis of the evidential matter examined and the applicable accounting standards, consider whether loss contingencies have been properly accrued and/or disclosed in the financial statements.

Effect on Opinion

13. If the client's lawyer refuses to furnish the information requested in the confirmation inquiry letter, the resultant limitation in scope of examination would preclude an unqualified opinion, and necessitate either a qualified opinion or a disclaimer.

14. If the client's lawyer is unable to form a judgment regarding the likelihood of an unfavorable outcome or the amount or range of possible loss, because of inherent uncertainties, and the effect of the matter on the financial statements could be material, a qualified ("subject to") opinion may have to be expressed.

Figure 2-9
Confirmation Letter to Client's Lawyer
(Client Listing of Certain Items Included)

(Client letterhead)

(Date)

(Addressed to attorney)

Gentlemen:

In connection with an examination of our (consolidated) financial statements (as well as those of our subsidiaries _____ and _____) at (date) and for the (period) then ended, management of the Company has prepared and furnished to our auditors, (name and address of auditors), a description and evaluation of certain contingencies, including those set forth below under the headings, "Pending or Threatened Litigation, Claims and Assessments" and "Unasserted Claims or Assessments". These involve matters which the Company regards as material, with respect to which you have been engaged and to which you have devoted substantive attention on behalf of the Company in the form of legal consultation or representation. Please forward directly to our auditors the information requested in this letter. Your response should cover matters that existed at the balance sheet date (date) and during the period to the date of your response.

Pending or Threatened Litigation, Claims, and Assessments

(The listing by the client should ordinarily include the following: nature of the litigation, claim or assessment: progress of the case to date; how management is responding or intends to respond to the litigation or other action—for example, to contest the case vigorously or to seek an out-of-court settlement; and an evaluation of the likelihood of an unfavorable outcome and an estimate, if one can be made, of the amount or range of possible loss.)

Please furnish to our auditors such explanation, if any, that you consider necessary to supplement the foregoing information, including an explanation of those matters as to which your views may differ from those stated and an identification of the omission of any pending or threatened litigation, claims, and assessments, or a statement that the list of such matters is complete.

Unasserted Claims and Assessments

(If no unasserted claims or assessments requiring disclosure exist, the following wording should be used in place of the sentence below: "Management believes that there are no unasserted claims and assessments that are probable of assertion and, if asserted, have at least a reasonable possibility of an unfavorable outcome.")

The following unasserted claims and assessments are considered by management to be probable of assertion and, if asserted, to have at least a reasonable possibility of an unfavorable outcome.

(The listing by the client should ordinarily include the following: nature of the matter; how management intends to respond if the claim is asserted; and an evaluation of the likelihood of an unfavorable outcome and an estimate, if one can be made, of the amount or range of potential loss.)

Please furnish to our auditors such explanations, if any, that you consider necessary to supplement the foregoing information, including an explanation of those matters as to which your views may differ from those stated.

It is our understanding that whenever, in the course of performing legal services for us with respect to a matter recognized to involve an unasserted possible claim or assessment that may call for financial statement disclosure, you have formed a professional conclusion that we should disclose or consider disclosure concerning such possible claim or assessment, as a matter of professional responsibility to us, you will so advise us. Moreover, you will consult with us concerning the question of such disclosure and the applicable requirements of Statement of Financial Accounting Standards No. 5. Please specifically confirm to our auditors that our understanding is correct.

Please specifically identify the nature of and reasons for any limitation on your response.

Other Matters

We would also appreciate your including in your reply information regarding the following matters:

(Such additional matters might relate to: illegal acts of company or key personnel; guarantees of indebtedness of others; contracts or legal documents; unpaid or unbilled charges for legal services.)

A return envelope addressed to our auditors is enclosed for your convenience. We appreciate your cooperation.

Very truly yours,

_____

(Client authorized
signature and title)

Figure 2-10
Confirmation Letter to Client's Lawyer
(Client Listing of Certain Items Not Included)

(Client letterhead)

(Date)

(Addressed to attorney)

Gentlemen:

In connection with an examination of our (consolidated) financial statements (as well as those of our subsidiaries _____ and _____) at (date) and for the (period) then ended, we respectfully request that you prepare and forward directly to our auditors, (name and address), a description and evaluation of pending or threatened litigation, claims and assessments and other contingencies with respect to which you have been engaged and to which you have devoted substantive attention on behalf of the Company in the form of legal consultation or representation. Include in your listing those matters that are considered material (management should specify materiality standard). Your response should cover matters that existed at the balance sheet date (date) and during the period to the date of your reply.

In describing pending or threatened litigation, claims and assessments, please provide the following information: nature of the litigation; progress to date; what response is being made or is intended to be made—for example, to contest the matter vigorously or to seek an out-of-court settlement; and an evaluation of the likelihood of an unfavorable outcome and an estimate, if one can be made, of the amount or range of possible loss.

Management of the Company believes, and we have so represented to our auditors, that there are no unasserted possible claims or assessments that you have advised are probable of assertion and, if asserted, have at least a reasonable possibility of an unfavorable outcome.

It is our understanding that, whenever in the course of performing legal services for us with respect to a matter recognized to involve an unasserted possible claim or assessment that may call for financial statement disclosure, as a matter of professional responsibility to us you will so advise us. Moreover, you will consult with us concerning the question of such disclosure and the applicable requirements of Statement of Financial Accounting Standards No. 5. Please specifically confirm to our auditors that our understanding is correct.

Please specifically identify the nature of and reasons for any limitation on your response.

We would also appreciate your including in your reply, information regarding the following matters: (To be specified).

We appreciate your cooperation. A return evelope addressed to our auditors is enclosed for your convenience.

Very truly yours,

_____

(Client-authorized
signature and title)

Figure 2-11
Updated Confirmation Letter to Client's Lawyer

(Client letterhead)

(Date)

(Addressed to attorney)

Gentlemen:

You previously furnished our auditors, (name and address), in a letter dated (date), information regarding legal matters existing at (date) and during the period to the date of your letter. Inasmuch as an updated letter from you is now required in connection with their regular examination of our financial statements, we would appreciate your writing directly to our auditors to inform them of any change in the status of, or in your views with respect to, any matters previously reported on in your letter of (date).

Moreover, we have provided our auditors with the following additional information regarding pending or threatened litigation, claims or assessments and/or unasserted claims and assessments arising (mainly) subsequent to our previous letter to you dated (dated):

(Provide description and use wording as in preceding Figures 2-9 and 2-10. If there were no changes or additional information, state: "We have informed our auditors that no changes have taken place since our previous letter to you with respect to matters previously covered in your letter or similar matters arising subsequently.)

Please furnish to our auditors such explanations, if any, that you consider necessary to supplement the foregoing information, including an explanation of those matters as to which your views may differ from those stated above.

A return envelope addressed to our auditors is enclosed for your convenience. Only a limited time remains for the completion of our financial statements and we would therefore appreciate a reply at your earliest convenience.

Very truly yours,

_____

(Client authorized
signature and title)

SUBSEQUENT EVENTS

Certain transactions or events may occur after the balance sheet date and prior to the issuance of the financial statements that may have a material effect on the financial statements and the auditor's report. The auditor's responsibilities in this area are discussed in AU 560. The period involved and audit objectives and procedures are dealt with in Figure 2-12, which should be incorporated in the Audit Program Guide. It is dealt with in this chapter because it is a general area of audit responsibility affecting the examination of all accounts.

Figure 2-12
Audit Program Guide—Subsequent Events

(*Note*: See Chapter 4 for a description of documentation requirements applicable to all sections of the Audit Program Guide.)

PERIOD COVERED

The subsequent events period extends from the balance sheet date to the date of the auditor's report, which in turn corresponds to the date of completion of the field work. The period may be of relatively short duration or may cover several months. For SEC registration statement filings, the period extends to the effective date of the registration.

AUDIT OBJECTIVES

1.   To obtain additional corroborative evidence relative to account balances and conditions existing at the balance sheet date. (Examples: cash collected from customers after balance sheet date; subsequent movements of merchandise previously on hand or held in warehouses.)

2.   To gather information regarding subsequent transactions or events that may directly affect the financial statements under examination and call for adjustment to those statements if not already adjusted. (Examples: previously unrecorded or understated liabilities; bankruptcy of customer, the condition having existed at the balance sheet date; final settlements in amounts differing materially from recorded estimates, as in settlement of lawsuits; finally determined income tax assessments; declines in sales prices affecting inventory valuation; retroactive wage adjustments; unusual or material sales returns and allowances.)

3.   To bring to light material matters that may require footnote disclosure in the financial statements (and sometimes, for reasons of emphasis, even in the auditor's report) and relate to conditions existing at the balance sheet date. (Example: contingencies that do not meet the criteria for recording an accrual.)

4.   To bring to light material matters that may require footnote disclosure in the financial statements (and sometimes in the auditor's report) and relate to conditions that arose subsequent to the statement date. (Examples: fire losses or other casualties; purchase of a company; litigation; sharp decline in sales volume; loss of major customers; bond or capital stock issuances.)

AUDITING PROCEDURES

	Performed by	NA
1. Synchronize post balance sheet review with procedures designed to uncover unrecorded or understated liabilities or contingent liabilities. (See Figure 4-8).		
2. Update listing of meetings of stockholders, board of directors and executive committees and examine minutes not previously reviewed. Inquire about matters covered at meetings for which minutes may not as yet have been prepared, but follow-up for later review of minutes.		
3. Make appropriate inquiries of president and other senior officers. Inquiries should be both general and specific in nature and should include reference to illustrative types of situations, transactions, and events.		
4. Include in management's representation letter a statement that no material transactions or events have occurred subsequent to the statement date requiring adjustment or disclosure in the financial statements except as noted. The letter should similarly include a comprehensive listing of illustrative events to facilitate a reliable response.		
5. Obtain an updated representation on subsequent events, where indicated.		
6. Date the letter to the client's attorney as close to the report date as practicable (and obtain updated letter where indicated), and include inquiries regarding claims, assessments and subsequent events for which the services of an attorney would have been required.		
7. Review interim statements for subsequent period, compare with audited statements, and inquire whether (a) the interim statements were prepared on the		

same basis as the audited statements; (b) adjustments usually made at year-end were made at the interim date; and (c) unusual adjustments or transactions were or should have been reflected in the interim statements. Identify in working papers the statements reviewed.

8. Review budget reports and compare with interim statements.

9. Scan the books and records and take note of any entries in the subsequent period that appear unusual or significant and warrant further inquiry or investigation.

10. Observe the operation of the company and take note of newspaper, trade, or other reports that may have a bearing on the subsequent events review.

INTERNAL ACCOUNTING CONTROL AND AUDITING STANDARDS AND PROCEDURES—GENERAL CONSIDERATIONS

The auditor's auditing responsibilities in regard to the client's system of internal accounting control rest upon the second standard of field work. The basic considerations are set forth in AU 320. Other aspects of the subject are dealt with in other AU sections as later noted. Essentially, the auditor is required to study and evaluate the system of internal accounting control to judge the extent to which he can rely upon that system in determining the nature, extent and timing of audit tests and procedures.

Internal control encompasses both administrative control and accounting control, and the establishment and maintenance of both types is the responsibility of management. However, AU 320 specifically states that the auditor's study and evaluation of the internal control takes in only the accounting control segment.

Administrative control includes those procedures and records concerned with management's business and operational decision-making leading to the authorization of transactions.

The AU 320 definition of internal accounting control—in effect, a statement of objectives—is stated in Figure 2-13. The major objectives reflected in that definition concern *authorization, accounting,* and *asset safeguarding.* Figure 2-13 also includes a more complete and pragmatic statement of objectives of an internal accounting control system for the working guidance of the auditor, as well as a listing of significant characteristics of an adequate system. Figure 2-13 can serve as a basic general introduction to an auditor's Internal Accounting Control Guide.

The Foreign Corrupt Practices Act uses the exact language of the AU 320 definition in requiring that public companies devise and maintain an adequate system of internal accounting control. It also includes a requirement—redundant because a good system would reflect this in any event—that public companies "make and keep books, records, and accounts, which, in reasonable detail, accurately and fairly reflect the transactions and dispositions of . . . assets . . .".

It is important to stress that even a satisfactory system of internal accounting control can provide only *reasonable* assurance that the objectives of the system have been achieved. Cost-benefit considerations must be taken into account so that the cost of internal controls does not exceed the expected benefits. But there are also inherent limitations that can impair the effectiveness of any system of internal accounting control. As stated in AU 320, they are:

1. Collusion may be present, thus nullifying the effectiveness of segregation of duties.

2.   Management ordinarily has the power to circumvent or override controls.

3.   Human factors such as the following may weaken controls: misunderstanding of instructions, mistakes of judgment, carelessness, distraction, or fatigue.

4.   Procedures may become inadequate because of a change in conditions.

5.   Degree of compliance can vary or actually deteriorate because of the sheer impact over time of carrying out routine procedures or of growing familiarity with and indulgent acceptance of fellow employees.

Figure 2-13
Internal Accounting Control:
Definition, Objectives, General Characteristics
Introductory Text for Internal Accounting Control Guide

DEFINITION (from AU 320.28)

Internal accounting control comprises the plan of organization and the procedures and records that are concerned with the safeguarding of assets and the reliability of financial records and consequently are designed to provide reasonable assurance that:

1. Transactions are executed in accordance with management's general or specific authorization.
2. Transactions are recorded as necessary (a) to permit preparation of financial statements in conformity with generally accepted accounting principles or any other criteria applicable to such statements, and (b) to maintain accountability for assets.
3. Access to assets is permitted only in accordance with management's authorization.
4. The recorded accountability for assets is compared with the existing assets at reasonable intervals and appropriate action is taken with respect to any differences.

In the context of internal accounting control, the objective of *safeguarding of assets* takes in avoidance of loss or impairment of assets through errors, irregularities, or inadequacies in processing transactions and handling assets. (*Errors* may be characterized as unintentional mistakes, and *irregularities* as intentional distortions of financial statements or as defalcations.) It does not ordinarily encompass loss of assets from management's business decisions, such as the decision to undertake a research and development program that may later turn out to be unproductive, or the decision to acquire equipment that may later prove to be unsatisfactory.

OBJECTIVES

The following is an elaboration of the succinct statement of objectives embodied in the foregoing definition. An adequate system of internal accounting control is one that is designed to provide reasonable assurance that:

1. Errors or irregularities affecting the safeguarding of assets and the reliability of the financial records are prevented or are detected early.

2. All transactions, and all matters requiring accounting entries, have in fact been properly recorded.

3. Proper recording signifies that a clear accountability for assets exists, and that entries have been made in proper amounts in conformity with generally accepted accounting principles, including proper classification, and in the correct accounting period. It also signifies that the soundness of accounting estimates and judgments by management has been enhanced by controls designed to ensure that those estimates and judgments are based on sufficient reliable information and deliberation and have been reviewed by appropriate executives.

4. All accounting entries are valid and are based upon bona fide transactions and circumstances.

5. Transactions are supported by appropriate and relevant records, documents, and other evidential matter.

6. Transactions require either general authorization (such as stated credit terms and limits) or specific authorization (such as authorization to acquire a building or to grant a customer a special allowance).

7. The terms and conditions of completed transactions are later compared with authorizations to see if transactions have been properly executed. This comparison may take the form of approval procedures or an internal audit or other type of review.

8. Assets are physically safeguarded by (a) physical segregation; (b) use of protective equipment or devices; (c) placement in secure custodial facilities such as banks and bonded warehouses; (d) use of physical facilities protected against improper intrusion, fire or other casualties, or spoilage; (e) limitation of access to assets to authorized personnel; (f) adequate casualty insurance coverage.

9. Losses are minimized. It would seem, however, that certain causes of losses, such as poor judgment of management in authorizing certain transactions, or an inefficient management generally, would fall outside the area of internal accounting control and, therefore, outside the scope of the auditor's more direct concern.

10. Assets are counted or inspected (as appropriate) and compared periodically with the recorded amounts. Material differences are investigated and appropriate action is taken.

11. The internal accounting controls are themselves periodically monitored to ensure their continued effectiveness.

BASIC CHARACTERISTICS

Underlying Features

1. *Documentation.* Whenever reasonable and practicable, all matters of importance relating to the system of internal accounting

control and to the transactions and operations of the entity should be in writing and/or supported by written documentation. Moreover, the information reflected in the written materials should be presented clearly so that misunderstanding may be avoided.

2. *Communication.* Policies, authorization, responsibilities, instructions, and procedures should be publicized and fully communicated to the appropriate persons.

3. *Reexamination.* Internal accounting controls and related policies, instructions, authorizations, procedures, and so on, should be periodically reexamined, monitored, redesigned if necessary, and republicized and recommunicated to prevent any slackening of responsibilities.

4. *Timeliness.* Timeliness is a vital element in carrying out accounting control procedures. Undue delays, as in the case of delayed cash deposits or in the recording of assets, can negate the effectiveness of otherwise adequate procedures. In general, assets acquired should come under immediate physical control and an immediate accountability should be established.

5. *Cycle control sequence.* Sequential controls should be established for the various steps involved in a transaction cycle to ensure both the safeguarding of assets and, concurrently, the creation of proper accountability by suitable documentation and by accounting entries. Thus in the revenue cycle these controls should operate at every stage, beginning with receipt of a customer's order, then the credit check, then the price and quantity check, and on through shipping, invoicing, accounting entries, and subsequent cash receipts.

Organization and Personnel

1. *Plan of organization.* The plan should be in writing and provide the structure through which company policies and plans are formulated, executed, and monitored. Some of its major features, as related to internal accounting controls, are noted below.

2. *Assignment and fixing of responsibilities.* Duties, powers, and responsibilities should be clearly assigned to promote effectiveness and efficiency of operations and to fix responsibility for failures or irregularities. Job descriptions and other such written documentation should be available as supporting evidence and to minimize any misunderstanding.

3. *Authorizations.* The plan of organization should provide for a system of authorization at various levels as a major control in preventing unauthorized actions or transactions.

4. *Supervision.* Personnel should be properly supervised to ensure that duties are being carried out as assigned.

5. *Monitoring and internal auditing.* Review procedures should be established to ensure that transactions have been consummated in accordance with the terms of prior authorization and, further, that transactions have been properly entered in the accounting records. The monitoring and review aspect of internal accounting control may take a variety of forms, including review by a responsible official, audit and review by internal auditors, involvement of the board of directors or its audit committee, or consideration of a given transaction or matter by a company executive or operating committee. The internal audit function adds immeasurably to the adequacy of a system of internal accounting control.

6. *Competence and training.* Employment policies should reflect an emphasis on executive and employee competence. Duties assigned should be commensurate with the capabilities of the personnel. Continued training should be part of the program.

7. *Honesty of personnel.* The background of prospective employees should be investigated to determine their honesty and integrity.

8. *Bonding.* Employees should be bonded to insure against embezzlement losses. Investigation by the bonding company will also screen out employees with questionable backgrounds.

9. *Segregation of duties.* This general control, often referred to as *division of duties*, is really made up of a number of different control features:

(a) *No one in complete control.* No one person should be in complete control of a transaction. Such complete control would permit a person to operate incompetently or fraudulently without detection.

(b) *Separate custodianship.* No one employee should be responsible for the multiple custody of assets that are susceptible to substitution. Thus if one person has custody of both negotiable securities and cash funds, a shortage in one can be made up by a transfer of assets from the other.

(c) *Single custodial responsibility.* Only one person should have custody of a cash or other fund, so that responsibility can be fixed more easily. Several persons may be assigned custodial responsibilities for a given fund if adequate controls can be instituted to ensure proper personnel accountability.

(d) *Operations and assets versus records.* The employees who are involved in company operations (including authorization of transactions) or in custody of assets should not be assigned any accounting or recordkeeping functions, and vice versa. The books and records provide an accountability for assets and transactions, and the failure to separate the operational and asset custody functions from recordkeeping simply provides an easy opportunity to cover up irregularities or errors.

(e) *Comparison of records (accountability) with assets.* Periodically, assets on hand (e.g., cash, securities and merchandise inventories) should be compared with the records and any material differences should be investigated and appropriate action taken. However, the officials responsible for counting or inspecting the assets and for comparison with the accounting records should have no responsibilities or duties pertaining to either asset custody or the accounting records. Similarly, they should not have had responsibility for authorizing the acquisition of the assets involved.

(f) *Double check.* To the extent practicable, one person should check on the accuracy of the work done by another. Sometimes, this can be done indirectly and without duplication of effort. The person performing a bank reconciliation, for example, is in effect checking on the work of employees who record or deposit cash receipts.

(g) *Rotation and vacations.* A policy of rotating employees and scheduling of vacations ensures that the work performed by an employee is checked by the person replacing him.

10. *Joint responsibility.* For some matters, assignment of joint responsibility to two or more persons makes for better control. Some examples are checks requiring two signatures, or the presence and signature of two persons required to open safety deposit box.

Accounting and Financial Function and Records

1. *Good accounting system.* A complete and integrated system of accounting is an essential internal control component. The system should be designed to create a clear accountability for the company's assets and operations and to ensure the accuracy of the accounting records and financial statements. The system should provide for subsidiary ledgers, where applicable, and for periodic reconciliation with controlling accounts.

2. *Reports.* Budgets, managerial accounting reports and financial accounting reports should be prepared annually and for interim periods on a timely basis, both for the company as a whole and for the appropriate operating divisions and levels of management. Periodic comparison of budgets and other plans should be made with reports portraying actual results and conditions, and differences should be thoroughly investigated. Analytical review procedures should be employed in examining and analyzing reports.

3. *Written manuals.* The accounting and operational procedures should be described in accounting and procedures manuals and charts.

4. *Forms and documentation.* Adequate forms, with such control features as prenumbering, should be made up for the various operations and business transactions (e.g., sales invoices, purchase orders, receiving records) to create a clear accountability.

5. *Indication of authorization and approval.* Documents (like purchase invoices or sales orders) should, where practicable, bear some indication (like initials, signatures, or attachments) that the item had been authorized and later approved, the approval implying that the actual transaction corresponded with the authorization terms. When an initial authorization is lacking, the subsequent approval of a completed transaction is somewhat in the nature of a delayed authorization.

6. *Assets and records.* Actual assets on hand or held by outside custodians should be periodically compared with accounting and other records and differences should be accounted for. This principle includes communications with outside parties (e.g., sending monthly statements to customers or receiving and reconciling monthly reports from warehouses).

Physical and Other Safeguards

1. *Custody devices.* Assets should be physically protected (e.g., securities placed in vaults, cash sales rung up in cash register, or cash deposited in bank).

2. *Facilities.* The physical facilities should be of such construction and have such safeguards as to minimize the possibility of loss, destruction or deterioration of assets by fire or other casualty, inadequate storage space, poor atmospheric conditions, and unauthorized access to or removal of assets.

3. *Adequate insurance.* The company should be adequately insured against fire and other hazards. Appropriate monitoring procedures should be instituted to ensure periodic review of insurance coverage.

SYSTEM REVIEW, COMPLIANCE TESTING, AND SUBSTANTIVE TESTING

AU 320 discusses the place of the study of internal accounting control within the total context of the auditor's examination of the financial statements. The following terms are used whose meaning, significance, and interrelationship must be understood if an informed audit is to be performed: study of internal control; review of internal control; compliance testing; system evaluation; and substantive testing. Figure 2-14 presents definitions of these and related terms in clarification of their meaning and interrelationships. Also included in Figure 2-14 is a listing of the several stages through which a study of the system of internal accounting control may go. The figure can serve as introductory text material for the Audit Program Guide.

Figure 2-14
System Review, Compliance Testing, and Substantive Testing: Definitions and Examination Stages—Introductory Text for Audit Program Guide

Definitions

1. *Study of system of internal accounting control.* The auditor's study of the system is a two-phase undertaking:

(a) Acquiring a knowledge and understanding of the system and of the component control procedures. This is referred to as a *review* of the system. The information may be obtained by inquiries and discussion with the client's officers and staff, examination of manuals and other documentation, preparation and/or review of flowcharts and narrative descriptions of the system, and completion of internal control questionnaires.

(b) Gaining reasonable assurance that the system is actually working as prescribed. This is referred to as *compliance testing*. To determine whether the prescribed accounting controls are actually being complied with, the auditor undertakes auditing procedures (i.e., compliance testing) in which transactions are tested to determine whether the control procedures were performed, how they were performed, and by whom. The tests usually entail the examination of documents supporting the transactions to note authorizations, approvals, appropriate initials or signatures, prenumbering, tie-in to supporting documents, and other such features. Compliance testing with respect to segregation of duties may be revealed by signatures noted on the documentation examined and by observation and careful inquiry.

2. *Evaluation of the System.* The auditor undertakes a study and evaluation of the system of internal accounting control, as stated in the second auditing standard of field work, so that he may determine the extent of reliance on the system in undertaking his other auditing procedures known as *substantive testing* (defined below). Complete reliance, however, can never be placed on the internal controls, and substantive testing must always be undertaken, although the amount of such testing, the timing of audit procedures, and sometimes the type of evidential matter examined, will be affected by the degree of reliance on the system. In forming his evaluation, the auditor considers the two components of the study, as previously defined:

(a) *Review.* After evaluating the data acquired during the review phase of the study, the auditor will proceed as follows: (i) If the system

as designed appears adequate, he will then undertake compliance testing; (ii) If the system appears to be inadequate, he will bypass compliance testing and proceed directly to substantive testing, with no reliance being placed upon the system.

(b) *Compliance testing.* Following compliance testing, the auditor
will then evaluate the results of the testing and proceed as follows: (i) If
the prescribed system is in fact being complied with, the substantive
testing will take that into account; (ii) If the prescribed system is not in
fact being followed satisfactorily, the auditor will proceed to substantive testing and those procedures will reflect his lack of reliance on the
system of internal accounting control.

3. *Substantive testing.* The third standard of field work, with its
emphasis on obtaining sufficient competent evidential matter as a
basis for the expression of an opinion regarding the financial statements, underlies those auditing procedures designated as *substantive
testing.* The term embraces three classes of auditing procedures, as
follows:

(a) *Tests of details of transactions.* Substantive testing in this
area may include the same items tested in *compliance testing,* but the
goals will usually be different. In compliance testing of transactions
the focus is on the internal control attributes (i.e., features) noted such
as indications of approval or of cancellation of vouchers (referred to
as *attribute testing*), whereas in substantive testing the focus is on the
validity of the *amounts* entered in the accounts and ultimately reflected
in the financial statements.

(b) *Tests of account balances.* These procedures focus directly
on the account balances appearing in the financial statements.

(c) *Analytical review.* These procedures entail a critical analysis
and review of ratios, trends, and account and other interrelationships
to determine their reasonableness or to reveal unusual or questionable
fluctuations or discrepancies requiring further inquiry and investigation.

Stages in Study of Internal Control System

The study of the system of internal accounting control is undertaken
in stages throughout the engagement. The schema may be described
as follows, subject to the caveats noted in Figure 2-15.

1. *Pre-engagement planning.* In this stage a broad insight is
gained regarding the control system. Many of the procedures undertaken in pre-engagement planning are pertinent to the study of the
system of internal accounting control, especially in acquiring an understanding, however limited and tentative, of the general internal

control environment. These procedures relate to: acquiring an understanding of the client's business (see Figure 1-7); inquiry regarding
related party transactions (Figure 1-12); identifying major trouble
or risk areas (Figure 1-8); and gaining some insight as to the condition of the records and the adequacy of the system of internal accounting control (Figure 1-2, item 6[a]).

2. *Audit planning*. After acceptance of the engagement, an
orientation-type review of the accounting records and the internal
accounting controls is undertaken as a basis for forming at least a
preliminary judgment as to whether a more detailed study of the system is to be undertaken. The objectives and procedures for such a
review appear in Figure 1-9.

3. *More detailed review*. If the orientation review leads to a preliminary conclusion that reliance can presumptively be placed on the
internal accounting controls, a more detailed review (to gain additional
and more definitive understanding of the prescribed system) will then
be undertaken.

4. *Compliance testing*. If the prescribed system appears to be
adequate, compliance testing will then be undertaken.

5. *Evaluation*. At each stage in the study of the system of internal
accounting control, the applicable results must be evaluated and a
conclusion formed as to whether the study is to be further pursued.
Thus a negative judgment following the second stage may have the effect of precluding a more detailed review. Similarly, knowledge that the
prescribed system is materially deficient, gained after a more detailed
review, would obviate the need for compliance testing. The basic question to be asked at each step is, "Will we as auditors ultimately place
any reliance on the system of internal accounting control in (as stated
in the second standard of field work) 'the determination of the resultant
extent of the tests (i.e., *substantive testing*) to which auditing procedures are to be restricted.'?"

The evaluation of internal accounting controls must take into account (a) the type of errors or irregularities that could occur; (b) the
potential materiality of any impact that such errors or irregularities
might have on the fairness of the financial statements if not prevented
or detected; and (c) the extent to which controls exist that can prevent
or detect such errors or irregularities.

6. *Reporting weaknesses*. Material weakness in internal accounting controls that come to the auditor's attention must be communicated to senior management and the board of directors or its audit
committee.

SOME CAVEATS FOR THE STUDY OF THE
INTERNAL ACCOUNTING CONTROL SYSTEM

In designing and undertaking procedures for the study of the system of internal accounting control, there can be a tendency to apply the theoretical framework too rigidly and mechanically, and thus impair the quality of the auditor's total examination. Such an approach tends to obscure the overlapping and interrelationships that exist among the various elements of the auditor's examination that may be involved in the study of the system. The caveats and elucidations in Figure 2-15 are presented for the purpose of reemphasizing certain fundamentals pertinent to the subject. The figure may be used as introductory text material for the Audit Program Guide as well as for the Internal Accounting Control Guide.

Figure 2-15
Caveats for the Study of the System of
Internal Accounting Control (Introductory
Text for Audit Program Guide)

1.   The various stages in the study of the system should not be artifically separated. Thus some auditors may combine the pre-engagement stage of system review with that of audit planning, especially if they have previously had some familiarity with the client.

2.   The transaction cycle approach to the study of internal accounting controls is in fact only one approach. There are other ways that can provide a valid focus, depending on the individual client, such as by function, department, operating unit, or by any combination.

3.   The two phases of internal control study—review of the system and compliance testing—should not be mechanically viewed as two disparate phases. They are often inseparable. This caveat is recognized explicitly in AU 320 which states that the two phases may sometimes be performed concurrently.

4.   There is no preferred device for documenting the review of the internal accounting control system. Some auditors use internal control questionnaires exclusively, while others may use narrative system descriptions or flowcharts or a combination of such devices. The questionnarie is perhaps the most popular tool (whether used exclusively or in combination) because it serves, in addition to other uses, as a checklist of essential control features.

5.   Whatever devices are used—questionnaires, flowcharts, and narrative descriptions—must later be updated or otherwise modified, based on findings subsequent to their initial preparation.

6.   Questionnaires or guides (and flowcharts and narrative descriptions) may be prepared at any appropriate stage. Some auditors may prepare them as part of the process of gaining knowledge of the prescribed system. Other auditors may prepare them in the process of concurrently undertaking a review of the system and compliance testing. Still others may, for example, use an internal control questionnaire as a means of documenting conclusions *after* completing compliance testing.

7.   Generalized evaluations of the overall system of internal accounting controls are not useful in the practical conduct of the audit. This caveat is expressed in AU 320. In considering the effect of reliance on the system on the auditing (substantive) procedures, the focus must be (apart from the general environment) on individual accounting controls as they relate to meaningful system segments such as cash receipts, cash disbursements, inventories, and the like. Moreover, strengths in one segment may have no bearing in overcoming weak-

nesses in another area. Further, considerable variation may exist among the several subsegments of a given area. For example, cash disbursements for fixed assets may have stronger controls than for payroll. In general, the evaluation of internal controls must be analytical in nature.

8. In certain respects, compliance testing and substantive testing are interrelated. AU 320 states that the test of details of transactions, which represents one of several aspects of substantive testing, can often be conducted concurrently with compliance testing, although the objectives will differ. But beyond that, substantive testing may often contribute substantially to a knowledge of both the prescribed system of internal accounting control and compliance with the system. For example, confirmation of accounts receivable may disclose poor cutoff procedures; or a count of cash and securities on hand may provide information regarding custodial devices and arrangements, as well as degree of compliance with the prescribed system.

9. The study of the system of internal accounting control should cover the system as it existed throughout the period covered by the engagement. However, if the study was carried out during an interim period and appropriate conclusions drawn at that time, the study of the balance of the period may be tailored to take the prior study and conclusions into account. Quite often, a carry-through can be accomplished via substantive testing that may also, as previously noted, yield additional internal control information.

10. The working papers should contain (a) appropriate documentation as evidence of the auditor's study and testing of the system of internal accounting control; (b) the auditor's conclusion on whether the prescribed system and compliance with it in each area are satisfactory; and (c) indication of the extent to which substantive auditing procedures have been affected by the system of internal accounting control.

COMMUNICATING MATERIAL WEAKNESSES
IN INTERNAL ACCOUNTING CONTROL

It is incumbent on the auditor to communicate to senior management and the board of directors or its audit committee, material weaknesses in internal accounting control that come to his attention during the examination of the financial statements conducted in accordance with generally accepted auditing standards. This requirement is established in AU 323.

As originally defined in AU 320.68, prior to an amendment by SAS 30 (see appendix to SAS 30), "a material weakness means a condition in which the auditor believes the prescribed (internal accounting control) procedures or the degree of compliance with them does not provide reasonable assurance that errors or irregularities in amounts that would be material in the financial statements being audited would be prevented or detected within a timely period by employees in the normal course of performing their assigned functions."

The SAS 30 amendment of AU 320.68 revised this definition to read: "A material weaknes in internal accounting control is a condition in which the specific control procedures or the degree of comliance with them does ot reduce to a relatively low level the risk that errors or irregularities in amounts that would be material in relation to the financial statments being audited may occur and not be detected within a timely period by employees in the normal course of performing their assigned functions." While one definition may focus on reasonable assurance and the other on risk and probability, the two definitions have the same practical significance and reflect identical goals.

Some basic considerations pertinent to this topic are presented in Figure 2-16. A suggested form of communication shown as Figure 2-17 is a modified version of an illustrative form that appeared in AU 323, paragraph 8, prior to the amendment of that paragraph by SAS 30. After restating the basic proposition that the form of communicating material weaknesses in internal accounting control to senior management and the board of directors or its audit committee is optional, SAS 30 suggests a report of the type shown as Figure 6-64 when the auditor communicates in writing. Nevertheless, Figure 2-17 may also be found helpful to the auditor in the fashioning of an appropriate report.

To facilitate the preparation of this report, a separate summary record of the type shown in Figure 2-18 should be maintained by the auditor in which weaknesses in internal accounting control should be listed as they are encountered.

Chapter 6 presents illustrative reports on an entity's system of internal accounting control issued in connection with engagements in which the accountant is requested to report on the system.

Figure 2-16
Communicating Material Internal
Accounting Control Weaknesses—
A Checklist Guide

1.   The communication by the auditor of material internal accounting control weaknesses that come to his attention during the examination, to senior management and the board of directors or its audit committee, is a requirement. But it is only incident to the auditor's
examination of the financial statements and to his study or evaluation
of internal accounting control. Such communication is entirely unrelated to the auditor's opinion on the financial statements or the reference in the report to generally accepted auditing standards.
2.   Material weaknesses may come to the auditor's attention at any
stage in the study of the internal accounting controls, or while performing the auditing procedures associated with substantive tests.
The auditor, however, is under no obligation to evaluate every control
or to identify all material weaknesses. In fact, because of cost-benefit
considerations, the auditor may decide to base his examination exclusively on substantive tests. He must, however, report material weaknesses that do in fact *come to his attention*.
3.   The material weaknesses reported on are those that were not
corrected before coming to the auditor's attention. As defined in AU
323 (as amended by SAS 30), a material weakness in internal accounting control "is a condition in which the specific control procedures
or the degree of compliance with them does not reduce to a relatively
low level the risk that errors or irregularities in amounts that would
be material in relation to the financial statements being audited may
occur and not be detected within a timely period by employees in the
normal course of performing their assigned functions."
4.   The auditor may, but is *not* required to, communicate immaterial
weaknesses or the fact that no material weaknesses came to his attention.
5.   Material weaknesses should be reported at the earliest practicable date following the completion of the examination, but preferably
in addition at interim dates if the examination is conducted in stages.
6.   There is no standard form of communication. Preferably, it
should be in writing but if the delivery is made orally, the working
papers should contain appropriate supporting notations.
7.   The communication may make reference to management's
belief, where applicable, that corrective action for certain specified
weaknesses is not practicable.
8.   Comments may also be included concerning corrective action
taken or in process, as well as the auditor's suggestions for corrective
action.

9. If the auditor's report has been qualified because of a scope restriction, that fact and its effect on the study and evaluation of the system of internal accounting control should be noted in the communication.

10. The auditor may wish to note in the communication: (a) that the internal accounting control system is a responsibility of management; (b) the basis for the auditor's interest in internal accounting control; and (c) the inherent limitations in any internal accounting control system. The report should state that it is intended solely for the use of management, the board of directors, or its audit committee. Illustrative reports are shown as Figures 2-17 and 6-64.

Figure 2-17
Report Communicating Material Weaknesses in
Internal Accounting Control

(Auditor's Stationery)

(Date)

(Addressed to senior management
and board of directors)

Gentlemen:

The purpose of this letter is to communicate certain conditions that came to our attention during our examination of your Company's financial statements which we believe to represent material weaknesses in your system of internal accounting control.

We have examined the financial statements of (client's name) for the year ended (date) and have issued our report thereon dated (date). As a part of our examination, we made a study and evaluation of the Company's system of internal accounting control to the extent we considered necessary to evaluate the system as required by generally accepted auditing standards. Under these standards, the purposes of such evaluation are to establish if a basis exists for reliance on the system of internal accounting control in determining the nature, timing, and extent of other auditing procedures that are necessary for expressing an opinion on the financial statements, and to assist the auditor in planning and performing his examination of the financial statements.

The objective of a system of internal accounting control is to provide reasonable, but not absolute, assurance as to the safeguarding of assets against loss from unauthorized use or disposition, and the reliability of financial records for preparing financial statements and maintaining accountability for assets. The concept of reasonable assurance recognizes that the cost of a system of internal accounting control should not exceed the benefits derived and also recognizes that the evaluation of these factors necessarily requires estimates and judgments by management.

There are also inherent limitations that should be recognized in considering the potential effectiveness of any system of internal accounting control. In the performance of most control procedures, errors can result from misunderstanding of instructions, mistakes of judgment, carelessness, or other personal factors. Control procedures whose effectiveness depends upon segregation of duties can be circumvented by collusion. Similarly, control procedures can be circumvented intentionally by management either with respect to the execution and recording of transactions or with respect to the estimates and judgments required in the preparation of financial statements. Further, projection of any evaluation of internal accounting control to future periods is subject to the risk that the procedures may become inadequate because of changes in conditions and that the degree of compliance with the procedures may deteriorate.

Our examination of the financial statements made in accordance with generally accepted auditing standards, including the study and evaluation of the Company's system of internal accounting control for the year ended (date), that was made for the purposes set forth earlier in this letter, would not necessarily disclose all weaknesses in the system for the reasons mentioned and because it was based on selective tests of accounting records and related data. However, such study and evaluation disclosed the following conditions that we believe to be material weaknesses. They do not include material weaknesses that were corrected before coming to our attention.

(At this point, material weaknesses that have come to the auditor's attention should be listed and described, accompanied by, if desired, indications of corrective actions taken or in process, or suggestions for corrective action.)

(If applicable) Our study and evaluation of internal accounting control also disclosed the following conditions that we believe to be material weaknesses for which management believes corrective action is not practicable in the circumstances.

(At this point, weaknesses should be summarized and the circumstances described.)

The foregoing conditions were considered in determining the nature, timing, and extent of audit tests to be applied in our examination of the financial statements, and this report of such conditions does not modify our report dated (date) on such financial statements.

This report is intended solely for the use and information of management and the board of directors and should not be used for any other purpose.

Sincerely,

_____

(Signature of accountant)

_____

Comment. See earlier reference to Figure 6-64 as the type of report suggested by SAS 30.

Figure 2-18
Internal Accounting Control Weaknesses—
Summary Record

(For use in preparing report letter communicating material weaknesses to senior management and board of directors.)

Client: _____

Prepared by: _____   Date: _____

Period of financial statements: _____

Reviewed by: _____   Date: _____

Note: Comments should provide clarification as to management's reaction; corrective plans; reasons for exclusion from report, if applicable, etc.

Documentation					
Internal Accounting Control Guide		M (Material) or NM	To be included	Description	
Section Item	W/P ref.	(Not Material)	in report?	of weakness	Comments

ANALYTICAL REVIEW PROCEDURES

As the term is defined in AU 320, *substantive testing* involves obtaining evidential matter through (*a*) tests of details of transactions and account balances, and (*b*) analytical review procedures applied to financial information. AU 318 provides some clarification of the nature and method of application of analytical review procedures that are undertaken in an examination made in accordance with generally accepted auditing standards.

Analytical review procedures are also undertaken for reviews of interim financial information of public entities and for reviews of financial statements (interim or annual) of nonpublic entities, and they are dealt with in, respectively, SAS No. 24 (AU 721), and Statement on Standards for Accounting and Review Services (SSARS) No. 1. For such review engagements, analytical review procedures are not associated with substantive testing—a term that applies to *audits*. Moreover, on review engagements the procedures are carried out with objectives and in a context that are different from those of an audit. The definition of analytical review procedures and the method of their application as presented in AU 318, AU 721 and SSARS No. 1, are so similar, however, in many fundamental respects, that the audit program guide for use and application of analytical review procedures provided by Figure 2-19 should also be helpful to the accountant in review engagements. The subject of review engagements is covered in Chapter 8.

Figure 2-19
Analytical Review Procedures

(Introductory Text For Audit Program Guide)

Definition

Analytical review procedures comprise one of the main categories of substantive testing in an examination made in accordance with generally accepted auditing standards. These procedures are also employed on *review* (as distinguished from *audit*) engagements where, together with *inquiries*, they constitute the means by which the objectives of the *review* of the financial statements are carried out by the accountant.

Analytical review procedures are, in the main, broad overview-type comparisons of current period financial information with similar or related information:

1. Within the current period (for example, sales by months, or repairs in relationship to plant and equipment).
2. In comparable prior periods.
3. Derived from trends, the entity's historical experience, or other such factors having predictive value.
4. Reflected in reports of anticipated results such as budgets or forecasts.
5. As stated in company policies (for example, policy as to sales discounts, sales returns, capital expenditures, dividends).
6. Contained in significant documents or sources such as corporate minutes, tax returns, and published investment services and data.
7. Of a nonfinancial nature (for example, number of employees or footage of inventory storage space).
8. Reported by other companies in the industry or by the industry as a whole.

The emphasis is on evaluating trends, ratios, and other relationships and forming a judgment on whether they are as expected—that is, meet the tests of normality, reasonableness, logic, conformity to predictable patterns, and inherent consistency—and therefore provide additional evidential support for the validity of the account balance or other data examined or reviewed. Unusual, unexpected, or otherwise questionable deviations or fluctuations, or the absence of expected fluctuations, are investigated further in order to achieve satisfaction in the given matter.

Entity and Segments

These procedures and the comparisons made may be applied to the financial statements as a whole, to segments of the statements (such as current assets, current liabilities, revenues, and operating results), or to account balances, and to subsidiaries, divisions, or other components of the entity considered appropriate by the accountant. The focus of the analytical review procedures will usually represent cumulative or final balances or other data for a given period—interim, annual, or span of years.

Timing

The procedures may be undertaken at various times during the examination:

1. In the preliminary planning stages of the engagement as an aid in identifying areas that will require special attention during the engagement.
2. During the conduct of the examination in conjunction with other types of procedures.
3. In the concluding stages of the examination as an overall review.

Methods and Techniques

In contrast to tests of details of transactions and balances, the emphasis in analytical review procedures is on gaining understanding and satisfaction in broad terms regarding the matters under review. The data compared, developed, or calculated in the analytical review may often be expressed as estimates or approximations inasmuch as the objective is to gain satisfaction as to the matter on an overall basis and within an acceptable *range*, rather than in terms of utmost precision or details. Hence, analytical review procedures can often be carried out relatively quickly. They may even yield, on occasion, results as precise or as convincing as any that may be derived from detailed tests.

The comparisons made and relationships considered (see *definition* section above) may be expressed in a number of ways, including dollar amounts, physical quantities, other quantitative data, ratios, and percentages. The comparisons are often tied in with a variety of techniques, such as scanning; independent calculations and approximations; reference to comparable or related data on documents such as tax returns or corporate minutes; consideration of company policy relating to the matter in question; judgment as to reasonableness, taking into account the nature of the business, the company's financial condition and other considerations; personal observation of the physical environment.

Procedural Steps—the General Pattern

1.   Identify the financial and nonfinancial information to which the analytical review is to be applied. The subject matter of the review may be an account balance for a given month or period, a ratio, a percentage, sundry items, results or classifications as reflected on the financial statements, in fact, any matter or data of importance to the accountant in his examination (or review).

2.   Obtain corresponding financial and nonfinancial information that is to serve as a basis for (or as an aid in making) a comparison with related information of the current period. Some examples of information to be obtained are prior period data and financial statements, current period data (such as monthly sales, or interim financial statements), budgets and forecasts, pertinent company policies and authorizations, industry data, data reflected on tax returns (e.g., total monthly, quarterly or annual payroll or payroll taxes) and in corporate minutes, and independent calculations of ratios, percentages, or other data.

3.   Consider the possibility that the "base" data on a given matter may require adjustment or, perhaps, may be unreliable and should not be used at all.

4.   Make the appropriate comparison and analyze the relationship under consideration, using the review technique appropriate in the circumstances, such as: compare; scan; calculate; roughly approximate; observe; refer to relevant documentation.

5.   Judge whether the information under review and the associated relationships (including trends) correspond with expectations—that is, meet the tests of reasonableness, logic, normality, conformity to predictable patterns, and inherent consistency.

6.   In forming such judgments, take the following into account:

(a)   The nature and strength of the entity's business and financial condition and operating results, the characteristics of the industry, the entity's position in the industry, and the trends in these respects.

(b)   Information derived from auditing or other procedures that may help to explain or contradict the findings of the analytical review procedure—such as knowledge of a labor dispute that would account for a sales decline, or increase in repairs and maintenance despite plant renovations in a prior period.

(c)   Changed circumstances that may be the cause of unusual or questionable variations or fluctuations, or may arouse suspicions if significant fluctuations do not occur.

(d) An awareness that the absence of an expected relationship or fluctuation may be just as significant as their presence, and that alertness must be exercised with respect to both.

(e) The *degree* of deviation, variation or fluctuation, using appropriate materiality standards (which may vary, depending on the item or matter reviewed), but also recognizing that the comparisions are often properly based on broad-gauged approximations and estimates.

7. Relate the results of the analytical review to the findings and evidential matter developed by means of other types of audit tests and procedures.

8. Investigate any unusual fluctuations, variations, or other relationships (including the absence of expected fluctuations, variations, or relationships), as well as anything else that appears unusual or questionable upon analytical review.

9. Discuss these matters with the client and obtain explanations for their occurrence.

10. Evaluate the reasonableness of management's responses and consider the need for corroboration, especially if the responses seem inadequate.

11. Obtain such corroboration, where necessary, by undertaking additional procedures and obtaining supporting evidential matter.

12. Consider the need to modify the audit program as a result of the findings developed through the analytical review procedures. For example, if current inventory turnover rates are considerably lower than in prior periods or the industry average, this knowledge may lead to expanded testing procedures for inventories, especially for obsolete or unsaleable merchandise that the client may continue to carry at cost.

Commonly Used Financial Ratios and Other Relationships

This section of the guide presents a selective listing of some financial ratios and other relationships commonly used in analytical reviews of financial information. The extent to which they apply will depend, of course, on the particular entity; moreover, others not listed here may be important and should be considered. For certain of the items mentioned, a brief description or explanation is provided, but it should be understood that the comment is limited in scope and is not intended to be an exhaustive explanation of the significance of the item or of any findings associated with its use.

Once computed or determined, the financial ratios and other relationships will, of course, then be compared with comparable "base" information, as outlined in the definition of analytical review procedures presented earlier in this guide (e.g., comparison with comparable data in prior periods, budgets, monthly and other interim information of current period, significant documents and published sources, industry figures, and so on to the extent appropriate). Further, in using financial ratios the accountant should not overlook the insights that may be gained for analytical review purposes, by taking into account the impact of price-level changes.

Selected Financial Ratios and Other Relationships

1. *An account or other item standing by itself.* Examples would be any account of the current period, the aggregate of a given financial statement classification such as total current assets, or an operating result such as gross profit or net income. While these may not be financial ratios or other relationships in themselves, they do represent important subject matter for appropriate comparisons with comparable prior period data, budgets, and so on, and for evaluations on an absolute basis, and are therefore included in this listing.

2. *Working capital.* Current assets minus current liabilities; a general indication of availability of current assets for business purposes, assuming current obligations have been met.

3. *Current ratio.* Current assets divided by current liabilities, expressed as *x* to 1 (e.g., 2.5 to 1); permits the adequacy of working capital to be gauged on a relative, rather than absolute, basis).

4. *Acid test ratio.* Quick current assets—that is, financial assets like cash, marketable securities, and receivables—divided by current liabilities; a measure of availability of current liquid assets to meet current liabilities immediately; also expressed as *x* to 1.

5. *Percentage distribution of current assets.* Each current asset account in a percentage relationship to total current assets; can suggest problems relating to individual accounts—for example, excessive inventories or mounting receivables.

6. *Ratio of property, plant and equipment to long-term liabilities.* This ratio can be expressed as a percentage or in the form of *x* to 1, and provides an indication of the security provided for long-term debt, or of security potentially available for future financing.

7. *Ratio of stockholders' equity to total assets.* Often called the "proprietary ratio" expressed as a percentage, this relationship indicates the extent of the stockholders' investment in the total enterprise in contrast to the investment of creditors, and is sometimes used, particularly by creditors, as a measure of financial strength of the enterprise.

8. *Average collection period.* Receivables/net sales x 360 days, with the result expressed in number of days, which is then evaluated taking into account the usual terms of sale. The figure of 360 is used if the given period is a year, but will be less for an interim period. This ratio is sometimes referred to as "number of days sales are outstanding in receivables," or as "turnover of receivables."

9. *Inventory turnover.* Cost of sales divided by average inventory; expressed as *x* times; may reveal excessive, unsaleable, or unusable inventories.

10. *Income statement items to revenues—sales or net sales.* Usually expressed as a percentage. All items of income may be important and the following are simply illustrative: sales returns and allowances; sales discounts; gross profit; selling expenses in the aggregate and also individually, especially sales commissions; bad debts; income before extraordinary items; net income. Also to be considered are data for number of units sold and average unit selling price.

11. *Gross profit ratio.* The relationship of gross profit to net sales, expressed usually as a percentage, requires special mention although included in the item above. The ratio has been often used, after comparison with the comparable ratio in prior years, to determine whether the ending inventory appears to be stated at a reasonable figure and is not materially understated or overstated; yet a questionable result could reflect on any of the factors entering into the computation of gross profit—sales as well as each element of cost of sales, including beginning and ending inventories.

12. *Expense and valuation accounts to related assets.* Expressed as a percentage, these relationships include: bad debts and allowance for doubtful accounts to accounts receivable; depreciation and allowance for depreciation to plant and equipment or to other related fixed asset accounts.

13. *Income or expense accounts to related assets or liabilities.* Some examples of the efficacy of the analytical review procedure as applied to this category: the relationship of interest income to bonds owned; interest expense to bonds issued; repairs and maintenance to plant and equipment; or dividend income to securities owned. Often, an independent overall calculation can be readily made and then compared with recorded amounts.

14. *Expenses to expenses.* This category includes the relationship of payroll taxes to payroll, repairs and maintenance to deprecia-

tion or to power consumption, power consumption to production, and purchase discounts to purchases.

15. *Cost accounts to cost of sales and to cost of manufacturing.* Expressed as a percentage, the items so related may be materials used, direct labor, manufacturing overhead in the aggregate as well as component overhead elements, and inventories. Also important are comparisons of product unit costs.

16. *Relationship to net income, income before extraordinary items, and funds provided from operations.* Items compared, usually as a percentage of the item to income or, if appropriate, as a percentage of income to the item: Federal income taxes, current assets, total assets, and stockholders' equity—return on investment. An important financial ratio in this category is earnings per share, both primary and diluted. While the price-earnings ratio is a significant ratio of special pertinence to the external investor, it too can have considerable analytical review value for the independent accountant; questionable variations, for example, may reveal developments affecting the financial statements that might otherwise not have come to his attention. The ratio "times interest charges earned" is a measure of the capability of the enterprise to continue to meet fixed interest obligations. An even broader ratio of this type is the relationship of earnings to total fixed obligations.

AUDIT COMMITTEE OF THE BOARD OF DIRECTORS

In recent years the value of a corporate audit committee—especially when composed entirely of outside (i.e., non-officer) directors—has received ever-increasing attention and recognition. The establishment of such committees by the board of directors has been recommended by the AICPA, the SEC, and the accounting profession generally. The New York Stock Exchange now requires that each company listed with it have an audit committee made up solely of outside directors. A major impetus in this development has been the revelation by SEC investigations and Congressional committee hearings of questionable and illegal corporate payments and practices, including the bribery of foreign officials, by a number of prominent corporations, and the passage of the Foreign Corrupt Practices Act of 1977.

A guide for the auditor for use in preparing for and participating in meetings with the corporate audit committee is presented as Figure 2-20. Inasmuch as the mode of operation of an audit committee has not been legislated or standardized and will vary from company to company, the guide must of course be adapted to the circumstances of the individual client. The guide can also be helpful even if a client has not as yet established an audit committee, for the issues reflected therein will be pertinent in any meetings the auditor may have with the full board of directors or any of its regular or ad hoc committees.

Figure 2-20
Meeting with the Corporate Audit
Committee—A Checklist Guide

	Performed by	NA

SAS References

1. Review the following references to audit committees in the Statements on Auditing Standards. The nature of the matter dealt with is briefly indicated.

(a) AU 311.04. Discuss with the board of directors or its audit committee the type, scope, and timing of the examination.

(b) AU 323.04. Report to the board of directors or its audit committee (preferably in writing) any material weaknesses in internal accounting control that were not corrected by management before coming to the auditor's attention. (This is stated as a requirement.)

(c) AU 327.14. The auditor should determine (presumably, by direct communication) that the board of directors or its audit committee is aware of material errors or irregularities that he believes may exist.

(d) AU 328.13. When the auditor has determined that an illegal act has occurred, the matter should be reported by him to a sufficiently high level of authority within the organization, including, in some circumstances (presumbly, in the event senior officers are involved), the board of directors or its audit committee.

Structure, Operation, and Responsibilities of Audit Committee

2. Gain an understanding of the structure, operations, and responsibilities

of the audit committee by employing the following procedures:

(a) Review the resolution of the board of directors creating the audit committee.

(b) Make inquiries of senior officers and members of the audit committee.

(c) Examine minutes of meetings of the audit committee and of the full board of directors.

(d) Review reports prepared by the audit committee or submitted to the audit committee by management, the internal auditors, and others.

(e) In undertaking the foregoing procedures, obtain data with respect to:

(i) Composition of the committee and especially regarding its independence of management. Optimally, its membership should be made up entirely of outside directors.

(ii) Number and type of meetings over a one-year period. Optimally, the committee should meet with the independent auditors at least three times a year—early during the auditor's examination, at an appropriate time later in the examination, and in the closing stage for review of the results of the audit. These meetings should be open, where appropriate, to representatives of management and the internal auditors, but the independent auditors should also have the opportunity to meet privately with the audit committee.

(iii) Availability of the audit committee to the auditors for discussion of major problems encountered by the auditors of the type that would normally be a concern of the committee or the board of directors.

(iv) Working relationship with the internal audit function.

(f) Ascertain and evaluate the scope, earnestness, and thoroughness of the committee's monitoring of the corporation's policies and procedures relating to:

(i) System of internal accounting control.

(ii) Condition and satisfactoriness of the books, records and accounting system in general.

(iii) Prevention and detection of: material errors or irregularities; conflicts of interest; questionable or illegal acts and practices including those falling within the purview of the Foreign Corrupt Practices Act of 1977.

Pertinent Matters for Discussion with Audit Committee

3. At a meeting scheduled prior to commencement of the examination or in the early stages of the engagement, discuss the following:

(a) Matters specified in engagement letter including fees, non-audit services, type of report and examination, responsibility for detection of irregularities, the financial statements as representations of the entity.

(b)   The general scope (but not the details) of the examination, including branch and subsidiary locations to be visited and plan, if any, for rotating such visits; also, the subsidiaries or other segments to be examined by other auditors, the reputation of those auditors, and the type of examination to be made by them.

(c)   Personnel to be assigned to the audit, by level, with special reference to their experience in the profession, and their experience and familiarity with companies in the industry and with the client.

(d)   Risk or trouble areas, and anticipated audit problems in general.

(e)   Problems or recent changes relating to the company's financial condition and operating results.

(f)   Review of the system of internal accounting control with indication of areas of special concentration, and impact of the system review on substantive testing.

(g)   Testing and sampling approaches to be applied.

(h)   Cooperation to be expected from management.

(i)   Utilization of the work of internal auditors and arrangements for cooperative procedures, where appropriate.

(j)   Review of major or unusual accounting policies and practices followed by the client and of any recent changes in that respect.

(k)   Recent pronouncements by the FASB, SEC and AICPA that may affect the company's financial statements including footnotes, or the auditor's examination and report.

4.   At a meeting scheduled at an advanced stage of the examination, discuss the following:

(a)   Action taken by management, and degree of success, in remedying in the current year material as well as immaterial weaknesses in internal accounting control reported by the independent auditors in the engagement for the prior period.

(b)   Weaknesses in the system of internal accounting control revealed during the current examination and management's plan and timetable for remedying those weaknesses.

(c)   The existence and quality of the company's policies and procedures designed to prevent or reveal conflicts of interest and questionable and illegal acts and practices. In discussing this topic, consider whether the system of internal control has the following features:

(i)   The company's policy is in writing.

(ii)   The written policy has been disseminated to all levels of personnel to whom it does or may apply.

(iii)   The policy has been promulgated at the highest level and reinforced, if deemed appropriate, by restatements by appropriate officials at lower levels of management.

(iv)   Evidence has been obtained (by signed representations of officers and employees or otherwise) that the policy statement has been received and understood.

(v) Written policies and procedures are clearly set forth and include sufficient examples of forbidden acts and practices to ensure that the spirit and letter of the policies are understood and that questionable matters are identified, reported, and dealt with on a timely basis.

(vi) Policies and procedures are periodically republicized.

(vii) A monitoring mechanism has been established to oversee compliance with the control system.

(d) Significant problems encountered during the examination.

(e) Restrictions on the examination imposed by management, or other indications of lack of cooperation.

(f) Significant changes in preliminary audit plan.

(g) Knowledge of material errors or irregularities, or questionable or illegal acts or practices of management personnel.

(h) Interim financial statements, including: interim financial condition and operating results; availability of information and adequacy of recordkeeping for the preparation of satisfactory interim reports; if applicable, the auditor's review of interim financial information and report thereon.

5. At a final meeting scheduled at the completion stage of the examination, discuss:

(a) Review of draft of auditor's report and financial statements and accompanying notes, with special attention paid to changes in form, presentation or content as compared with preceding period.

(b) Review of draft of auditor's report communicating material weaknesses in internal accounting control.

(c) Discussion of material errors, irregularities, conflicts of interest, and questionable and illegal acts and practices of which the auditor is aware.

(d) Material adjustments to the accounts developed during the examination.

(e) Differences of opinion between the auditors and management with respect to accounting principles or practices, the examination, or other services, and the manner of their resolution.

(f) The results of other services performed by the auditors—tax, management consulting, and the like.

(g) Analytical review of the financial statements, and explanations of unusual or unfavorable fluctuations, variations, and trends.

(h) Material or unusual contingencies, uncertainties, and commitments.

(i) Matters and suggestions relating to the engagement for the following period.

CHAPTER **3**

Internal Accounting
Control Guide

INTERNAL ACCOUNTING CONTROL GUIDE—
STRUCTURE AND CONTENTS

An internal accounting control guide—sometimes referred to as an internal accounting control questionnaire or checklist—is used by many auditors as the centerpiece in their study and evaluation of the system of internal accounting control. It can serve as a comprehensive checklist of controls pertinent to each given area but it must, of course, be adapted and made relevant to the particular client, type of business, industry category, and accounting system.

As previously noted in the listing in Figure 2-15 of caveats for the study of the system of internal accounting control, practice varies on when the auditor will prepare the guide—in gathering information on the system, in the compliance testing stage, or throughout the examination. There is no approved way of using an internal accounting control guide, and its appropriate and effective use will depend on the judgment of the auditor.

In some guides the control features are expressed in the form of inquiries as to whether the particular control exists, while others may state the control in a declarative sentence, the inquiry being implied. In either case, a "Yes" or "No" column is checked, the Yes signifying that the control is present, and the No signifying a deficiency. An NA column can be checked if the control does not apply to the particular client.

Although many accountants do not include in their guides, for each of the areas studied, a listing of objectives which the listed controls are designed to achieve, it probably would be helpful to do so even though many of the same objectives will be repeated in the various control areas. It would be unrealistic, however, to attempt to match each control feature with one or more objectives. The reason is that the objectives are in the main interrelated while each control is usually associated with multiple objectives.

The instructions and explanations that might be used by an auditor as an introduction to an internal accounting control guide are presented in Figure 3-1. The instructions as well as the comments and documentation forms pertaining to and in support of the conclusions reached, as illustrated in Figure 3-2, apply to each of the sections making up the internal accounting control guide and should be completed for each section. However, in this book they will not be reproduced later in the interest of conserving space.

The cycle approach in a somewhat modified form has been attempted as a framework for the study of the system of internal accounting control, but the very same guide can be used for other approaches. The auditor who focuses on specific accounts in his review of internal accounting control will find those accounts represented in the guide as sections within the relevant transaction cycle. Thus controls for sales and accounts receivable are to be found within the revenue cycle. Similar representation exists for the auditor whose approach may be expressed in terms of function or department. The transaction cycle approach simply places added emphasis on the importance of seeing the relationships that exist between one area and another as the transaction cycle unfolds, and the need to maintain continuing control at each step in the cycle and at each transaction point. But this kind of emphasis can and should also be present for any other meaningful approach to the study of the system.

Inasmuch as too rigid and mechanical an application of the cycle concept could easily hamper the examination, a modified cycle approach to the study of the system of internal accounting control has been adopted. The type of modifications may be illustrated by reference to the revenue cycle.

A revenue cycle typically covers the following activities and transactions: Receipt of customer orders, credit granting, price setting and approvals, shipments, recording and collections. But the cycle must be modified to take into account matters and transactions falling outside the basic cycle flow, such as bad debts, returned merchandise, allowances, commissions, discounts, warranties, and the like. Further, while cash receipts are part of the revenue cycle, a proper understanding of the internal accounting controls for cash receipts requires that they be viewed within the total context of the internal accounting controls for cash in all of its aspects, including disbursements and cash balances. For these reasons the Cash section of the Internal Accounting Control Guide covers cash as a whole, including cash disbursements, but appropriately classified under the several aspects. Nevertheless, when covering the Expenditure Cycle later in this chapter, selected internal accounting controls for cash disbursements are reemphasized in order to stress their relevance to expenditure transactions, even though some slight duplication may result. Similarly, splitting investments into various balance sheet categories for purposes of reviewing the system of internal accounting control could also result in the creation of artificial and confusing distinctions.

As mentioned earlier (see Figure 2-15), generalized evaluations of the overall system of internal accounting control are not useful in the practical conduct of the audit. Each section within each transaction cycle will have its individual impact upon the audit program and substantive testing. Hence, for each section an internal accounting control "package" should be assembled; this package can serve as a basis for evaluating controls in the given section, as a record of conclusions reached, as documentary support for the evaluation, and as a record of the impact, if any, of the evaluation on the audit program. The details of the "package" are noted in Figure 3-1 as part of the instructions for the completion of the guide.

Figure 3-1
Internal Accounting Control Guide
Introduction and Instructions

_____   _____

(Client)   (Period)

_____   _____

(Prepared By)   (Reviewed by)

INSTRUCTIONS

1. Except for the general introductory section, this guide consists of a series of sections classified as follows by transaction cycle:

(a) General environment, accounting records, and financial reporting.

(b) Revenue cycle: sales and accounts receivable; cash; investments.

(c) Expenditure cycle: purchases, expenses, and accounts payable; payroll.

(d) Production cycle: inventories; property, plant and equipment; prepaid expenses, deferred costs, and intangible assets.

(e) Financing cycle: long-term debt; stockholders' equity.

2. Each section of the guide is made up of a "package" of materials, each item of which is to be utilized and completed with due care. The package consists of the following:

(a) _The basic questionnaire guide itself._ The appropriate column —Yes, No, or NA (not applicable)—is to be checked. A check in the Yes column signifies that the control is presumably present, while a No response indicates a weakness in the control element in question.

(b) _Segregation of function form._ The form lists the names of persons performing specified functions and indicates whether the individuals are associated with any inappropriate duties.

(c) _Comments and documentation form._ This form consists of several parts as follows:

(i) Comments on guide: for comments on No answers and any other matters requiring clarification or special consideration.

(ii) Comments on segregation of function form: for comments on apparent weaknesses relating to segregation of duties.

(iii) Description of compliance testing: for recording information as to sampling plan and testing procedures.

(iv) Evaluation of internal accounting controls: for comments on the adequacy of internal accounting controls, weaknesses in the system, compensating controls, and impact on substantive testing.

(v)   Working paper documentation: for reference to working papers containing documentation in support of the study of internal accounting control in the indicated area.

3.   The signature of the auditor completing each section of the guide (including the related forms making up the entire package for that section), as well as the signature of the reviewer, should be recorded in the indicated space.

4.   The listing of objectives in each section is a selective one and is not intended to be comprehensive. In addition to keeping in mind the listed objectives as well as others that may apply, the auditor should, as he makes his study of the system and examines individual controls, take into account (a) the type of errors or irregularities that could occur; (b) the potential materiality of any impact that such errors or irregularities may have on the fairness of the financial statements if not prevented or detected; and (c) the extent to which the control or controls in question can prevent or detect such errors or irregularities.

5.   Descriptions of weaknesses in the internal accounting controls that come to the attention of the auditor and are noted on the Comments and Documentation Form should also be recorded on the Internal Accounting Control Weaknesses—Summary Record form. (See Figure 2-18.)

Figure 3-2
Internal Accounting Control Guide—
Comments and Documentation Form

(to be completed for, and attached to, each section of the Guide)

Cycle _____   Section _____

Prepared by _____   Reviewd by _____

COMMENTS ON GUIDE

(Clarifying comments are generally required with respect to: No answers (including reference to compensating controls, if any); qualifications or other clarifications of Yes answers; in general, any matter or condition of significance requiring special attention and consideration.)

Guide Item No.	Comments

COMMENTS ON SEGREGATION OF FUNCTION FORM

(Note here the apparent weakness relating to segregation of duties as well as compensating controls, if any.)

Item No.	Comments

DESCRIPTION OF COMPLIANCE TESTING

(Describe here—or refer to pertinent working papers—the compliance testing undertaken, making reference where applicable to the relevant numbered auditing procedure in the Audit Program Guide. The description should encompass the sampling plan; the auditing procedures performed (cross-referenced to Audit Program Guide); documentary and other evidence examined.)

_____

_____

EVALUATION OF INTERNAL ACCOUNTING CONTROLS

(Comment here on the adequacy of the internal accounting controls. Weaknesses should be listed and clearly described. For each weakness (or related group of weaknesses) indicate the degree of materiality, compensatory controls, if any, and the effect upon substantive testing. List material weaknesses on the Internal Accounting Control Weakness—Summary Record form. Indicate the extent to which substantive testing may have been restricted or otherwise modified by reliance upon adequate internal accounting controls.)

_____

_____

WORKING PAPER DOCUMENTATION

(List here the title and reference symbol for working papers that provide documentation pertaining to the study of the system of internal accounting control for this section other than the internal accounting control guide and attached forms or the related section of the Audit Program Guide. Illustrative of such working papers are narrative descriptions of the system, flowcharts, descriptions of compliance testing, and audit notes and memoranda.

_____

_____

Figure 3-3
Internal Accounting Control Guide
General Environment, Accounting Records, and
Financial Reporting

(Prepared by)	(Date)	(Reviewed by)	(Date)

OBJECTIVES

(*Note*: See Figure 2-13 for a more comprehensive listing of objectives.)

1. A clearly defined plan of organization and associated procedures spell out personnel duties, responsibilities, and acceptable segregation of function.
2. Transactions are executed in accordance with management's general or specific authorization, and such authorizations are clearly expressed in writing.
3. An adequate accounting system is maintained; all transactions and all matters requiring accounting entries are properly recorded on a timely basis.
4. Assets, accounting records, and other tangible things of value are safeguarded, and access to them is adequately controlled.
5. Transactions and accounting procedures and entries are monitored to ensure that the terms of transactions correspond with authorization and that they are properly recorded.
6. Assets are periodically accounted for and compared with recorded amounts.

INTERNAL ACCOUNTING CONTROLS

	Yes	No	NA
Plan of Organization			
1. The company has a written plan of organization.			
2. Duties, responsibilities, and supervisory and monitoring functions are clearly defined in:			
(a) The written plan of organization.			
(b) Organization charts.			
(c) Job descriptions.			

(d)   Minutes of board of directors.

(e)   Other (fill in) _____.

(f)   Other (fill in) _____.

3.   The items listed in 2 above are revised periodically as designated duties and responsibilities are changed.

4.   The written plan of organization and related documents reflect a concern for appropriate segregation of function with respect to both departments and personnel.

5.   Continuing authority to authorize or approve transactions, sign checks, and so on, is periodically reviewed and is withdrawn when the executive has left the company.

6.   Close relatives to executives or other personnel are not employed by the company.

7.   Employees in positions of trust are bonded for sufficient amounts.

8.   Executives and other personnel are required to take their scheduled annual vacations, at which time their duties are taken over by others.

9.   A written policy exists on conflicts of interest, and this policy is periodically republicized.

10.   Where practicable, an effort is made to rotate personnel, and this policy is set forth in writing.

Policies and Authorizations

11.   Policies, as well as general and specific authorization to undertake actions or consummate transactions, are in writing for important matters.

12.   Written documentation for policies and authorizations are contained in:

(a)   Minutes of board of directors.

(b)   Policy and systems manuals.

(c)   Departmental manuals.

(d)   Other _____.

13.   Policies and authorizations are periodically reviewed and, if necessary or desirable, republicized.

14.   Matters authorized in minutes of the board of directors, executive committees, or otherwise, are followed up by designated persons to determine if corresponding transactions have been consummated in accordance with authorization and have been properly recorded in the accounts.

Accounting and Financial Statements

15.   The accounting function is completely separate from any function having responsibility for authorizing or consummating transactions and for custody of or control over assets.

16. The accounting principles and methods used are stated in writing.

17. The company maintains:

(a) an accounting manual.

(b) a detailed chart of accounts.

18. Difficult or unusual questions or problems relating to accounting matters, including accounting estimates, accruals, and disclosures, are taken up with senior officers.

19. Prenumbered forms or other documentation are used to provide a record and accountability for transactions.

20. Accounting entries, including general journal entries, are supported by documentation bearing authorization and/or approval signatures or initials.

21. Files containing forms and documents supporting accounting entries are well maintained and readily accessible.

22. Trial balances of the general ledger and subsidiary ledgers are prepared and reconciled monthly.

23. Financial statements are prepared monthly.

24. Monthly, quarterly, and annual financial statements are analytically reviewed by top executives.

25. Budgets are prepared on an annual and monthly basis and are compared with interim and annual financial statements.

26. The company uses a formal cost accounting system, the procedures for which are detailed in a cost accounting manual.

27. Asset writeoffs and other significant account adjustments are specifically authorized by a top-level executive not involved in the original acquisition of assets or their custody or recordkeeping.

Asset and Records Safeguarding

(Controls designed to safeguard specific assets are presented later in sections of the guide dealing with those assets.)

28. Formal written procedures exist to ensure that assets are adequately insured against loss by fire or other casualties.

29. The responsibility for periodically reviewing insurance coverage is specifically assigned to an official knowledgeable in insurance.

30. A written records retention program is maintained.

31. Accounting records and files are kept in fireproof premises and cabinets.

32. Access to accounting records and files is restricted to authorized personnel.

Internal Auditing

33. The board of directors has an audit committee.

34. Internal auditors are employed by the company.

35. The internal auditors are completely independent of other functions and departments.

36. They report to the audit committee or to a senior officer who is independent of the accounting department.

37. Formal written audit programs and procedures are followed.

38. Internal audit reports are prepared for each project and are reviewed by senior officers.

39. The operation of the internal audit function is periodically reviewed by a senior officer.

Figure 3-4
Internal Accounting Control Guide
Segregation of Function Form
General Environment, Accounting Records,
and Financial Reporting

INSTRUCTIONS

1. For each activity or area of responsibility, blank spaces are to be filled in specifying the person(s) directly involved and the department head.

2. Inappropriate or conflicting duties for any persons mentioned should be commented on in the indicated blank space.

3. If many persons are directly involved in the given activity, cross-reference the item to the detailed listing on an attached sheet.

4. Note on Segregation of Function Form attached any apparent weaknesses relating to segregation of duties and compensating controls, if any, as well as any other matters of audit significance.

SEGREGATION OF FUNCTION FORM

Activity or Area of Responsibility	Person Responsible	Department Head	Inappropriate Duties
1. Makes decisions on complex accounting matters.	_____	_____	_____
2. Maintains general ledger.	_____	_____	_____
3. Authorizes nonstandard journal entries.	_____	_____	_____
4. Reconciles subsidiary ledgers with controlling accounts	_____	_____	_____
5. Prepares monthly financial statements	_____	_____	
6. Reviews financial statements.	_____	_____	
7. Compares budgeted figures with financial statements.	_____	_____	_____
8. Heads EDP function.	_____	_____	_____
9. Directs internal audit function.	_____	_____	_____
10. Reviews insurance coverage.	_____	_____	_____

Revenue Cycle/Sales and Accounts Receivable, Cash, Investments

Figure 3-5
Internal Accounting Control Guide
Sales and Accounts Receivable

OBJECTIVES

1. Sales or services are provided only for approved customers.
2. Sales quantities, prices, credit standing, credit terms, sales and shipping terms, and discounts and allowances are authorized and/or approved.
3. A proper, accurate, and timely follow-through is maintained to ensure an unbroken chain of control for the following so that each link leads to the next: approved sales orders, to shipment, to billing, to recording, to collections. Related review procedures cover quantities, unit prices, aggregate amounts, and arithmetical accuracy of documents.
4. Adequate prenumbered forms under proper control are used for orders, shipments, invoicing, etc.   *Purchasing*
5. Sales, receivables, and related accounts (e.g., cost of sales, discounts, commissions, warranty costs) are recorded in the proper accounting period and are properly classified in the accounts.
6. Adequate records are maintained to provide information regarding the status and collectibility of accounts receivable, and the accounts are periodically reviewed.
7. Cash receipts are safeguarded and promptly deposited and recorded.
8. Write-offs or adjustments of accounts receivable in the form of bad debts, allowances, special discounts, or other credits are not granted or recorded without specific authorization or approval.
9. An appropriate segregation of function exists.

INTERNAL ACCOUNTING CONTROLS

	Yes	No	NA
1. The company has written policies covering: (a) Criteria for customer acceptance including credit terms and limits.			

(b) Types of sales, such as exports, nonstandard merchandise or services, and related parties.

(c) Authorized unit sales prices.

(d) Terms of sale—freight, services, warranties, returns and allowances, discounts.

(e) Authorization and/or approval procedures for deviations from standard policies.

2. An approved customer list is kept.

3. A separate credit department or function is maintained.

4. Acceptance of sales orders requires prior approval by credit departments.

5. Sales orders, sales contracts, shipping documents, and invoices are prenumbered and provide informative data.

6. Logs or listings are separately maintained in numerical sequence for sales orders and for shipping advices, and disposition of each item is promptly recorded (e.g., on sales order log, the corresponding shipping advice number and other data; on shipping log, corresponding invoice number, etc.).

7. Shipments are made only on the basis of approved sales orders.

8. Access to shipping area is restricted to authorized persons.

9. Guards are under orders to inspect authorized passes before permitting parcels to be removed from the plant.

10. Invoices bear notations and initials to fix responsibility for and to ensure that invoices have been:

(a) Matched with sales orders and shipping documents.

(b) Double checked for unit prices, quantities, extensions and total amounts, and terms of sale.

11. Controlled prenumbered invoices are prepared and recorded for sales to employees and for miscellaneous sales including scrap.

12. The listings, documents, and records pertaining to orders, shipments, billings, and recording of invoices are reviewed periodically, as appropriate, to ensure that a proper follow-through has been accomplished and that unfilled or incomplete items are investigated.

13. The persons responsible for the foregoing review are not connected with the functions being reviewed.

14. Subsidiary accounts receivable and notes receivable ledgers or records are kept.

15. Subsidiary records are reconciled at least monthly with the general ledger controlling accounts.

16. Monthly statements are sent to customers.

17. Monthly statements are reviewed and controlled by a person not connected with recordkeeping or cash control functions.

18. Accounts receivable are periodically confirmed on a surprise basis by internal auditors.

19. A monthly aged schedule of accounts receivable is prepared, and is reviewed by a responsible person. Follow-up and investigation is undertaken, as appropriate.

20. The credit department is regularly informed about delinquent accounts.

21. Credit department policies and credit limits are periodically reviewed by an official not directly involved with credit, sales, or receivables.

22. Bad-debt write-offs require specific authorization.

23. Controls over accounts previously written off are maintained for subsequent follow-up.

24. Credits to customer accounts for allowances, returns, special discounts, or other adjustments require:

(a) Use of prenumbered credit memos numerically controlled.

(b) Specific authorization.

(c) Documentary support such as receiving advices and correspondence.

(d) Written indication of comparison of price and other data on credit memos with original invoices. *Purchasing*

25. Book entries and supporting documentation for credits and write-offs of accounts receivable are periodically reviewed for propriety by a person not associated with cash, sales, or accounts receivable transactions or accounting.

26. A similar critical review is periodically made of customers' credit balances. *See p 273 (each 6 months)*

27. For cash sales:

(a) A cash register is used.

(b) The amount rung up is clearly visible to the customer.

(c) The customer is given an invoice.

(d) Invoices are prenumbered and cash sales are reconciled daily with invoice totals.

(e) Cash register receipts are deposited daily and intact.

28. Cutoff procedures exist to ensure that sales transactions are recorded in the proper month.

29. Separate records and other controls are maintained for consignment sales and consignment accounts.

30. With respect to miscellaneous sales of scrap, equipment and other such items, a control system similar to that for regular sales and trade receivables exists, including the use of authorization forms (equivalent to approved sales orders), shipping advices and invoices, all prenumbered and periodically accounted for.

31. Interest income, rent income, dividend income, gain or loss on sale of securities and equipment, and miscellaneous income in general are reviewed monthly by a responsible official to determine whether:

(a) Appropriate authorization exists where applicable.

(b) Amounts received correspond to expectations based on interest or dividend rates relative to assets, lease terms, and other factors.

32. Income accruals are reflected in the preparation of interim statements.

Bookkeeper could cheat/payment could go to ...

more specific breakdown of drawer tickets

33. A note register or other subsidiary ledger is maintained for notes receivable, and is reconciled at least monthly with the controlling account. Past due notes are promptly investigated.

34. Notes or loans receivable from officers, employees, related companies, other related parties, or of an unusual nature, require specific authorization of the board of directors or senior officials, as appropriate in the circumstances. Similar approval is required for renewal of notes or loans.

35. Notes and collateral (for notes or other receivables) are kept in a secure place by an official not associated with the accounting function or with cash or other fund custodial responsibilities.

36. Notes and collateral are periodically inspected and compared with the accounting records by an official not associated with the accounting function or custodianship of assets.

37. An overall review of sales and other revenues and receivables, employing sundry ratio and comparison tests as well as internal statistical data, is undertaken monthly by a responsible official in order to appraise the reasonableness of the recorded data.

38. In undertaking the overall review, independent estimates are calculated monthly for sales discounts and sales commission expense, and are compared with recorded amounts.

39. Functions have been properly segregated. (See Segregation of Function Form attached.)

Figure 3-6
Internal Accounting Control Guide
Sales and Accounts Receivable
Segregation of Function Form

In general, an association of any one of the following functions with any of the others would be inappropriate: handling cash or incoming mail; recordkeeping; credit function; sales and orders; shipping, bad-debt write-offs or other adjustments to receivable accounts; inspection of or other contact with assets; authorization or approval of transactions.

Activity or Area of Responsibility	Person Responsible	Department Head	Inappropriate Duties
1. Approves credit.			
2. Accepts sales orders.			
3. Authorizes shipments.			
4. Prepares billings.			
5. Checks billings for prices, quantites and extensions, and compares with sales orders and shipping advices.			
6. Controls logs for:			
(a) Shipping advices.			
(b) Sales orders.			
7. Reviews logs for:			
(a) Sales orders.			
(b) Shipping advices.			
8. Posts to or maintains subsidiary receivable ledgers.			
9. Reconciles subsidiary ledgers with controlling accounts.			
10. Reviews monthly statements.			
11. Arranges for mailing statements.			
12. Reviews aged receivable scheddule.			
13. Authorizes or approves bad debt write-offs.			
14. Approves credit memos.			
15. Reviews dividend, interest, rent, and miscellaneous income accounts.			
16. Has custody of notes receivable and collateral.			
17. Inspects notes and collateral for comparison with records.			
18. Authorizes (or approves renewal of) notes or loans receivable to related parties or any of an unusual nature.			
19. Undertakes overall review of revenue and receivable accounts.			

Figure 3-7
Internal Accounting Control Guide
Cash

OBJECTIVES

1. Cash receipts and cash funds are safeguarded.

2. Disbursements of funds are authorized and/or approved and are supported by pertinent documentation.

3. Authorization is required for opening and maintenance of bank accounts and for designation of check signers and of officers permitted to negotiate bank loans.

4. The accounting for cash transactions is thorough and is undertaken promptly.

5. An appropriate segregation of function is maintained including especially separation of recordkeeping from cash funds and cash transactions.

INTERNAL ACCOUNTING CONTROLS

Cash Receipts

K other employee
(Job 13 to sort"

1. The mail is opened by a responsible person having no recordkeeping or asset custodial responsibilities.

2. A remittance list of incoming currency and checks is immediately made up by the person opening the mail. (Also applicable where a lock box is in use.)

3. Checks are immediately stamped with a restrictive endorsement "For Deposit Only".

4. Company's banks have been advised that they are not to cash checks made payable to the company.

5. Cash receipts are deposited daily and intact.

6. Authenticated deposit slips are obtained from the bank.

7. Until deposit, cash is safeguarded and under the control of a responsible

	Yes	No	NA

person not connected with the accounting records or custodianship of other assets.

8. Daily accounting entries are made for cash receipts by persons who do not have access to cash and do not maintain accounts receivable records.

9. Accounting entries for cash receipts are compared ~~daily~~ *weekly* with authenticated deposit slips and remittance lists (and later with bank statement) by a person not connected with cash remittances or the accounting records.

10. Cash proceeds totals from customers are reconciled with credits to controlling accounts.

11. Cash discounts or other deductions taken by customers as entered in the accounting records are periodically reviewed by a person not associated with cash or with the accounts receivable records.

12. Complaints and other such correspondence from customers are initially routed by the person opening the mail to a responsible offical not associated with the sales, accounts receivable, or cash functions.

13. For over-the-counter sales, cash registers are used as well as prenumbered sales invoices.

14. A daily comparison is made of proceeds from cash sales with register tapes and prenumbered invoices.

Cash Disbursements

15. All cash disbursements are made by check except for petty cash items below a designated amount.

16. Checks are prenumbered and their sequence is periodically accounted for.

17. Voided or spoiled checks are marked as such and retained.

18. Unissued blank checks are safeguarded under the control of a responsible official, and the stock is periodically checked.

19. Check signers are authorized by the Board of Directors and their names formally communicated to the company's banks.

20. Persons authorized to sign checks have no direct involvement with other cash functions, other asset custodianship, accounting records, or purchasing.

21. Company's banks are immediately advised when an authorized check signer has left the company or authorization is to be withdrawn for other reasons.

22. Signing blank checks is against company policy.

23. Checks require two signatures except for amounts below an established figure, and instructions to that effect have been communicated to the company's banks.

24. Manual signatures are required for unusual or sensitive dis-

bursements such as special payroll checks, customer adjustments, and so on.

25. Check protectors are used.

26. Where check-signing machines are used:

(a) Signature plates are safeguarded when not in use and are under the control of a responsible official.

(b) The usual internal accounting controls for disbursements also apply to check-signing by machine.

(c) Only checks below a designated amount may be issued.

(d) Machine counts and amounts are independently reconciled with completed checks by a responsible official.

27. Checks can be drawn only to the order of specific parties and not to "Cash" or "Bearer."

28. All disbursements are properly authorized, the particular type of authorization being dependent on the amount and character of the disbursement.

29. Appropriate authorization, vouchers and other supporting documentation are examined and approved by the check signer before signing checks.

30. Loss of purchase discounts due to delay in submitting vouchers for payment is investigated by the check signer.

31. Vouchers and other documentation are cancelled by the check signer when signing checks.

32. Signed checks are mailed directly without first returning them to those preparing checks or to anyone connected with the cash or accounting functions.

33. Checks that have been signed and mailed are recorded daily in the accounting records.

34. Check disbursements are reconciled periodically with charges to the accounts payable controlling account or, as appropriate, to other accounts. *at months end*

35. For signed checks not mailed:

(a) Safeguarding and control is overseen by check signers.

(b) A listing or other control record is maintained and periodically reviewed.

(c) A comparison of the listing with accounting records is made at the close of accounting periods to ensure a proper cutoff.

36. Disbursements from branch bank accounts, other than limited imprest bank accounts, may be made only by the home office and for deposit only to a home office bank account.

Cash Balances and General Matters

37. Authorization is required by Board of Directors for opening bank accounts.

38.   Bank accounts are reconciled monthly by persons not involved with cash receipts or disbursements or the accounting records for cash or accounts receivable.

39.   Bank statements are forwarded by the banks directly to persons responsible for reconciling the accounts.

40.   The bank reconciliation procedures are carried out in depth and involve:

(a)   Examination of signatures and endorsements.

(b)   Review of check number sequence.

(c)   Comparison of names, amounts, and so on, with corresponding cash entries.

(d)   Comparison of bank deposits, bank charges, charge-backs, and so on, with cash entries.

(e)   Scrutiny of bank transfers, matching of deposits and disbursements, and investigation of time lags.

(f)   Follow-up and investigation of reconciling items.

41.   Questionable matters noted in reconciling bank accounts are communicated directly to an official not connected with cash receipts, disbursements, customer accounts, or the accounting records.

42.   Long-outstanding checks are investigated and, where appropriate, stop-payment orders are issued and corresponding entries are recorded.

43.   Cash budgets are prepared, book and budgeted figures are compared monthly, and significant variations are investigated.

44.   An overall review of the accounting entries for cash receipts and disbursements is undertaken monthly (by a person not associated with cash transactions or their recordkeeping), encompassing the propriety of the entries especially as to material or nonstandard transactions, and the correctness of their account classification.

Petty Cash and Cash on Hand

45.   Petty cash expenditures are made from an imprest fund.

46.   The amount of the fund has been limited so as to require reasonably frequent reimbursement.

47.   The maximum amount of any expenditure has been specifically set.

48.   Where an imprest fund is represented by a bank account, the bank has been instructed that no checks payable to the company may be accepted for deposit in that account, and that a designated maximum limit has been set on the amounts of issued checks.

49.   The petty cash custodian does not have custody over other assets and does not maintain any accounting records.

50.   Controls are maintained to fix responsibility if more than one custodian handles the petty cash fund.   *only goyle*

51. A policy is maintained prohibiting the use of petty cash funds for check cashing or loans.

52. If checks are in fact cashed from petty cash funds, they are immediately deposited.

53. Petty cash vouchers are:

(a) Approved prior to payment.

(b) Used for all petty cash disbursements.

(c) Prenumbered.

(d) Supported by invoices or other supporting documentation, as applicable.

(e) Written in ink and the amounts spelled out as well as recorded in numerals.

(f) Signed by the payee.

54. Vouchers and supporting documents submitted for reimbursement are reviewed, approved, and cancelled by the person signing the reimbursement check.

55. Reimbursement checks are made out to the order of the petty cash custodian, the purpose of the check being specified on its face.

56. A postage meter machine is used.

57. Surprise counts are periodically made of petty cash funds as well as undeposited cash on hand, and reconciled with book entries.

Figure 3-8
Internal Accounting Control Guide

Cash
Segregation of Function Form

In general, an association of any one of the following functions with any of the others would be inappropriate: handling cash or incoming mail; recordkeeping; custodianship of other assets; check signing; preparation of checks; responsibility for bank reconciliations; authorization or approval of cash transactions; functions associated with sales and accounts receivable; functions associated with purchasing and accounts payable; responsibility for count of petty cash or cash funds on hand; comparison review of accounting entries and supporting documentation.

Activity or Area of Responsbility	Person Responsible	Department Head	Inappropriate Duties
1. Opens mail.			
2. Prepares remittance list.			
3. Safeguards cash prior to deposit.			
4. Deposits cash in bank.			
5. Records cash receipts entries.			
6. Compares entries with remittance lists and deposit slips.			
7. Reviews cash discounts.			
8. Reviews correspondence and complaints from customers.			
9. Compares cash sales proceeds with register tapes and invoices.			
10. Safeguards unissued blank checks.			
11. Signs checks.			
12. Controls check-signing machine.			
13. Controls unmailed signed checks.			
14. Reconciles bank accounts.			
15. Receives report of questionable items noted in bank reconciliation.			
16. Investigates long-outstanding checks.			
17. Undertakes cash budgetary review.			
18. Undertakes monthly overall review of accounting entries for cash receipts and disbursements, for propriety of entries and correctness of account classification.			

19. Has custody of petty cash fund.
20. Signs checks drawn on petty cash imprest bank account.
21. Reviews petty cash vouchers submitted for reimbursement.
22. Controls postage meter machine.
23. Performs surprise count of petty cash and cash on hand.

Figure 3-9
Internal Accounting Control Guide
Investments

OBJECTIVES

1. Authorization is required for acquisition, sales and other investment transactions.
2. Adequate records and accounting entries provide a proper accountability for investments and related income.
3. Investment policy, investment holdings, and actual transactions are periodically reviewed.
4. Securities are safeguarded.
5. An appropriate segregation of function is maintained, especially separation of custodianship of securities from recordkeeping and from custodianship of other assets.

INTERNAL ACCOUNTING CONTROLS

	Yes	No	NA
1. The company has a formal investment policy in writing covering such matters as use of idle cash, types of investments, income yields, and holding periods.			
2. Investment purchases, sales, and other transactions are authorized by the Board of Directors or finance or other committee designated by the Board.			
3. Consummated transactions are reviewed by a responsible person to see if they correspond to prior authorization, and if price and other data are supported by acceptable documentary evidence.			
4. Detailed subsidiary records are maintained independently of the custodian and contain a full description, including certificate numbers, and related income data.			
5. Detailed records are reconciled monthly to controlling accounts by a person who is not the custodian and does not keep the subsidiary records.			

6. Securities are kept in a bank safe deposit box.

7. Securities not kept in a bank safe deposit box are safeguarded by a responsible official who is not associated with custodianship of other assets, recordkeeping, or investment transactions.

8. A record is maintained of all visits to the safe deposit vault, and the presence of at least two designated officials is required.

9. A similar record and control is kept by the custodian for movements of securities under his care.

10. All securities except bearer bonds are required to be registered in the name of the company.

11. Securities held for others as collateral are properly safeguarded and under accounting control.

12. Securities are periodically inspected and counted on a surprise basis or confirmed with outside custodians, and a comparison is made with the accounting records by a responsible official not associated with the custody of securities, investment transactions, or their accounting.

13. Investment income is periodically reviewed and compared with owned investments to determine whether all income has been received and fully and promptly accounted for.

14. Income accruals are properly recorded and/or reflected in interim financial statements.

15. Authorization is required for write-downs of investments, and adequate control records are maintained for investments that have been completely written off so that appropriate follow-up may later be made.

16. The company's investment policy, holdings, and operating results are periodically reviewed and evaluated.

17. The accounting for, and account classification of, the various types of investment are periodically reviewed to ensure that investments are carried on a basis that conforms with generally accepted accounting principles.

Figure 3-10
Internal Accounting Control Guide
Investments
Segregation of Function Form

An association of any one of the following functions with any of the others would generally be inappropriate: authorization or approval of investment transactions; custodianship of securities; recordkeeping for investments; custodianship of cash or other funds.

Activity or Area of Responsibility	Person Responsible	Department Head	Inappropriate Duties
1. Authorizes investment transactions.			
2. Reviews consummated transactions.	_____	_____	_____
3. Maintains detailed investment records.	_____	_____	_____
4. Reconciles subsidiary records to controlling accounts.	_____	_____	_____
5. Has access to safe deposit box.	_____	_____	_____
6. Has custody of securities.	_____	_____	_____
7. Periodically makes a surprise inspection and count of securities.	_____	_____	_____
8. Authorizes write-downs or write-offs of investments.	_____	_____	_____
9. Reviews company's investment policy, holdings, and operating results.	_____	_____	_____
10. Reviews the accounting for, and account classification of, investments.	_____	_____	_____

Expenditure Cycle/Purchases, Expenses and Accounts Payable; Payroll

Figure 3-11
Internal Accounting Control Guide

Purchases, Expenses, and Accounts Payable

OBJECTIVES

1. Purchase of goods, other assets, and services are properly authorized, such authorization encompassing significant acquisition features such as type of item, vendor, quantity, terms of purchase, and price.

2. A proper, accurate, and timely follow-through is maintained to ensure an unbroken chain of control for the following so that each link leads to the next: approved purchase orders (or, as applicable, special contracts), to receipt of services, merchandise or other assets, to recording in the accounts, to disbursements. Related review and approval procedures cover quantities, unit prices, aggregate amounts, and arithmetical accuracy of documents.

3. Adequate prenumbered forms under proper control are used *terms due dates* for requisitions, purchase orders, receiving advices, vouchers, etc.

4. Purchases of goods, other asset acquisitions, and services received are recorded promptly and in the applicable accounting period, and properly classified in the accounts.

5. Adequate records are maintained to provide information regarding the accounts payable, payment due dates, and duplicate or improper payments.

6. Purchases of goods, other assets and services are authorized, accepted and paid for only if they are for business purposes of the company and not for the personal benefit of officers or any other persons or parties.

7. An appropriate segregation of function exists.

INTERNAL ACCOUNTING CONTROLS

	Yes	No	NA
1. The company has written policies covering purchasing procedures, including explicit requirements for a sys-			

tem of authorization and approval at specified levels of authority for given categories of goods, assets, and services acquired.

2.   An approved vendor list is kept and periodically updated.

3.   The vendor list is based on established criteria as to quality of products and services, past performance, credit standing, and price competitiveness.

4.   A clear and publicized written policy is in force on purchase dealings with related parties.

5.   Purchase requisitions, purchase orders, receiving records, and vouchers are prenumbered and provide informative data.

6.   Purchases are made only on the basis of purchase requisitions approved by department heads or other responsible officials or, for material nonroutine acquisitions, on the basis of written authorization at a level of authority commensurate with the nature of the transaction.

7.   There is a separate purchasing department or function that is independent of the accounting, receiving, shipping, accounts payable, and cash disbursement functions.

8.   Purchase orders are approved by the purchasing function supervisor and are confirmed by vendors.

9.   Nonstandard purchase contracts and any unusual, special, or material purchase transactions are also approved by originating departments, legal department when necessary, and other responsible officers or the board of directors, as appropriate in the circumstances.

10.   Competitive bidding procedures are followed, where practicable.

11.   An independent review is periodically made of the pricing policies, practices, and controls of the purchasing department by responsible persons not associated with it.

12.   The receiving department has been instructed to question and report any unanticipated or unauthorized deliveries.

13.   A prenumbered receiving report is made up for all incoming items.

14.   An independent count and inspection of goods or other items received is made by the receiving department, and copies of the receiving report are sent to the purchasing and accounting departments.

15.   Logs or listings are separately maintained in numbered sequence for purchase requisitions, purchase orders, and receiving reports; disposition of each item is promptly recorded (e.g., on requisition log, the corresponding purchase order number and other data; on purchase order log, the corresponding receiving report; on receiving report, the corresponding invoice/voucher number; etc.).

16.   Similar controls are maintained for purchase returns and other credits due from vendors, and prenumbered debit memos are prepared, processed, and controlled.

17.   Vendor invoices are forwarded directly to the accounts payable department.

18.   Extra copies of invoices are clearly stamped as duplicates.

19. Invoices are matched by the accounts payable department with purchase requisitions, orders, and receiving reports.

20. Vouchers or invoices bear notations and initials to fix responsibility and to ensure that the following matters have been checked and matched with supporting documentation:

(a) Receipt of merchandise or other items and name of vendor.

(b) Description, quantities and condition.

(c) Unit prices and freight and other charges or credits.

(d) Discounts.

(e) Extensions and arithmetical accuracy.

(f) Account distribution.

(g) Overall review of voucher and approval for payment.

21. The responsibility for designating the account classification is assigned to a knowledgeable accountant fully acquainted with the chart of accounts and company policy on accounting matters.

22. Invoices for services and expense items, for which receiving reports are inapplicable, are specifically approved by designated responsible persons prior to processing for payment.

23. Discrepancies or errors in the vouchering process are investigated before payment is approved, and, where indicated, questionable matters are reported to responsible officials outside the purchasing and receiving functions.

24. Vouchers approved for payment are promptly entered in a voucher register or purchase book.

25. Controls are maintained to ensure that payment is made within the discount period.

26. The logs or listings for purchase requisitions, purchase orders, receiving reports, and vouchers are reviewed on a regular basis to ensure that a proper follow-through has been accomplished and that unmatched or incomplete items are investigated. The persons responsible for this review are not connected with the functions being reviewed.

27. A schedule of accounts payable is reconciled at least monthly with the controlling account.

28. Vendor statements are reconciled with accounts payable records.

29. The accounts payable schedule and unpaid voucher file are periodically reviewed, and appropriate inquiries made with respect to long-outstanding accounts, lost discounts, debit balances, or any questionable matters.

30. Cutoff procedures exist to ensure that purchase transactions and corresponding liabilities and accruals are entered in the proper month. In that connection, unentered and unprocessed invoices as well as unmatched receiving reports are reviewed.

31. Expense accruals are reflected in interim financial statements.

32. Separate records and other controls are maintained for consignment purchases.

33. Purchase and expense accounts are reviewed monthly by a responsible official and appropriate ratio and comparison tests are made using budget figures, prior period data, and so on, in order to appraise the reasonableness and validity of the recorded data and financial reports.

34. In undertaking the overall review, independent estimates are calculated for accounts such as interest, commissions, purchase discounts, rent, and other expense accounts for which such calculations can be made.

35. Functions have been properly segregated. (See Segregation of Function form attached.)

Notes: (1) The internal accounting controls for Notes and Loans Payable are included in the financing cycle. (2) The controls for cash disbursements may be found under that classification in the Cash section of the revenue cycle.

Figure 3-12
Internal Accounting Control Guide
Purchases, Expenses and Accounts Payable
Segregation of Function Form

An association of any one of the following functions with any of the others would generally be inappropriate: involvement with cash disbursements and check signing; recordkeeping for purchases, accounts payable and disbursements; requisitions; purchasing; receiving; vouchering and preparation of vouchers for payment; review of foregoing functions.

Activity or Area of Responsibility	Person Responsible	Department Head	Inappropriate Duties
1. Updates approved vendor list.			
2. Authorizes major or nonstandard acqusitions.			
3. Prepares purchase orders.			
4. Approves purchase orders.			
5. Reviews nonstandard purchase contracts.			
6. Inspects and counts items received and prepares receiving reports.			
7. Maintains listings or logs for:			
(a) Purchase requisitions.			
(b) Purchase orders.			
(c) Receiving reports.			
8. Reviews listings and logs.			
9. Receives vendor invoices.			
10. Matches invoices with supporting documentation.			
11. Receives reports of errors or discrepancies uncovered in vouchering process.			
12. Prepares vouchers for payment.			
13. Records accounting entries for purchases, expenses, and accounts payable.			
14. Reconciles accounts payable schedule with controlling account.			
15. Checks on adequcy of cutoff.			
16. Maintains records for consignment purchases.			
17. Reviews accounts payable schedule and unpaid voucher file for lost discounts, long outstanding balances, debit balances, and questionable matters.			

18. Undertakes overall review of propriety of account balances for purchases, expenses and accounts payable.

Figure 3-13
Internal Accounting Control Guide

Payroll

OBJECTIVES

1. Authorization is required for engaging employees, terminating employment, setting compensation rates, and providing fringe benefits.

2. A system of approval, documentation, and adequate record-keeping ensures that only employees legitimately employed who have actually been working on behalf of the company are in fact paid, and that the amounts correspond to approved rates and period of time actually employed.

3. Gross compensation, tax and other withholdings, and net amounts payable are double-checked for accuracy.

4. Payroll costs are properly classified and recorded in the accounts.

5. An appropriate segregation of function exists.

INTERNAL ACCOUNTING CONTROLS

	Yes	No	NA

1. The company's personnel policies are incorporated in a personnel manual which is periodically updated.

2. A personnel department or function is maintained that is independent of the payroll department and operating departments.

3. Detailed personnel records are kept for all employees.

4. Personnel may not be employed without prior written authorization (and specification of compensation rates and employment terms) from department heads or other officials having this responsibility.

5. Prior to employment, application forms are submitted, individuals are interviewed, and background and references are checked.

6. Written authorization and advice is similarly submitted for changes in status or rates and for terminations.

7. Compensation of officers is authorized by the board of directors and recorded compensation is later compared with authorized amounts. Similar authorization and review policies in writing apply to executive perquisites.

8. The payroll department is required to await formal written advice from personnel department before adding employees to payroll, recording compensation rates, or adjusting such rates.

9. A time clock system is in use.

10. Time cards are prepared and controlled by the payroll department independently of foremen or other operating department personnel.

11. Time cards are punched by employees in the presence of timekeepers.

12. Time cards are signed by foremen or department heads.

13. Time cards, piecework tickets, or other such documentation are compared and reconciled with foremen's records and production reports.

14. Salesmen's commissions are similarly reconciled with sales figures.

15. The preparation of payrolls is divided among a number of employees whose duties are periodically rotated.

16. Payroll and supporting documentation (e.g., time cards) are double-checked for hours, rates, withholdings, net payment, clerical accuracy, etc.

17. Payrolls bear the signature of persons preparing payroll, performing calculations, and reviewing and approving payrolls.

18. A periodic test review of the payroll function is made (including a comparison of names, rates, hours, etc., with personnel records and time cards) by a responsible person independent of the personnel, payroll, or operating departments.

19. Employees are paid by check.

20. An imprest bank account is used for payroll disbursements.

21. Instructions have been issued to bank to allow only payroll checks below a specified maximum amount to clear, and to reject deposts of checks drawn to the company's order.

22. The payroll disbursement function, including check preparation and check signing, as well as bank reconciliations, are performed by persons independent of the personnel, payroll, or operating departments.

23. The person responsible for signing payroll checks, or for controlling the check-signing machine, compares individual amounts with corresponding payroll entries.

24. The aggregate of payroll check amounts (or cash payments) is reconciled with payroll totals.

25. Payroll receipts are obtained for wages paid in cash.

26. Distributions of wage payments, upon proper employee identification, are made by specially designated employees not associated with personnel, payroll, accounting, or operating functions.

27. Internal auditors or others performing that function periodically witness payroll distributions.

28. Unclaimed wages are turned over to a responsible official independent of personnel or payroll functions.

29. Unclaimed wages are subject to a variety of controls, including entry in supporting records, requiring satisfactory identification by claimants, follow-up inquiries, and reversal of cash entry and corresponding recording of a liability.

30. The customary internal accounting controls for regular cash disbursement and bank accounts are equally applicable to payroll bank accounts, and persons reconciling payroll accounts are instructed to compare names and amounts on checks with payrolls and to note numerical sequence, check signatures, and endorsements.

31. Mailing of W-2 statements is controlled outside the personnel, payroll, and disbursement functions, and returns or other questionable matters are followed up.

32. Payroll accounting entries are supported by approved payrolls, account distributions are coded in accordance with a chart of accounts, and account classification is subsequently reviewed for propriety.

33. Accruals for payroll and related tax and other expense accounts are reflected in interim financial statements.

34. An overall analytical review of payroll and related tax accounts is undertaken monthly and quarterly by a responsible official who is independent of any incompatible function. The review encompasses reference to production records and statistical data, comparison of recorded amounts with budget figures and with independently calculated estimates, and reconciliation of payroll shown on tax returns with recorded payroll for the period in question.

35. The confidentiality of personnel and payroll records is maintained by pertinent publicized written instructions and other controls, and payroll records are under strict physical control.

36. Responsibilities for overseeing the following and for undertaking periodic reviews are assigned to higher level officials:

(a) Compliance with labor laws and regulations.

(b) Employee benefits.

(c) Conformity of pension fund and transactions with pension plan provisions, pension laws and regulations, and actuarial requirements.

Figure 3-14
Internal Accounting Control Guide

Payroll
Segregation of Function Form

An association of any one of the following functions with any of the others would generally be inappropriate: Personnel; payroll; operations; cash disbursements including check signing and check distribution; payroll bank account reconciliation; review and approval of payrolls.

Activity or Area of Responsibility	Person Responsible	Department Head	Inappropriate Duties
1. Has a position of responsibility in personnel department.			
2. Prepares payrolls.			
3. Prepares time cards.			
4. Serves as timekeeper.			
5. Compares time cards, piecework tickets, etc., with foremen's and production records.			
6. Reconciles salesmen's commissions with sales figures.			
7. Doublechecks payroll and time cards for accuracy.			
8. Reviews and approves each payroll.			
9. Periodically undertakes a test review of payroll function.			
10. Prepares payroll checks for signature.			
11. Signs payroll checks.			
12. Distributes payroll checks.			
13. Periodically witnesses payroll distribution.			
14. Takes custody of unclaimed wages.			
15. Reconciles payroll bank account.			
16. Records accounting entries for payroll and determines proper account classification.			
17. Reviews accounting entries for payroll for validity and propriety of account classification.			
18. Undertakes a monthly overall analytical review of payroll and related accounts.			

19. Has responsibility for oversee-
    ing:
    (a) Compliance with labor laws.
    (b) Employee benefits.
    (c) Pension plan and pension fund.

Production Cycle/Inventories; Property, Plant and Equipment; Prepaid Expenses, Deferred Costs, and Intangible Assets

Figure 3-15
Internal Accounting Control Guide

Inventories

OBJECTIVES

1. Proper authorization is required for production scheduling, including specification of types and quantities of goods to be manufactured and materials to be applied to production.

2. Movements of inventories require prior authorization or approval and are supported by properly completed prenumbered forms.

3. Adequate accounting records and a satisfactory cost accounting system are maintained:

   (a) To establish a clear accountability.

   (b) To provide information regarding inventory quantities, costs, condition, and classification.

   (c) To ensure that inventories and related accounts are stated in conformity with generally accepted accounting principles.

4. Records are periodically substantiated by physical count and outside confirmations.

5. Inventories are adequately protected against theft, misuse, spoilage, and fire or other casualty.

6. An appropriate segregation of function exists.

INTERNAL ACCOUNTING CONTROLS

	Yes	No	NA
1. There is a separate production control function.			
2. Short-term and long-range written plans and policies are formulated covering production and inventories.			
3. Production schedules or job orders are prepared and approved by designated persons.			

4. Material requisitions are:
(a) Used for obtaining materials from storerooms.
(b) Prenumbered, and sequence is periodically checked.
(c) Approved prior to submission.
(d) Written in ink with amounts spelled out to preclude alteration.
(e) Signed by recipient of materials.
(f) Forwarded also to accounting department for perpetual inventory and recordkeeping purposes.

5. Merchandise inventories are stored in an orderly way in storerooms with restricted access and under the custody of storekeepers not connected with perpetual inventory records or other recordkeeping functions.

6. Other physical security controls exist for safeguarding inventories, including:
(a) Use of guards at key exit points.
(b) Separate enclosed receiving and shipping areas with restricted access.
(c) Written authorization required for acceptance or shipment of inventories.
(d) Use of fire alarm and protective equipment and devices for fire, atmospheric, and similar controls.
(e) Periodic inspection and appraisal of physical security conditions.

7. Merchandise held on consignment is physically segregated.

8. Perpetual inventory records are maintained for all classes of inventory by persons having no contact with physical inventories (e.g., storekeeping, receiving, and shipping functions) or having responsibility for authorizing or approving inventory acquisitions or movements.

9. Perpetual inventory records show both quantity and cost.

10. Entries in perpetual inventory records are made only against approved and numerically accounted for receiving, requisition, and shipping advices.

11. Perpetual inventory records are balanced periodically and totals reconciled with controlling accounts.

12. A complete physical inventory count is:
(a) Made at least once a year (which may be on a cycle basis if well-kept perpetual inventory records are maintained) for inventories on hand or in warehouses.
(b) Carried out independently of personnel with stores, receiving, shipping, or recordkeeping responsibilities.
(c) Adequately prepared for and detailed written instructions are issued.
(d) Compared and reconciled with perpetual inventory records, and material discrepancies are investigated by designated persons.

13. Inventories are periodically inspected and records reviewed to identify and investigate goods that are obsolete, excessive, unsaleable, shopworn, deteriorated, or slow-moving.

14. Adjustments to perpetual inventory records require specific authorization by a responsible person not associated with the physical inventories or inventory recordkeeping.

15. Details regarding inventories held by public warehouses are periodically confirmed by letter or by examination of monthly statements received from warehouses.

16. Adequate and separate records are kept for consigned goods as well as for inventories in warehouses or with other outside custodians.

17. A good cost system is used for accumulation and allocation of costs and for use in pricing inventories.

18. Standard costs are used and periodically updated, and variances are investigated.

19. Cost system data are reconciled monthly with the financial accounting records.

20. Adjustments to inventory accounts in the financial accounting records are authorized and supported by appropriate documentation.

21. Adequate written documentation provides support for entries and transfers to cost of sales and ensures a clear coordination of sales, cost of sales, and inventory entries for transfer to work-in-process and to finished goods.

22. Priced inventory listings reflect all pertinent cost elements, including overhead, freight, and discounts, are based on perpetual inventory records and/or physical count, and are double-checked for description, quantity, unit cost, unit market value, and extensions and footings.

23. Controls designed to ensure the conformity of inventory and related accounts with generally accepted accounting principles on a consistent basis, include updated accounting manuals, chart of accounts, and review by accounting executives.

24. Cutoff procedures at financial statement dates are reviewed to ensure that transactions are recorded in the proper period and inventories are fairly stated.

25. The adequacy of insurance coverage is periodically reviewed by a designated executive.

26. Sales, cost of sales, and inventory accounts are reviewed monthly by a designated executive, and appropriate ratio and comparison tests are made using forecast and budget figures, prior period data, and turnover and gross profit statistics, in order to appraise the overall reasonableness and validity of recorded data and financial reports.

Figure 3-16
Internal Accounting Control Guide

Inventories
Segregation of Function Form

An association of any one of the following functions with any of the others would generally be inappropriate: physical contact with inventories (including storekeeping, receiving, shipping, or production); maintenance of inventory records; authorization for acquisition or movement of goods; physical count of inventory; cash receipts or disbursements.

Activity or Area of Responsibility	Person Responsible	Department Head	Inappropriate Duties
1. Prepares production schedules.			
2. Approves production schedules.			
3. Approves material requisitions.			
4. Functions as storekeeper.			
5. Periodically inspects and appraises physical security conditions.			
6. Maintains perpetual inventory records.			
7. Reconciles perpetual inventory records with controlling accounts.			
8. Supervises physical count.			
9. Authorizes adjustments to perpetual inventory records.			
10. Authorizes adjustments to inventory accounts in the financial accounting records.			
11. Reconciles cost system data with financial accounting records.			
12. Reviews adequacy of insurance coverage.			
13. Performs monthly overall ratio and comparison tests and review of sales, cost of sales, and inventory accounts.			

Figure 3-17
Internal Accounting Control Guide

Property, Plant, and Equipment

OBJECTIVES

1. A written company policy is in force covering:
(a) Acquisition and disposition of property, plant, and equipment.
(b) Authorization for such acquisition or disposition.
(c) Depreciation and amortization.
(d) Accounting distinction between capital and revenue expenditures.
(e) Repairs and maintenance.
2. Capital expenditures are under budgetary control.
3. Detailed subsidiary records are maintained and reconciled periodically with controlling accounts.
4. Assets are clearly identified and periodically inspected, and tied in, at least on a test basis, with the records.
5. Periodic appraisals are made for insurance and control purposes.
6. Assets are adequately safeguarded against theft, misuse, physical deterioration, and fire or other casualty.
7. Asset condition and continued usefulness are under periodic review.
8. Controls exist to ensure that assets are stated at cost and are depreciated over their useful lives on a systematic basis.
9. An appropriate segregation of function exists.

INTERNAL ACCOUNTING CONTROLS

	Yes	No	NA
1. A written policy covers: (a) Acquisition and disposition of property, plant and equipment. (b) Repairs and maintenance. (c) Distinction between capital and revenue expenditures. (d) Depreciation. 2. Authorization of the Board of Directors or specified senior officers is required for major property acquisitions and dispositions.			

3. Actual property transactions (acquisitions and dispositions) are compared by the Board or designated officers with prior authorization specifications.

4. Assets constructed by the company are subject to the same authorization and other pertinent controls as are other acquisitions.

5. A work-order system and procedures for issuing informative progress reports are in effect for construction or major repairs undertaken by the company, and these orders and reports are reviewed for propriety, conformity with authorization, and inclusion of relevant overhead and other costs.

6. Adequate documentation under numerical and other control is maintained in support of property, plant and equipment acquisitions, dispositions, movements, and repairs, including requisitions, work orders, purchase orders and contracts, receiving reports, vouchers, etc.

7. Equipment items are tagged and clearly identified by serial numbers and technical description.

8. Subsidiary plant and equipment ledgers are maintained and periodically reconciled with controlling accounts.

9. Equipment is periodically inspected and inventoried and compared with the records.

10. Records are kept of equipment not carried on the books such as fully depreciated, idle, or obsolete assets, and are regularly reviewed and tied in with assets on hand.

11. Periodic appraisals are obtained for insurance and control purposes.

12. Physical security controls exist for safeguarding plant and equipment, including use of guards and fire alarm and protection devices.

13. The responsibility for designating the account classification for plant and equipment transactions has been assigned to a knowledgeable accountant fully acquainted with the chart of accounts and company policy and accounting matters.

14. Accounting entries are supported by appropriate documentation properly approved.

15. Depreciation schedules supporting monthly depreciation entries are reviewed and double-checked for underlying validity and mathematical accuracy.

16. Accounting entries for fixed asset transactions and depreciation are periodically reviewed for validity and propriety.

17. Designated executives have the responsibility to review and report on:

(a) Condition of plant and equipment and adequacy of repairs and maintenance policy and practices.

(b) Plant obsolescence.

(c) Depreciation policies.

(d) Acquisition and replacement policies.

18. Leased plant and equipment are covered by controls similar to those maintained for owned assets, including authorization and adequate recordkeeping.

Figure 3-18
Internal Accounting Control Guide

Property, Plant, and Equipment
Segregation of Function Form

An association of any one of the following functions with any of the others would generally be inappropriate: authorization for acquisitions or dispositions; recordkeeping; receiving, shipping, inspection or count of equipment; and cash disbursements.

Activity or Area of Responsibility	Person Responsible	Department Head	Inappropriate Duties
1. Authorizes plant and equipment acquisitions or dispositions.	_____	_____	_____
2. Controls work orders.	_____	_____	_____
3. Approves work orders.	_____	_____	_____
4. Maintains plant and equipment subsidiary ledgers.	_____	_____	_____
5. Reconciles subsidiary ledgers with controlling accounts.	_____	_____	_____
6. Periodically inspects and inventories equipment, and compares with records.	_____	_____	_____
7. Codes fixed asset transactions for accounting entries.	_____	_____	_____
8. Reviews and double-checks depreciation schedules.	_____	_____	_____
9. Approves accounting entries.	_____	_____	_____
10. Reviews accounting entries.	_____	_____	_____
11. Reviews and reports on: (a) Condition of plant and equipment and repairs and maintenance policies and practices.	_____	_____	_____
(b) Plant obsolescence.	_____	_____	_____
(c) Depreciation.	_____	_____	_____
(d) Acquisition and replacement policies.	_____	_____	_____

Figure 3-19
Internal Accounting Control Guide
Prepaid Expenses, Deferred
Costs, and Intangible Assets

OBJECTIVES

1. A written policy is in force covering:
(a) Acquisition and disposition of deferred costs and intangibles.
(b) Authorization for such acquisition or disposition.
(c) Amortization and write-offs.
2. Actual expenditures and accounting entries are compared with authorization.
3. Detailed subsidiary records are maintained which are reconciled periodically with controlling accounts.
4. Adequate support exists to ensure that, as of date of acquisition, cost corresponds to value.
5. Periodic review is undertaken of the continued utility of assets, for amortization or write-off purposes.
6. Income and expense accounts are reviewed in relationship to corresponding assets.
7. An appropriate segregation of function exists.

INTERNAL ACCOUNTING CONTROLS

	Yes	No	NA

1. A written policy is in force covering acqusition, disposition, and amortization of intangible assets.
2. Authorization of Board of Directors or specified senior officers is required for material acquisitions, dispositions, and lump-sum write-offs of intangible assets and deferred costs.
3. Accounting entries for prepaid expenses, deferred costs, and intangibles are based on adequate documentation, properly approved, in support of acquisitions, dispositions, amortization, or write-offs. Accounting entries are coded by knowledgeable accountants.
4. Detailed subsidiary records are maintained which are balanced monthly with controlling accounts.

5. The continued usefulness of intangibles is periodically reviewed and amortization rates are adjusted, as required.

6. Accounting entries for lump-sum write-downs or write-offs of deferred costs or intangibles require special approval.

7. Revenue and expense accounts pertinent to prepaid expenses, deferred costs, and intangible assets are periodically reviewed in relationship to the corresponding assets.

8. Amortization and prepaid expense schedules and corresponding entries are double-checked and reviewed for validity and mathematical accuracy.

9. The responsibility for the casualty insurance program, adequacy of insurance coverage, and insurance premium costs is assigned to an executive who is well-versed in insurance.

10. An insurance register and supporting insurance records in adequate detail are maintained.

11. Periodic appraisals are obtained for insured assets.

12. Adequacy of insurance coverage is periodically reviewed.

13. Policy cancellations and return premiums are under adequate control by a designated person.

Figure 3-20
Internal Accounting Control Guide

Prepaid Expenses, Deferred Costs, and Intangible Assets Segregation of Function Form

An association of any one of the following functions with any of the others would generally be inappropriate: authorization for acquisitions, dispositions or write-offs; recordkeeping; cash receipts or disbursements; responsibility for insurance coverage.

Activity or Area of Responsibility	Person Responsible	Department Head	Inappropriate Duties
1. Authorizes acquisitions or dispositions.			
2. Maintains subsidiary records.			
3. Reconciles supporting records with controlling accounts.			
4. Codes transactions for accounting entries.			
5. Periodically reviews continued usefulness of intangibles.			
6. Approves accounting entries for lump-sum write-downs or write-offs.			
7. Reviews revenue and expense accounts in relationship to corresponding assets.			
8. Double-checks and reviews amortization and prepaid expense schedules.			
9. Has the responsibility for casualty insurance program.			
10. Maintains insurance register and records.			
11. Reviews adequacy of insurance coverage.			
12. Keeps controls over policy cancellations and insurance premium refunds.			

Financing Cycle Long-Term Debt; Stockholders' Equity

Figure 3-21
Internal Accounting Control Guide

Long-Term Debt

OBJECTIVES

1. Established policies exist covering short- and long-term financing, and these policies are periodically reviewed.

2. Authorization is required by the Board of Directors for major debt financings (including lease transactions), and by designated executives for incurring liabilities of lesser significance. Such authorization covers financing terms, pledging of assets, and authorization limits for designated officers.

3. Entries in the accounting records for debt and related accounts like interest and discount or premium are supported by adequate documentation and are properly recorded and classified.

4. Detailed records are maintained to provide information regarding covenant requirements, interest and repayment due dates, prepayment privileges, and other important matters, and these records are periodically reviewed by specified persons and reconciled with controlling accounts.

5. An appropriate segregation of function exists.

INTERNAL ACCOUNTING CONTROLS

	Yes	No	NA
1. Short-term and long-range written policies and plans are formulated for debt financings.			
2. Budgets, forecasts, and cash flow analyses are used in the planning process.			
3. Significant loan agreements (including leasing arrangements) are authorized by the Board of Directors, while financing transactions of lesser importance are authorized by specified officers.			

4. Similar authorization is required for the pledging or mortgaging of assets.

5. Approval by counsel of legal features is obtained prior to consummation of debt arrangements.

6. Entries in the records are supported by adequate documentation and pertinent approvals, and are properly recorded and classified.

7. A review is undertaken to determine whether the proceeds of incurred debt have actually been used in accordance with prior plans.

8. Detailed supporting records are maintained that provide necessary information as to covenant terms and conditions, interest and installment due dates, and other important matters.

9. Detailed records are reconciled periodically with general ledger accounts.

10. Entries and balances in general ledger and in supporting records are periodically reviewed to determine their propriety and their conformity with transactions as authorized, and to ensure that requirements such as timely payments and covenant restrictions are complied with.

11. Borrowing policies and outstanding debt are periodically reviewed with respect to borrowing needs, current interest rates, and other features.

12. Related interest, discount, and premium accounts are periodically reviewed and reconciled with outstanding debt.

13. An executive has been designated to oversee the return and cancellation of notes on repayment of debt.

Figure 3-22
Internal Accounting Control Guide

Long-Term Debt
Segregation of Function Form

An association of any one of the following functions with any of the others would generally be inappropriate: authorization for borrowings; recordkeeping; cash receipts or disbursements.

Activity or Area of Responsibility	Person Responsible	Department Head	Inappropriate Duties
1. Authorizes borrowings.	⎯⎯⎯⎯	⎯⎯⎯⎯	⎯⎯⎯⎯
2. Codes transactions for accounting entries.	⎯⎯⎯⎯	⎯⎯⎯⎯	⎯⎯⎯⎯
3. Maintains subsidiary records.	⎯⎯⎯⎯	⎯⎯⎯⎯	⎯⎯⎯⎯
4. Reviews transactions and accounting records for propriety and for conformity with authorization.	⎯⎯⎯⎯	⎯⎯⎯⎯	⎯⎯⎯⎯
5. Reconciles subsidiary records with general ledger accounts.	⎯⎯⎯⎯	⎯⎯⎯⎯	⎯⎯⎯⎯
6. Periodically reviews borrowing policies and outstanding debt.	⎯⎯⎯⎯	⎯⎯⎯⎯	⎯⎯⎯⎯
7. Reviews interest, discount, and premium accounts and reconciles with outstanding debt.	⎯⎯⎯⎯	⎯⎯⎯⎯	⎯⎯⎯⎯
8. Oversees the return and cancellation of notes on repayment of debt.	⎯⎯⎯⎯	⎯⎯⎯⎯	⎯⎯⎯⎯

Figure 3-23
Internal Accounting Control Guide
Stockholders' Equity

OBJECTIVES

1. Equity transactions are authorized by the Board of Directors and, where applicable, by the stockholders.
2. Accounting entries are supported by adequate documentation and are properly recorded and classified.
3. Detailed supporting records are maintained, and these are periodically reviewed and reconciled with controlling accounts.
4. An appropriate segregation of function exists.

INTERNAL ACCOUNTING CONTROLS

	Yes	No	NA
1. Equity transactions are authorized by the Board of Directors or, where applicable, by stockholders.			
2. Legal counsel reviews proposed capital stock transactions for compliance with legal requirements including conformity with debt covenant restrictions.			
3. The company uses:			
(a) An independent registrar.			
(b) An independent transfer agent.			
(c) An independent dividend disbursing agent.			
4. Reports from registrar and transfer agent are regularly reconciled with general ledger accounts.			
5. Stock certificates are signed and controlled by designated officers.			
6. A stockholders ledger and stock certificate book are maintained and regularly reconciled with general ledger accounts.			
7. Detailed supporting records are kept for stock options.			

8. Stock certificates are prenumbered, and unused certificates as well as treasury stock are safeguarded and periodically accounted for.

9. Surrendered certificates are cancelled and retained.

10. Entries in the accounting records are supported by adequate documentation, are properly recorded and classified, and periodically reviewed.

11. A review is undertaken to determine whether the proceeds of stock issuances have actually been used in accordance with prior plans.

12. An imprest bank account is used for dividend payments, and the account is subject to the same internal accounting controls as the regular bank accounts, including authorized signatures, control over unclaimed checks, etc.

13. Dividends paid are reconciled in the aggregate with amounts authorized by the Board of Directors, with outstanding shares, and with recorded amounts.

Figure 3-24
Internal Accounting Control Guide

Stockholders' Equity
Segregation of Function Form

An association of any one of the following functions with any of the others would generally be inappropriate: authorization of stock transactions; recordkeeping; registrar agent or function; stock; transfer agent or function; cash receipts or disbursements; custodianship of certificates.

Activity or Area of Responsibility	Person Responsible	Department Head	Inappropriate Duties
1. Authorizes capital stock transactions.	_____	_____	_____
2. Acts as registrar or company equivalent.	_____	_____	_____
3. Acts as transfer agent or company equivalent.	_____	_____	_____
4. Acts as dividend disbursing agent or company equivalent.	_____	_____	_____
5. Signs stock certificates.	_____	_____	_____
6. Maintains stockholder records.	_____	_____	_____
7. Has custody of stock certificates.	_____	_____	_____
8. Reviews accounting records.	_____	_____	_____
9. Reviews equity transactions and related recording for conformity with authorization.	_____	_____	_____
10. Supervises dividend disbursements.	_____	_____	_____
11. Signs dividend checks.	_____	_____	_____
12. Controls unclaimed dividend checks.	_____	_____	_____
13. Reconciles dividends paid with authorization, with outstanding shares, and with recorded amounts.	_____	_____	_____

Figure 3-25
Internal Accounting Control Guide
For Use in Review of Client's
EDP Department or Function

OBJECTIVES

1. Organization and general controls, systems, programs, and operating standards and procedures are formalized in writing and adequately documented.

2. The EDP function is under the overall supervision and control of high level non-EDP management.

3. An adequate segregation of function exists between EDP department and personnel and any of the following: non-EDP management; involvement with business or operating transactions or functions; custody of or control over assets; user departments; the accounting function.

4. An adequate segregation of duties exists within the department.

5. Input is properly authorized and approved by non-EDP personnel, and accurately processed in accordance with authorized specifications.

6. Ouput is examined and reviewed by non-EDP personnel for correspondence with authorized and approved input.

7. Procedures have been adopted and actions taken to (a) safeguard facilities, equipment, documentation materials, and files against physical damage, destruction or other loss; (b) to maintain adequate insurance coverage; and (c) to facilitate reconstruction of records and data in the event of damage or loss.

CONTROLS

	Yes	No	NA
Organization and General Controls			
1. Control over the EDP department is exercised by higher level non-EDP management, and such control is specified formally in writing (e.g., organization charts or manuals).			
2. The organization of the EDP department is similarly formalized in writing.			
3. Updated and approved job descriptions are on file for the various EDP personnel classifications.			

4. The EDP department (function) is independent of user departments.

5. The EDP department and the EDP personnel are not permitted to engage in, and are not involved in, the following business, operating, or accounting functions:

(a)   Originating or otherwise participating in transactions.

(b)   Authorizing transactions.

(c)   Approving transactions.

(d)   Performing original data preparation and documentation for transactions.

(e)   Creating, selecting, authorizing, or approving input data or documents submitted to the EDP department for processing.

(f)   Having access to, custody of, control over, or other operating involvement with, non-EDP assets.

(g)   Having general ledger or other accounting responsibilities other than properly controlled routine EDP processing.

(h)   Authorizing, approving, or originating accounting entries or adjustments to the accounting records.

(i)   Having access to or control over signature plates or check protection devices.

(j)   Maintaining inventory records for stored blank checks to be drawn on for periodic EDP processing.

6. The authority for originating master file changes lies outside the EDP department.

7. The following functions are segregated: systems analysis and design; programming; equipment operator; control group; librarian.

8. A control group is maintained.

9. The control group is organizationally independent of EDP operations.

10. Responsibilities of the control group relate to:

(a)   Receiving data to be processed.

(b)   Noting authorization for input.

(c)   Ensuring the recording of data received.

(d)   Following up on errors uncovered during processing.

(e)   Verifying proper distribution of output.

(f)   Maintaining adequate logs and control records relating to input and output.

11. The internal audit function periodically examines the operations of the EDP department and reports its findings to non-EDP management.

12. The internal audit department has a written program covering all phases of the EDP department.

13. Internal auditors use their own special software packages in undertaking audit tests.

14. In the event that documents for certain types of transactions are permitted to be automatically generated by computer (e.g., initi-

ation of purchase orders when inventory quantities fall below a specified level, or preparation of payroll or other checks), such permissible circumstances are:

    (a)   Clearly identified.

    (b)   Specifically authorized by higher level management unrelated to either the EDP department or the user department involved.

    (c)   Effectively publicized.

    (d)   Recorded in writing in operating manuals or other such documents, with specification as to authorization and control procedures.

    (e)   Periodically monitored and reviewed by higher-level management.

    (f)   Actual output is subject to controls (including review, approval, and appropriate reconciliation procedures) exercised by user department and, where indicated, by independent management personnel.

    15.   Operators are periodically rotated, especially with respect to applications of a risk nature.

    16.   EDP personnel are required to take their vacations.

    17.   For services rendered by an outside service bureau:

    (a)   A contract covers such arrangements.

    (b)   The contract and other arrangements have been approved by EDP and non-EDP management.

    (c)   The reputation of the service bureau has been verified by management.

    (d)   The service bureau is adequately insured to cover casualty losses.

    (e)   A performance bond has been provided.

    (f)   Adequate internal controls are in force and they correspond to the applicable controls set forth in the guide.

System Development Controls

    18.   Written procedures for requesting, authorizing, testing, and approving all new systems and computer programs as well as changes in systems and programs are maintained and periodically reviewed and updated.

    19.   Written specifications for new systems or for system changes:

    (a)   Are prepared.

    (b)   Are reviewed and approved by an appropriate level of non-EDP management and by affected user departments.

    20.   User departments, as well as the accounting department and internal auditors, actively participate and are consulted in EDP system design and development including the acquisition of software packages.

    21.   System testing:

    (a)   Is a joint effort of users and EDP personnel.

    (b)   Includes both manual and computerized aspects of the system.

    (c)   Is designed to ensure that input, if correct, will produce the desired correct output, and that incorrect input, processing, or output will be detected.

22.   Final approval of non-EDP management is obtained before a new system or system change is put into operation.

23.   Such final approval is recorded in writing and is based on review of prior authorization, specifications, testing results, and documentation.

24.   Master file and transaction file conversions necessitated by system changes are subject to controls to prevent unauthorized changes and to ensure the correspondence of transferred data.

25.   Data on converted files are reconciled with original files.

Input, Output, and Processing Controls

26.   Input is not accepted for processing without prior written authorization by the user department.

27.   Input is submitted on specially designed forms bearing an identification code and the forms are retained for future reference.

28.   Input is subject to batch and other controls.

29.   Input record counts are made and later compared with output:

(a)   By computer program.

(b)   By manual operation.

30.   Source documents are key-verified.

31.   Key-verification is undertaken by persons other than those performing initial key operation.

32.   Output control totals are reconciled to input control totals by:

(a)   Control group.

(b)   Computer program.

(c)   User department.

33.   The EDP processing of bank checks or other negotiable paper is subject to the usual internal accounting controls. In particular:

(a)   Checks and other negotiable paper are prenumbered.

(b)   Two or more persons are present during processing, one of the persons being a properly authorized non-EDP supervisory employee not assigned to any incompatible function.

(c)   Spoiled paper is cancelled, retained, and accounted for.

(d)   Appropriate reconciliations are made to verify correctness of totals for papers used and dollar amounts.

34.   Programs provide editing routines for:

(a)   Code or serial continuity check.

(b)   Field check: testing for valid characters, field size, sign, transaction, and combination of fields.

(c)   Limit (reasonableness) check; detecting input with dollar amounts or other quantitative data exceeding a predetermined amount.

(d)   Logic check: noting illogical conditions such as credit balances in perpetual inventory file.

(e) Missing or inactive items check: reporting inactive master records or absence of documentation on time cards.

(f) Identification check: comparing identifying data with authorized master data.

35. Computer hardware checks used include:

(a) Parity bit.

(b) Read-after-write.

(c) Echo.

(d) Character validity.

(e) Overflow test.

(f) Dual read.

(g) Hole count.

36. The accuracy of random access files is checked by periodic balancing.

37. The console log is reviewed daily by supervisory personnel.

38. Documented control is maintained over errors to ensure their review, correction, reprocessing and, where applicable, notification of user department.

39. Machine utilization logs, console print-outs, and error listings are retained and reviewed.

40. Logs and other appropriate records are kept and periodically reviewed, and show time and other operating statistics for:

(a) Regular production.

(b) Reruns.

(c) Testing and similar programmer needs.

(d) Maintenance.

(e) Scheduled downtime.

(f) Idle time.

(g) Outside users.

(h) Special use.

(i) _____.

41. Statistics are maintained and reviewed for errors and halts.

42. Internal leader label provides file name, date, identification number, and reel and sequence number.

43. Internal trailer label provides record count, control totals, and end-of-file code.

44. Internal labels are program-checked.

45. Operating personnel do not have access to program documentation materials, and programmers are not permitted to serve as operators.

46. Periodic review of EDP-generated reports is undertaken by higher level management to evaluate:

(a) Adequacy of form and content.

(b) Continued usefulness.

(c) Timeliness.

(d) Distribution methods.

(e) Need for revision of listings of approved distributees.

47. Controls have been established to account for processing performed for outside parties, and to prevent commingling and confusion with own work.

Documentation Controls

48. A standard documentation manual is kept.
49. Problem definition documentation includes:
(a) Reasons for system implementation.
(b) Project proposals.
(c) Description of system operations.
50. System documentation includes:
(a) Flow charts.
(b) Description of controls.
(c) Authorization.
(d) Coding conventions.
51. Program documentation includes:
(a) Narrative description.
(b) Flowcharts.
(c) Decision table or logic narrative.
(d) Parameter listings.
(e) Control features.
(f) Description of file formats and record layouts.
(g) Operating instructions.
(h) Listing of program changes and related testing.
52. Operations documentation includes:
(a) Description of required inputs and outputs.
(b) Sequence of cards.
(c) Information on tapes, disks, and other files.
(d) Control procedures.
(e) Recovery and restart procedures.
(f) Normal and maximum run time.
(g) Run manual.
53. Operator run manuals describe:
(a) Input and output files, and their disposition.
(b) Set-up procedures.
(c) Halt conditions and related actions.
(d) Typical console messages and related actions.
54. Override conditions are specified in writing, and overrides are subject to supervisory review and approval.
55. An adequate audit trail is maintained.
56. User documentation includes:
(a) Description of system and input and output data and format.
(b) System flowchart.
(c) Control procedures.

    (d) Error correction procedures.

    (e) Review procedures.

Physical and Environmental Controls

57. A periodic review is undertaken by non-EDP management of the adequacy of the physical and environmental controls.

58. A written report on the review is prepared and subsequently followed up to ensure that recommendations for improvement have been carried out.

59. Access to the EDP department is restricted to properly authorized and designated individuals.

60. Equipment, files, and documentation materials are physically safeguarded by use of:

    (a) Fireproof and atmospherically controlled facilities.

    (b) Heat and smoke detectors, and fire and burglar alarm devices.

    (c) Fireproof vaults and cabinets.

    (d) Secure off-premises storage facilities.

    (e) Guards and other security personnel.

61. An EDP librarian function exists with responsibilities clearly fixed for safeguarding and controlling data files, usage logs, and documentation materials.

62. Library records are maintained showing:

    (a) Items stored.

    (b) Individuals authorized to obtain files and documents.

    (c) Data regarding movements of materials: names, dates, file identification, reason obtained, proper return.

63. Library records are periodically reviewed by internal auditors or appropriately authorized officials.

64. Reconstruction procedures in adequate detail are periodically updated and reviewed.

65. Back-up files are kept.

66. Copies of critically important files and documentation are stored off premises.

67. Authorization is required for duplication of data or program files.

68. An approved updated records-retention program is in effect for EDP files, source documents and other EDP-related materials.

69. Computer files have external labels showing file name, date, identification number, and retention date.

70. File protection rings are used to prevent accidental erasure.

71. EDP personnel are bonded.

72. An insurance program adequately covers losses due to fire, theft, physical damage, loss or destruction of files and records, employee irregularities, and other casualties.

73. The insurance program is under the control of and regularly reviewed and monitored by non-EDP management.

Application (User Department) Controls

74. Transmittal forms and documents are regularly prepared for submission to the EDP department for processing.

75. Transmittal papers:

(a) Are preprinted.

(b) Are signed by preparer and supervisor.

(c) Are prenumbered and properly identified.

76. Copies of transmittal forms and documents are retained in user department.

77. A control log is kept of all transmittals and associated control data including batch totals and document counts.

78. EDP output is compared and reconciled by user department with transmittal forms and other manual records and control data for correspondence as to details of individual records as well as record count and dollar amount totals.

79. Only authorized personnel are permitted to handle output received from EDP department.

Figure 3-26
Internal Accounting Control Guide

Segregation of Function Form
for Use in Review of Client's
EDP Department or Function

In general, an involvement of the EDP department or personnel with any of the following functions or activities would be inappropriate:

1. User department responsibilities and activities.

2. Originating, authorizing, approving, or otherwise participating in business dealings or transactions of the firm.

3. Performing original data preparation and documentation for transactions.

4. Creating, selecting, authorizing, or approving input data or documents submitted for computer processing.

5. Having access to, custody of, control over, or other operating involvement with, non-EDP assets.

6. The accounting or internal auditing function.

7. Moreover, within the EDP department the following functions should be segregated: systems analysis and design, programming, equipment operators, control group, and librarian.

Activity or Area of Responsibility	Person Responsible	Department Head	Inappropriate Duties
1. Exercises higher level, non-EDP control over EDP department.			
2. Heads EDP department.			
3. Is assigned to:			
(a) System analysis and design.			
(b) Programming.			
(c) Equipment operating.			
(d) Control group.			
(e) Librarian function.			
4. Has access to, or control over, signature plates or check protection devices.			
5. Maintains inventory records for, or control over, blank checks stored for computer processing.			
6. Supervises:			
(a) Key-punch operations.			
(b) Acceptance of input.			
(c) Processing of input.			
(d) Processing of output.			
(e) Reconciliation of input and output.			
(f) Distribution of output.			

 7. Authorizes arrangements with outside service bureaus.
 8. Monitors controls over processing by outside service bureau.
 9. Authorizes system development or system changes, including programming.
10. Prepares written specifications for new systems or system changes.
11. Reviews and approves new systems or system changes (other than EDP management).
12. Supervises system testing.
13. Gives final approval before a new system or system change is put into operation.
14. Supervises master file and transaction file conversions.
15. Supervises handling and processing of bank checks or other negotiable paper and applies appropriate controls to ensure proper accounting for quantities and dollar amounts.
16. Reviews and evaluates editing routines.
17. Periodically balances random access files.
18. Reviews console log.
19. Maintains documented controls over errors and their correction and reprocessing.
20. Periodically reviews logs and other records showing time and other operating statistics.
21. Ensures that operating personnel do not have access to program documentation materials.
22. Has responsibility for periodically reviewing the usefulness of computer-produced reports.
23. Oversees adherence to documentation standards.
24. Authorizes and reviews override conditions.
25. Periodically reviews adequacy of audit trail.
26. Periodically reviews (i.e., by non-EDP management) adequacy of physical and environmental safeguards and controls.
27. Periodically inspects and evaluates operations and records of the EDP librarian. function.
28. Monitors EDP insurance programs.

CHAPTER 4

Audit Program Guide

AUDIT PROGRAM GUIDE—STRUCTURE AND CONTENTS

The structure and contents of an audit program guide may vary considerably. Some accountants simply list the auditing procedures for specific accounts and areas without noting the audit objectives. Others may prefer to prepare guides in which only the audit objectives are presented for the various accounts, leaving it to the auditor on the engagement to develop the pertinent auditing procedures based on those objectives. Similar variations can be found in the extent to which audit guides differentiate between compliance testing and substantive testing, or between interim and year-end procedures.

Introductory instructions for an Audit Program Guide are detailed in Figure 4-1. Each section of the Guide includes the following:

1. Audit objectives.
2. Auditing procedures.
3. Specification of auditing procedures appropriate for compliance testing and for interim work.
4. Audit comments and documentation form. This form, which is illustrated in Figure 4-2, should be provided for each section of the Audit Program Guide, but it is not reproduced later in this book in the interest of conserving space. Its contents are as follows:
    (a) Audit comments.
    (b) Audit testing and sampling.
    (c) Analytical review procedures.
    (d) Audit conclusions.
    (e) Working paper documentation.

No attempt has been made to identify each auditing procedure with one or more objectives, since the audit objectives are in the main interrelated and, moreover, each auditing procedure can usually be associated with multiple objectives.

As previously pointed out (Figure 2-15), in the tests of details of transactions, *substantive testing* may often include the very same items tested in *compliance testing*. Although the focus in the former is on amounts and the validity of the transaction, and in the latter on internal accounting control features, it is often difficult and counterproductive to distinguish between them too sharply. The lack of an invoice number, for example, may reflect on compliance with sequential prenumbering of documents as an internal accounting control, but it could also fall into the *substantive* domain and evoke questions about the bona fides of the transactions. The audit program guide does list at the end of each section the procedures (by numbered item) that may fall into the compliance testing category, but it should be understood that this does not imply that the procedure has no applicability to substantive testing. This method of identification has been chosen, rather than a separate listing of compliance testing procedures, because it better reflects the foregoing caveats, avoids arbitrary distinctions, and provides greater flexibility for the practitioner who may wish to restructure the audit program guide to meet the requirements of his practice.

For similar reasons, procedures that clearly can be profitably performed at interim dates are likewise identified by numbered item at the end of each section. Some procedures can be undertaken at both interim and year-end dates, some mainly at interim dates, and others mainly at year-end, and so on. The designated items should therefore be looked upon as possible candidates for inclusion by a practitioner in an audit program for work to be performed at an interim date.

The introductory section of the audit program guide, as shown in Figure 4-3, covers general matters of audit concern. It also serves as a reminder checklist to ensure that certain specialized sections of the audit program guide, on which some work had already been done in the pre-engagement or audit planning stages, are reviewed and updated. Following the introductory general section of the guide, accounts are presented in the same order as in the Internal Accounting Control Guide.

Figure 4-1
Audit Program Guide

Introduction and Instructions

_____   _____
(Client)   (Period)

_____   _____
(Guide preparation   (Reviewed by)
supervised by)

INSTRUCTIONS

    1.   This is a pattern audit program guide which must be individually tailored for each audit engagement, although many of the auditing procedures usually will require little or no modification. It has been designed mainly for commercial and industrial companies but can easily be adapted for appropriate use on engagements for clients in specialized enterprises.

    2.   At the end of each section of the Guide, those procedures that most clearly seem to be associated with compliance testing are identified by numbered item. But the distinction between compliance testing and substantive testing, it should be recognized, sometimes cannot be sharply drawn.

    3.   Those procedures that might profitably be performed at interim dates are likewise identified by numbered item at the end of each section of the Guide. But here, too, a caveat must be expressed, since some procedures may be performed at both (or either) interim and year-end dates, and their character and scope may vary depending on when they are carried out.

    4.   The use of the Audit Program Guide, section by section, should be synchronized, where appropriate, with that of related sections of the Internal Accounting Control Guide.

    5.   The "Performed by" column should be initialed for each procedure as an indication of satisfactory performance.

    6.   The "NA" column should be initialed only when the auditing procedure in question does not at all apply to the entity. If it is believed that a procedure conceivably does apply but it is unreasonable or impracticable to perform it, a conspicuous reference should be made on the "NA" line to the Audit Comments and Documentation Form, which should provide an appropriate explanation as well as the comments and opinion of the engagement partner.

    7.   The Audit Comments and Documentation Form that follows

each section of the Guide is an integral and vital segment of the Guide and should be carefully completed. The component parts of the form are:

(a) Audit comments.
(b) Audit testing and sampling.
(c) Analytical review procedures.
(d) Audit conclusions.
(e) Working paper documentation.

Instructions are provided for each of these segments of the Audit Comments and Documentation Form, and they should be carefully read and followed.

8. The audit program guide as a whole and its various sections are to be signed in the indicated spaces by appropriate staff and supervisory personnel as evidence of their assumption of full responsiblity for satisfactory preparation or review.

Figure 4-2
Audit Program Guide

Audit Comments and Documentation Form

(To be completed for, and attached to, each section of the Guide)

Section: _____

_____		_____	
(Prepared by)	(Date)	(Reviewed by)	(Date)

AUDIT COMMENTS

(Use this space to comment on and clarify any problems or questions that may have arisen with respect to any of the auditing procedures in this section of the guide.)

Guide Item No.   Comments
_____   _____

_____

_____

AUDIT TESTING AND SAMPLING

(Describe here—or refer to the description in working papers—the sampling plan followed for those procedures where quantitative scope is not already clearly indicated in the Guide. The description should be keyed to the numbered auditing procedure. Where applicable, appropriate cross reference should be made to the description of the compliance testing plan as recorded on Comments and Documentation Form attached to the Internal Accounting Control Guide.)

_____

_____

ANALYTICAL REVIEW PROCEDURES

(Review carefully the discussion on analytical review procedures presented in Figure 2-19. Describe below the analytical review procedures employed, follow-up inquiries and investigations, if any, and conclusions as to audit satisfaction with the evidential findings developed by the analytical review procedures. If the foregoing matters are covered in the working papers, so indicate below and refer to the pertinent working papers.)

AUDIT CONCLUSIONS

(State here whether the audit findings pertinent to this section of the Guide permit the auditor to express satisfaction that the audit objectives have been achieved, and to express an opinion that the accounts examined are presented fairly in accordance with generally accepted accounting principles on a basis consistent with the prior period. Any reservations should be clearly recorded.)

WORKING PAPER DOCUMENTATION

(List here the title and reference symbol for working papers that provide documentation for the accounts covered in this section of the audit program guide.)

Figure 4-3
Audit Program Guide
General Matters

AUDIT OBJECTIVES

The following audit objectives, which are expressed in general terms, underlie the more specific audit objectives pertinent to the individual accounts dealt with later in the Guide. The objectives are interrelated and some may therefore seem redundant, but each renders a significant contribution to a total understanding of what the auditing procedures are designed to accomplish.

1. To determine whether the financial statements are presented fairly in conformity with generally accepted accounting principles.
2. To learn whether accounting principles have been applied on a basis consistent with the prior period.
3. To ascertain whether all material matters have been disclosed in the financial statements whose disclosure is necessary to make the statements fair and not misleading.
4. To study and evaluate the system of internal accounting control as a basis for reliance, or lack of reliance, on those controls and for determination of the effect on the other auditing procedures to be employed.
5. To obtain information about the client and its background, policies, practices, and key personnel as a basis for effective and alert examination.
6. To determine the genuineness (bona fides) of the transactions and account balances.
7. To verify the client's ownership of the recorded assets and that all owned assets have been properly recorded.
8. To determine that the owned assets truly exist and are on hand or otherwise properly accounted for.
9. To verify that liabilities and transactions truly pertain to (are those of) the client.
10. To detect possible material overstatement of net assets (and net income) through overstatement of assets or understatement of liabilities.
11. To detect possible material understatement of net assets (and net income) through failure to record all owned assets, improper expensing of assets, or overstatement of liabilities.
12. To discover material errors, fraud, or other irregularities.
13. To determine whether there is a proper cutoff of transactions and that they have been recorded in the proper accounting period.

14. To review subsequent events of a material nature and to determine whether adjustment of, or disclosure in, the financial statements is indicated.

15. To be alert to the possibility that illegal acts by the entity and its key personnel may have occurred that might have a material effect on the financial statements, and to adopt appropriate procedures if it is believed that such acts have occurred.

16. To identify and examine transactions with related parties.

AUDITING PROCEDURES

The auditing procedures in this section of the guide touch upon general and often overlapping matters of broad interest, and will be carried out at various stages of the examination. Some of the procedures serve in effect as checklist reminders that other sections of the guide are to be reviewed, updated and completed.

	Performed by	NA

1. Review the Pre-Engagement Planning and Control Guide (Figure 1-2) and related working papers.

2. Review Audit Planning and Control Guide (Figure 1-6) and related working papers and, to the extent indicated, update or complete procedures and matters contained therein.

3. Review and update throughout the examination the guides covering areas such as:

(a) Understanding the Client's Business—A Checklist Guide (Figure 1-7).

(b) Risk Areas Questionnaire Guide (Figure 1-8).

(c) Detection of Errors or Irregularities—A Planning and Control Guide (Figure 1-10).

(d) Illegal Acts: Identification, Auditing Procedures, and Reporting—A Planning and Control Guide (Figure 1-11).

(e) Related Party Transactions—A Planning and Control Guide (Figure 1-12).

4. With respect to the internal auditors:

(a) Undertake the procedures specified in the section of the Audit Program Guide on Evaluating the Work of Internal Auditors (Figure 2-7).

(b) Prepare a memorandum covering (i) the results of the evaluation; (ii) the details of the plan, if any, for using the work of the internal auditors; (iii) a description of how the internal auditors were actually utilized in the conduct of the examination; and (iv) the extent to which the evaluation of the system of internal accounting control and the nature, timing, and extent of the independent auditor's auditing procedures have been affected by the client's internal audit function.

5. Obtain authenticated copies of all minutes of stockholders, board of directors, committees of directors, and executive committees; prepare excerpts and take note of and cross reference to working papers, material matters affecting the examination and the financial statements.

6. Review monthly and quarterly reports prepared by the client during the current year; investigate unusual or questionable data and fluctuations.

7. Obtain the working papers specified in the written request previously submitted to the client (Figure 1-14), and note whether they are in the proper form.

8. Obtain a working trial balance and compare with general ledger balances.

9. If this is a recurring engagement, compare opening balances with prior year's report and adjusted balances per prior year's working papers.

10. Determine that adjustments of prior year's audit have been properly recorded in the accounts.

11. If this is a first engagement, verify the fairness of opening balances as follows:

(a) Compare opening balances with:

(i) General ledger closing balances of prior year.

(ii) The company's financial statements of prior year.

(iii) Relevant data on prior year's income and business tax returns.

(iv) The report of predecessor independent auditor. (Note the type of opinion expressed and take into account the reputation of predecessor auditor (Figure 1-5).

(b) Determine whether accounting principles and methods followed in the prior year(s) are consistent with those of the current year.

(c) Review correspondence with client's attorneys, corporate minutes, and other corporate records.

(d) Review the cutoff of transactions at the beginning of the year to determine whether transactions have been recorded in the proper accounting period.

(e) In undertaking the regular examination for the current year, include a "subsequent events" type of review with respect to transactions in the early part of the year.

(f)   Obtain and review schedules and reconciliations as of the prior year-end for such accounts as cash, receivables, payables, investments, and inventories; and, as appropriate in the circumstances, obtain corroborative evidential matter.

(g)   Determine whether a physical count of inventories was undertaken by the client as of the beginning of the year; if so, make appropriate inquiries to ascertain the reliability of the count and examine evidential matter in support of quantities and pricing. If a physical count was not made, determine and evaluate the basis for arriving at inventory balances.

(h)   Test accruals and prepayments as of the beginning of the year by independent calculations and approximations.

(i)   Analyze (going back as far as necessary to verify the fairness of the opening balances), and examine supporting evidential matter for, such accounts as investments, property, plant and equipment, intangibles, stockholders' equity, long-term debt, receivables and payables of an unusual or nonrecurring nature, and allowances for depreciation and for doubtful accounts.

(j)   Test prior years' transactions for accounts such as repairs and maintenance and bad debts expense for the possibility of improper expensing of assets.

(k)   Examine revenue agents' reports, review prior income tax returns, and determine the propriety of recorded amounts including deferred taxes.

(l)   Undertake comparison tests, compute appropriate ratios, and perform other such analytical procedures with respect to financial statements of prior years.

12.   Test postings from posting sources to general ledger and from general ledger to posting sources.

13.   Test footing and cross-footing of journals.

14.   Test general journal entries and take note especially of nonstandard, material, or unusual entries; authorizations and approvals; adequacy of supporting evidence; and the type and frequency of adjusting entries.

15.   Review management letter (and/or memoranda) reporting on and making recommendations with respect to weaknesses (material and immaterial) in internal accounting controls for the prior year and ascertain whether reported weaknesses have been remedied (similarly review any interim report on internal accounting control covering an early period of the current year).

16.   Review and/or undertake the procedures necessary to complete the following introductory or general sections of the Audit Program Guide.

(a)   Using the work of a specialist (Figure 2-5).

(b)   Litigation, claims, and assessments, including confirmation letter to company's attorneys (Figure 2-8, 2-9, 2-10, 2-11).

(c)   Subsequent events (Figure 2-12).

(d)   An overview guide to internal accounting control (Figure 2-13).

(e)   System review, compliance testing, and substantive testing (Flgure 2-14).

(f)   Audit committee of the board of directors (Figure 2-20).

17.   For consolidated statements:

(a)   Obtain consolidating working papers.

(b)   Trace individual accounts to year-end adjusted trial balance figures of individual entities.

(c)   Review propriety of elimination, reclassification, and adjusting entries made for consolidation purposes.

(d)   Ascertain that intercompany balances (income and balance sheet) have been properly eliminated.

18.   Obtain representation letters (Figures 2-1, 2-3, 2-4).

19.   Undertake analytical review procedures with respect to the financial statements taken as a whole (Figure 2-19).

20.   Resolve problems and questions recorded in audit notes, and in comments and documentation forms completed for each section of the Internal Accounting Control Guide (Figure 3-2) and of the Audit Program Guide (Figure 4-2).

21.   Give client a copy of adjusting entries accumulated during the audit and obtain signature of appropriate officer on working paper copy to signify approval and acceptance of adjusting entries for recording in the accounts.

22.   Obtain representation letter covering corporate minutes (Figure 2-2).

23.   Follow procedures outlined in checklist guide dealing with communication of material weaknesses in internal accounting control (Flgure 2-16) and prepare report communicating such weaknesses (Figure 2-17).

24.   Perform the reviews needed to properly complete the following review guides:

(a)   Auditor's report checklist review guide (Figure 7-3).

(b)   Financial statements checklist review guide (Figure 7-4).

(c)   Financial statement disclosures checklist reminder and review guide (Figure 7-5).

(d)   Working papers checklist review guide (Figure 7-6).

25.   Prepare memorandum containing suggestions for use by the auditor on subsequent audit engagements.

Noted below are suggested auditing procedures that would seem to be especially appropriate for compliance testing and for interim work. They have been selected from the foregoing audit program and are identified by corresponding number.

Compliance testing: 12, 13, 14

Interim work: 1, 2, 4, 5, 6, 7, 9, 10, 11, 12, 13, 14, 15

Figure 4-4
Audit Program Guide

Sales and Accounts Receivable

AUDIT OBJECTIVES

1. To determine the genuineness (bona fides) of receivables and of related sales transactions.

2. To ascertain the collectibility of receivables and to evaluate the allowances for doubtful accounts and discounts so that receivables may be properly stated at realizable amount.

3. To see if an adequate cutoff has been established so that receivables and sales are recorded in the proper accounting period.

4. To determine whether receivables and sales have been overstated due to error, improper cutoff, improper recording of consignment sales, recording of fictitious transactions, failure to write off uncollectible accounts; or understated due to error, improper cutoff, failure to account for all shipments, improper bad debt or other write-offs of receivables.

5. To determine whether account balances are fairly stated with appropriate classifications and/or disclosure of noncurrent and non-trade receivables, related party receivables and sales, pledging of receivables, and unfavorable sales commitments.

AUDITING PROCEDURES

	Performed by	NA
1. Review prior and current year's audit memoranda, audit programs and other working papers contained in permanent and current files bearing on sales and accounts receivable.		
2. Review memorandum on Understanding the Client's Business (Figure 1-7) and take note particularly of sales methods; terms of sale including cash and trade discounts, freight charges, and sales return policy; types of customers; major customers; sales trends; sales to related parties; warranties; and customer services.		

3. Examine a sample of sales drawn from sales journals and verify invoice data by comparison with supporting sales orders or contracts, approved price lists, bills of lading, and shipping advices. Take note of:

(a) Indications on invoices and documents of compliance with internal accounting controls (e.g., credit and sales order approvals; matching of documents; unit price verification; and mathematical check).

(b) Customer name, product description, dates, unit price, and quantities.

(c) Credit and sales order approvals.

(d) Terms of sale and shipment, including freight charges, FOB specifications, trade and cash discounts.

(e) Numerical sequence of invoices and supporting documents.

(f) Mathematical accuracy of invoices; check by independent computation.

(g) Proper ledger posting; trace to accounts receivable ledgers.

(h) Proper inventory posting (at cost); trace to perpetual inventory records.

4. Examine samples of sales orders, shipping advices, and bills of lading drawn from the files and, for each sample, match with corresponding sales orders, shipping documents, sales invoices and entry in sales journal. Take note of correspondence of the invoices and supporting documents with respect to customer, products, terms, unit prices, and quantities. (See auditing procedure 3, above, for additional audit features to be considered, depending on the testing plan.)

5. Examine a sample of credit memos drawn from the sales returns and allowances register and verify book entries as follows:

(a) Compare sales register entries with corresponding credit memos, noting numerical sequence, name, amount, and authorization and/or approval on face of credit memo or attached documents.

(b) Examine documents in support of sales returns or allowances, including receiving records, correspondence, and authorization.

(c) Compare data on credit memos with original invoices, sales orders, and shipping documents, concerning name, product, quantity, unit price, and terms of sale.

(d) Check mathematical accuracy of credit memos by independent computation.

(e) Consider whether the credits are unusual in amount or nature and whether they are indicative of serious shortcomings in product acceptance or other sales factors.

(f) Trace postings to accounts receivable ledgers and, where applicable, to perpetual inventory records.

6. Trace postings for a sample of cash receipts book entries to accounts receivable ledgers, and trace postings for a sample of ledger entries to cash receipts book.

7. For sales journals and sales returns and allowances journals, for a test period:

(a) Foot and crossfoot journals.

(b) Check postings to general ledger, and from general ledger back to journals; investigate unmatched entries.

8. Obtain an aged schedule of accounts receivable.

(a) Foot schedule and compare total with general ledger balance.

(b) Test aging of accounts.

(c) Compare balances with subsidiary ledgers (part of aging test).

(d) Test individual ledger accounts by tracing balances to accounts receivable schedule and by tracing selected entries to posting sources.

(e) Scan aged schedule and, for items listed, scan subsidiary ledgers, noting any unusual features such as material past-due balances, significant variations in periodic sales charges, questionable posting sources, material or unusual noncash credits, peculiarities in payment, signs of pledging, nontrade or related-party receivables, indications of consignment sales improperly recorded as regular sales, and credit balances.

(f) Undertake follow-up verification where indicated for questionable matters, by examination of supporting documents and by making inquiries of appropriate personnel.

9. Confirm by direct communication with customers and other parties a sample of accounts drawn from the schedule of accounts receivable.

(a) Review guidelines on confirmation of receivables as developed in AU 331 and discuss with manager or partner in charge of engagement any departures from those standards, which may be summarized as follows:

(i) Confirmation of receivables is a generally accepted auditing procedure.

(ii) The burden of justifying the failure to confirm is generally insurmountable, and that failure may result in a qualified opinion or, depending upon materiality and other considerations, in a disclaimer of opinion.

(iii) Confirmation may be undertaken during or after the period under audit; the choice of confirmation date, the use of positive or negative method, and the sample size, are determined after consideration of a number of factors, such as adequacy of internal accounting controls, possibility of customer disputes, indications of inaccuracies or irregularities in the accounts, and materiality of amounts.

(iv) The negative form is especially applicable in the case of mass accounts with small balances subject to good controls and if customers are of the type that would be apt to respond in the event of differences.

(v) Second and sometimes third requests should be sent when replies have not been received; supporting evidence should be examined for signficant accounts that have failed to respond.

(b) Prepare a memorandum describing the sampling plan and methods of confirmation (i.e., positive and negative).

(c) Arrange for client to fill in form confirmation letters and to attach monthly statements.

(d) Test names, balances, and details of confirmation letters and attached statements by comparison with auditor's confirmation control listing.

(e) Enclose confirmation requests and reply envelopes addressed to the auditor in envelopes bearing auditor's return address, and bring directly to a post office for mailing.

(f) Send second request confirmations if replies to positive confirmations have not been received within a given period.

(g) Investigate reply comments and differences by appropriate inquiries and by reference to relevant documents and records such as subsidiary ledgers, sales and shipping documents, cash receipts records, and correspondence. Investigate also requests returned by post office as undeliverable.

(h) Appraise the significance of reported differences as possibly indicating inadequate internal accounting controls, poor cutoff procedures, inaccurate recordkeeping, and irregularities. Record adjusting journal entries where indicated.

(i) For significant accounts not responding to original and follow-up confirmation requests, examine adequate evidence in support of balances, such as cash collected after confirmation date, sales and shipping documents, credit reports, scrutiny of the account, and inquiry of management. Where indicated, obtain client's permission to telephone customer.

(j) Depending on results of confirmation at an interim date and other considerations, such as the emergence of new customers with material balances, consider sending additional confirmations at year-end.

(k) Summarize and evaluate confirmation test.

10. Determine the adequacy of the allowance for bad debts, the propriety of bad debt write-offs, and the collectibility of receivables, as follows:

(a) Review cash collections after balance sheet date for past due accounts and for a selected number of other accounts of material amount listed on aged schedule.

(b) Determine whether bad debt or other write-offs of receivables were recorded after the statement date by reviewing journal and general ledger entries.

(c) Review aged schedule with credit manager and other appropriate personnel and obtain pertinent information and explanations regarding past due accounts and collectibility of accounts.

(d) Test collectibility of past due and other selected accounts by evaluating reasonableness of client's explanations, examining sales and shipping records, reviewing account payment and transaction history, inspecting collateral, reviewing credit reports, and examining correspondence with customers, attorneys and collection agencies.

(e) Record adjusting entries to write off uncollectible accounts.

(f) Obtain an analysis of the allowance for doubtful accounts.

(g) Verify validity of write-offs to the allowance account by examining authorization and undertaking procedures mentioned in item (d) above.

(h) Consider sending confirmations to accounts written off.

(i) Ascertain and evaluate the basis for management's estimate of an adequate allowance for doubtful accounts.

(j) Independently judge the adequacy of the allowance account after taking into account the findings developed by the foregoing procedures, the bad debt history of the firm, the type of customers, external and economic conditions generally and in the industry, and changes in sales and credit policies.

11. Independently determine the adequacy of allowances for sales discounts, returns, freight, and warranties by reference to sales arrangements and contracts, comparison tests with prior years and industry data, independent overall calculations such as ratio of sales discounts to sales (or cash collections), inquiries, and other corroborative evidential matter.

12. Review the cutoff of sales and sales return transactions for a test period before and after the balance sheet date.

13. Perform post balance sheet review procedures for sales and sales return transactions (Figure 2-12). Take note of any unusual sales and sales returns and material price declines.

14. Determine whether receivables have been pledged or hypothecated.

15. For receivables from officers, employees and related companies:

(a) Analyze accounts.

(b) Determine the reason for the transactions.

(c) Examine authorization.

(d) Examine collateral.

(e) Obtain specific approval from appropriate officials.

(f) Send confirmation requests.

(g) Reconcile intercompany balances.

(h) Examine and evaluate evidence in support of collectibility.

(i) Note whether receivables purportedly reduced or liquidated shortly before the balance sheet date were subsequently restored.

16. For notes receivable, undertake the same procedures, where applicable, as for accounts receivable, including confirmation, and in addition:

(a) Inspect notes.

(b)   Confirm with banks any notes discounted or held for collection.

(c)   Examine authorization for loans and determine business purpose.

(d)   Independently test calculations for interest income and accrued income.

17.   Perform analytical review procedures for accounts receivable, sales, sales returns, sales discounts, and related accounts, using Figure 2-19 as a guide. Specifically, compare monthly and annual sales and sales returns with prior years, forecasts, and industry data; note monthly variations; compute and compare ratios such as receivable turnover, receivables to current and total assets, gross profit percentage, and ratio of returns, discounts, and bad debts and allowances to sales and receivables.

18.   Determine that financial statements reflect a proper segregation of current and noncurrent receivables, receivables from related parties, and credit balances, and that assigned or hypothecated receivables are disclosed.

_____

Noted below are suggested auditing procedures that would seem to be especially appropriate for compliance testing and for interim work. They have been selected from the foregoing audit program and identified by corresponding number.

Compliance testing: 2, 3, 4, 5, 10c, d, g.

Interim work: 2, 3, 4, 5, 6, 7, 8, 9, 10c, d, 15, 16.

Figure 4-5
Audit Program Guide

Cash

AUDIT OBJECTIVES

1. To determine that cash balances truly represent cash in banks and on hand and belong to the client company, and that cash transactions are bona fide and are recorded in conformity with generally accepted accounting principles.

2. To ascertain whether there are any cash withdrawal restrictions.

3. To determine whether all cash that should have been received has been properly accounted for, and that all cash received has been deposited and properly recorded.

4. To see whether an adequate cutoff has been established so that cash receipts and disbursements have been recorded in the proper accounting period.

5. To determine whether cash balances have been overstated or understated because of error or irregularities.

6. To utilize cash transactions and related evidential matter as additional verification of other accounts and for revealing matters or events that call for adjustment of or disclosure in the financial statements.

AUDITING PROCEDURES

	Performed by	NA
1. Review prior and current years' working papers in permanent and current files bearing on cash.		
2. Send the following confirmation letters to all banks with which the company has maintained an account or engaged in borrowing transactions during the period under review, requesting confirmation of the following as of the confirmation date:		
(a) Bank balances and other data as specified on standard AICPA confirmation form letter.		

(b)   Authorized signatures.

(c)   Information regarding credit and compensating balance arrangements.

3.   Obtain cutoff bank statements directly from the bank for a given period after the confirmation date.

4.   Review information confirmed by banks, compare with corresponding recorded data, and make note of matters requiring statement disclosures.

5.   Obtain bank statements from client and undertake the procedures specified below, which are designed to verify the accuracy and validity of bank reconciliations, cash receipts and disbursements entries, and general ledger cash balances. Certain of the procedures are to be undertaken on a test basis in accordance with the sampling plan contained in the working papers and not necessarily in conjunction with review of bank reconciliations. Moreover, a proof of cash should be prepared for a selected period.

6.   For cash balances:

(a)   Check clerical accuracy of bank reconciliation including footing of outstanding check list.

(b)   Compare bank and book balances per reconciliation with balances per bank statement, bank confirmation, and general ledger.

(c)   Test accuracy and completeness of bank statement and cleared checks by independently agreeing cleared checks and debit advices with total of bank charges and by review of cancellation dates.

(d)   Perform appropriate analytical review procedures using Figure 2-19 as a guide. Comparison and ratio tests should include working capital, current ratio, cash to total current assets, and cash to total financial assets.

7.   For cash receipts:

(a)   Foot and cross-foot cash receipts journals for a test period and trace postings to general ledger.

(b)   Match deposit entries on bank statement with daily totals per cash receipts journal, stamped duplicate deposit slips, and the corresponding remittance lists, and take note of any time lags or discrepancies.

(c)   Perform the reverse procedure and match deposits per books with bank statement, remittance lists, and duplicate deposit slips.

(d)   Select a sample number of days' entries in cash receipts journal and compare individual items with details of corresponding duplicate deposit slips and remittance lists, noting agreement of names, dates and amounts.

(e)   Select a sample number of remittance lists and compare individual items with details of corresponding duplicate deposit slips and cash book entries.

(f)   Test validity of entries by examination of customers' remittance vouchers and, for miscellaneous receipts, contracts, cash register tapes, cash or miscellaneous sales invoices, and shipping or other documents.

(g) For a selected period, check numerical sequence and recording of remittance lists.

(h) Test sales discounts by scanning cash book entries and, for a selected sample of entries, by comparing net cash received per books with remittance lists; examine sales orders and invoices (and/or subsidiary ledger accounts) for terms of sale and elapsed time; and independently calculate discounts.

(i) Trace deposits in transit to remittance lists, duplicate deposit slips, and cutoff bank statement, and investigate delayed deposits.

(j)   Test accuracy of account distribution.

8.   For cash disbursements:

(a) Foot and cross-foot cash disbursements journal for a test period and trace postings to general ledger.

(b) Compare paid checks with listing of outstanding checks of prior bank reconciliation and with entries in cash disbursements journal, noting payee, endorsements, authorized check signer, amount, and check number.

(c) Examine supporting documentation and authorization for cash, bearer, or bank transfer checks, and trace bank transfer checks to corresponding deposit.

(d) For a period before and after the confirmation date, prepare a schedule of bank transfer checks (and, separately, of NG checks and other debit advices) that have cleared in the monthly bank statement and cutoff statement and/or have been recorded in the cash disbursements journal; match checks with related deposits, noting whether checks and deposits correspond and were recorded as of the same dates and properly entered in the accounts.

(e) Test validity of entries in cash disbursements journal by tracing a selected sample of entries to supporting vouchers and underlying documentation. (To be synchronized with corresponding procedure in the audit program for purchases, expenses, and accounts payable.)

(f) Test purchase discounts by reference to terms of purchase and by independent calculation.

(g) Check accuracy of carryforward of open items to list of outstanding checks.

(h) Trace checks cleared in cutoff bank statement to list of outstanding checks, and take note of any discrepancies as to name, dates, amounts, and clearance lags.

(i) Follow up on outstanding checks that did not clear in cutoff statement by reviewing checks clearing in subsequent bank statement, making appropriate inquiries and examining supporting vouchers.

(j) Obtain details regarding checks written but not issued at statement date or entered at that date but not issued, so that appropriate cutoff adjusting entries may be recorded where indicated.

(k) Test accuracy of account distribution.

9. Scan cash journals for the period after the statement date in accordance with subsequent events procedures outlined in Figure 2-12. Take note of and review material or unusual entries, including those reflecting bank borrowings, loans to officers and related parties (especially if purportedly repaid prior to the statement date), stock issuances, and significant sales or purchases of assets not held or acquired for resale.

10. For cash on hand and petty cash funds:

(a) Obtain a list of cash funds, select a sample number for count, and arrange for simultaneous control over cash funds and negotiable securities.

(b) Make a surprise count of cash on hand and selected petty cash funds in the presence of custodians.

(c) Prepare cash count working papers listing cash, vouchers and other reconciling items.

(d) Reconcile cash count with general ledger balances and cash book entries.

(e) Examine supporting authorization, approvals, and vouchers for expenditures, loans or advances, and cashed checks, and evaluate reasonableness and propriety of disbursements.

(f) Obtain specific approval of responsible executive for loans and any unusual items included in the count; also, obtain signature of custodian on completion of count.

(g) Consider confirming loans, cashed checks, and unusual disbursements with parties involved.

(h) For cash sales or miscellaneous receipts included in cash on hand or cash funds, compare with amount to be accounted for by reference to prior entries and examination of prenumbered sales invoices and other supporting documentation accumulated since the last book entry for such proceeds.

(i) Trace vouchers and other open items to subsequent reimbursement.

(j) Trace cashed checks to deposit entries.

(k) Note whether loans have been entered as such on the books.

(l) Trace cash on hand held for deposit to deposit slip and cash receipts journal.

(m) Consider undertaking a second surprise count of cash on hand and petty cash funds at a later date.

(n) Obtain confirmation from custodians of funds not selected for count.

(o) Obtain a sample of reimbursed vouchers for the period under review, drawn from the cash disbursements journal; trace to voucher register and cancelled checks; and examine supporting documentation for authorization, approval, cancellation of documents, and general validity and propriety. Undertake the same procedure for a sample drawn from the files to be traced to book entries.

Noted below are suggested auditing procedures that would seem to be especially appropriate for compliance testing and for interim work. They have been selected from the foregoing audit program and are identified by corresponding number.

Compliance testing: 5, 6, 7, 8, 10.

Interim work: 5, 6, 7, 8, 10.

Figure 4-6
Audit Program Guide

Investments

AUDIT OBJECTIVES

1. To determine the genuineness of investment transactions and account balances and to verify that client actually owns and has valid title to recorded investments.
2. To determine that owned securities and other indicia of investment ownership truly exist and are on hand or otherwise accounted for at the statement date.
3. To ascertain whether investments are stated in conformity with generally accepted accounting principles and on a consistent basis—the equity method for certain common stock investments, and at cost for other investments (with proper adjustment, where required by GAAP, for market declines and amortization of discount or premium).
4. To determine whether investments are fairly stated and properly classified as between current and noncurrent assets, with adequate disclosure of related party investments, nature of investment, basis of valuation, pledging, and other material factors.
5. To verify whether gains and losses on sale of investments and investment income are fully accounted for and accurately recorded.
6. To ascertain whether investments have been pledged to secure liabilities or are otherwise subject to encumbrances.

AUDITING PROCEDURES

	Performed by	NA
1. Review prior and current years' working papers in permanent and current files bearing on investments and related income accounts.		
2. Review AC 5131 on the equity method of accounting for investments in common stock, AC 5132 on accounting for certain marketable securities, and AU 332 on evidential matter for long-term investments.		
3. Obtain a schedule-analysis of investments showing opening balances,		

transactions for the period, and ending balances, market values (for traded securities), and related gain or loss data and investment income.

4. Foot and crossfoot schedule, test extensions, and reconcile beginning and ending balance totals with general ledger accounts.

5. Compare schedule with investment ledger entries and balances.

6. Select a sample of investment purchase and sales transactions drawn from general ledger accounts and traced to cash and other journals, and a sample similarly drawn from investment schedule.

(a) Vouch purchase and sales transactions by examining supporting evidence including brokers' advices and statements.

(b) For investments in real property, mortgages, and related companies, examine, as applicable, such evidences as contracts of purchase and sale, legal correspondence and documents, title papers, closing statements, notes and mortgages.

(c) Refer to minutes of board of directors or other evidence to ascertain whether transactions have been properly authorized and approved.

(d) Note whether investments have been recorded at cost, including acquisition taxes, commissions and other expenses and, similarly, that commissions and other costs pertaining to sales have been properly recorded.

(e) Test correspondence of purchase cost with the then market value, and of sales proceeds with market value at time of sale by examination of such evidences as market quotations, appraisal reports, insurance coverage, property tax bills, and audited financial statements of investee companies.

(f) Determine that the investment account has been credited with full cost on disposal of investments and the gain and loss properly recorded.

7. Inspect and count securities on hand or in safety deposit box in the presence of the custodian and authorized executives, and obtain signature of custodian on completion of count.

(a) Where appropriate, arrange for concurrent control of securities and cash funds.

(b) Record serial numbers of certificates, note whether certificates are in the name of the client, and account for bond interest coupons.

(c) Compare details of count with corresponding items appearing on investment schedule and in investment ledger for securities on hand at the verification date.

(d) Undertake a similar inspection of notes, mortgages and title documents for investments other than securities, and compare details with investment schedule.

(e) Inspect collateral in client's possession relating to investment loans and notes, bonds and mortgages receivable, and examine evidences in support of market value of such collateral.

(f) Determine propriety and business purpose of related party investments, examine authorization for transactions, and critically evaluate evidences in support of cost and market value for such investments.

8. Confirm securities held by brokers, banks, or other independent custodians. Confirmation request should call for details on quantities, description, certificate numbers, ownership, and reasons for holding securities. Compare returned confirmations with investment schedule and ledger.

9. Consider arranging with client for actual inspection and count, by the auditor in the presence of client's personnel, of securities held by outside custodians.

10. Confirm the terms and balances of mortgages and investment loans with mortgagors and debtors.

11. Test dividend and interest income received and accrued by independent estimation and calculation both overall and for individual investments, taking into account capital change reports, dividend declarations, interest rates, and period of elapsed time.

12. Review investment transactions for a period subsequent to the statement date and relate sales of securities to balances outstanding at the statement date.

13. Ascertain that investments are stated at the balance sheet date at cost, lower of cost or market value, or on the equity basis, as appropriate in applying generally accepted accounting principles.

(a) Verify market values for investments by reference to market quotations for marketable securities and, for other investments, by examination of audited financial statements, collateral value, credit reports, and inquiries of client personnel.

(b) Determine that current and noncurrent marketable equity securities have been properly differentiated and that a separate allowance for market decline has been recorded (or adjusted) for each where market values are, in the aggregate, lower than cost.

(c) Determine whether investments in common stock of subsidiaries or of controlled companies are carried on the equity method and whether appropriate adjustments have been made to carrying value for proportionate share of investee gains, losses, and dividends paid since acquisition date, and for unrealized intercompany profits and losses. For supporting evidence relating to the investee financial operating results and condition and to degree of control of a nonsubsidiary investee, examine audited financial statements of investee, make inquiries of client officers, and, where indicated, request additional financial information regarding the investee from the client and from the investee company itself.

(d) Determine whether long-term investments have been written down and losses have been recorded for permanent declines in market value below cost or carrying amount.

14. By inquiries, confirmations, and review of evidential matter,

ascertain whether investments have been pledged or are subject to restrictions on their disposition.

15. Note whether appropriate financial statement classifications and disclosures have been made, including those relating to current and noncurrent investments, method of valuation, related party investments, cost and market value, and so on. (See AC 5131 and 5132 for specification of required disclosures.)

16. Perform appropriate analytical review procedures using Figure 2-19 as a guide. Especially consider investment earnings relative to both cost and market value of investments; character and risk factor of investments made; business purpose; comparison with prior year investments and investment policies.

Noted below are suggested auditing procedures that would seem to be especially appropriate for compliance testing and for interim work. They have been selected from the foregoing audit program and are identified by corresponding number.

Compliance testing: 6, 11.

Interim work: 6, 7, 11.

Figure 4-7
Audit Program Guide

Purchases, Expenses, and Accounts Payable

AUDIT OBJECTIVES

1.   To determine the genuineness (bona fides) of payables and of related purchase and expense transactions, and that the assets and services acquired belong to the company and were recorded at the proper amount. (*Purchases*, in this context, is intended to apply not only to inventories but also to the acquisition of other assets and services.)

2.   To see whether an adequate cutoff has been established and accruals have been properly recorded so that payables, purchases, and expenses are recorded in the proper accounting period.

3.   To determine whether liabilities and contingencies have been unrecorded, understated, or undisclosed.

4.   To determine whether liabilities have been overstated because of error or irregularity.

5.   To determine whether the accounts reflect a proper differentiation between capital and revenue expenditures.

6.   To ascertain whether costs and expenses have been properly classified and appropriate disclosures made as to liabilities to related parties, subordination of liabilities, pledging of assets, unfavorable purchase commitments, and material contingencies.

AUDITING PROCEDURES

	Performed by	NA
1. Review prior and current years' working papers in permanent and current files bearing on purchases, expenses, and accounts payable.		
2. Examine a sample of purchase vouchers drawn from the voucher register and verify details by comparison with supporting vendors' invoices, purchase orders or contracts, bills of lading, receiving reports, and purchase requisitions, taking note of:		

(a) Vendor name, product description, dates, unit price, and quantities.

(b) Client's name appearing on invoices and other documents.

(c) Requisition, purchase order, and voucher authorization and/or approvals by appropriate personnel, including, where applicable, authorization in minutes of board of directors.

(d) Terms of purchase, including freight charges, FOB specification, and trade and cash discounts.

(e) General reasonableness of prices and product or services within the context of client's business needs and prior practices.

(f) Numerical sequence of vouchers and supporting documents.

(g) Mathematical accuracy of vouchers and invoices; check by independent computation.

(h) Account coding and proper classification.

(i) Proper posting; trace to, if maintained, accounts payable subsidiary ledger and perpetual inventory records.

(j) Cash disbursements; note indication of voucher approval for payment by authorized person; see whether payment has been noted in voucher register; review purchase discounts taken; trace to cash disbursements journal and cancelled check. (These steps should be coordinated with audit program for cash disbursements.)

3. Examine a sample of purchase requisitions, purchase orders, receiving reports, and purchase vouchers drawn from the files and from the cash disbursements journal, match with supporting documents, and follow the same steps as in the foregoing auditing procedure.

4. Examine a sample of credit memos drawn from the voucher register or other journal used to record purchase credits and verify book entries as follows:

(a) Relate data on credit memos to original purchase invoices, shipping advices for returned purchases, correspondence, and other supporting documentation.

(b) Note whether the credits have been properly reviewed and approved by appropriate personnel.

(c) Check mathematical accuracy of memos.

(d) Trace credits to subsequent payments to determine whether they were properly applied.

(e) Trace postings to (if maintained) accounts payable subsidiary ledger and perpetual inventory records.

5. For a test period, foot and crossfoot voucher register (purchase journals) and check postings to general ledger.

6. Obtain a schedule of accounts payable with notations as to due dates.

(a) Foot schedule and compare total with general ledger balance.

(b) Compare individual balances with open items in voucher register (or, as applicable, with subsidiary accounts payable ledger).

(c)   Examine vouchers, invoices, receiving records, authorization, and other evidences in support of balances.

(d)   Reconcile balances with monthly vendor statements.

(e)   Trace vouchers making up creditor balances to subsequent payments as recorded in disbursements journal and to cancelled checks.

(f)   Make inquiries regarding accounts past due, refer to correspondence and other evidences in support of explanations and of the validity of the liability, and follow-up to determine disposition.

7.   Send confirmation letters to vendors and creditors with whom the client has had purchase transactions for a determined period prior to the statement date (for six to twelve months), whether or not a balance exists at that date, requesting a statement of balances owing and also data on purchase commitments. In addition to verifying recorded balances, this procedure can help in uncovering unrecorded liabilities.

8.   Reconcile confirmation replies with the records and investigate differences.

9.   Review the cutoff of purchase and purchase return transactions for a test period before and after the statement date.

10.   Perform subsequent events review procedures for purchase transactions (Figure 2-12).

11.   Determine whether any assets have been pledged and whether liabilities have been subordinated.

12.   For liabilities to officers, related companies, and other related parties, undertake procedures as shown in Figure 1-12.

13.   For notes and loans payable undertake essentially the same procedures as for accounts payable, including:

(a)   Review schedule of notes payable, foot schedule, and reconcile total with controlling account.

(b)   Examine authorization and supporting evidence going back to the original transactions giving rise to the liability, such as vouchers and loan agreements.

(c)   Determine the reason for, and business purpose of, liabilities incurred; trace cash proceeds to cash journal and deposits; examine evidences in support of recorded cost of services or assets received in the transaction.

(d)   Inspect note stubs and prenumbering and compare with open items.

(e)   Select a sample of completed note and loan transactions as recorded, and test to underlying documents.

(f)   Confirm notes and loans payable as of the statement date.

(g)   Test interest expense, prepaid interest, and accrued interest by reference to loan agreements and terms of notes and loans, and by independent calculation.

14.   Complete the comprehensive audit program presented in Fig-

ure 4-8 for uncovering and disclosing understated and unrecorded liabilities and contingencies. Many of the procedures listed will already have been performed in connection with the examination of other areas and accounts, and the work, of course, should not be duplicated. Figure 4-8 can nevertheless serve as a useful reminder checklist. Its use should be synchronized with that of Figure 2-8, the section of the audit program guide dealing with litigation, claims, and assessments.

15. For costs and expenses, the following basic procedures are to be undertaken:

(a) Compare current period expenses with budgets and with prior years in total amount and on a percentage and ratio basis relative to revenue, aggregate cost classifications, and other relevant bases.

(b) Scan general ledger entries and note monthly variations and unusual entries or fluctuations.

(c) Obtain either complete or partial analyses as indicated for the particular account, and test-vouch entries by examination of documentary evidence, including authorizations, purchase orders, approved vouchers, invoices, receiving reports, rental lease and other agreements, and the evidences of disbursement. Such analyses should be obtained for legal and professional fees, contributions, travel and entertainment, and accounts containing miscellaneous entries whose nature is unclear or unexplained.

(d) Obtain, for voluminous and routine expense accounts not ordinarily analyzed in some detail, a sample of entries in the account and verify their validity by examination of supporting evidences.

(e) Evaluate the validity, propriety, and accuracy of expense entries based on transfers or allocations from other accounts.

(f) In analyzing or testing expense accounts, consider whether capital items have been improperly expensed.

(g) Confirm expense liabilities outstanding at the statement date.

(h) Make an overall estimate of expenses for the period where this is feasible (as in the case of rent expense, based on contractual amounts, or commission expense, based on percentages applied to sales volume, etc.), and compare estimate with recorded expense.

(i) Obtain computation of prepaid and accrued expenses and verify validity and accuracy by independent calculation and by examining evidences supporting the various factors entering into the calculation.

(j) Undertake analytical review procedures to verify the reasonableness and validity of costs and expenses for individual accounts and for broad classifications such as cost of sales, the several categories of operating expenses, extraordinary items, etc. Figure 2-19 may be used as a guide. Tests should include comparison of amounts and relevant ratios (using revenue, assets, selected operating statement aggregates, and other data as relevant bases) with prior periods, budgets and forecasts, and industry data, taking into account trends and changed circumstances. Investigate inconsistencies and significant fluctuations.

(k)   Determine that costs and expenses have been properly classified in the income statement and that appropriate disclosures (such as those required by FASB No. 13 (AC 4053.16) for operating leases and rental payments) have been made.

16.   With respect to the Federal income tax provision and liability:

(a)   Analyze accounts.

(b)   Review current and prior years' tax returns and reports by the Internal Revenue Service.

(c)   Review reconciliation of accounting income and taxable income; take note of reconciling items and evaluate propriety of treatment.

(d)   Determine if the proper tax treatment has been accorded operating losses and investment and other credits.

(e)   Independently calculate Federal income tax provision and liability, including deferred taxes, and compare with recorded amounts.

(f)   Compare provisions and accruals with corresponding amounts in prior years, taking into account variations in taxable income and income tax rates.

(g)   Arrange for a review by the tax partner of the client's income tax situation and income tax returns, and the fairness of recorded amounts.

Auditing procedures from the foregoing suggested for:
Compliance testing: 2, 3, 4c, 13.
Interim work: 2, 3, 4, 5, 13, 15.

Figure 4-8
Audit Program Guide

Determination of Unrecorded, Under-
stated, or Undisclosed Liabilities
and Contingencies

(*Note*: Many of the procedures listed below will already have been performed in connection with the examination of other areas and accounts, and the work, of course, should not be duplicated. The listing can nevertheless serve as a useful reminder checklist the use of which should be coordinated with that of Figure 2-8, the section of the Audit Program Guide dealing with litigation, claims, and assessments.)

AUDITING PROCEDURES

	Performed by	NA
1. Compare book entries with related invoices for a test period prior to the statement date. The full invoice amount may not have been recorded.		
2. Examine unpaid "open invoice" file for unentered invoices applicable to the prior period.		
3. Examine requisitions, purchase orders, contracts, and significant correspondence files, and follow through to see if title has passed or service was received as of the statement date.		
4. Examine sales order and contract file for disclosure of guarantee and warranty provisions or unfavorable sales commitments.		
5. Review corporate minutes and follow through on authorizations to determine whether the liability for fixed asset or other significant acquisitions has been incurred and recorded, and to obtain information regarding lawsuits, long-term leases, pension plans, and the like.		

6. Compare statements from creditors with accounts payable balances.

7. Examine treasury department reports on tax examination for possible unrecorded assessments or items in dispute.

8. Circularize suppliers with whom the company has transacted business during a determined past period; request statements of account balances and data on outstanding purchase commitments. These confirmation requests should be sent even to those suppliers whose accounts show zero balances.

9. Send confirmation forms to banks with which the company maintained any cash balances during a determined past period. The confirmation form will normally be the same AICPA standard form for confirmation of cash balances. It also provides for information on bank loans, discounting of notes, guarantees, unutilized letters of credit, and so on.

10. Communicate with client's attorneys requesting information on past or pending lawsuits and other transactions; the information may disclose contingencies or unrecorded liabilities. (Review of invoices from attorneys will also be helpful in this connection.)

11. Confirm bonds or mortgages payable.

12. Compare receiving records for a period before the statement date with book entries to see if the liability has been recorded as of the statement date.

13. Review receiving records for merchandise received after the balance sheet date to pick up merchandise in transit and related unrecorded liabilities.

14. Review purchase book and cash disbursements book for a post balance sheet period, noting particularly the more material items; relate to invoices and other evidences for unentered liabilities applicable to the prior period.

15. Review cash receipts book after the statement date and, particularly for entries to liability accounts, refer to remittance lists, agreements, and other evidences to see if the liability was applicable to the prior period. The proceeds may have been received prior to, but deposited subsequent to, the statement date.

16. Determine by inquiries and dates of clearance of cancelled checks whether the cash disbursements book had been held open, thereby erroneously reducing both cash and liability balances at the statement date.

17. In analyzing and reviewing interest expense accounts, relate the interest to applicable liabilities.

18. Scrutinize insurance policies; the absence of policies or notation of co-beneficiary other than the client may suggest liabilities that may not have been recorded.

19. Review real estate tax bills that may be in the name of mortgagee although the mortgage liability may not have been recorded.

20. Vouch deposit accounts and such assets as advances for future purchases, and follow through to determine whether the transaction and passing of title have materialized and whether there has been a failure to record the corresponding liability.

21. In analyzing property, plant, and equipment accounts, it may be determined that installment notes were issued but that the full amount was not recorded, the asset being charged only with actual installment payments.

22. Review credit balances in accounts receivable; the liabilities may have been concealed by erroneous offsets against receivables.

23. In analyzing expense accounts, where payments are made on a "period basis" (e.g., professional retainer fees, subscriptions, rent expense, etc.), determine whether there remains an unrecorded liability for the balance of the period.

24. Examine accounts with consignors to determine whether the liability for merchandise sold for their account has been recorded. A review of post balance sheet settlement disbursements would aid in such verification.

25. Ascertain by reference to labor contracts, pension plans and agreements, and so on, whether related liabilities have been recorded and whether any contingencies are indicated.

26. Account for and independently check computations of accruals for payroll, interest, taxes, and other expenses.

27. Independently compute liabilities for Federal income taxes, including deferred income taxes, and compare with recorded amounts.

28. Review debit balances in accounts payable; they may represent payments to vendors, along with failure to record the related liability.

29. Make suitable inquiries of management regarding the recording of all liabilities and the existence of pending lawsuits, unfavorable purchase and sales commitments, and contingencies in general.

30. Ascertain whether there have been changes in company policy or operations for which liabilities may have been incurred or commitments undertaken and then follow through to see if they have been recorded.

31. Determine whether the client has complied with pertinent laws and governmental regulations.

32. Obtain a written representation from the client to the effect that all liabilities have been recorded, noting all material contingencies.

33. Perform analytical review procedures, including appropriate ratio and comparison tests; material discrepancies or unusual fluctuations may be related to unrecorded liabilities.

34. Basic to the problem, of course, is a system of internal accounting control that can provide additional assurance that the controls serve to minimize the likelihood that liabilities and contingencies will be unrecorded, understated, or undisclosed. The review of the system should certainly encompass this segment.

Figure 4-9
Audit Program Guide
Payrolls

AUDIT OBJECTIVES

1. To determine whether disbursements for wages, salaries, and other payroll costs were made in accordance with proper authorization and for services actually rendered on behalf of and for the benefit of the company.

2. To determine whether payroll and related costs were recorded in conformity with generally accepted accounting principles, including appropriate account classification, accrual of pertinent liabilities, and disclosure of stock options, pension plan, and other commitments.

AUDITING PROCEDURES

	Performed by	NA
1. Review prior and current years' working papers in permanent and current files dealing with wages, salaries, and related accounts. Make inquiries regarding new union contracts, employment contracts, and changes in compensation for officers and employees.		
2. Scan general ledger entries for payroll, accrued payroll, salaries, and so on, and take note of unusual monthly variations and posting sources.		
3. Trace entries in general ledger payroll accounts on a test basis to payroll journals, voucher register (as applicable), cash disbursements journal, and other posting sources.		
4. Trace monthly payroll journal totals to summary payroll sheets and trace weekly entries on summary sheets to corresponding payrolls.		
5. For a test period, foot and cross-foot payroll journals, payroll summaries and individual payrolls.		

6. Determine whether payroll entries have been properly coded and classified as to direct and indirect labor, administrative and selling expense, and appropriate capitalization of labor expended on construction or installation of plant and equipment.

7. Review cost records for propriety of standard costs for labor.

8. Examine a sample of payroll entries and supporting evidences as follows:

(a) Employee names, classification, and salary and wage rates: Personnel records, noting authorization and comparing with union contracts.

(b) Hours worked: Approved time cards or piece work records; test mathematical accuracy of totals recorded on time cards. Take note of correspondence of time card dates with payroll period.

(c) Gross wages (and overtime): Independent computation reflecting hours, rate, etc.

(d) Tax withholdings: Independent computation for payroll taxes, and exemption certificates and withholding tables for income taxes withheld.

(e) Advances and other withholdings: Authorization memoranda, union contracts, and supporting documentation, as relevant.

(f) Net cash: Arithmetical computation.

(g) Check disbursements: Obtain cancelled payroll checks for the foregoing sample and compare details with payroll, taking note of name, payroll identification number, check number, amount, authorized check signer, endorsement, questionable second endorsement, if any, and numerical sequence of checks.

(h) Account classification: Note whether employee has been entered on proper payroll for account distribution purposes.

9. Examine a sample of personnel records for terminated employees and trace to appropriate payrolls to verify date of actual removal from payroll.

10. Coordinate test reconciliations of payroll bank accounts with audit program for cash.

11. Examine a sample of reimbursement payroll checks (for imprest payroll bank accounts), compare with payroll totals, and trace deposit into payroll bank account.

12. Consider witnessing a payroll distribution on a surprise basis.

13. Verify accrued payroll (and any accruals for vacation pay or retroactive increases) by independent computation and reference to supporting evidences.

14. Reconcile recorded payroll for interim periods and for the year with payroll totals on payroll tax returns, compensation insurance reports, and production records.

15. Examine a sample of W-2 forms and reconcile data with payroll records.

16. Perform analytical review procedures for payroll and related costs, using Figure 2-19 as a guide. Especially compare monthly and

yearly data with prior years, budgets, and industry figures in the aggregate and on a percentage and ratio basis relative to sales and production volumes, manufacturing costs, and other meaningful bases.

17. Obtain an analysis of officers' salaries:

(a) Reconcile with authorization by the board of directors.

(b) Test account entries by examination of disbursement records and cancelled checks.

(c) Obtain confirmation of liabilities or advances to officers that are outstanding at the statement date.

18. Review salesmen's commissions:

(a) Test commissions by reference to agreements, authorization, and appropriate sales and commission records.

(b) Obtain confirmation of liabilities or advances to salesmen that are outstanding at the statement date.

(c) Reconcile totals of salesmen's commission sales and house sales with recorded sales for the period.

(d) Reconcile an overall independently calculated estimate of commissions for the period (based on rates applied to total sales by salesmen) with recorded commissions.

19. Obtain from client calculations of bonuses and bonuses payable:

(a) Examine related employment contracts, authorization of the board of directors and other relevant documentation.

(b) Independently compute bonus amounts.

(c) Confirm details of bonus arrangement and liability outstanding at the statement date.

20. With respect to pension plan costs and related liabilities:

(a) Review AC 4063 on the accounting for cost of pension plans.

(b) Obtain copy of pension plan and related documents, and excerpt for the permanent file significant provisions of the plan.

(c) Determine whether the plan has been authorized in the minutes of the board of directors.

(d) Examine IRS ruling and correspondence to verify qualification of the plan for income tax purposes.

(e) Obtain satisfaction regarding the qualifications of the plan's actuary by inquiry and review of professional background and professional society affiliations.

(f) Consider engaging an independent actuary as a specialist consultant to assist in evaluating actuarial aspects that must be considered by the auditor. If a specialist-actuary is to be used, follow the auditing procedures outlined in Figure 2-5 on using the work of a specialist, and refer to Figure 2-6 for form of confirmation letter covering understanding with the specialist.

(g) Send confirmation letter to plan's actuary and review report which should contain data and information helpful in evaluating the current year's provision and accruals for pension costs and liabilities, and the adequacy of financial statement disclosures in accordance with the principles and disclosure requirements in AC 4063.

(h) With the aid of an actuary-consultant, or independently, review for propriety the plan's actuarial cost and funding methods, actuarial assumptions, and changes in actuarial assumptions.

(i) Include a test of pension plan contributions by employees as part of the regular payroll audit program.

(j) Test employer contributions by reference to cash disbursements records and trustee reports.

(k) Gather and evaluate information regarding the pension plan fund and the valuation of fund assets. Obtain copy of trustee report certified by an independent auditor.

Auditing procedures from the foregoing suggested for:

Compliance testing: 6, 7, 8, 9, 11.

Interim work: 3, 4, 5, 6, 7, 8, 9, 10, 11, 11, 14, 17, 18.

Figure 4-10
Audit Program Guide

Inventories

AUDIT OBJECTIVES

1. To determine whether the client actually owns the inventories, whether all inventories owned at the statement date have been included in the ending balances, and whether any of the inventories on hand are not owned but held on consignment or for the account of others.

2. To determine whether the owned inventories truly exist and are on hand at the statement date.

3. To see whether a proper coordinated purchases-sales-inventory cutoff has been achieved.

4. To gain assurance that inventories are not overstated or understated because of errors or irregularities.

5. To ascertain whether inventories have been valued in accordance with generally accepted accounting principles and on a consistent basis.

6. To determine whether inventories have been fairly stated and classified on the financial statements with adequate disclosures, including basis of valuation, costing method, and pledging or assignment of inventories.

AUDITING PROCEDURES

	Performed by	NA
1. Review prior and current years' audit and internal accounting control notes, memoranda, guides and other materials in permanent and current files dealing with inventories.		
2. Scan inventory accounts in general ledger and investigate unusual features such as questionable posting sources; abnormal monthly variations; substantial adjustments to bring accounts into agreement with perpetual inventory records or physical count or to correct inter-account		

transfers such as those from work in process to finished goods or to cost of sales.

3. Trace general ledger entries for inventory and cost of sales accounts to posting sources on a test basis, and similarly from posting sources to general ledger.

4. Foot and crossfoot, on a test basis, records accumulating costs for transfers to, and between, inventory accounts and cost of sales, and trace to supporting weekly or other cost accumulation records.

5. Examine a sample of job orders or other cost accumulation records, as applicable, and supporting evidences for entries in these records; also reverse the order and examine a sample of supporting evidences drawn from the files or other sources, and match with corresponding entries on job order or other cost accumulation records.

(a) For charges to raw materials inventory, the applicable evidences and examination are described in the audit program for purchases and accounts payable.

(b) For charges to work in process for materials, direct labor, and overhead, evidences to be examined include: purchase requisitions, payroll records (to be coordinated with audit program for payrolls), and computations for overhead charges. Production orders should also be tested and the examination of production orders and cost accumulation records are to be coordinated.

(c) Evaluate the fairness and reasonableness of standard costs used by comparison with prior periods; review of procedures followed by the client in setting standards; review and analysis of cost variance accounts and investigation of material variances; comparison of standard and actual costs on a test basis by reference to purchase invoices and payroll records; and review of basis of establishing overhead rates. In investigating significant overhead variances, account should be taken of possible improper capitalization of loss factors relating to idle plant or other circumstances.

(d) For charges to finished goods inventory, examine production reports and cost accumulation reports, noting whether work in process was relieved of all finished goods and particularly of finished goods sold.

(e) For charges to cost of sales, correlate examination with that of sales. Relate shipping advices, sales records, and cost records to transfers of finished goods to cost of sales and, as indicated, reverse the procedure and trace cost of sales entries to supporting records.

(f) Determine whether partial shipments have been properly recorded.

(g) Test numerical sequence and mathematical accuracy of records and documents examined.

(h) Trace inventory and cost of sales entries covered in the sample to applicable perpetual inventory records and, for a selected sample, trace entries in perpetual inventory records back to original posting sources. These procedures should be coordinated with comparable steps in audit program for purchases.

6. Carry out preparatory planning steps for observation of physical inventory count.

(a) Review guidelines on observation of physical count as developed in AU 331 and discuss with engagement manager or partner any departures from these standards. The standards may be summarized as follows:

(i) It is the client's responsibility to make the actual count and to ensure that the count is properly made, and this is consistent with the basic concept that the financial statements are management's representations.

(ii) Observation of inventory count is a generally accepted auditing procedure and, as stated in AU 331, tests of accounting records alone are insufficient to gain satisfaction as to inventory quantities.

(iii) When the system of internal accounting control for inventories is good, and well-kept perpetual inventory records are maintained and checked periodically by the client to quantities determined by physical count, the auditor's observation procedures can be undertaken either during the period under audit or after the end of the period, with appropriate tests of intervening transactions and review of the records on which the year-end inventories are based. (See AU 331 for reference to use of statistical sampling by the client in inventory taking.)

(iv) In the absence of well-kept perpetual inventory records, the inventory count and the auditor's observation should be carried out relatively close to the statement date.

(b) Review prior year's working papers to ascertain the type and relative materiality of inventories and the nature of problems and difficulties previously encountered during the count.

(c) Meet with the client and review and discuss the written inventory instructions.

(d) Obtain a complete listing of locations for all inventories, including any at public warehouses or held by other custodians, with an indication of type and value of inventory at each location. Where warranted, building diagrams should be made available by the client.

(e) Tour selected locations and take note of inventory stacking and physical arrangements, relative inventory values, and need for special cutoff controls.

(f) Inform client regarding confirmation procedures for inventories held by warehouses or other parties, as well as physical count and observation procedures.

(g) Discuss with client the procedures to be adopted for proper stacking of inventories and for segregation and identification of inventories that are obsolete, damaged or slow-moving; intercompany; pledged; not owned, including consignments.

(h) Determine the details of count procedures including client personnel involved and names of supervisors and department heads; use of prenumbered tags and sheets, and controls over blank and completed copies; method of count and recheck; the auditor's role during the count; retention of copies; and cooperation of client's staff.

(i) Emphasize the need for the assignment of client personnel who are fully acquainted with the inventories and can deal knowledgeably with inventory problems encountered, especially those relating to obsolete merchandise or work in process inventories.

(j) Discuss the detailed controls to be adopted to ensure a reliable cutoff with respect to receipts, shipments, and movements of inventories during the count.

(k) Consider the need for using the services of an outside specialist to assist the auditor in identification and valuation problems of inventories of a highly technical nature.

(l) Review the procedures to be followed for reconciliation and investigation of differences between physical count and perpetual inventory records.

(m) Discuss the proper form to be used in listing quantities and cost, market and other data on the priced copy of the inventory, and the need to provide copies of summary and accumulation working papers to facilitate subsequent checking of quantities carried over to the priced copy.

7. Observe the physical inventory count.

(a) Make an early record, for later follow-up, of recent shipping and receiving reports, noting details including dates and number sequence.

(b) Station staff assistants at appropriate locations.

(c) During the course of the count and at the close, add to the listing of shipping and receiving reports and make appropriate notes as to inventories to be included or excluded from count so that duplication may be avoided. Consider whether these and other controls ensure an adequate cutoff.

(d) Note whether the written inventory instructions are being followed and whether the client's count is being undertaken conscientiously, reliably, and efficiently.

(e) Make selective test counts, especially of high value inventories, and compare (using, as appropriate, approximation "sight" tests) with client's count. Arrange for test opening of containers and cartons.

(f) Determine that inventories on railroad cars or trucks outside the plant have been properly accounted for.

(g) Obtain a record of issued inventory tags and subsequently determine that all have been properly accounted for.

(h) Obtain a descriptive schedule of work in process inventories and make a test comparison with supporting production and job orders and relate data to inventories on hand. Evaluate the reasonableness of client's estimate of stage of completion by inquiries, reference to production and job orders, and observation.

(i) Take note of inventories that appear to be or have been identified as obsolete or slow-moving, consignments and otherwise not owned, intercompany, or pledged, and see whether they have been properly marked as such on inventory tags.

(j) Make a test comparison of physical count with perpetual inventory records. (This procedure will also be undertaken after receipt of the priced copy of the inventories.)

(k) Arrange for pulling of tags in the presence of the auditors, after it has been determined by inspection that all inventories in the given area have been counted and tagged.

(l) Retain control copies for later comparison with final priced inventory sheets. If the size and complexity of the inventories and company operations are such as to make it impracticable to obtain complete control copies, include in working papers a sufficient test listing of details for later follow-up.

(m) Check off blank, voided, and completed count tags against schedule of issued tags maintained for control purposes, and note whether all tags have been properly accounted for.

(n) Prepare a memorandum in which conclusions are expressed on the adequacy of the inventory-taking and observation procedures. It should also make note of matters, such as cutoff data, that must be correlated with the records or otherwise taken cognizance of in later audit work on inventories.

8. With respect to inventories held by public warehouses or other outside custodians, undertake the following procedures (which include those set forth in AU 331 and 901):

(a) Obtain from the client a complete listing of inventories held by warehouses and other custodians and compare data with inventory records.

(b) Review the client's internal accounting controls for the inventories held by outsiders, including documentation gathered by the client in investigating the business reputation and financial standing of the warehouses or other custodians.

(c) Inquire into the reason inventories are being held by outside custodians.

(d) Send confirmation requests to warehouses and custodians concerning inventories held and whether there are any restrictions on withdrawal.

(e) Observe the physical count of the goods held, wherever practicable and reasonable, if the inventories held by warehouses and custodians are of material amount.

(f) Compare and reconcile details on inventory schedule with confirmation responses, data derived from observation of physical count, warehouse receipts, and monthly statements from custodians.

(g) Confirm with lenders pertinent details of warehouse receipts pledged as collateral.

(h) Examine supporting evidence for a sample of entries in records maintained for inventories held by warehouses and others, including receiving and shipping reports, instructions to warehouses, periodic correspondence and reports, and warehouse receipts.

(i) Relate sales invoices and shipments from warehouses after the statement date to inventories held by them at that date.

(j) Perform the other procedures undertaken for inventories generally.

9. Obtain a final priced copy of the inventory listings and detailed papers supporting the summaries.

(a) Check footings and extensions of summaries and detailed listings.

(b) Trace totals of detailed listings to summary sheets.

(c) Trace control copies of tags (or, if applicable, details recorded in working papers during count observation), as well as test counts, to inventory sheets. Note whether description of items and quantities have been properly carried forward.

(d) Similarly, for a selected sample trace items appearing on final inventory sheets to control copies of tags.

(e) Tags covering work in process should also be matched with schedule of work in process made available during the count and retained for control purposes.

(f) Review memorandum on observation of physical inventory count and cutoff and other data in working papers relating to the count. Determine whether cutoff adjustments have been made. (Coordinate this step with additional cutoff procedures listed later in this audit program.)

(g) Compare a sample of items on final inventory with perpetual inventory records, and compare a sample drawn from the records with corresponding items on the final inventory sheets. Investigate significant differences.

(h) Determine the basis for valuing the inventories and whether they are stated on a basis consistent with the prior period.

(i) Examine a sample of inventory items on the final priced copy for verification of pricing. Determine whether cost includes all appropriate elements such as invoice cost of materials acquired less purchase discounts, freight charges, purchasing expenses, warehousing costs, and manufacturing costs, including applicable manufacturing overhead; ascertain that inventories are not inflated by inclusion of selling or administrative expenses. In verifying market and the application of the principle of "lower of cost or market," take into account the definition of market (see AC 5121) as current replacement cost but not to exceed net realizable value (selling price less costs of completion and disposal), and not to be less than net realizable value reduced by an allowance for an approximately normal profit margin.

(j) For raw materials and purchased items verify cost—for FIFO inventories—by reference to latest purchase invoices, going back far enough to account for quantities on hand; for LIFO inventories, by reference to opening inventories and earliest purchase invoices. Determine replacement value by examination of recent invoices and purchase contracts (but consider whether prices were based on earlier commitments), newspaper or trade journal market quotations and inquiries of purchasing department.

(k) For work in process and finished goods, test individual costs for materials, labor and overhead by:

(i)   Review production and job orders.

(ii) Compare with prior period costs.

(iii) Check quantities of materials required to bills of material.

(iv) Refer to payroll records, material requisitions, and purchase invoices.

(v)   Review overhead rate computations.

(vi) Determine replacement cost for raw materials and purchased parts in reviewing pricing of raw materials component of work in process and finished goods.

(vii) Determine current replacement cost for the labor and manufacturing overhead elements by noting recent revisions in labor and overhead cost rates and review of cost, payroll, and accounting records.

(viii) Make appropriate computations in verification of costs of completion and disposal, refer to sales records for realizable value, and determine whether market has been stated at the proper amount.

(l) Test compare inventories with inventories as of the beginning of the period with respect to quantities and pricing and consistency of valuation methods.

(m) Compare inventory totals with general ledger and perpetual inventory record balances and investigate significant differences.

(n) See that the lower of cost or market has been properly extended and that the rule has been applied on either an item-by-item basis or in the aggregate for given inventory categories, as appropriate in the circumstances.

10. Determine whether obsolete, damaged, and slow-moving inventories have been properly identified, segregated, and accounted for, and recorded at realizable value by:

(a) Observations at physical inventory count.

(b) Inquiries of management.

(c) Client's written representations.

(d) Review of perpetual inventory records and prior period inventories, noting activity and static items.

(e) Examination of sales invoices before and after the statement date.

(f) Review of price lists and catalogues, noting selling price reductions and style changes.

(g) Calculating inventory turnover ratios.

(h) Sales and sales returns analyses that may evoke questions as to saleability and customer acceptance of products.

11. Determine whether consigned and intercompany inventories have been properly accounted for (exclusion of consignments in, inclusions of consignments out at cost, and adjustments for intercompany profit in inventories).

12. Complete the cutoff examination initiated in connection with the physical observation procedures by undertaking a review of a period before and after the inventory count dates and, similarly, for a period before and after the statement date to determine that purchase and sales transactions were recorded in the proper accounting period with appropriate inclusions or exclusions from inventory.

13. Review and test entries in general ledger inventory accounts and perpetual inventory records for the period intervening between the count and the statement date.

14. Obtain an inventory representation letter.

15. In undertaking the subsequent events review (Figure 2-12), watch out especially for any unusual developments relating to inventories, such as significant sales returns, product changes, and material price declines.

16. Determine whether inventories have been pledged.

17. Review purchase and sales commitments for unfavorable features as to price, or as to quantities in excess of requirements.

18. Review insurance policies and note whether coverage bears a reasonable relationship to inventory balances and whether there is any indication of pledging of inventories.

19. Undertake an analytical review of inventories in the aggregate and by product lines. Especially consider the following: gross profit test; inventory turnover ratio; monthly variations and final balances compared with prior periods, budgets, forecasts, and industry data.

20. Consider whether inventories are presented in the financial statements in accordance with generally accepted accounting principles applied on a basis consistent with the preceding period, and are properly classified with adequate disclosures such as basis of valuation, method of costing, and pledging.

Auditing procedures from the foregoing suggested for:
Compliance testing: 4, 5, 6, 7.
Interim work: 2, 3, 4, 5, 6, 7.

Figure 4-11
Audit Program Guide

Property, Plant, and Equipment

AUDIT OBJECTIVES

1.   To verify that the client actually owns and has valid title to recorded property, plant, and equipment.

2.   To ascertain whether owned assets truly exist and are on hand at the statement date.

3.   To determine whether all owned fixed assets have been recorded.

4.   To determine whether assets are stated in accordance with generally accepted accounting principles, that is, at cost, including all costs of acquisition and placement such as freight and installation, less cash and other discounts, and reduced by related depreciation allowances.

5.   To ascertain whether assets are being systematically depreciated over their useful lives in accordance with acceptable depreciation methods and on a consistent basis, and that depreciation has been properly classified in the accounts.

6.   To determine whether all retirements or dispositions have been recorded, that asset costs and related allowances have been eliminated upon retirement or disposal, and related gains and losses have been properly recorded.

7.   To ascertain that repairs and maintenance expenditures have not been improperly capitalized and that capital items have not been improperly expensed.

8.   To determine whether assets have been mortgaged or are otherwise encumbered.

9.   To determine whether rental or other income from property, plant, and equipment is properly accounted for.

AUDITING PROCEDURES

	Performed by	NA
1. Review prior and current year's audit and internal accounting control notes, memoranda, guides, and other materials in permanent and current files dealing with property, plant, and equipment.		

2. Review data gathered on company retirement, capitalization, and other policies relating to fixed assets. (The term *fixed* assets will be used interchangeably with *property, plant, and equipment*.)

3. Obtain an analysis of entries in the fixed asset accounts showing additions, retirements and other changes, and an analysis of gain or loss on sale of fixed assets. Check the arithmetical accuracy of the analyses and compare balances with the general ledger. The analyses should contain specific identifying information such as name of supplier, technical descriptive data, serial number, and cost details.

4. Test entries on analysis to corresponding entries in general ledger accounts and trace to voucher register and cash and other journals; similarly, reverse the procedure and test compare entries in general ledger fixed asset accounts with analysis and trace to posting sources. If the auditor prepares the analysis himself, these steps would be performed concomitantly with preparation of the analysis.

5. Test additions by examination of supporting evidence.

(a) Examine purchase orders, contracts, receiving records, approved invoices and vouchers, and cancelled checks. Documents and other evidences should be in the name of the client. For real property, examine contracts, closing statements, deed with official notation of recording in the public records, title policies, appraisal reports, if any, related tax bills and mortgage documents, and insurance policies for changes in coverage. Examine registration licenses for vehicles.

(b) For assets constructed by the client and for installation costs, examine construction job orders or similar records, reconcile with general ledger entries, and vouch costs by test examination of approved invoices, receiving records (for purchased items), material requisitions, payroll records, and calculations of overhead allocations. Determine whether costs actually pertain to construction or installation of assets and are entered in the proper accounts.

(c) Note whether additions have been properly authorized, especially in the minutes of the board of directors for material acquisitions.

(d) Determine whether all costs of acquisition have been capitalized, including freight-in, installation, allowable overhead for assets constructed and, for real estate, title search fees, brokerage commissions, and attorney fees relating to purchase, and that purchase discounts have been recorded as cost offsets so that recorded cost corresponds to "cash" cost.

(e) Observe accuracy of account distribution. Note whether fixed assets have been improperly expensed and whether expense items have been improperly capitalized.

(f) For assets acquired in exchange for other assets or capital stock, in addition to the foregoing procedures and evidences examined, obtain satisfaction that the recorded cost of assets acquired bears a reasonable correspondence to their market value (or utility) and that the transaction has been consummated on an arms-length basis.

6. Test sales, retirements or other disposition of property, plant, and equipment by examination of supporting evidence.

(a) Examine sales orders, contracts, shipping records, and invoices. For real property, examine closing statements and legal documents.

(b) Note whether sales, retirements, or other dispositions and sales prices have been properly authorized, especially in the minutes of the board of directors for material sales.

(c) Determine whether the full cost of assets sold or disposed of and the applicable allowance for depreciation (after recording depreciation to date of disposal) have been eliminated from the accounts. Verify such costs by reference to auditor's current and prior year analyses, plant ledger, and original purchase documents. Verify the applicable allowance for depreciation by reference to depreciation records and independent calculation.

(d) Coordinate verification of sales and retirement entries in fixed asset accounts with review of gain or loss account on sale or retirement of fixed assets. Trace recorded amount for proceeds to cash receipts journal and to evidence in support of sales.

7. Test compare additions and retirements per account analyses to plant ledger; review plant ledger and test compare entries for current period to account analyses.

8. Physically inspect a sample of additions for the current year (including significant acquisitions) selected from the account analyses. In touring the plant, select a sample of fixed assets seemingly recently acquired and trace to additions in account analyses. Assets included in the test samples should be identified by serial numbers or other appropriate identifying data.

9. Make inquiries of management and plant personnel regarding changes in production methods or plant layout, and significant acquisitions or sales and retirements of property, plant, and equipment.

10. Relate asset additions to retirements, and retirements to additions, and determine whether such related additions and retirements have been properly recorded.

11. Obtain a summary depreciation schedule and supporting schedules.

(a) Test arithmetical accuracy.

(b) Reconcile balances for assets, depreciation, and allowances for depreciation with general ledger accounts.

(c) Scan general ledger depreciation and allowance accounts and trace postings on a test basis to posting sources.

(d) Relate charges to depreciation expense to corresponding credits to allowance accounts, and relate charges to the allowance accounts for sales and retirements to corresponding entries in the analyses of the asset accounts and gain or loss account on sale or retirement of property, plant, and equipment.

(e) Test client's depreciation computations recorded on supporting schedules (or subsidiary records, as applicable), test footings, and trace totals to summary schedule.

(f) Evaluate the overall reasonableness of the total depreciation recorded for the period for each classification and in the aggregate by overall calculations and comparison with prior periods, taking into account current year's additions and retirements.

(g) Note whether acceptable depreciation methods have been used and whether they have been applied on a consistent basis.

(h) Consider whether the depreciation methods and rates and the accumulated allowances are adequate to ensure that fixed assets are being depreciated over their useful lives.

(i) Compare data on income tax return depreciation schedules with corresponding book balances for assets, depreciation, gains and losses, and accumulated allowances. Review and independently calculate tax allocation entries and affected account balances based on differences in depreciation methods between books and income tax return.

12. Obtain an analysis of repairs and maintenance accounts and vouch a sample of entries, including especially material items, by examination of authorizations, purchase orders, approved vouchers, and maintenance work orders. Work order entries should similarly be vouched to supporting evidences. Ascertain whether capital expenditures have been improperly expensed. Review for reasonableness selected individual repairs and maintenance entries as well as total expense for the period.

13. Obtain a summary analysis of rental income account.

(a) Relate analysis data to entries in the account and test entries to cash journal.

(b) Examine lease provisions and note description of property leased, parties involved, rentals, duration of lease, and special terms for insurance, taxes, heating and maintenance.

(c) Reconcile total recorded income for the period with amount due per lease agreement.

14. With respect to leased property, plant, and equipment:

(a) Discuss with management its lease versus purchase policies.

(b) Review thoroughly the provisions in FASB Statement No. 13 (AC 4053) regarding the accounting for and capitalization of capital leases.

(c) Determine whether one or more of the criteria for capitalization (AC 4053.007) have been met, and whether leased property has been recorded at the present value, at the beginning of the lease term, of the aggregate of minimum lease payments over the lease term, but no higher than the fair value of the property at the inception of the lease (AC 4053.101).

(d) Review amortization rate for assets capitalized. (Such assets should be amortized in a manner consistent with the depreciation policy for owned assets, but subject to certain restrictions specified in AC 4053.011.)

(e) Examine relevent evidential matter, including lease agreements, other documents drawn up by attorneys for the company, pertinent correspondence, authorization in minutes of the board of directors, rental notices, and cancelled checks. Such evidential matter should relate to lease arrangement, arms-length relationship, rental and other disbursements, fair value of property, and appropriateness of interest rate used in arriving at present value.

(f) Confirm lease arrangements and terms with lessor.

(g) Discuss with management its lease versus buy policies.

(h) Ascertain whether the capitalized obligation is stated at the proper amount and that the allocation between reduction of the obligation and interest expense has been correctly computed.

(i) To the extent relevant, apply to capitalized leased assets the usual auditing procedures employed for the examination of property, plant, and equipment.

15. Examine insurance policies for adequacy of coverage as well as for data regarding mortgaging of property or indication of unrecorded additions or retirements.

16. Compare account balances for property, plant, and equipment, depreciation, and accumulated allowances, as well as current year's additions and retirements, with prior years, budgets, forecasts, and industry data. A similar comparison should be made using meaningful ratios such as fixed assets to total assets, and depreciation to manufacturing cost. In performing these analytical review procedures, use Figure 2-19 as a guide.

17. Determine whether property, plant, and equipment, allowances for depreciation, and depreciation provisions, are properly classified and disclosed in the financial statements, and that with respect to major classifications of depreciable assets, a general description of the depreciation methods used is presented.

Auditing procedures from the foregoing suggested for:
Compliance testing: 5, 6, 7
Interim work: 2, 3, 4, 5, 6, 7, 8, 12

Figure 4-12
Audit Program Guide

Prepaid Expenses, Deferred Costs, and
Intangible Assets

AUDIT OBJECTIVES

1. To ascertain whether these assets are owned by (or, depending on the type of asset, pertain to) the client.

2. To determine that they are stated at cost less amounts properly amortized or otherwise written off or expensed.

3. To verify that cost:

(a) Includes all costs of acquisition.

(b) Was arrived at on a bargained and arms-length basis (especially applicable to intangibles).

(c) Corresponds to the utility of the asset as of date of acquisition.

4. To ascertain whether these assets are being systematically amortized over the period expected to be benefited, and on a consistent basis; whether amortization rates are adjusted for changes in estimates of the period of expected utility; whether lump-sum write-offs in whole or in part are recorded in the event of substantial or complete loss of remaining benefit; and whether the unamortized asset balance is consistent with and is supported by the underlying remaining benefit to be derived.

5. To determine whether income associated with these assets is properly accounted for.

6. To determine whether these assets and related allowances and expenses are presented and classified in the financial statements in conformity with generally accepted accounting principles and that all necessary disclosures are made.

AUDITING PROCEDURES

	Performed by	NA
1. Review prior and current year's audit and internal accounting control notes, memoranda, guides, and other materials in permanent and current files dealing with prepaid expenses, deferred costs, and intangible assets.		

2. Review APB Opinion No. 16 as amended (AC 1091) and APB Opinion No. 17 as amended (AC 5141) for accounting principles pertaining to intangible assets, including goodwill, and FASB Statement No. 2 (AC 4211) on the accounting for research and development costs.

3. Obtain an analysis of entries in the asset accounts showing additions, amortization, and other charges and credits. For certain accounts, especially with routine voluminous entries such as prepaid insurance, it may be more practicable to obtain a summary analysis.

4. Obtain a summary analysis of entries in the related expense accounts (e.g., amortization of intangibles, deferred cost write-offs, and insurance, tax, and interest expense). Unless acquisition costs of prepaid expenses are initially charged to the expense accounts, the summary analysis should be adequate to permit a ready correlation of expense charges with corresponding amortization credits to the asset accounts.

5. Obtain schedules listing the component elements making up the balance in each asset account. Where applicable, this schedule should also reflect current and cumulative amortization. Check arithmetical accuracy and compare balances with general ledger account balances.

6. Test-trace entries on analyses to corresponding entries in general ledger accounts and to posting sources; similarly, reverse procedure and test-trace entries in general ledger accounts to posting sources and analyses. If the auditor prepares the analyses himself, these steps would necessarily be performed concomitantly with the preparation of the analyses.

7. Test asset acquisition entries:

(a) By examination of supporting evidence:

(i) For prepaid insurance: Insurance brokers' and underwriters' invoices and statements, insurance policies, and reference to insurance register.

(ii) For prepaid interest: Bank or other advices and loan agreements specifying terms, cancelled notes, and independent computation.

(iii) For prepaid taxes: Tax bills, copies of tax returns, and independent computation.

(iv) For prepaid rent: Lease agreement, rental notices.

(v) Deferred costs and intangibles: In general—purchase agreements and contracts, receiving records (where applicable), invoices, closing statements, legal and attorney-related correspondence and documents, appraisal reports (where applicable), and registered copyright, patent, and similar documents of title.

(b) Note whether acquisitions have been properly authorized, especially in the minutes of the board of directors for purchase of intangibles and similar additions.

(c) For assets constructed or developed by the client, examine job orders or similar records, reconcile with general ledger entries, and vouch costs by test examination of approved invoices, receiving records (for purchased items), material requisitions, payroll records, and calculations of overhead allocations. Determine whether costs actually pertain to construction, creation, or installation of assets (e.g., leasehold improvements) and are entered in the proper accounts.

(d) Determine whether all relevant costs of acquisition have been capitalized.

(e) Observe accuracy of account distribution and note whether assets have been improperly expensed or expense items improperly capitalized. Take cognizance of the principle (AC 4211) that research and development costs may not be capitalized.

(f) For assets (especially intangibles) acquired in exchange for other assets or capital stock, obtain satisfaction that the transaction has been consummated on an arms-length basis and that the recorded cost bears a reasonable correspondence to the market value (or utility).

8. Relate credits to asset accounts representing periodic amortization or write-offs to the corresponding charges to related expense accounts, and reconcile differences, if any. Refund credits (for example, insurance refunds) should be supported by reference to policies and brokers' advices. For credits representing sales, say of certain intangibles, follow corresponding procedures included in the program for property, plant, and equipment.

9. With respect to amortization and write-offs:

(a) Test arithmetical accuracy of computations by independent computation.

(b) In evaluating estimates of the useful lives of intangible assets and of the benefit reflected in the unamortized balances, see whether the minutes of the board of directors reflect any action, judgment, or resolution of the board pertinent to this question.

(c) Make appropriate inquiries of management and ascertain whether management periodically reviews amortization rates as well as the need for significant additional writeoffs in the event of material declines in recorded asset values.

(d) Examine production, sales, income and other records of operations and profitability, where applicable (e.g., goodwill, patents, or copyrights), for indications of continued utilization, utility and benefit derived from the given asset.

(e) Determine whether the client has considered factors such as the following in estimating the useful lives of intangible assets (AC 5141.27):

(i) Legal, regulatory, or contractual provisions that may limit the maximum useful life (period may never exceed 40 years—AC 5141.28).

(ii) Renewal or extension provisions.

(iii) Economic factors such as obsolescence, demand, and competition.

(iv)   Service life expectancies of individuals or groups of employees.

(f)   Determine whether the assets are being amortized (or properly expensed—periodically or otherwise—as in the case of prepaid insurance and other prepaid expenses) on a systematic basis over the period of expected benefit and whether there is a need for a change in amortization rate to reflect a change in remaining period of useful life, or a need for lump-sum write-offs, apart from periodic amortization, to reflect substantial additional declines in remaining utility.

10.   With respect to prepaid insurance, insurance in force, at the statement date, and insurance expense:

(a)   Obtain analyses of prepaid insurance and insurance expense accounts and vouch the entries by reference to invoices, cash disbursement records, policies, and insurance register entries, and by tracing periodic transfers from prepaid insurance to expense accounts.

(b)   Obtain a schedule of insurance in force reflecting, among other data, description of policies, coverage, premium, period of policy, and unexpired insurance.

(c)   Relate items included in schedule to, and examine, insurance policies including endorsements.

(d)   In examining policies note:

(i)   Whether policies are in the name of the client; if a co-beneficiary is recorded, or if the original of the policy is not on hand, it may suggest the pledging or mortgaging of insured assets.

(ii)   Co-insurance provisions as well as any restrictions affecting recoverability.

(e)   Independently compute prepaid insurance and compare with schedule and recorded amount.

(f)   Request confirmation from insurance brokers and underwriters on details of insurance in force, including parties insured, assets covered, amount of coverage, premiums, accounts payable, and refundable amounts.

(g)   Coordinate information obtained from account analyses, schedule, confirmation, and evidential matter, and investigate differences and inconsistencies.

(h)   Evaluate the adequacy of insurance coverage by inquiries of and discussion with management, and by comparison with book values of assets covered (at least as a rough guide) and, if available, with market values and appraisal reports. Take into account the impact of inflation on current values.

(i)   Examine insurance accounts and insurance policies from the standpoint of their representing additional evidential matter in support of assets—either in terms of bona fides of assets or in revealing unrecorded asset acquisitions or retirements through unexplained increases or reductions in insurance coverage.

(j)   Determine whether insurance expense has been properly allocated to the appropriate cost and expense classification in the income statement.

11. With respect to officers' life insurance:

(a) Analyze the relevant accounts—cash surrender value, life insurance expense, and prepaid life insurance expense.

(b) Obtain a schedule of officers' life insurance showing the pertinent data as listed below in the confirmation procedure.

(c) Examine insurance policies and compare data with details recorded in the schedule of insurance.

(d) Vouch premium payments and charges to expense by reference to policies, premium notices and, selectively, cancelled checks.

(e) Note whether the company is the beneficiary of the policies. (If the company is not the beneficiary, premium payments would then fall into the category of compensation and should be audited as such; moreover, cash surrender value should not then be recognized as an asset of the company.)

(f) Review entries adjusting the account balance for cash surrender value and compare the account balance with amount specified in the policies. Take into account added increments based on dividend accumulations and relate such additions to policy provisions and premium advices.

(g) Examine authorization in the minutes of the board of directors (or other appropriate documentation) for taking out officers' life insurance.

(h) Ascertain from senior management the reasons for acquiring insurance and examine related agreements, if any, on future disposition of proceeds.

(i) Confirm details of policies with life insurance companies, using the standard confirmation inquiry form. The details should include policy number, names of insured and beneficiaries, face amount, premiums and date to which paid, policy surrender value, dividend accumulations, prepaid insurance, and outstanding loans.

(j) Confirm with insured officers the details of coverage. (Although a desirable procedure, this confirmation step is often considered as optional in view of the direct confirmation with the insurance company.)

(k) Relate evidential findings to information reflected on insurance schedule, account analyses, and confirmation replies, and investigate differences and inconsistencies.

(l) Ascertain whether cash surrender value of life insurance policies (including accumulated dividends) has been properly reflected as a noncurrent asset, and insurance expense as an operating expense, although the expense is not deductible in computing taxable income.

12. Where practicable and applicable, confirm *material transactions* relating to deferred costs and intangibles involving especially such matters as terms of acquisition agreements and royalty arrangements.

13. Determine whether the asset balances and related expense accounts have been classified properly in the financial statements (as applicable—current and noncurrent, cost of sales, operating expense, and extraordinary items) and have been presented in con-

formity with generally accepted accounting principles applied on a consistent basis, including required disclosures of material matters.

Auditing procedures from the foregoing suggested for:
Compliance testing: 7, 9, 10.
Interim work: 6, 7, 8, 9, 10.

Figure 4-13
Audit Program Guide
Long-Term Debt

AUDIT OBJECTIVES

1. To determine whether the obligations are bona fide liabilities of the client and are stated at the proper amount.

2. To ascertain whether assets received in connection with the transaction giving rise to the indebtedness are fairly stated.

3. To ascertain whether long-term debt has been properly classified in the financial statements and with current maturities shown as a current liability, and whether appropriate disclosures have been made as to maturity dates, interest rate, mortgaging of assets, covenant restrictions, and items of similar importance.

4. To determine whether interest and other expenses as well as accruals pertaining to long-term debt have been properly recorded.

5. To determine whether material liabilities and contingencies have been unrecorded, understated, or undisclosed.

AUDITING PROCEDURES

	Performed by	NA
1. Review prior and current year's audit and internal accounting control notes, memoranda, guides, and other materials in permanent and current files dealing with long-term debt.		
2. Obtain a schedule-analysis of each of the long-term debt accounts (mortgages, bonds, capitalizable leases, etc.) showing major provisions, opening balances, transactions for the period, and ending balances, as well as applicable interest paid and accrued.		
3. Foot and cross-foot schedule and compare beginning and ending balances with general ledger accounts.		
4. Compare data on schedule with detailed subsidiary records and with general ledger entries.		

5. Vouch additions to long-term debt by examination of supporting evidence.

(a) Note whether the transaction and the important provisions of the debt agreement were authorized by the board of directors.

(b) Obtain copies of mortgage documents, bond indentures, leases, loan agreements and related basic documents, prepare abstracts of major provisions (including asset mortgaging or other encumbrances and subordination agreements) and relate those provisions to data recorded on schedule-analysis and to other evidences examined. Determine whether specified restrictions or requirements (such as limitations on dividend payments or reacquisition of capital stock) have been complied with or whether defaults have occurred.

(c) Make inquiries about the reasons for incurrence of debt and the utilization of the proceeds received, evaluate the reasonableness of the explanations, and undertake follow-up verification as necessary.

(d) Trace entries to cash receipts journal or other posting sources, noting amounts recorded for cash or other assets received in connection with debt incurred. Note deposit entry on bank statement and examine underwriters' or other statements and documents in support of cash entry. For noncash assets acquired, examine deeds or other documents of title, attorney documents, closing statements and other such evidences customarily examined for property acquired. (See audit program for property, plant, and equipment.)

(e) For debt securities issued, examine certificate book, reconcile with recorded data, and account for numerical sequence.

6. Vouch reductions in long-term debt as a result of amortization payments, retirements or reacquisition of debt securities, by examining supporting evidence, including terms of original agreements, authorization in the minutes, trustees' report, cancelled checks, correspondence, cancelled notes and certificates, and inspection of treasury bonds.

7. Independently compute (on an overall basis, if practicable, or on a test basis) for each of the long-term obligations, the interest expense for the period and accrued interest, and reconcile with amounts reflected in those accounts. Make similar computations for any discount or premium relating to indebtedness as well as for any gain or loss in extinguishment of debt.

8. Determine by inquiries of management and reference to published data whether interest rates are reasonable.

9. Obtain from mortgagees, bondholders, holders of notes and other creditors, written confirmation of important provisions of long-term debt agreements, transactions during the year in summary form, and balances as of the end of the period. Obtain such confirmation from the trustee if one is involved, as well as information regarding compliance with terms of the indenture.

10. Complete the comprehensive audit program presented in Figure 4-8 for uncovering and disclosing understated and unrecorded liabilities and contingencies, although many of the procedures contained therein may already have been performed in connection with the examination of other areas.

11. Ascertain whether long-term debt has been fairly stated, classified, and disclosed in the financial statements (e.g., current maturities shown as current liabilities and disclosure of important data such as mortgaging of assets, other asset encumbrances, agreement restrictions, defaults, due dates, interest rates, and amortization and retirement provisions).

Auditing procedures from the foregoing suggested for:
Compliance testing: 5, 6.
Interim work: 5, 6.

Figure 4-14
Audit Program Guide

Stockholders' Equity

AUDIT OBJECTIVES

1. To determine whether the stockholders' equity accounts are stated in accordance with generally accepted accounting principles and in conformity with the corporate charter and applicable statutes.

2. To determine whether transactions affecting capital stock and related accounts have been properly authorized and approved.

3. To ascertain whether the equity accounts have been properly classified with appropriate distinctions maintained between paid-in capital and retained earnings.

4. To ascertain whether adequate disclosures have been made in the financial statements regarding such matters as dividends in arrears, stock options, treasury stock, stock repurchase plans, liquidation preferences, restrictions (by statute or loan or other agreements) affecting dividends, retained earnings, and reacquisition of shares.

AUDITING PROCEDURES

	Performed by	NA
1. Review prior and current year's audit and internal accounting control notes, memoranda, guides, and other materials in permanent and current files dealing with stockholders' equity accounts.		
2. Obtain a schedule-analysis of each of the stockholders' equity accounts showing opening balances, entries for the period, and ending balances.		
3. Foot and crossfoot schedule and compare opening and closing balances with the general ledger accounts.		
4. Compare data on schedule with general ledger entries and vouch to supporting evidences, as indicated below.		
5. Obtain, review, and prepare abstracts of copies of certificate of incorpo-		

ration and amendments thereto, State permits to issue capital stock where required, subscription agreements, stock option plans, and other documents pertaining to the capital accounts; relate this review and the relevant provisions of these documents to recorded entries and to the other evidences examined.

6. Vouch stock issuances by examination of relevant documents and agreements, authorization in the corporate minutes, cash receipts records, and underwriters' statements.

7. For noncash assets acquired, examine deeds or other documents of title, attorney documents, closing statements and other such evidence customarily examined for property acquired. Determine whether such assets have been recorded in accordance with generally accepted accounting principles (see AC section 1041), and examine evidence in support of their fair value. (See audit program for property, plant, and equipment.)

8. Vouch entries for reacquisition of stock as treasury stock or for retirement by examination of purchase agreements, authorization in the minutes, brokers' advices, and disbursement records and cancelled checks.

9. Inspect treasury certificates, noting whether they are carried in the company's name or properly endorsed over, and reconcile with stockholder records and with analysis of the account.

10. Ascertain whether stock issuances and reacquisitions have been made on an arms-length basis and whether transaction prices are supported by objective evidence.

11. Confirm details of shares issued and outstanding with registrar and transfer agent and reconcile replies with the accounting records.

12. If the company acts as its own registrar and transfer agent:

(a) Obtain a listing of stockholders and compare data with stockholders ledger and stock certificate book, and reconcile with outstanding shares.

(b) Account for issued certificates (noting revenue stamps affixed to stubs) including those turned in for transfer or reacquired (noting cancellations of certificates where applicable).

(c) Account for unissued certificates.

13. With respect to dividends paid or declared:

(a) Examine minutes of the board of directors for authorization and declaration details.

(b) Independently compute total dividends for the period and compare with account balance.

(c) Undertake a test examination of dividend cash disbursements (follow customary program for examination of cash in bank):

(i) Inspect reimbursement check deposited in dividend bank account and relate amount to dividend declaration.

(ii) Reconcile dividend bank account.

(iii) Make a test comparison of cancelled checks with stockholder records, noting name, endorsement, and correspondence of amount with number of shares owned.

(iv) Inspect unclaimed checks, relate them to stockholder records, make appropriate inquiries, and determine if they are under adequate control.

14. If dividend payments are made by independent paying agent, examine cancelled check payable to agent, reconcile amount with dividend declaration, and review agent's reports.

15. Determine the amount, if any, of dividends in arrears on preferred stock.

16. Obtain an analysis of the retained earnings account; relate included data as well as opening and closing balances to general ledger entries and balances; review entries for propriety and conformity with generally accepted accounting principles.

17. Determine whether the stockholders' equity accounts have been properly classified in the financial statements, and if adequate disclosures have been made regarding: dividends in arrears, stock options, stock repurchase plans, liquidation preferences, restrictions by statute or loan or other agreements affecting dividends, retained earnings, and reacquisition of shares, and similar important matters.

18. Determine whether earnings per share data have been properly computed and disclosed in the financial statements in conformity with requirements of AC section 2011.

Auditing procedures from the foregoing suggested for:
Compliance testing: 6, 7, 8, 9, 13.
Interim work: 5, 6, 7, 8, 12, 13.

CHAPTER **5**

Confirmation Forms and Letters

See page 250 for a listing of representation letters and additional confirmation letters included in other chapters; but see Chapter 8 Contents for engagement letters and representation letters for use on compilation and review engagements.

INTRODUCTION

Audit confirmation letters or forms are written communications by the auditor addressed to outside parties requesting them to send information, about which they should have knowledge, directly to the auditor. The information may relate to an account balance, transactions, events, agreements, or other matters that are pertinent to the auditor's examination of the financial statements. In this context, the term *outside parties* includes parties within the client organization, such as the client entity's officers and employees of whom written confirmation may be requested of receivables from or payable to them and of other such matters affecting the financial statements.

The written confirmation procedure has fundamental support in the third standard of field work of the generally accepted auditing standards, which reads as follows: "Sufficient competent evidential matter is to be obtained through inspection, observation, inquiries, and *confirmations* to afford a reasonable basis for an opinion regarding the financial statements under examination." [italics supplied] It should not be inferred, however, that it is generally accepted practice to confirm *every* material or otherwise significant account or matter that is susceptible to confirmation. For certain accounts like accounts receivable, confirmation is a generally accepted and authoritatively mandated auditing procedure, unlike, for example, the confirmation of trade accounts payable which, while practiced by perhaps the majority of auditors, does not enjoy the same emphasis or support in authoritative auditing pronouncements. The fact, however, that confirmation of certain accounts or matters may not be a generally accepted auditing practice in ordinary circumstances cannot be used as an excuse to avoid such confirmation if reasonable professional judgment in the circumstances of the individual engagement requires that the confirmation procedure be undertaken as a means of obtaining sufficient competent evidential matter.

Figure 5-1, which may appropriately be located in an introductory section of an audit program guide, provides a more comprehensive introduction to this chapter and to the illustrative confirmation forms and letters that follow. It can be used as a checklist guide to the basic principles, procedures, and caveats that apply to confirmations in general. Additional expository comments have also been appended, selectively, to certain of the forms and letters.

Figure 5-1
Confirmation Guide: Principles,
Procedures, and Caveats

Basic Principles

1.   Review carefully AU 330 on evidential matter in general and AU 331 on evidential matter for receivables and inventories. These sections expand on the third standard of field work and express some fundamental principles relating to confirmation. The auditing standard requires that sufficient competent evidential matter be obtained by confirmations (as well as other cited evidences) as a reasonable basis for forming an opinion as to the fairness of the financial statements.

2.   For certain accounts, especially for accounts receivable, confirmation is a generally accepted auditing procedure. The burden of justifying the omission of such a generally accepted auditing procedure must be borne by the auditor and this burden may often be insurmountable. Depending on materiality and other considerations, the failure to employ a generally required confirmation procedure where it is reasonable and practicable to do so, may result in a qualified opinion or a disclaimer of opinion (including, in certain circumstances, the characterization of the financial statements as being *unaudited*).

3.   There is a danger, however, that too literal a reading of the third standard of field work can lead to the erroneous belief that confirmation alone represents conclusive evidence, and that internally available documentary or other evidence relating to the matter confirmed has minimal or relatively less value than confirmations as evidential value.

4.   While providing highly persuasive evidential matter, confirmations also represent *additional* evidences that serve as corroboration of the other evidences gathered by the auditor, many of which, together with the books and records, constitute the representations of management. In general, one type of evidential matter alone cannot be considered as conclusive verification. It is the combination of evidences—some, perhaps, more reliable than others but with each affecting the credibility of the others (enhancing or detracting)—that permits a judgment to be made as to the *competence*, and to some extent the *sufficiency*, of evidential matter.

5.   Confirmation replies, it should be recognized, may sometimes be misleading and even fraudulent. For example:

(a)   The asset or other matter confirmed may be fictitious and the outside party nonexistent, but the mailing address may be under the control of the wrongdoers within the client's organization.

(b)   The item may be fictitious but the outside party purportedly involved may be real; however, the confirmation letter may be received and responded to by an employee of the outside party who is in collusion with client personnel.

(c) Even if deliberate irregularity is not present, account balances or other data may be confirmed as being correct without proper (or perhaps any) scrutiny or investgation by the outside party. The latter may be indifferent, careless, or unwilling to expend the necessary effort to review the matter, or may simply rely on the integrity of the client. Moreover, the accounting and other records of the outside party may be unreliable or not kept in a manner that permits confirmation in the form and for the data requested.

(d) The confirming party may misread or misinterpret the confirmation request.

6. The fact that certain accounts or matters stand out as being traditionally subject to confirmation as a generally accepted auditing procedure or practice should not inhibit the auditor in exercising his professional judgment on extending the confirmation scope to other accounts or matters not generally confirmed by direct communication with outside parties. A decision to extend the confirmation scope may depend upon such considerations as:

(a) Adequacy of the system of internal accounting control.

(b) Reliability and sufficiency of other evidential matter.

(c) Presence or suspicion of errors, irregularities, related parties, illegal acts, uncertainties and contingencies, and any other questionable matters.

(d) Materiality of the accounts or other subject matter—materiality being judged quantitatively, qualitatively, and in terms of both present and potential circumstances.

7. Even though outside confirmation may have been obtained regarding assets of the client held by others for safekeeping, to secure liabilities or for other reasons, the auditor nevertheless will usually wish to arrange for his inspection of, say, securities held by outside parties, or for the observation and test count procedures for inventories in the hands of public warehouses or outside custodians. As previously emphasized, confirmation should not be considered as being so conclusive an evidence as to warrant the omission of other relevant and competent evidential matter.

8. The subject matter confirmed may be anything of significance to the auditor in his examination of the financial statements: account balance; account balance plus transactions making up the balance; individual transactions; agreements and pertinent provisions thereof; contingencies; and so on. Thus, for example, the fact that most confirmations relate to account balances should not deter the auditor from confirming, in a given circumstance, say, a specific transaction or a series of transactions or anything else that is significant and relevant to the examination.

9. Many confirmation requests are made properly as of the date of the balance sheet, but for some accounts like accounts receivable,

the confirmation procedure may be undertaken at an interim date depending on the system of internal accounting control and other considerations. But the fact that certain accounts may be confirmed as of an interim date should not preclude the auditor from confirming the same type of accounts again as of the year-end if, in his judgment, it would be necessary or even desirable to do so (e.g., because of deterioration in the internal accounting controls or recordkeeping, poor cutoff procedures, new or material accounts).

Confirmation Preparation and Mailing

10. A confirmation and sampling plan should be prepared, and reviewed by the engagement partner.

11. Except for confirmations like the standard bank confirmation request, confirmation forms and letters need not be standard in design, and the auditor should feel free to modify any model illustrative forms and letters to meet the requirements of the individual engagement.

12. Precise instructions should be given to the client regarding the form, wording, and content of the confirmation letters and forms, any attached statements or schedules, and the parties to be addressed.

13. Control copies and listings should be made up for the auditor's use and retention.

14. The data on the confirmations should be compared by the auditor with the control copies and listings and with the books and records of the client. Among the details to be tested are name and address of outside party, account balances and other quantitative data, descriptive matter, and confirmation date.

15. Sufficient information should be furnished to the confirming party to facilitate a proper and informed response. This may require, for certain accounts, preparing and attaching a statement detailing the transactions making up an account balance.

16. The confirmation should advise the party that replies are to be sent only to the offices of the auditor; a stamped envelope addressed to the auditor should be enclosed. Moreover, the original mailing envelope should bear his return address so that any undeliverable mail would be returned by the post office to the auditor and not the client.

17. The confirmation letter or form should be signed by a properly designated officer of the client organization, the signature serving as official authorization to the outside party to communicate and disclose the requested information to the auditor. Most accountants arrange for confirmation letters and forms to be typed on the client's stationery, but some accounting firms use their own stationery but provide space, usually at the bottom of the letter or form, for insertion of the client's authorization and signature.

18. The confirmation letters should be taken to the post office by the auditor himself.

19. The mailing should be as close as possible to the confirmation date; the greater the delay, the more difficulty would the outside party have in checking the confirmation.

Confirmation Replies and Results

20. Second and even third follow-up confirmation requests should be sent if no reply is initially received. Selectively, and with permission of the client, the party may be contacted by telephone or telegraph. The failure to receive replies in the case of material matters or accounts should be thoroughly investigated. Moreover, the scope and nature of the examination of other evidential matter should be expanded to achieve alternative satisfaction as to the bona fides and fairness of the account in question.

21. Replies should be compared with and reconciled with the retained control listings and the accounting records.

22. Any differences, exceptions, questions, or suspicions revealed or evoked by confirmation returns or undelivered mail should be reconciled and investigated by the auditor himself by inquiries and by reference to internal supporting records and other evidences, and satisfactorily resolved. For some types of confirmation response, as in the case of voluminous accounts having small balances, the detailed reconciliation of differences can be initially undertaken by the client's personnel, but the findings should be reviewed by the auditor and the validity tested by reference to internal records and other evidential matter.

23. Any additional comments made by the confirming party should be carefully reviewed even though, say, the account balance has been confirmed. The added comment, when investigated, may reveal information that is significant for the examination.

24. Client explanations of questions raised by a confirmation response should be evaluated for reasonableness, but they may also need to be validated by examination of supporting evidence.

25. Reported differences should also be reviewed for indications of inadequacies in, say, the client's system of internal accounting control, cutoff procedures, and recordkeeping.

26. The confirmation results should be summarized—for accounts receivable, for example—and evaluated by the auditor in a memorandum to be incorporated in the working papers and reviewed by the engagement partner.

Figure 5-2
Standard Bank Confirmation Inquiry

STANDARD BANK CONFIRMATION INQUIRY
Approved 1966 by
AMERICAN INSTITUTE OF CERTIFIED PUBLIC ACCOUNTANTS
and
BANK ADMINISTRATION INSTITUTE (FORMERLY NABAC)

```
ORIGINAL
To be mailed to accountant
```

_____ 19____

Your completion of the following report will be sincerely appreciated. IF THE ANSWER TO ANY ITEM IS "NONE," PLEASE SO STATE. Kindly mail it in the enclosed stamped, addressed envelope *direct* to the accountant named below.

Report from

Yours truly,

_____

(Bank)

By _____
Authorized Signature

_____
(ACCOUNT NAME PER BANK RECORDS)

Accountant

Bank customer should check here if confirmation of bank balances only (item 1) is desired. ☐

NOTE—If the space provided is inadequate, please enter totals hereon and attach a statement giving full details as called for by the columnar headings below.

Dear Sirs:

1. At the close of business on_____19____ our records showed the following balance(s) to the **credit** of the above named customer. In the event that we could readily ascertain whether there were any balances to the credit of the customer not designated in this request, the appropriate information is given below.

AMOUNT	ACCOUNT NAME	ACCOUNT NUMBER	Subject to Withdrawal by Check?	Interest Bearing? Give Rate
$				

2. The customer was directly liable to us in respect of loans, acceptances, etc., at the close of business on that date in the total amount of $_____, as follows:

AMOUNT	DATE OF LOAN OR DISCOUNT	DUE DATE	INTEREST		DESCRIPTION OF LIABILITY, COLLATERAL, SECURITY INTERESTS, LIENS, ENDORSERS, ETC.
			Rate	Paid to	
$					

3. The customer was contingently liable as endorser of notes discounted and/or as guarantor at the close of business on that date in the total amount of $_____, as below:

AMOUNT	NAME OF MAKER	DATE OF NOTE	DUE DATE	REMARKS
$				

4. Other direct or contingent liabilities, open letters of credit, and relative collateral, were

5. Security agreements under the Uniform Commercial Code or any other agreements providing for restrictions, not noted above, were as follows (if officially recorded, indicate date and office in which filed):

_____

Yours truly, (Bank) _____

Date _____ 19____   By _____
                              Authorized Signature

Additional copies of this form are available from the American Institute of CPAs, 1211 Avenue of the Americas, New York, N. Y. 10036

Comment. The standard bank confirmation inquiry form may be sent to all banks with which the client maintained any cash balances or otherwise engaged in any loan or banking transactions during the period under examination, even if no cash or loan balances are outstanding at the confirmation date. Unrecorded or understated liabilities or contingencies may thereby be disclosed, as well as cash balances for seemingly inactive accounts having zero book values.

**Figure 5-3
Standard Bank Confirmation
Inquiry—Follow-up Request
for Clarification, Corrections,
or Additional Information**

(Client name and address)

(Date)

(Name and address of bank)

Gentlemen:

Our auditors, (name and address), have indicated that they wish to receive from you clarification and further information on the following matters pertaining to the enclosed photocopy of the standard bank confirmation inquiry form dated (date) which you had completed and forwarded to them at our request.

_____

_____

_____

Your prompt response will be appreciated. An envelope addressed to our auditors is enclosed for your convenience.

Very truly yours,

_____
(Authorized signature and title)

_____

Comment. If an amended confirmation form is desired, the first sentence of the last paragraph should read: "We are enclosing another confirmation form (bearing the word *Amended* at the top) and request that it be fully completed."

Figure 5-4
Cutoff Bank Statement Request

(Client name and address)

(Date)

(Name and address of bank)

Gentlemen:

Our auditors, (name and address), are making an examination of our financial statements. In that connection, please send directly to them statements of all our accounts, together with cancelled checks and other customary enclosures, for the period from (date) through (date).

Account name	*Account number*
_____	_____
_____	_____
_____	_____

Your prompt response will be appreciated.

Very truly yours,

_____
(Authorized signature and title)

Figure 5-5
Authorized Bank Signatures Confirmation

(Client name and address)

(Date)

(Name and address of bank)

Gentlemen:

Our auditors, (name and address), are making an examination of our financial statements. For verification purposes, please furnish them with a list of the persons who, according to your records, are authorized to sign checks on each of our accounts, including those accounts listed below; any co-signature or other requirements should also be specified.

Account name   *Account number*

_____   _____
_____   _____

Your prompt response will be appreciated. An envelope addressed to our auditors is enclosed for your convenience.

Very truly yours,

_____
(Authorized signature and title)

_____

Comment. The confirmation of authorized signatures according to the bank's records will enable the auditor to determine whether they correspond with audit tests of bank transactions and with prior written authorization, and whether there has been any failure to notify the bank of withdrawal of authorization for persons leaving the organization or for any other reason.

Figure 5-6
Bank Duplicate Deposit Slips Confirmation

(Client name and address)

(Date)

(Name and address of bank)

Gentlemen:

Our auditors, (name and address), are making an examination of our financial statements. For verification purposes, please compare the detailed items on the enclosed duplicate deposit slips with those shown on the original deposit slips in your files and advise our auditors, by completing the confirmation section below, whether or not they are in agreement. If this is not feasible, please send them a photocopy of the original deposit slips with attachments.

A return envelope is enclosed for your convenience in replying directly to our auditors. Your prompt response will be appreciated.

Very truly yours,

_____
(Signature and title)

_____

CONFIRMATION

The deposit slips are in agreement (subject to differences, if any, noted below).

Date _____ Signature and title _____

Details of exceptions or differences, if any _____

_____

Figure 5-7
Petty Cash Custodian Confirmation

(Client name and address)

(Date)

(Name and address)

Dear _____:

   Our auditors, (name and address), are making an examination of our financial statements. For verification purposes, please advise them, by completing and signing the confirmation section below, whether or not the following information is correct.

   You were holding as custodian a petty cash fund of ($ amount) as of (date).

   This letter should be forwarded directly to our auditors in the enclosed, stamped envelope. Your prompt attention will be appreciated.

Very truly yours,

_____
(Signature and title)

_____

CONFIRMATION

   The above information is correct (subject to differences, if any, noted below).

Signature _____
Date _____

Details of exceptions or differences, if any _____
_____
_____

_____

   Comment. If desired, the letter may be modified to request that the custodian of the fund (or of cash on hand) provide an analysis of the contents as of the given date, including currency and other items. The above letter would generally not be used if the audit test were to include a count of the specific fund.

Figure 5-8
Safe Deposit Box Entry Inquiry

(Client name and address)

(Date)

(Name and address)

Gentlemen:

Our auditors, (name and address), are making an examination of our financial statements. For verification purposes, please furnish them with a listing by dates of persons entering our safe deposit boxes or vaults during the period (date) through (date). Please provide this listing separately for each of the safe deposit boxes or vaults.

A return envelope is enclosed for your convenience in replying directly to our auditors. Your prompt response will be appreciated.

Very truly yours,

_____

(Signature and title)

Figure 5-9
Bank Credit and Compensating Balance
Arrangements—Form of Confirmation Letter

(From AICPA's CPA Letter, as modified; see
comment below following the letter)

(Client name and address)

(Date)

Appropriate bank lending or
account officer and name
and address of bank)

Dear _____:

Generally accepted accounting principles require that disclosures be made in the financial statements of certain information with respect to credit arrangements (including compensating balances), whether written or oral. In that connection, the term *compensating balance* may be defined as follows:

"A compensating balance is defined as that portion of any demand deposit (or any time deposit or certificate of deposit) maintained by a corporation (or by any other person on behalf of the corporation) which constitutes support for existing borrowing arrangements of the corporation (or any other person) with a lending institution. Such arrangements would include both outstanding borrowings and the assurance of future credit availability."

In connection with an examination of the financial statements of (name of Company or Companies) as of (balance sheet date) and for the (period) then ended, please confirm the following information as of dates indicated below by signing and returning the enclosed copy of this letter directly to our independent auditors, (name and address of CPA firm).

I. Lines of Credit

A. Description [unless covered by a document that can be referred to, include such information as amount of total line, fee (if any), expiration date (if any), conditions under which line may be withdrawn]

B. Related debt outstanding at close of business on (date)
C. Amount of unused line of credit, subject to terms of the related document, at (date)
D. Interest rate at close of business on (date)
E. If the arrangement specifies that this line supports commercial paper or other borrowing arrangements, describe

II. Commitments

A. Description (in general, reference to a specific agreement is sufficient)
B. Related debt outstanding at close of business on (date)
C. Amount of unused commitment, subject to terms of the related agreement, at (date)
D. Interest rate at close of business on (date)
E. Commitment or other related fees, if any

III. Other Existing Debt

A. Description
B. Balance outstanding at close of business on (date)
C. Interest rate at close of business on (date)

IV. Compensating Balance Arrangements

A. There (were) (were no) compensating balance arrangements at (date)
B. Withdrawal by the Company of the compensating balance (was) (was not) legally restricted at (date)
C. The terms of the compensating balance arrangements at (date) were:

Selected Examples

1—The Company has been expected to maintain an average compensating balance of 20 percent of its average bank loan outstanding, as determined from the bank's ledger records adjusted for estimated average uncollected funds.

2—The Company has been expected to maintain an average compensating balance of $100,000 during the year, as determined from the bank's ledger records without adjustment for uncollected funds.

3—The Company has been expected to maintain a compensating balance, as determined from the bank's ledger records without adjustment for uncollected funds, of 15 percent of its outstanding loans plus 10 percent of its unused line of credit.

4—The Company has been expected to maintain as a compensating balance non-interest bearing time deposits of 10 percent of its out-standing loans.

D. (Not applicable if compensating balances are based on bank ledger records without adjustment for uncollected funds.)

    In determining compliance with compensating balance arrangements, the Company uses a factor for uncollected funds of _____ (business) (calendar) days and we understand this to be a reasonable method.

    (If some other method is used for determining collected funds for compensating balance purposes, the method actually used should be described.)

E. There (were the following) (were no) significant changes in the compensating balance arrangements during the (period) and subsequently through the date of this letter.

F. The Company (was) (was not) in substantial compliance with the compensating balance arrangements during the (period) and subsequently through the date of this letter.

G. (Applicable only if the response to F discloses noncompliance with compensating balance arrangements.)

    The Company has no knowledge of any imminent sanctions by the bank because of noncompliance with compensating balance arrangements.

    (If the bank has applied sanctions during the (period) or notified the Company that sanctions may be applied, indicate details.)

V. *Compensating Balance Arrangements by or for the Benefit of Others*

During the (period), and subsequently through the date of this letter, (no) (the following) compensating balances were maintained by the Company at the bank on behalf of an affiliate, director, officer, or any other third party and (no) (the following) third party maintained compensating balances at the bank on behalf of the Company. (Withdrawal of such compensating balances (was) (was not) legally restricted.)

                                 Yours very truly

                                 (Name of Company)

                                 _____

          By: _____
                               (Officer)

CONFIRMATION

(Name of CPA firm)
(Address)

Gentlemen:

The above description of the terms of the credit arrangements and related matters with this bank are in accordance with our understanding except as noted below or in an attached letter.

_____

_____

_____

(If applicable, phraseology similar to the following may be added to the confirmation reply by either the company or the bank:)

This confirmation does not relate to arrangements, if any, with other branches or affiliates of this Bank. Information should be sought separately from such branches or affiliates with which any such arrangements might exist. Moreover, this confirmation is not, and should not be taken as, advice with respect to any aspect of any relationship between this Bank and the Company except as expressly stated herein.

(Name of Bank)

_____

By: _____
    (Officer)

Date _____

_____

Comment. The foregoing form letter for confirmation of bank credit and compensating balance arrangements is a modified version of a suggested letter prepared by the compensating balances task force of the AICPA's auditing standards division and published in the December 17, 1973 issue of the *CPA Letter*. Its preparation was in response to the issuance by the SEC of Accounting Series Release (ASR) No. 148 requiring the disclosure of such arrangements in financial statements filed with the Commission. The AICPA suggested form letter differs from the foregoing modified version mainly in stating, in the opening paragraph, that: "Securities and Exchange Commission Accounting Series Release No. 148 requires disclosure . . ." In referring to generally accepted accounting principles, the modified version has broadened its application to nonpublic as well as public companies.

The following are some of the confirmation guidelines suggested by the AICPA task force:

1.   The confirmation letter should be mailed separately from any other bank confirmations.

2.   Because of the special nonroutine nature of the inquiries, the letter should be addressed to the appropriate bank lending or account officer responsible for the company's account. This may involve more than one officer or branch of the bank.

3.   If there are separate credit arrangements for a parent company and its subsidiaries, the name should be specified or separate letters prepared.

4.   The items listed in the foregoing letter are simply reminders of data to be provided and filled in by the client in the actual letter, as illustrated in Figure 5-10.

Figure 5-10
Bank Credit and Compensating Balance Arrangements—
Illustrative Confirmation Letter with Data Inserted

(From AICPA's CPA Letter, as modified; see
comments below following the letter)

(Client name and address)

January 4, 198Y

Mr. John Doe, Vice President
ABC Bank
Anytown, New York 10000

Dear Mr. Doe:

Generally accepted accounting principles require that disclosures be made in the financial statements of certain information with respect to credit arrangements (including compensating balances), whether written or oral. In that connection, the term *compensating balance* may be defined as follows:

"A compensating balance is defined as that portion of any demand deposit (or any time deposit or certificate of deposit) maintained by a corporation (or by any other person on behalf of the corporation) which constitutes support for existing borrowing arrangements of the corporation (or any other person) with a lending institution. Such arrangements would include both outstanding borrowings and the assurance of future credit availability."

In connection with an examination of the financial statements of XYZ Company as of December 31, 198X and for the year then ended, please confirm the following information as of the dates indicated below by signing and returning the enclosed copy of this letter directly to our independent auditors, Jones and Jones, 200 Main Street, Anytown, New York 10000.

I. Lines of Credit

A. Description

The Company has available at the Bank a line of credit totaling $35,000,000. The terms of the line of credit are contained in a letter dated May 25, 198X. This line can be withdrawn at the Bank's option.

B. Related debt outstanding at close of business on December 31, 198X

$25,000,000

C. Amount of unused line of credit, subject to terms of the related document, at December 31, 198X

$10,000,000

D. Interest rate at close of business on December 31, 198X

9½% per annum

E. The arrangement does not specify that this line of credit supports commercial paper or other borrowing arrangements.

II. Commitments

A. Description

The Company has a commitment from the Bank for $50,000,000 in borrowings. Terms of the commitment are described in the letter agreement dated September 30, 198X.

B. Related debt outstanding at close of business on December 31, 198X

None

C. Amount of unused commitment, subject to terms of the related agreement, at December 31, 198X

$50,000,000

D. Interest rate at close of business on December 31, 198X

Not applicable

E. Commitment or other related fees, if any

½ of 1 percent per annum of the average daily unused amount

III. Other Existing Debt

There was no other debt payable to the Bank by the Company at December 31, 198X.

IV. *Compensating Balance Arrangements*

A. There were compensating balance arrangements at December 31, 198X under the line of credit. There were no compensating balance arrangements under the commitment at December 31, 198X.
B. Withdrawal by the Company of the compensating balances was not legally restricted at Dec. 31, 198X.
C. The terms of the compensating balance arrangements at December 31, 198X were:

> The Company has been expected to maintain an average compensating balance of 20 percent of the debt outstanding under its line of credit as determined from the bank ledger records adjusted for the estimated average uncollected funds.

D. In determining compliance with compensating balance requirements, the Company uses a factor for uncollected funds of 1.5 business days and we understand this to be a reasonable method.
E. There were no significant changes in the compensating balance arrangements during the year and subsequently through the date of this letter.
F. The company was in substantial compliance with the compensating balance arrangements during the year and subsequently through the date of this letter.

V. *Compensating Balance Arrangements by or for the Benefits of Others*

During the year, and subsequently through the date of this letter, no compensating balances were maintained by the Company at the bank on behalf of an affiliate, director, officer, or any other third party and no third party maintained compensating balances at the bank on behalf of the Company.

Yours very truly,

XYZ Company

By: _____
   Joe Smith, Treasurer

CONFIRMATION

Jones and Jones
200 Main Street
Anytown, New York 10000

Gentlemen:

The above descriptions of the terms of the credit arrangements and related matters with this bank are in accordance with our understanding except as noted below or in an attached letter.
No exceptions

_____

_____

_____

ABC Bank

By: _____

John Doe, Vice President

DATE January 15, 198Y

_____

Comment. See comments following Figure 5-9. The foregoing letter is similarly a modified version of the illustrative letter prepared by the compensating balances task force of the AICPA's auditing standards division and published in the December 17, 1973 issue of the *CPA Letter.*

Figure 5-11
Accounts Receivable Positive Confirmation—
With Statement Attached

(Client name and address)

(Date)

(Name and address of customer)

Gentlemen:

Our auditors, (name and address), are making an examination of our financial statements. For verification purposes, please advise them, by completing and signing the confirmation section below, whether or not the enclosed statement showing a balance of ($ amount) due us at the above date (or specify date) is correct.

This letter should be forwarded directly to our auditors in the enclosed stamped, addressed envelope. Your prompt response will be appreciated.

Very truly yours,

_____

(Signature and title)

_____

CONFIRMATION

The enclosed statement with the balance due you in the amount shown above is correct (subject to differences, if any, noted below).

Customer _____

Signature _____

Details of exceptions or differences, if any _____

_____

_____

_____

Comment. AU 331 should be reviewed for basic guidance on confirmation of receivables and the use of positive or negative methods of confirmation.

Figure 5-12
Accounts Receivable Positive Confirmation—
Without Attached Statement

(Client name and address)

(Date)

(Name and address of customer)

Gentlemen:

Our auditors, (name and address), are making an examination of our financial statements. For verification purposes, please advise them, by completing and signing the confirmation section below, whether or not the following information is correct:

A balance of ($ amount) is due us on your account at the above date (or specify date).

This letter should be forwarded directly to our auditors in the enclosed stamped envelope. Your prompt response will be appreciated.

Very truly yours,

_____

(Signature and title)

_____

CONFIRMATION

The balance due you as shown above is correct (subject to differences, if any, noted below).

Customer _____

Signature and title _____

Date _____

Details of exceptions or differences if any _____
_____
_____

Figure 5-13
Accounts Receivable Positive Confirmation—
With Gummed Perforated Edge Attached to Statement

AUDIT CONFIRMATION REQUEST

Auditors' No. _____

After you examine the attached statement carefully, please advise our auditors, by completing and signing the confirmation section below, whether or not the statement is correct. After signing below, detach this AUDIT CONFIRMATION REQUEST and mail it in the enclosed, stamped return envelope directly to our auditors.

(Auditors' name)

(Auditors' address)

Please do not send them your remittances. Your prompt response will be appreciated.

CONFIRMATION

The statement is correct (subject to differences, if any, noted below).

Date _____   Customer _____

Signature and title _____

Details of exceptions or differences, if any _____

_____

_____

Detach Here

Figure 5-14
Accounts Receivable Positive Confirmation of Open Items
(For customers on voucher system)

(Client name and address)

(Date)

(Name and address of customer)

Gentlemen:

Our auditors, (name and address), are making an examination of our financial statements. You have indicated that the voucher system you maintain for vendor accounts makes it difficult for you to confirm to our auditors the correctness of the balance due us. We would, however, appreciate your verification of the following items of your account with us that were open and unpaid by you at (date).

         Item   Amount

_____

_____

_____

_____

Please complete and sign the confirmation section below and forward this letter directly to our auditors in the enclosed stamped, addressed envelope. Your prompt response will be appreciated.

Very truly yours,

_____

(Signature and title)

_____

CONFIRMATION

The items listed above were properly invoiced to us and were unpaid at the date indicated. (Differences, if any, are noted below.)

Date _____   Customer _____

Signature and title _____

Details of exceptions or differences, if any _____

_____

_____

Figure 5-15
Accounts Receivable Negative Confirmation

(To be placed on customer's statement by
rubber stamp or gummed sticker)

AUDIT CONFIRMATION REQUEST

Please examine this statement carefully. IF IT IS NOT CORRECT, please report any differences directly to our auditors,

(Auditors name)

(Auditors' address)

An envelope addressed to our auditors is enclosed for your convenience. Please do not send them your remittance.

Figure 5-16
Accounts Receivable—
Subsequent Payments Confirmation

(Client name and address)

(Date)

(Name and address of customer)

Gentlemen:

Our auditors, (name and address), are making an examination of our financial statements. For verification purposes, please advise them, by completing and signing the confirmation section below, whether or not the following information is correct regarding payments on your account with us received from you from (date) through (date).

Date Received	Amount Received	Discount or Other Deductions	Gross Amount Credited	Invoice No.
_____	_____	_____	_____	_____
_____	_____	_____	_____	_____

This letter should be forwarded directly to our auditors in the enclosed, stamped envelope.

Very truly yours,

_____
(Signature and title)

CONFIRMATION

The above information is correct (subject to differences, if any, noted below.)

Date _____ Company _____

Signature and title _____

Details of exceptions or differences, if any _____

_____

_____

_____

Comment. This form of confirmation may be used if there is a need to verify book entries for cash collections received after the balance sheet date.

Figure 5-17
Notes Receivable Confirmation

(Client name and address)

(Date)

(Name and address)

Gentlemen:

Our auditors, (name and address), are making an examination of our financial statements. For verification purposes, please advise them, by completing and signing the confirmation section below, whether or not the following information as to your notes payable to us at the above date (or specify date) is correct.

Date of Note	Due Date	Original Amount	Unpaid Balance	Interest Rate	Date Interest Paid to	Collateral
_____	_____	_____	_____	_____	_____	_____
_____	_____	_____	_____	_____	_____	_____

This letter should be forwarded directly to our auditors in the enclosed stamped envelope. Your prompt response will be appreciated.

Very truly yours,

_____
(Signature and title)

_____

CONFIRMATION

The above information is correct (subject to differences, if any, noted below.)

Date _____   Customer _____

Signature and title _____

Details of exceptions or differences, if any _____
_____
_____

Figure 5-18
Miscellaneous Receivables Confirmation

(Client name and address)

(Date)

(Name and address)

Gentlemen: (or Dear _____:)

Our auditors, (name and address), are making an examination of our financial statements. For verification purposes, please advise them, by completing and signing the confirmation section below, whether or not the following information is correct.

You owed our company ($ amount) as of (date). This liability to us represents (describe).

This letter should be forwarded directly to our auditors in the enclosed stamped envelope. Your prompt response will be appreicated.

Very truly yours,

_____
(Signature and title)

_____

CONFIRMATION

The above information is correct (subject to differences, if any, noted below).

Signature and title _____

Date _____

Details of exceptions or differences, if any _____

_____

_____

Figure 5-19
Collection Agency (or Collection Lawyer) Confirmation

(Client name and address)

(Date)

(Name and address)

Gentlemen:

Our auditors, (name and address), are making an examination of our financial statements. For verification purposes, please furnish them with a list (showing accounts involved, disposition, and status) of all accounts and notes receivable referred to you for collection from (date) to the present date.

A return envelope is enclosed for your convenience in replying directly to our auditors. Your prompt response will be appreciated.

Very truly yours,

_____
(Signature and title)

Figure 5-20
Inventories Held by Public Warehouses or Others
(Inventory Listing Submitted)

(Client name and address)

(Date)

(Name and address)

Gentlemen:

Our auditors, (name and address), are making an examination of our financial statements. For verification purposes, please complete and sign the confirmation section below relative to the following inventories owned by us and held by you for our account as of (date):

Description	Quantity
_____	_____
_____	_____
_____	_____
_____	_____

This letter should be forwarded directly to our auditors in the enclosed stamped envelope. Your prompt response will be appreciated.

Very truly yours,

_____
(Signature and title)

_____

CONFIRMATION

We confirm the following (subject to any exceptions or differences, if any, noted below):

1.   The above inventory listing is correct and represents all inventories owned by your company and held by us for your account as of the date mentioned above.

2.   There are no liens or other restrictions on merchandise withdrawals by your company.

3.   The merchandise is being held by us for the following reason: _____

_____

_____

4.   A statement of amounts due to or from you as of the above-mentioned date is attached.

Date _____   Company _____

Signature and title _____

Details of exceptions or differences, if any _____

_____

_____

_____

_____

_____

Comment.   See AU 331 and 901 for additional guidance relating to confirmation of inventories, including supplemental inquiries as to the bona fides of the custodian, and observation of physical count.

Figure 5-21
Inventories Held by Public Warehouses
or Others Confirmation
(Inventory Listing Requested)

(Client name and address)

(Date)

(Name and address)

Gentlemen:

Our auditors, (name and address), are making an examination of our financial statements. For verification purposes, please furnish them with the following information relative to inventories owned by us and held by you for our account as of (date):

1.   Inventory description and quantities.
2.   A statement confirming that the inventory listing represents all our owned inventory held by you for our account; the reason you are holding the inventories; and details of any liens or other restrictions on inventory withdrawals by us.
3.   Details of any amounts due to or from you as of (date).
4.   Any other information that may be helpful to our auditors.

A return envelope is enclosed for your convenience in replying directly to our auditors. Your prompt response will be appreciated.

Very truly yours,

_____
(Signature and title)

Figure 5-22
Merchandise Consignor Confirmation

(Client name and address)

(Date)

(Name and address)

Gentlemen:

Our auditors, (name and address), are making an examination of our financial statements. For verification purposes, please advise them, by completing and signing the confirmation section below, whether or not the following information is correct as of (date).

1. We were holding your merchandise on consignment for your account as follows:

Merchandise Description	*Quantity*
_____	_____
_____	_____

2. A balance of ($ amount) is due you (or us) at the above date as shown on the attached statement.

This letter should be forwarded directly to our auditors in the enclosed stamped envelope. Your prompt response will be appreciated.

Very truly yours,

_____

(Signature and title)

_____

CONFIRMATION

The above information is correct (subject to differences, if any, noted below).

Date _____ Company _____

Signature and title _____

Details of exceptions or differences, if any _____
_____
_____

Figure 5-23
Securities Held for Others Confirmation

(Client name and address)

                                                    (Date)

(Name and address)

Gentlemen:

Our auditors, (name and address), are making an examination of our financial statements. For verification purposes, please furnish them with the following information for each security held by you for our account at (date).

1. Name and description.
2. Serial number.
3. Principal amount or number of shares.
4. In whose name security is registered.

Please also advise our auditors as to: the reason the securities are being held by you; the details regarding pledging or assignment of the securities, if applicable; and names of persons authorized to withdraw the securities.

A return envelope is enclosed for your convenience in replying directly to our auditors. Your prompt response will be appreciated.

                              Very truly yours,

                              _____
                              (Signature and title)

_____

Comment. In addition to confirmation of securities held by others, it may be necessary to arrange to visit the outside party and inspect and count the securities.

Figure 5-24
Stockbroker's Statement Request

(Client name and address)

(Date)

(Name and address)

Gentlemen:

Our auditors, (name and address), are making an examination of our financial statements. In that connection, please send directly to them the regular statements of all our accounts with you for the period (date) through (date).

A return envelope is enclosed for your convenience in replying directly to our auditors. Your prompt response will be appreciated.

Very truly yours,

_____
(Signature and title)

Figure 5-25
Accounts Payable Confirmation

(Client name and address)

(Date)

(Name and address)

Gentlemen:

Our auditors, (name and address), are making an examination of our financial statements. For verification purposes, please furnish them with the following information as of the above-mentioned date (or specify date).

1. Itemized statement of our indebtedness to you on open ac-acount.
2. Details of notes and acceptances payable to you.
3. Details of collateral or guarantees provided in connection with amounts owing to you.
4. Listing of purchase commitments outstanding at the above date.
5. Any other information that may be helpful to our auditors.

A return envelope is enclosed for your convenience in replying directly to our auditors. Your prompt response will be appreciated.

Very truly yours,

_____

(Signature and title)

_____

Comment. The confirmation procedure for accounts payable will also serve to uncover understated or unrecorded payables. Hence, the test should include suppliers with whom the client has transacted business for a given period even though a zero balance may exist at the statement date.

Figure 5-26
Notes Payable Confirmation
(Information Supplied)

(Client name and address)

(Date)

(Name and address)

Gentlemen:

Our auditors, (name and address), are making an examination of our financial statements. For verification purposes, please advise them, by completing and signing the confirmation section below, whether or not the following information regarding our notes payable to you as of (date) is correct.

Date of Note	Due Date	Original Amount	Unpaid Balance	Interest Rate	Date Interest Paid To
_____	_____	_____	_____	_____	_____
_____	_____	_____	_____	_____	_____

Also, please furnish our auditors with the details regarding collateral, any contingent liability to you on discounted notes, acceptances or otherwise, and any other information that may be helpful.

This letter should be forwarded directly to our auditors in the enclosed stamped envelope. Your prompt response will be appreciated.

Very truly yours,

_____
(Signature and title)

_____

CONFIRMATION

The above information is correct (subject to differences, if any, noted below). The following is additional information regarding collateral, contingent liabilities, etc., as requested. _____

_____

_____

Company _____

Signature and title _____

Date _____

Details of exceptions or differences, if any _____

_____

_____

Figure 5-27
Notes Payable Confirmation
(Information Requested)

(Client name and address)

(Date)

(Name and address)

Gentlemen:

Our auditors, (name and address), are making an examination of our financial statements. For verification purposes, please furnish them with the following information regarding our notes payable to you (or other indebtedness) as of (date).

1. Date of note.
2. Due date.
3. Original amount of note.
4. Unpaid balance.
5. Interest rate and date to which interest has been paid.
6. Details of collateral.
7. Contingent liability to you on discounted notes, acceptances, or otherwise.
8. Any other information that may be helpful to our auditors.

A return envelope is enclosed for your convenience in replying directly to our auditors. Your prompt response will be appreciated.

Very truly yours,

_____

(Signature and title)

Figure 5-28
Miscellaneous Payables Confirmation

(Client name and address)

(Date)

(Name and address)

Gentlemen: (or Dear _____:)

Our auditors, (name and address), are making an examination of our financial statements. For verification purposes, please advise them, by completing and signing the confirmation section below, whether or not the following information is correct.

Our company owed you ($ amount) as of (date). This liability to you represents (describe).

This letter should be forwarded directly to our auditors in the enclosed stamped envelope. Your prompt response will be appreciated.

Very truly yours,

_____
(Signature and title)

_____

CONFIRMATION

The above information is correct (subject to differences, if any, noted below).

Signature and title _____

Date _____

Details of exceptions or differences, if any _____

_____

_____

Figure 5-29
Mortgage Payable Confirmation

(Client name and address)

(Date)

(Name and address)

Gentlemen:

Our auditors, (name and address), are making an examination of our financial statements. For verification purposes, please furnish them with the following information as of (date) relative to our mortgage indebtedness to you.

1. Description of property mortgaged.
2. Original mortgage liability.
3. Unpaid balance.
4. Interest rate.
5. Due dates of interest and amortization payments.
6. Terms of amortization of principal.
7. Date to which interest has been paid.
8. Nature of defaults, if any.
9. Details of any changes in original mortgage agreement.
10. Any other information that may be helpful to our auditors.

A return envelope is enclosed for your convenience in replying directly to our auditors. Your prompt response will be appreciated.

Very truly yours,

_____
(Signature and title)

_____

Comment. This letter may be readily adapted for use in confirming mortgages receivable.

Figure 5-30
Bond Trustee Confirmation

(Client name and address)

(Date)

(Name and address)

Gentlemen:

Our auditors, (name and address), are making an examination of our financial statements. For verification purposes, please furnish them with the following information as of (date) concerning our issue of (bond description) for which you are acting as trustee.

1. The amount of bonds authorized.
2. Maturity dates and amounts.
3. The amount issued and certified by you as trustee, and the amount retired and cancelled.
3. The amount in your custody, uncancelled.
4. Interest rate and date to which interest has been paid.
5. Details as to any matured and past-due interest or other required payments.
6. Amount of cash or other assets held by you for unredeemed interest coupons, bond retirement, or otherwise. (Please provide details.)
7. Description of any property pledged, and of securities or other property held as collateral under the indenture terms.
8. Details of any default or violations of any covenants or restrictions of the trust indenture.

A return envelope is enclosed for your convenience in replying directly to our auditors. Your prompt response will be appreciated.

Very truly yours,

_____

(Signature and title)

Uniform Commercial Code (Form UCC 11)—Request for Information or Copies of Financing Statements and Statements of Assignment Filed with State

REQUEST FOR COPIES OR INFORMATION. Present in DUPLICATE to Filing Officer.

1 Debtor (Last Name First) and Address	Party requesting information or copies: (Name and Address)	For Filing Officer, Date, Time, No.-Filing Office

☐ INFORMATION REQUEST:　　　　　☐ COPY REQUEST:

Filing officer please furnish certificate showing if there is on file under the code as of _____, 19___ at _____ M., any presently effective financing statement filed pursuant to the UCC naming the above named debtor and any statement of assignment thereof; and if there is, giving the date and hour of filing of each such statement and the name(s) and address(es) of each secured party(ies) therein. Enclosed is uniform fee of $3.00.

Filing officer please furnish exact copies of each page of financing statements and statements of assignment listed below, at the rate of $1.00 each, which are on file with your office. Enclosed is $_____ fee for copies requested. In case any of said statements contain more than one page the undersigned agrees to pay the sum of $1.00 for each additional page payable in advance.

Date_____

(Signature of Requesting Party)

File No.	Date and Hour of Filing	Name(s) and Address(es) of Secured Party(ies) and Assignees, if any

CERTIFICATE: The undersigned filing officer hereby certifies that:

☐ the above listing is a record of all presently effective financing statements and statements of assignment which name the above debtor and which are on file in my office as of _____, 19___ at _____ M.

☐ the attached _____ pages are true and exact copies of all available financing statements or statements of assignment listed in above request

_____　　　　_____
Date　　　　　　　　　　　　Signature of Filing Officer

Approved by New York Secretary of State

APPROVED FOR USE IN MOST STATES

COPY 2

9/65 STANDARD FORM NEW YORK STATE FORM UCC-11

Comment. The above form is issued by New York State. UCC forms and provisions vary from state to state.

297

Figure 5-32
Pension Plan Trustee Confirmation

(Client name and address)

(Date)

(Name and address)

Gentlemen:

Our auditors, (name and address), are making an examination of our financial statements. For verification purposes, please furnish them with the following information on our (name of plan) pension plan of which you are trustee.

1.   Detailed statement of transactions between us (including payments made by us or refunds credited to us, with indication of period to which applicable) from (date) through (date).
2.   Detailed statement of amounts due you under the plan as of (date).
3.   Amounts owing to you for fees or other charges as of (date).
4.   Statement of assets in the pension fund.
5.   Description of amendments to the plan for the period (date) through (date).
6.   Any other information that may be helpful to our auditors.

A return envelope is enclosed for your convenience in replying directly to our auditors. Your prompt response will be appreciated.

Very truly yours,

_____

(Signature and title)

Figure 5-33
Pension Plan Actuary Confirmation

(Client name and address)

(Date)

(Name and address)

Gentlemen:

Our auditors, (name and address), are making an examination of our financial statements. For verification purposes, please furnish them with the following information as of (date) and for the year then ended, relative to our (name of plan) pension plan for which you are serving as actuary. Appropriate crossreferences may be made to sections of your report containing the information requested on any of the items listed, in which case a copy of your report should also be forwarded to our auditors.

1. Date of last actuarial valuation.
2. Actuarial cost method used.
3. Method of recognizing actuarial gains or losses including realized and unrealized gains or losses on securities.
4. Details of current provision including current service cost, past service cost and amortization period for past service cost, interest provision and reason therefor, and actuarial gains and losses.
5. Unfunded past service costs.
6. Actuarially computed value of vested benefits and the amount of any excess of that value over the total of the pension fund.
7. Amount of the net assets of the pension fund, the basis at which they are carried, and their aggregate market value.
8. Details of changes in any of the following during the period (date) through (date), with indication of the effect of such changes:
(a) Actuarial cost method.
(b) Amortization of past and prior service cost.
(c) Treatment of actuarial gains and losses.
(d) Actuarial assumptions.
(e) Plan provisions.
(f) Funding policies.

9. Description of employee categories and number of employees reflected in calculations.

A return envelope is enclosed for your convenience in replying directly to our auditors. Your prompt response will be appreciated.

Very truly yours,

_____

(Signature and date)

Figure 5-34
Landlord (or other Lessor) Confirmation

(Client name and address)

(Date)

(Name and address)

Gentlemen:

Our auditors, (name and address), are making an examination of our financial statements. For verification purposes, please furnish them with the following information as of (date) relative to the premises at (address), which we have leased from you.

1. Brief description of premises.
2. Lease period.
3. Rental terms.
4. Date to which rents have been paid and amounts due, if any.
5. Security deposits held.
6. Any other information that may be helpful.

A return envelope is enclosed for your convenience in replying directly to our auditors. Your prompt response will be appreciated.

Very truly yours,

_____

(Signature and title)

_____

Comment. Figures 5-34 and 5-35 may readily be adapted to apply to other types of leased property by substituting a description of the leased property for the reference to *premises.*

Figure 5-35
Tenant (or Other Lessee) Confirmation

(Client name and address)

(Date)

(Name and address)

Gentlemen:

Our auditors, (name and address), are making an examination of our financial statements. For verification purposes, please advise them, by completing and signing the confirmation section below, whether or not the following information as of (date) is correct relative to the premises at (address), which we have leased to you.

1. Premises _____
2. Lease period _____
3. Rental terms _____
4. Rent paid to _____
5. Rents due _____
6. Security deposits held _____
7. Other data _____

This letter should be forwarded directly to our auditors in the enclosed stamped envelope.

Very truly yours,

_____
(Signature and title)

_____

CONFIRMATION

The above information is correct (subject to differences, if any, noted below).

Date _____ Company _____

Signature and title _____

Details of exceptions or differences, if any _____
_____
_____

Figure 5-36
Business Insurance Confirmation

(Client name and address)

(Date)

(Name and address of
broker or underwriter)

Gentlemen:

Our auditors, (name and address), are making an examination of our financial statements. For verification purposes, please furnish them with the following information regarding our insurance policies in force with you at (date).

1. Name of insurance company.
2. Policy number.
3. Type of insurance.
4. Amount of coverage.
5. Period of policy.
6. Premium for the policy period.
7. Parties covered by policy.
8. Details as to:
(a) Claims pending at above date, and claims paid during the preceding (specify period).
(b) Premium refunds or other amounts due us at the above date.
(c) Amount and nature of indebtedness to you, if any, at the above date.

A return envelope is enclosed for your convenience in replying directly to our auditors. Your prompt response will be appreciated.

Very truly yours,

_____
(Signature and title)

Figure 5-37
Standard Confirmation Inquiry for Life Insurance Policies

STANDARD CONFIRMATION INQUIRY
FOR LIFE INSURANCE POLICIES

Developed by

AMERICAN INSTITUTE OF CERTIFIED PUBLIC ACCOUNTANTS
LIFE OFFICE MANAGEMENT ASSOCIATION
MILLION DOLLAR ROUND TABLE

> **ORIGINAL**
> To be mailed to accountant
>
> _____ 19___

Please furnish the information requested below in items 1 through 9 (and also in items 10 through 12 if any of those items are checked) for the policies identified on lines A, B and C. This information is requested as of the date indicated. IF THE ANSWER TO ANY ITEM IS "NONE," PLEASE SO STATE. The enclosed envelope is provided for the return of one copy of this form to the accountant named below.

(Ins. Co.) _____

_____
(Name of owner as shown on policy contracts)

Information requested as of _____

(Accountant) _____

Request authorized by _____

		Col. A	Col. B
A.	Policy number		
B.	Insured		
C.	Beneficiaries as shown on policies (if verification requested in item 11) Col. A— Col. B—		
1.	Face amount of basic policy	$	$
2.	Values shown as of (insert date if other than date requested)		

304

3. Premiums, including prepaid premiums, are paid to (insert date) _____

4. Policy surrender value (excluding dividends, additions and indebtedness adjustments) $____ $____

5. Surrender value of all dividend credits, including accumulations and additions $____ $____

6. Termination dividend currently available on surrender $____ $____

7. Other surrender values available to policyowner
   a. Prepaid premium value $____ $____
   b. Premium deposit funds $____ $____
   c. Other $____ $____

8. Outstanding policy loans, excluding accrued interest $____ $____

9. If any loans exist, complete either "a" or "b"
   a. Interest accrued on policy loans $____ $____
   b. 1.) Loan interest is paid to (enter date) _____
       2.) Interest rate is (enter rate) _____

The accountant will indicate by a check (✓) which if any of items 10-12 are to be answered

☐ **10.** Is there an assignee of record? (enter Yes or No) _____

☐ **11.** Is beneficiary of record as shown in item C above? (enter Yes or No*) ____ *

☐ **12.** Is the name of policyowner (subject to any assignment) as shown at the top of the form? (enter Yes or No) ____
     If No, enter name of policyowner of record. _____

*If answer to 11 is No, please give name of beneficiary or date of last beneficiary change. _____

Date _____   By _____   Title _____

For the insurance company addressed

Additional copies of this form are available from the American Institute of CPAs, 1211 Avenue of the Americas, New York, N. Y. 10036

305

Figure 5-38
Registrar and Transfer Agent Confirmation

(Client name and address)

(Date)

(Name and address)

Gentlemen:

Our auditors, (name and address), are making an examination of our financial statements. For verification purposes, please furnish them with the following information as of (date) relative to each class of our capital stock (or relative to our (description) capital stock).

1. Description of each class of stock and number of shares authorized.
2. Number of shares issued.
3. Number of shares outstanding.
4. Number of shares issued in the name of our company.
5. Number of shares reserved for certain purposes (please indicate the nature of the reservation).
6. Number of shares held by each of our officers and directors.
7. Stockholders holding 5% or more of the outstanding shares.

Also, please advise our auditors as to the amount of any indebtedness to you as of the above date for services rendered.

A return envelope is enclosed for your convenience in replying directly to our auditors. Your prompt response will be appreciated.

Very truly yours,

_____
(Signature and title)

Auditors' Reports

See Chapter 8 for accountants' reports on compilation and review of financial statements of nonpublic entities and for reports on unaudited financial statements of public entities.

SOME BASIC REPORTING PRINCIPLES

The auditor's responsibilities with respect to his report and opinion are based on the four standards of reporting. The first three require the auditor (a) to state whether the financial statements are in conformity with generally accepted accounting principles; (b) to report whether those principles have been applied on a basis consistent with the preceding period; and (c) to disclose in the report material matters that should have been disclosed by the client in the financial statements including notes to financial statements. It is the fourth reporting standard, however, that provides an explanation of the need for a clear differentiation among types of auditors' reports. That standard reads as follows:

"The report shall either contain an expression of opinion regarding the financial statements taken as a whole, or an assertion to the effect that an opinion cannot be expressed. When an overall opinion cannot be expressed, the reasons therefor should be stated. In all cases where an auditor's name is associated with financial statements, the report should contain a clear-cut indication of the character of the auditor's examination, if any, and the degree of responsibility he is taking."

The key idea expressed is that the auditor must report clearly and unambiguously on two matters with which, as auditor, he is plainly identified—the character of his examination, and the expression of an opinion.

The phrase in the fourth reporting standard, "financial statements taken as a whole," is interpreted (AU 509) as applying to a complete set of statements as well as to an individual statement. Moreover, under appropriate circumstances, the auditor may, in a single report, give one type of opinion (say, unqualified) for one of the financial statements, and a different opinion (say, qualified, adverse or disclaimer) on another statement.

Further, in clarifying the degree of responsibility he is assuming, if the auditor is expressing an opinion other than unqualified, all reasons therefor must be reported. Thus, if the report contains a qualified opinion or an adverse opinion because of material departures from generally accepted accounting principles, all such departures must be disclosed. Similarly, if the report is qualified or a disclaimer issued because of a scope limitation, the auditor must also disclose any departures from GAAP that may be known to him.

In deciding whether to issue a qualified opinion or, on the other hand, to deepen the qualification so that the report expresses, depending upon the reasons for the qualification(s), a disclaimer or an adverse opinion, a number of factors should be considered. A major factor is the degree of materiality of the matter or items in question. However, materiality is a complex concept encompassing the magnitude of a given item or matter either absolutely or relative to current and/or prior period income, assets, or other bases. The auditor must also consider if the exceptions are so pervasive as to affect many accounts, or if there are a number of exceptions which, in the aggregate, have so material an overall impact as to warrant the issuance of a disclaimer of opinion or an adverse opinion.

It is also important to note that when a qualified opinion is expressed for either a scope limitation or a departure from GAAP, a phrase bearing the words *except* or *exception* must appear in the opinion paragraph, just before or just after the phrase "in our opinion." However, the phrase "subject to" is used for an opinion qualified because of material uncertainties; and in a qualification as to consistency, the phrase "except for" appears in the latter part of the opinion paragraph since the qualification relates only to consistency.

AU 509 cautions that phrases such as the following should not be used in the opinion paragraph because they are not clear and depart from the required phraseology: "With the foregoing explanation," or "fairly presented when read in conjunction with Note X."

In addition to the required modification of the opinion paragraph for a report that is other than unqualified, an explanatory paragraph should be used to disclose the reasons for the exceptions and to describe the effects on the financial statements. But if a scope limitation is involved, an appropriate reference should also be included in the scope paragraph of the report. In the case of a qualification as to consistency, if the accounting change and the effects are described in a note to financial statements, the opinion paragraph should make reference to that note, and there would therefore be no need to repeat the information in an explanatory paragraph.

For illustrative auditors' reports and associated commentary on audited financial statements prepared in accordance with a comprehensive basis of accounting—such as cash basis or income tax basis—other than generally accepted accounting principles, see later section in this chapter on Special Reports.

Accountants' reports on unaudited financial statements are discussed and illustrated in Chapter 8, which covers unaudited financial statements of public companies as well as compilation and review of the (unaudited) financial statements of nonpublic companies.

The illustrative reports in Chapter 6 drawn from the Statements on Auditing Standards have been identified by an appropriate AU or SAS reference.

UNQUALIFIED OPINION REPORTS

The standard short-form report generally consists of two paragraphs—scope of examination paragraph and the opinion paragraph—but the separate paragraphs need not be, and usually are not, captioned as such. The illustrative reports in this book occasionally carry such captions but only for explanatory or identification purposes.

If the auditor is expressing an unqualified opinion, he nevertheless may introduce a separate report paragraph (usually a middle paragraph) if he wishes to emphasize some matter regarding the financial statements. But if such comments are made because of reservations or qualifications which preclude an unqualified opinion, they must also be referred to in the opinion paragraph whose wording should then correspond to the type of opinion deemed appropriate in the circumstances—that is, qualified, adverse, or disclaimer.

The report should be dated and should be signed by the auditor. The principles covering dating of the auditor's report are set forth in AU 530. The general principle is that the date of completion of the field work should be used as the report date.

The report may be addressed to the company or, if engaged by them, to its board of directors or stockholders, or to both the board and stockholders. If the report is on the financial statements of a sole proprietorship or partnership, it should be addressed, as indicated by the circumstances, to the proprietor, the partners, or the general partner. AU 509 states that if, as happens occasionally, the auditor is asked by a client to examine the financial statements of another company that is not his client (perhaps in connection with a contemplated acquisition), the report is customarily addressed to the client and not to the company examined or the latter's directors or stockholders.

The standard short-form report expressing an unqualified opinion is often referred to by bankers and other credit grantors as a *clean certificate* (i.e., one without qualification). It is submitted if the auditor has performed an examination in accordance with generally accepted auditing standards, including all procedures necessary in the circumstances, and has formed the opinion that the financial statements are fair presentations in conformity with generally accepted accounting principles applied on a basis consistent with the preceding period.

For reasons that will be apparent, several of the reports included in the classification, Unqualified Opinion Reports, have explanatory middle paragraphs or may not make reference to consistency, but they are unqualified in character and are properly included in this classification.

Figure 6-1
Unqualified Opinion

Standard Report—Single Year (AU 509)

August 25, 198Y

To the Stockholders and Board of Directors
The X Corporation
Chicago, Illinois

(SCOPE PARAGRAPH)

We have examined the balance sheet of the X Corporation as of (at) June 30, 198Y, and the related statements of income and retained earnings and changes in financial position for the year then ended. Our examination was made in accordance with generally accepted auditing standards and, accordingly, included such tests of the accounting records and such other auditing procedures as we considered necessary in the circumstances.

(OPINION PARAGRAPH)

In our opinion, the financial statements referred to above present fairly the financial position of the X Corporation as of (at) June 30, 198Y, and the results of its operations and the changes in its financial position for the year then ended, in conformity with generally accepted accounting principles applied on a basis consistent with that of the preceding year.

(Signature of auditor)

Figure 6-2
Unqualified Opinion

Standard Report—Comparative Financial
Statements (AU 505)

February 25, 198Y

To the Stockholders and Board of Directors
ABC Corporation
Chicago, Illinois

We have examined the balance sheets of ABC Company as of (at) December 31, 198Y and 198X, and the related statements of income, retained earnings, and changes in financial position for the years then ended. Our examinations were made in accordance with generally accepted auditing standards and, accordingly, included such tests of the accounting records and such other auditing procedures as we considered necessary in the circumstances.

In our opinion, the financial statements referred to above present fairly the financial position of ABC Company as of (at) December 31, 198Y and 198X, and the results of its operations and the changes in its financial position for the years then ended, in conformity with generally accepted accounting principles applied on a consistent basis.

Figure 6-3
Unqualified Opinion

Parent Company and Consolidated Statements

We have examined the balance sheet of X Company, Inc. (a (Delaware Corporation) and the consolidated balance sheet of X Company, Inc. and subsidiaries as of December 31, 198Y and 198X, and the related statements of earnings, retained earnings, and changes in financial position for the years then ended. Our examination was made . . .

In our opinion, the financial statements referred to above present fairly the financial position of X Company, Inc. and the consolidated financial position of X Company, Inc. and subsidiaries at December 31, 198Y and 198X, and the respective results of their operations and the changes in their financial position for the years then ended. . .

Figure 6-4
Unqualified Opinion

Single Balance Sheet; Comparative Income
and Other Statements

We have examined the balance sheet of X Company as of December 31, 198Y and the related statements of income, retained earnings, and changes in financial position for the years ended December 31, 198Y and 198X. Our examination was made. . .

In our opinion, the financial statements referred to above present fairly the financial position of X Company as of Dec. 31, 198Y and the results of its operations and the changes in its financial position for the years ended December 31, 198Y and 198X, in conformity with generally accepted accounting principles applied on a consistent basis.

Figure 6-5
Unqualified Opinion

Two Comparative Balance Sheets; Comparative
Income and Other Statements for Five Years

We have examined the consolidated balance sheets of ABC Company and subsidiaries as of Dec. 31, 198Y and 198X, and the related statements of income and retained income, and changes in financial position for the five years ended December 31, 198Y. Our examination was made in accordance with generally accepted auditing standards and, accordingly, included such tests of the accounting records and such other auditing procedures as we considered necessary in the circumstances.

In our opinion, the aforementioned consolidated financial statements present fairly the financial position of ABC Company and subsidiaries as of December 31, 198Y and 198X, and the results of operations and changes in financial position for the five years ended December 31, 198Y, in conformity with generally accepted accounting principles applied on a consistent basis.

Figure 6-6
Unqualified Opinion

First Examination of Newly-Formed Company

We have examined the balance sheet of X Company as of December 31, 198Y, and the related statements of income and retained earnings and of changes in financial position for the period from March 15, 198Y, the date of incorporation, to December 31, 198Y. Our examination. . .

In our opinion, the financial statements referred to above present fairly the financial position of X Company as of December 31, 198Y, and the results of its operations and changes in its financial position for the period from March 15, 198Y to December 31, 198Y, in conformity with generally accepted accounting principles.

Comment. Inasmuch as the report covers the first period of the company's existence, obviously no reference can be made to consistency.

Figure 6-7
Unqualified Opinion

Balance Sheet Only

We have examined the balance sheet of X Company as of December 31, 198Y. Our examination was made. . .

In our opinion, the balance sheet referred to above presents fairly the financial position of X Company as of December 31, 198Y, in conformity with generally accepted accounting principles applied on a basis consistent with that of the preceding year.

Figure 6-8
Unqualified Opinion

Comparative Statements of Income Only

We have examined the statements of income of X Company for the years ended December 31, 198Y and 198X. Our examination was made. . .

In our opinion, the statements of income referred to above present fairly the results of operations of X Company for the years ended December 31, 198Y and 198X, in conformity with generally accepted accounting principles applied on a consistent basis.

Figure 6-9
Unqualified Opinion

Sole Proprietorship or Partnership Statements
Prepared In Conformity with GAAP

We have examined the balance sheet of the X Company, a partnership (sole proprietorship), as of December 31, 198Y, and the related statements of income, changes in partners' equity (owner's equity), and changes in financial position, for the year then ended. Our examination. . .

We did not examine the personal accounting records of the partners (proprietor) or any of the other activities in which they (he) may have been engaged. The aforementioned financial statements relate only to the business of X Company and do not include any assets, liabilities, or results of operations attributable to the partners' (proprietor's) individual activities. No provision has been made, moreover, for Federal and State income taxes inasmuch as these taxes are computed on income from all sources and are the personal responsibility of the partners (proprietor). Similarly, the income statement does not reflect any salary to partners (the proprietor).

In our opinion, the financial statements referred to above present fairly the financial position of the X Company. . .

Comment. Even though the financial statements of a partnership or sole proprietorship may have been prepared in conformity with GAAP, some accountants prefer to describe the statement of financial position as a Statement of Assets and Liabilities. For statements prepared on a comprehensive basis of accounting other than GAAP (e.g., tax basis or cash basis), see section in this chapter on Special Reports, or Chapter 8 on reports on compilation or review of such financial statements.

LIMITATION IN SCOPE OF EXAMINATION

Limitations in the scope of examination may arise because of circumstances like:
1. Client restrictions.
2. Timing problems such as late retention of the auditor, which make it impracticable for him to undertake certain major procedures like confirmation of receivables.
3. Poor accounting records.
4. Unavailability of desired evidential matter.

These limitations, if material, may require the auditor to issue a qualified opinion or to disclaim an opinion.

An auditor may conceivably find that in circumstances which make it impracticable, unreasonable, or impossible to undertake certain customary auditing procedures, he has nevertheless been able to satisfy himself by the application of other auditing procedures. Under such circumstances, he can theoretically issue an unqualified opinion, but he must recognize that he bears a greater burden than otherwise if called upon to justify the report rendered. Two additional points should be noted. First, client restrictions can rarely if ever be used to justify the omission of customary or necessary auditing procedures. Further, AU 331 makes it quite clear that satisfaction as to ending inventory quantities cannot be achieved without making or observing some physical counts of the inventory.

As stated in AU 509, the wording in the opinion paragraph should indicate that the qualification relates to the possible effects on the financial statements rather than to the scope limitation itself.

When the auditor qualifies his opinion or disclaims an opinion because of scope limitation, he should give in a separate report paragraph *all* substantive reasons for doing so, as well as any reservations he may have as to fair presentation in conformity with generally accepted accounting principles or as to consistency.

Accountants' reports on unaudited financial statements are discussed and illustrated in Chapter 8, which covers unaudited statements of public companies as well as compilation and review of the financial statements of nonpublic companies.

Figure 6-10
Limitation in Scope of Examination

Inventories Not Observed—
Qualified Opinion (AU 509)

(SCOPE PARAGRAPH)

Except as explained in the following paragraph, our examination . . . and other such auditing procedures as we considered necessary in the circumstances. . .

(SEPARATE PARAGRAPH)

We did not observe the taking of the physical inventories as of December 31, 198Y, (stated at $_____), and December 31, 198X (stated at $_____), since those dates were prior to the time we were initially engaged as auditors for the Company. Due to the nature of the Company's records, we were unable to satisfy ourselves as to the inventory quantities by means of other auditing procedures.

(OPINION PARAGRAPH)

In our opinion, except for the effects of such adjustments, if any, as might have been determined to be necessary had we been able to observe the physical inventories. . .)

_____

Comment. Depending upon the materiality factor, the effects of the scope limitation mentioned above might also have led to a disclaimer of opinion.

Figure 6-11
Limitation in Scope of Examination

No Physical Inventory; Missing Records—
Disclaimer of Opinion (AU 509)

(SCOPE PARAGRAPH)

. . . Except as set forth in the following paragraph, our examination was made . . . considered necessary in the circumstances.

(SEPARATE PARAGRAPH)

The Company did not take a physical inventory of merchandise, stated at $_____ in the accompanying financial statements as of December 31, 198X, and at $_____ as of December 31, 198Y. Further, evidence supporting the cost of property and equipment acquired prior to December 31, 198X is no longer available. The company's records do not permit the application of adequate alternative procedures regarding the inventories or the cost of property and equipment.

(DISCLAIMER PARAGRAPH)

Since the Company did not take physical inventories and we were unable to apply adequate alternative procedures regarding inventories and the cost of property and equipment, as noted in the preceding paragraph, the scope of our work was not sufficient to enable us to express, and we do not express, an opinion on the financial statements referred to above.

Comment. The procedures actually performed should not be specified since such information would tend to overshadow and negate the disclaimer of opinion. Also, piecemeal opinions (on specific accounts) should not be issued in conjunction with a disclaimer or adverse opinion. (AU 509.48)

Figure 6-12
Limitation in Scope of Examination

Limited Scope as to Opening Inventories—
Split Opinion: Unqualified Opinion on Balance Sheet,
Disclaimer on Other Statements (AU 542)

(SCOPE PARAGRAPH)

We have examined the balance sheet of X Company as of September 30, 198Y, and the related statements of income and retained earnings and changes in financial position for the year then ended. Our examination was made in accordance with generally accepted auditing standards, and accordingly included such tests of the accounting records and such other auditing procedures as we considered necessary in the circumstances, except as stated in the following paragraph.

(MIDDLE PARAGRAPH)

Because we were not engaged as auditors until after September 30, 198X, we were not present to observe the physical inventory taken at that date and we have not satisfied ourselves by means of other procedures concerning inventory quantities. The amount of the inventory at September 30, 198X enters materially into the determination of the results of operations and changes in financial position for the year ended September 30, 198Y. Therefore, we do not express an opinion on the accompanying statements of income and retained earnings and changes in financial position for the year ended September 30, 198Y.

(OPINION PARAGRAPH)

In our opinion, the accompanying balance sheet presents fairly the financial position of X Company at September 30, 198Y, in conformity with generally accepted accounting principles applied on a basis consistent with that of the preceding year.

Comment. It is assumed, in the foregoing report, that the auditor was able to satisfy himself with respect to consistency.

Figure 6-13
Limitation in Scope of Examination

Investee Not Examined—Qualified Opinion

. . . necessary in the circumstances, except as described in the following paragraph.

In accordance with the terms of our engagement we did not undertake an examination of the financial statements and records of the ABC Joint Venture, the company's investment in which, as described in Note X to the financial statements, is stated at ($ amount) and ($ amount) as of, respectively, December 31, 198Y and 198X. Accordingly, we are unable to, and do not, express an opinion as to this investment.

In our opinion, except for the effects of such adjustments, if any, as might have been determined to be necessary had we been able to examine the financial statements of the joint venture referred to in the preceding paragraph, the financial statements referred to above present fairly. . .

DEPARTURE FROM GAAP

When the financial statements reflect a material departure from generally accepted accounting principles, the auditor should either qualify his opinion or express an adverse opinion (depending upon materiality and other factors) and give the reasons therefor in his report.

GAAP also encompasses the principle that information essential for a fair presentation should be disclosed in the financial statements including accompanying notes. The third reporting standard states, in effect, that if such disclosures are not made in the financial statements, the auditor similarly should express a qualified or adverse opinion and should disclose the information in his report. But see AU 545 for an exception to this rule for omission of a statement of changes in financial position, and AU 435 which refers to the suspension by FASB Statement No. 21 (AC 2083) of the reporting of earnings per share and segment information by nonpublic enterprises.

Rule 203 of the AICPA Code of Professional Ethics states that the auditor shall not express an unqualified opinion that the financial statements are in conformity with GAAP if the statements reflect a departure from an officially promulgated (e.g., by the Financial Accounting Standards Board) principle, with material effect on the financial statements, unless the auditor can demonstrate that due to unusual circumstances the statements would otherwise be misleading. He can then issue an unqualified opinion but he must disclose in his report the departure, the effect, and the reasons the statements would otherwise have been misleading. See Figure 6-18 for an illustration of such a report. It should be cautioned, however, that expressing an unqualified opinion in the event of a departure from an officially promulgated principle should be considered an extremely rare occurrence.

Figure 6-14
Departure from GAAP

Lease Obligations Not Capitalized—
Qualified Opinion (AU 509)

(SEPARATE PARAGRAPH)

The Company has excluded from property and debt in the accompanying balance sheet certain lease obligations, which, in our opinion, should be capitalized in order to conform with generally accepted accounting principles. If these lease obligations were capitalized, property would be increased by $_____$, long-term debt by $_____$, and retained earnings by $_____$ as of December 31, 198Y, and net income and earnings per share would be increased (decreased) by $_____$ and $_____$ respectively for the year then ended.

(OPINION PARAGRAPH)

In our opinion, except for the effects of not capitalizing lease obligations, as discussed in the preceding paragraph, the financial statements present fairly. . .

Comment. If the company were to disclose the above-noted facts in a note to financial statements, the opinion would remain qualified but the separate paragraph might read somewhat as follows:

(SEPARATE PARAGRAPH)

As more fully described in Note X to the financial statements, the Company has excluded certain lease obligations from property and debt in the accompanying balance sheet. In our opinion, generally accepted accounting principles require that such obligations be included in the balance sheet.

Figure 6-15
Departure from GAAP

Inadequate Disclosure: Dividend Restrictions—
Qualified Opinion (AU 545)

(EXPLANATORY PARAGRAPH)

On July 15, 198Y, the company issued debentures in the amount of $_____ for the purpose of financing plant expansion. The debenture agreement restricts the payment of future cash dividends to earnings after June 30, 198Y.

(OPINION PARAGRAPH)

In our opinion, except for the omission of the information in the preceding paragraph, the aforementioned financial statements present fairly. . .

Figure 6-16
Departure from GAAP

Inadequate Disclosure: Omission of Statement
of Changes in Financial Position—
Qualified Opinion (AU 545)

We have examined the balance sheet of X Company as of December 31, 198Y, and the related statements of income and retained earnings for the year then ended. Our examination was made in accordance with generally accepted auditing standards, and accordingly included such tests of the accounting records and such other auditing procedures as we considered necessary in the circumstances.

The company declined to present a statement of changes in financial position for the year ended December 31, 198Y. Presentation of such statement summarizing the company's financing and investing activities and other changes in its financial position is required by Opinion No. 19 of the Accounting Principles Board.

In our opinion, except that the omission of a statement of changes in financial position results in an incomplete presentation as explained in the preceding paragraph, the aforementioned financial statements present fairly the financial position of X Company at December 31, 198Y, and the results of its operations for the year then ended, in conformity with generally accepted accounting principles applied on a basis consistent with that of the preceding year.

Figure 6-17
Departure from GAAP

Fixed Assets at Appraisal Value; Deferred
Taxes Not Provided for—
Adverse Opinion (AU 509)

(SEPARATE PARAGRAPH)

As discussed in Note X to the financial statements, the Company carries its property, plant and equipment accounts at appraisal values and provides depreciation on the basis of such values. Further, the Company does not provide for income taxes with respect to differences between financial income and taxable income arising because of the use, for income tax purposes, of the installment method of reporting gross profit from certain types of sales. Generally accepted accounting principles, in our opinion, require that property, plant and equipment be stated at an amount not in excess of cost, reduced by depreciation based on such amount, and that deferred income taxes be provided. Because of the departures from generally accepted accounting principles identified above, as of December 31, 198Y, inventories have been increased $_____ by inclusion in manufacturing overhead of depreciation in excess of that based on cost; property, plant and equipment, less accumulated depreciation, is carried at $_____ in excess of an amount based on the cost to the Company; and allocated income tax of $_____ has not been recorded; resulting in an increase of $_____ in retained earnings and in appraisal surplus of $_____. For the year ended December 31, 198Y, cost of goods sold has been increased $_____ because of the effects of the depreciation accounting referred to above and deferred income taxes of $_____ have not been provided, resulting in an increase in net income and earnings per share of $_____ and $_____ respectively.

(OPINION PARAGRAPH)

In our opinion, because of the effects of the matters discussed in the preceding paragraph, the financial statements referred to above do not present fairly, in conformity with generally accepted accounting principles, the financial position of X Company as of December 31, 198Y, or the results of its operations and changes in its financial position for the year then ended.

Comment. In order to highlight the fact that an adverse opinion is being expressed, some accountants head such reports with the caption ADVERSE OPINION. Further, when an adverse opinion is expressed, no reference should be made to consistency in the opinion paragraph inasmuch as an opinion as to consistency implies adherence to GAAP. But exceptions as to consistency can be reported in the explanatory paragraph. (AU 509).

Figure 6-18
Departure from GAAP

Departure from Promulgated Accounting Principle, But Not From GAAP— Unqualified Opinion

(EXPLANATORY PARAGRAPH)

The company is accounting for (identify) on the basis of (describe). This treatment does not correspond with the accounting method adopted by the Financial Accounting Standards Board in its Statement No. X, which states that (describe). If Statement No. X had been followed, net income for the year 198Y and retained earnings as of December 31, 198Y would have been increased (decreased) by $ (amount) and $ (amount), respectively. It is the Company's judgment, in which we concur, that the application of the accounting method prescribed by the FASB would have resulted in misleading financial statements for the reason that (explain), and it is therefore our opinion that the Company's treatment is in conformity with generally accepted accounting principles.

(OPINION PARAGRAPH)

In our opinion, the financial statements referred to above present fairly. . .

Comment. It is only in extremely rare circumstances that the auditor can issue an unqualified opinion if the financial statements reflect a departure (having material effects) from an accounting principle promulgated by the FASB (or official body designated by AICPA Council to issue GAAP pronouncements). See AU 509; Rule 203 of the AICPA's Code of Professional Ethics; and Code Rule Interpretations Nos. 203-1 and 203-2.

MATERIAL UNCERTAINTIES CONCERNING FUTURE EVENTS

When, with respect to the financial statements, there are material uncertainties concerning future events, and reasonable estimates cannot be made as to their outcome and impact on the financial statements, the auditor should disclose the circumstances and their possible impact in a separate paragraph of his report, and he ordinarily would issue a qualified opinion. However, while AU 509 states that the report disclosure and a qualified opinion should serve adequately to inform users of the financial statements, it also indicates that the auditor is not precluded from issuing a disclaimer rather than a qualified opinion.

The phrase "subject to" rather than "except for" is used in the opinion paragraph to denote the qualification based on uncertainties.

Uncertainties of the type considered here, whose outcome may have a material effect upon the financial statements depending upon the individual circumstances, may include, as mentioned in AU 509, such matters as: recoverability of a deferred cost; the likelihood that material sums may become collectible or payable as a result of litigation or income tax adjustments; going concern difficulties resulting from recurring operating losses, inability to obtain adequate financing, working capital deficiencies, or lack of compliance with provisions of loan agreements; development-stage financial problems. (Fully relevant to this subject is AC 4311 which incorporates FASB Statement No. 5, as amended, on Accounting for Contingencies.)

Figure 6-19
Material Uncertainties Concerning Future Events

Lawsuit—Qualified Opinion (AU 509)

(EXPLANATORY PARAGRAPH)

As discussed in Note X to the financial statements, the Company is defendant in a lawsuit alleging infringement of certain patent rights and claiming royalties and punitive damages. The Company has filed a counter action, and preliminary hearings and discovery proceedings on both actions are in progress. Company officers and counsel believe the Company has a good chance of prevailing, but the ultimate outcome of the lawsuits cannot presently be determined, and no provision for any liability that may result has been made in the financial statements.

(OPINION PARAGRAPH)

In our opinion, subject to the effects, if any, on the financial statements of the ultimate resolution of the matter discussed in the preceding paragraph, the financial statements referred to above present fairly. . .

or

In our opinion, subject to the effects of such adjustments, if any, as might have been required had the outcome of the uncertainty referred to in the preceding paragraph been known, the financial statements referred to above present fairly. . .

Figure 6-20
Material Uncertainties Concerning Future Events

Uncertainty As to Going Concern Status—
Qualified Opinion

(EXPLANATORY PARAGRAPH)

The financial statements identified above have been prepared on the basis of generally accepted accounting principles applicable to a going concern which contemplates the realization of assets and the liquidation of liabilities in the normal course of business. However, the company has incurred losses from operations in each of the five years ended December 31, 198Y, and the deficit in stockholders' equity amounts to ($ amount) and ($ amount) as of December 31, 198Y and 198X, respectively. Moreover, as described in Note X to the financial statements, the Company does not meet the working capital requirements under long-term debt agreements, although these requirements have been waived until December 31, 198Z. The foregoing circumstances indicate that continuation of the Company as a going concern is dependent upon a combination of profitable operations and additional financing from stockholders or other outside sources.

(OPINION PARAGRAPH)

In our opinion, subject to the effects, if any, on the financial statements of the ultimate resolution of the uncertainties as to the Company's status as a going concern described in the preceding paragraph, the aforementioned financial statements present fairly. . .

Figure 6-21
Material Uncertainties Concerning Future Events

Company in Development Stage—
Qualified Opinion

(EXPLANATORY PARAGRAPH)

The aforementioned financial statements have been prepared on the basis of generally accepted accounting principles applicable to a going concern, which contemplates the realization of assets and the liquidation of liabilities in the normal course of business. The Company, however, has been in the development stage since its organization on March 15, 198W, and the recoverability of the cost of its assets as well as the achievement of profitable operations are dependent upon such future events as obtaining adequate financing and experiencing a significant increase in revenue, the outcome of which is indeterminable as of December 31, 198Y.

(OPINION PARAGRAPH)

In our opinion, subject to the ultimate resolution of the uncertainties described in the preceding paragraph relating to the Company's status as a going concern, the financial statements referred to above present fairly. . .

Comment. As defined in FASB Statement No. 7 (AC 2062), an enterprise is in the development stage if it is devoting substantially all its efforts to establishing a new business, and either principal operations have not begun or have commenced but have not yielded significant revenue. AC 2062 also specifies additional information and disclosures to be made by the company relating to its status as a development-stage enterprise.

REPORTING ON INCONSISTENCY

The second reporting standard reads: "The report shall state whether such principles have been consistently observed in the current period in relation to the preceding period." The standard is elaborated upon in AU 546.

When a change in accounting principle (which includes accounting methods) has occurred, the auditor should modify the opinion paragraph of his report as to consistency (often termed a "qualification as to consistency") and refer to the explanation presented in a footnote to the financial statements or, in the absence of such a footnote, to an explanatory paragraph in the auditor's report. The auditor should indicate his concurrence with the change by using a phrase such as "with which we concur" even though such concurrence is implied. But if the auditor does not concur because either the newly adopted principle or the method of accounting for the change is not in conformity with generally accepted accounting principles, then the report would have to express either a qualified opinion on the statements as a whole or an adverse opinion and not simply a qualification as to consistency alone.

As required by APB Opinion No. 20 and the auditing standards, all of the following must be disclosed in the financial statements regarding the change (or in the auditor's report): the nature of the change; effect on financial statements; and justification for the change including a clear explanation of why the newly adopted method is preferable.

It is beyond the scope of this book to outline in any detail the methods of accounting for different types of changes in accounting methods as discussed particularly in APB Opinion No. 20, but the method to be employed can be gleaned from the illustrative reports presented in this chapter. It may be helpful, however, to note briefly the accounting for some of the major types of accounting changes.

1. Some changes (as from LIFO to another inventory pricing method or a change in method of accounting for long-term construction-type contracts) are accounted for by restating financial statements of prior periods.

2. Other changes are accounted for by including the cumulative effect of the change in net income for the period as a separate item (and reflecting on the face of the statements certain pro-forma effects of retroactive application).

3. A change in the reporting entity (which includes a business combination accounted for as a pooling-of-interests) comes under the consistency standard, but there is no change in the reporting entity, in terms of consistency, as a result of purchase, disposition, or liquidation of a subsidiary or branch.

4. Changes in accounting estimates, while not an inconsistency, must be reported in the year of change and in the affected future years, but prior years' statements should not be restated.

5. A correction of an error in previously issued financial statements is treated as a prior year adjustment and not as an inconsistency, but the financial statements of the year the error was discovered and corrected should dislcose the effect of the correction on the income of the current and prior periods.

6. Changes in statement classification ordinarily affect comparability rather than consistency, and should be disclosed in notes to financial statements, if material.

It should be emphasized that comparability must be considered whether or not the consistency standard is applicable. Any significant circumstances affecting the comparability of the financial statements with prior periods (and, in some situations, with future periods) should be disclosed in notes to the financial statements. If the auditor wishes to emphasize the matter, he may make reference to it in an explanatory paragraph of his report, but if the consistency standard is not involved, the opinion paragraph would not ordinarily be affected.

Figure 6-22
Reporting on Inconsistency

Prior Years Restated—Single Year Statements (AU 546)

(OPINION PARAGRAPH)

. . . applied on a basis consistent with that of the preceding year after giving retroactive effect to the change, with which we concur, in the method of accounting for long-term construction contracts as described in Note X to the financial statements.

Comment. Inasmuch as the statements are consistent after giving retroactive effect to the accounting change, the opinion is not "qualified as to consistency," but the opinion paragraph must be appropriately modified.

Figure 6-23
Reporting on Inconsistency

Prior Years Restated—Comparative Statements (AU 546)

(OPINION PARAGRAPH)

. . . applied on a consistent basis after restatement for the change, with which we concur, in the method of accounting for long-term construction contracts as described in Note X to the financial statements.

Comment. According to AU 546, in a report covering comparative statements, no reference need be made to a change in accounting principle or the related restatement if the report includes the statements for the year of change together with the statements for a year subsequent to the year of change.

Figure 6-24
Reporting on Inconsistency

Prior Years Not Restated—
Single Year Statements (AU 546)

(OPINION PARAGRAPH)

. . . in conformity with generally accepted accounting principles which, except for the change, with which we concur, in the method of computing depreciation as described in Note X to the financial statements, have been applied on a basis consistent with that of the preceding year.

Figure 6-25
Reporting on Inconsistency

Prior Years Not Restated—
Comparative Statements (AU 546)

(OPINION PARAGRAPH)

. . . in conformity with generally accepted accounting principles consistently applied during the period except for the change, with which we concur, in the method of computing depreciation as described in Note X to the financial statements.

Comment. According to AU 546, if comparative statements for two or more years are being reported on, reference should continue to be made to the change (where restatement is not required) as long as the year of change is included. If the year of change is other than the earliest year reported on, the opinion paragraph should read as shown above. But if the year of change is the earliest year included in the report, there is no inconsistency and the opinion paragraph might read:

(OPINION PARAGRAPH)

. . . in conformity with generally accepted accounting principles consistently applied during the period subsequent to the change, made as of January 1, 198 , in the method of computing depreciation as described in Note X to the financial statements.

Figure 6-26
Reporting on Inconsistency

Accounting Change From FIFO to LIFO

(OPINION PARAGRAPH)

. . . in conformity with generally accepted accounting principles which, except for the change, with which we concur, in the method of valuing inventories as described in Note X to the financial statements, have been applied on a consistent basis.

NOTE X TO FINANCIAL STATEMENTS (AU 9420-3)

In 198Y, the Company adopted the last in, first out (LIFO) method of costing inventory. Previously, the first in, first out (FIFO) method of costing inventory was used. Management believes that the LIFO method has the effect of minimizing the impact of price level changes on inventory valuations and generally matches current costs against current revenues in the income statement. The effect of the change was to reduce net income by $xxxx ($.xx per share) from that which would otherwise have been reported. There is no cumulative effect on prior years since the December 31, 198X inventory value is the beginning inventory value under the LIFO method.

Comment. AU 9420-3 states that for a change from FIFO to LIFO made in the earliest year presented and reported on, the auditor need make no reference to the change inasmuch as there is no inconsistency in the application of accounting principles and, moreover, comparability is not affected since no cumulative effect is reported in the year of the change. For this special case of a change from FIFO to LIFO, see AU 9420-3 and AC 1051.26.

Figure 6-27
Reporting on Inconsistency

Change in Presentation of Statement of
Changes in Financial Position

(OPINION PARAGRAPH)

. . . in conformity with generally accepted accounting principles applied on a consistent basis after restatement for the change, with which we concur, in the presentation of the statements of changes in financial position as described in Note X to the financial statements.

Comment. AU 420 restates the conclusion in APB No. 20 (AC 1051) that material changes in classification should be explained in the financial statements or accompanying notes but that they do not affect the opinion as to consistency. However, certain changes in the statement of changes in financial position—for example, from *cash* to *working capital* as the basis for describing the changes in financial position—do involve the consistency standard and, if material, call for an exception as to consistency. But if the prior years' statements reported on have been restated, as in the illustrative report above, the auditor's report should make reference to the change even though the restatement has placed the statements on a consistent basis.

Figure 6-28
Reporting on Inconsistency

First Examination; Scope Limitation
as to Prior Year(s)—
Consistency Disclaimer; Opinion on
Balance Sheet Only (AU 546)

(SCOPE PARAGRAPH)

. . . and such other auditing procedures as we considered necessary in the circumstances, except as indicated in the following paragraph.

(EXPLANATORY PARAGRAPH)

Because of major inadequacies in the Company's accounting records for the previous year, it was not practicable to extend our auditing procedures to enable us to express an opinion on results of operations and changes in financial position for the year ended December 31, 198Y or on the consistency of application of accounting principles with the preceding year.

(OPINION PARAGRAPH)

In our opinion, the accompanying balance sheet presents fairly the financial position of X Company as of December 31, 198Y in conformity with generally accepted accounting principles.

Comment. The disclaimer in the explanatory paragraph applies to consistency as well as to the financial statements other than the balance sheet.

Figure 6-29
Reporting on Inconsistency

Change to Acceptable Principle; Consistency Reference Omitted If Prior Years Are Not Restated (AU 546)

(EXPLANATORY PARAGRAPH)

The Company has kept its records and has prepared its financial statements for previous years on the cash basis with no recognition having been accorded accounts receivable, accounts payable, or accrued expenses. At the beginning of the current year the Company adopted the accrual basis of accounting. Although appropriate adjustments have been made to retained earnings as of the beginning of the year, it was not practicable to determine what adjustments would be necessary in the financial statements of the preceding year to restate results of operations and changes in financial position in conformity with the accounting principles used in the current year.

(OPINION PARAGRAPH)

In our opinion, the aforementioned financial statements present fairly the financial position of X Company as of October 31, 198Y, and the results of its operations and the changes in its financial position for the year then ended, in conformity with generally accepted accounting principles.

Figure 6-30
Reporting on Inconsistency

Accounting Change Not Justified—
Opinion Qualified As to Both GAAP
and Consistency (AU 546)

(EXPLANATORY PARAGRAPH)

As disclosed in Note X to the financial statements, the Company has adopted (description of newly adopted method), whereas it previously used (description of previous method). Although use of the (description of newly adopted method) is in conformity with generally accepted accounting principles, in our opinion the Company has not provided reasonable justification for making a change as required by Opinion No. 20 of the Accounting Principles Board.

(OPINION PARAGRAPH)

In our opinion, except for the change in accounting principles as stated above, the aforementioned financial statements present fairly the financial position of X Company at December 31, 198Y, and the results of its operations and changes in its financial position for the year then ended, in conformity with generally accepted accounting principles applied on a basis consistent with that of the preceding year.

Figure 6-31
Reporting on Inconsistency

Accounting Change To An Unacceptable
Accounting Principle—
Opinion Qualified As to Both GAAP
and Consistency (AU 546)

(EXPLANATORY PARAGRAPH)

The Company previously recorded its land at cost but adjusted the amounts to appraised values during the year, with a corresponding increase in stockholders' equity in the amount of $_____. In our opinion, the new basis on which land is recorded is not in conformity with generally accepted accounting principles.

(OPINION PARAGRAPH)

In our opinion, except for the change to recording appraisal values as described above, the aforementioned financial statements present fairly the financial position of X Company at December 31, 198Y, and the results of its operations and changes in its financial position for the year then ended, in conformity with generally accepted accounting principles applied on a basis consistent with that of the preceding year.

Comment. If the effect of the adoption of the unacceptable principle is sufficiently material, an adverse opinion should be expressed. In that event, no reference to consistency should be made in the opinion paragraph. (AU 546.)

UTILIZING REPORTS OF OTHER AUDITORS

Presented in AU 543 are the reporting guidelines for the principal auditor who utilizes the work and reports of other independent auditors who have examined the financial statements of one or more subsidiaries, divisions or branches included in the consolidated or combined statements of the company as a whole. The method of reporting will depend on some basic decisions that the principal auditor must make.

He must first decide whether he should in fact serve as the principal auditor and report on the enterprise as a whole, taking into account the materiality of the portion of the financial statements examined by him as compared with that of the other auditors, as well as his knowledge of the financial statements as a whole.

Then he must decide whether to accept responsibility for the work of the other auditor. If he does, and is in a position to express an overall opinion on the financial statements, he should refrain from making mention of the other auditor. But if the principal auditor is unwilling to assume the responsibility for the work and report of the other auditor, he may decide to utilize that report on the basis of a divided responsibility, assuming that he has satisfied himself as to the reputation and independence of the other auditor.

In that event, the principal auditor must disclose in both the scope and opinion paragraphs of the report the fact of the divided responsibility. Dollar amounts or percentages of total assets, revenues or other important data that indicate the magnitude of the portion examined by the other auditor should be disclosed. The other auditor's name may be mentioned provided he consents and his report accompanies the principal auditor's report. But it should be emphasized that, by itself, the reference to the other auditor in the opinion paragraph does not signify a qualified opinion. Of course, if the other auditor's opinion was qualified (or adverse) that fact would have to be taken into account (based on its materiality in relation to the statements of the enterprise as a whole) by the principal auditor in determining whether the overall opinion will be affected or, even if not, whether some reference should be made to the other auditor's qualified opinion.

Figure 6-32
Utilizing Other Auditors' Reports

Divided Responsbility with Another Auditor—
Unqualified Opinion (AU 543)

We have examined the consolidated balance sheet of X Company and subsidiaries as of December 31, 198Y, and the related consolidated statements of income and retained earnings and changes in financial position for the year then ended. Our examination was made in accordance with generally accepted auditing standards and accordingly included such tests of the accounting records and such other auditing procedures as we considered necessary in the circumstances. We did not examine the financial statements of B Company, a consolidated subsidiary, which statements reflect total assets and revenues constituting 20 percent and 22 percent, respectively, of the related consolidated totals. These statements were examined by other auditors whose report thereon has been furnished to us, and our opinion expressed herein, insofar as it relates to the amounts included for B Company, is based solely upon the report of the other auditors.

In our opinion, based upon our examination and the report of other auditors, the accompanying consolidated balance sheet and consolidated statements of income and retained earnings and changes in financial position present fairly. . .

Comment. As stated in AU 509 and reiterated in AU 543, the reference in the report of the principal auditor to the examination of another auditor, as well as the modification of the opinion paragraph incorporating the phrase "based upon. . . ," are not to be construed as a qualification of the opinion but rather as an indication of divided responsibility.

Figure 6-33
Utilizing Other Auditors' Reports

Restated Financial Statements of Prior Years Following a Pooling of Interests; Other Auditors Involved—Opinion Only as to Compilation of Statements (AU 543)

We previously examined and reported upon the consolidated statements of income and changes in financial position of XYZ Company and subsidiaries for the year ended December 21, 19 , prior to their restatement for the 19   pooling of interests. The contribution of XYZ Company and subsidiaries to revenues and net income represent X percent and Y percent of the respective restated totals. Separate financial statements of the other companies included in the 19   restated consolidated statements of income and changes in financial position were examined and reported upon separately by other auditors. We also have reviewed, as to compilation only, the accompanying consolidated statements of income and changes in financial position for the year ended December 31, 19   , after restatement for the 19   pooling of interest; in our opinion, such consolidated statements have been properly compiled on the basis described in Note X of notes to consolidated financial statements.

Comment. The foregoing is an additional paragraph to be presented following the standard scope and opinion paragraph covering the consolidated financial statements for the current year. It is noted in AU 543 that the auditor assumes no responsibility for the work of other auditors and does not express an opinion on the restated financial statements taken as a whole. His opinion in this supplementary paragraph relates only to the compilation, his auditing procedures in that respect having been limited to checking the compilation for mathematical accuracy and seeing whether the methods of compilation (such as elimination of intercompany transactions and balances and manner and extent of disclosures in the restated financial statements) conform with generally accepted accounting principles.

COMPARATIVE FINANCIAL STATEMENTS

A continuing auditor (i.e., one who has examined the financial statements of the current period and of one or more consecutive periods immediately prior to the current period), as stated in AU 505, should update his report of the prior period statements presented on a comparative basis with the statements of the current period. During his current year's examination, he should be alert to circumstances that may affect the prior period statements and disclosures relating to them and the need to reflect them in updating his report on those statements.

Circumstances such as the following may cause the auditor, in updating his reports on prior periods, to modify previously expressed opinions. A material uncertainty may have subsequently been resolved, permitting an unqualified opinion rather than a previously issued qualified opinion or disclaimer. A prior period uncertainty discovered in a subsequent period will then call for a qualified opinion as to the prior period statements. The restatement of prior period statements in conformity with GAAP permits the substitution of an unqualified opinion in place of the previously expressed qualified opinion (or adverse opinion) based on a departure from GAAP.

Illustrative reports on comparative financial statements are also included elsewhere in this chapter, including the section on Unqualified Opinions. The illustrations that follow deal with reports on comparative financial statements with differing opinions, and with reports with updated opinions different from previously expressed opinions.

Figure 6-34
Comparative Financial Statements

Qualified Opinion, Current Year; Unqualified
Opinion, Prior Year (AU 505)

(EXPLANATORY PARAGRAPH)

As discussed in Note X, during 198Y the Company became a defendant in a lawsuit relating to the sale in 198Y of a wholly owned subsidiary. The ultimate outcome of the lawsuit cannot be determined, and no provision for any liability that may result has been made in the 198Y financial statements.

(OPINION PARAGRAPH)

In our opinion, subject to the effects on the 198Y financial statements of such adjustments, if any, as might have been required had the outcome of the uncertainty referred to in the preceding paragraph been known, the financial statements referred to above present fairly the financial position of ABC Company as of December 31, 198Y and 198X, and the results of its operations and the changes in its financial position for the years then ended, in conformity with generally accepted accounting principles applied on a consistent basis.

(ALTERNATIVE WORDING OF OPINION PARAGRAPH)

In our opinion, subject to the effects, if any, on the 198Y financial statements of the ultimate outcome of the uncertainty referred to in the preceding paragraph, the financial statements referred to above present fairly. . . .

Figure 6-35
Comparative Financial Statements

Unqualified Opinion, Current Year; Disclaimer on Prior Year Income and Other Statements Except Balance Sheet—Limited Scope (AU 505)

(SCOPE PARAGRAPH)

. . . Except as explained in the following paragraph, our examinations were made in accordance with generally accepted auditing standards and, accordingly, included such tests of the accounting records and such other auditing procedures as we considered necessary in the circumstances.

(EXPLANATORY PARAGRAPH)

We did not observe the taking of the physical inventory as of December 31, 198W, since that date was prior to our appointment as auditors for the Company, and we were unable to satisfy ourselves regarding inventory quantities by means of other auditing procedures.

(OPINION PARAGRAPH)

In our opinion, the balance sheets of ABC Company as of December 31, 198Y and 198X, and the related statements of income, retained earnings, and changes in financial position for the year ended December 31, 198Y, present fairly the financial position of ABC Company as of December 31, 198Y and 198X, and the results of its operations and the changes in its financial position for the year ended December 31, 198Y, in conformity with generally accepted accounting principles applied on a consistent basis.

(DISCLAIMER PARAGRAPH)

Because of the matter discussed in the second paragraph, the scope of our work regarding inventories as of December 31, 198W, was not sufficient to enable us to express, and we do not express, an opinion on the statements of income, retained earnings, and changes in financial position for the year ended December 31, 198X.

Figure 6-36
Comparative Financial Statements

Qualified Opinion for Both Years—
GAAP Departure and Material Uncertainties (AU 505)

(EXPLANATORY PARAGRAPHS)

The Company has excluded from property and debt in the accompanying 198Y balance sheet certain lease obligations that were entered into in 198Y, which, in our opinion, should be capitalized in order to conform with generally accepted accounting principles. If these lease obligations were capitalized, property would be increased by $_____, long-term debt by $_____, and retained earnings by $_____ as of December 31, 198Y, and net income and earnings per share would be increased (decreased) by $_____ and $_____, respectively, for the year then ended.

As discussed in Note X, the Company is involved in continuing litigation relating to patent infringement. The ultimate outcome of this litigation cannot be determined, and no provision for any liability that may result has been made in the 198Y or 198X financial statements.

(OPINION PARAGRAPH)

In our opinion, except for the effects on the 198Y financial statements of not capitalizing certain lease obligations, as described in the second paragraph, and subject to the effects on the 198Y and 198X financial statements of such adjustments, if any, as might have been required had the outcome of the uncertainty referred to in the preceding paragraph been known, the financial statements referred to above present fairly the financial position of ABC Company as of December 31, 198Y and 198X, and the results of its operations and the changes in its financial position for the years then ended, in conformity with generally accepted accounting principles applied on a consistent basis.

Figure 6-37
Comparative Financial Statements

Updated Opinion; Resolution of Prior
Period Uncertainty (AU 505)

(EXPLANATORY PARAGRAPH)

In our report dated March 1, 198Y, our opinion on the 198X financial statements was qualified as being subject to the effects on the 198X financial statements of such adjustments, if any, as might have been required had the outcome of certain litigation been known. As explained in Note X, the litigation was settled as of November 198Y, at no material cost to the Company. Accordingly, our present opinion on the 198X financial statements, as presented herein, is different from that expressed in our previous report.

(Or, with uncertainty resolved and recognized in current years.)

In our report dated March 1, 198X, our opinion on the 198X financial statements was qualified as being subject to the realization of the investment in DEF Company. As explained in Note X, the carrying amount of that investment has been charged to operations in the current year as required by generally accepted accounting principles. Accordingly, our present opinion on the 198X financial statements, as presented herein, is different from that expressed in our previous report.

Comment. If the opinion in an updated report differs from that previously expressed, all substantive reasons for the change should be disclosed in an explanatory paragraph. Also, if the updated opinion is other than unqualified, the opinion paragraph should make reference to the explanatory paragraph in which the circumstances and the date of the prior report would be noted.

Figure 6-38
Comparative Financial Statements

Updated Opinion; New Uncertainty Affecting
Current and Prior Year (AU 505)

(EXPLANATORY PARAGRAPH)

As discussed in Note X, a number of legal actions were filed against the Company subsequent to the date of our report on the 198X financial statements. These actions claim substantial damages as a result of alleged violations of antitrust laws during prior years. The Company is in the process of litigating these actions, but the ultimate outcome is uncertain at this time. In our report dated March 1, 198Y, our opinion on the 198X financial statements was unqualified; however, in view of the litigation referred to above, our present opinion on the 198X financial statements, as presented herein, is different from that expressed in our previous report.

Figure 6-39
Comparative Financial Statements

Updated Opinion; Prior Period
Statements Restated to Conform
With GAAP (AU 505)

(EXPLANATORY PARAGRAPH)

In our report dated March 1, 198Y, we expressed an opinion that the 198X financial statements did not fairly present financial position, results of operations, and changes in financial position in conformity with generally accepted accounting principles because of two departures from such principles: (1) the Company carried its property, plant, and equipment at appraisal values, and provided for depreciation on the basis of such values, and (2) the Company did not provide for deferred income taxes with respect to differences between income for financial reporting purposes and taxable income. As described in Note X, the Company has restated its 198X financial statements to conform with generally accepted accounting principles. Accordingly, our present opinion on the 198X financial statements, as presented herein, is different from that expressed in our previous report.

REPORTING ON INFORMATION ACCOMPANYING THE BASIC
FINANCIAL STATEMENTS IN AUDITOR-SUBMITTED DOCUMENTS

Guidance is provided in SAS 29 for the independent auditor when he submits to a client or others a document that contains information in addition to the basic financial statements and the report on those statements. This area of interest was formerly referred to as additional information in *long-form reports.*

The basic financial statements are identified as including the balance sheet, statement of income, statement of retained earnings, statement of changes in financial position, disclosures of changes in owners' or stockholders' equity, notes to financial statements, and schedules and explanatory material identified as being part of the basic statements. The additional information referred to accompanies but is presented outside the basic statements and is not necessary for a fair presentation of those statements. Some examples of such additional information are statistical data, details of items appearing in or related to the basic statements, historical summaries of such items, and consolidating information. A later section of this chapter deals with FASB-required supplementary information included in documents containing audited financial statements.

The following is a summary of the major principles applicable to additional information included in auditor-submitted documents. Pertinent illustrative reports are presented in Figure 6-41 and 6-42.

1. The additional information constitutes management's representation just as much as the basic financial statements, and their reliability and fairness are management's responsibility. When the auditor includes in his report detailed comments on the scope of his examination of, for example, specific items in the financial statements, such comments should be presented separately from the additional information in order to maintain a clear distinction between the auditor's representations (that is, the character of the examination) and management's representations (that is, the financial statements and financial information).

2. In any document submitted by him containing audited financial statements, the auditor must report on all the included information and, in accordance with the fourth reporting standard, must indicate clearly in his report the character of his examination and the degree of responsibility he is assuming (that is, expression of opinion or disclaimer). This principle applies equally to the additional information. In particular, the report on the additional information should:

(a) Identify the additional information.

(b) State that the examination was undertaken in order to express an opinion on the basic financial statements taken as a whole.

(c) Specify that the additional information is included for supplementary analysis purposes and is not a required part of the basic financial statements.

(d) Describe the character of the examination; for example, whether the information has been subjected to the auditing procedures applied to the basic financial statements; whether the information has not been audited; and so on.

(e) Express an opinion (unqualified, qualified, or adverse) on whether the information is stated fairly in all material respects in relation to the basic financial statements taken as a whole, or a disclaimer of opinion. In the case of a disclaimer, the additional information should be marked unaudited or include a reference to the disclaimer. If the information is materially misstated and the client refuses to revise it, the auditor should either refuse to include the information or revise his report on the information so that the circumstance is described and an adverse opinion is expressed.

3. The report on the additional information (including the opinion or disclaimer) may either be added to the standard report or presented separately in the document. In this connection a clear separation should be achieved in the document between the basic financial statements and the additional information. Such separation may be achieved by separate placement, appropriate titles, or distinctive captions such as ADDITIONAL FINANCIAL INFORMATION.

4. The effect of any qualified opinion, adverse opinion, or disclaimer expressed by the auditor with respect to the basic financial statements should be taken into account in his reporting on the accompanying information. The auditor is precluded from expressing an opinion that the accompanying information is fairly presented if either an adverse opinion or a disclaimer is expressed in the report on the basic statements.

5. When the basic financial statements are accompanied by FASB-required supplementary information in an auditor-submitted document, a disclaimer of opinion should be expressed on such information, unless the auditor has been engaged to examine and express an opinion on it. (A later section of this chapter deals with SAS 27 and the subject of reporting on supplementary information required by the FASB.) An illustrative disclaimer is presented as part of Figure 6-40. Also, the report on the FASB-required information should be expanded along the lines required by SAS 27 in the three circumstances noted in Figure 6-62.

6. When the same audited basic financial statements coexist in more than one type of document, the auditor should make sure that all the informative disclosures that are required for their fair presentation in conformity with GAAP are made in all such coexisting documents. He should also be satisfied that any additional information provided in an auditor-submitted document is not required for fairness of presentation of the basic financial statements contained either in that document or in other coexisting documents.

Figure 6-40
Reporting on Information Accompanying The Basic
Financial Statements In Auditor-Submitted
Documents: Illustrative Opinions (SAS 29)

(The following are illustrative paragraphs to be added to the auditor's standard report or presented separately in the auditor-submitted document.)

Unqualified Opinion

Our examination was made for the purpose of forming an opinion on the basic financial statements taken as a whole. The (identify accompanying information) is presented for purposes of additional analysis and is not a required part of the basic financial statements. The information has been subjected to the auditing procedures applied in the examination of the basic financial statements and, in our opinion, is fairly stated in all material respects in relation to the basic financial statements taken as a whole.

Qualified Opinion

Our examination was made for the purpose of forming an opinion on the basic financial statements taken as a whole. The schedule of investments as of December 31, 198X is presented for purposes of additional analysis and is not a required part of the basic financial statements. The information has been subjected to the auditing procedures applied in the examination of the basic financial statements and, in our opinion, except for the effects of not acounting for the investments in certain companies by the equity method as explained in the second preceding paragraph [second paragraph of our report on page xx], the information in the schedule is stated fairly in all material respects in relation to the basic financial statements taken as a whole.

Disclaimer

Our examination was made for the purpose of forming an opinion on the basic financial statements taken as a whole. The (identify information) is presented for purposes of additional analysis and is not a required part of the basic financial statements. The information has not been subjected to the auditing procedures applied in our examination of such statements and, accordingly, we express no opinion on it.

Disclaimer on Part of the Additional Information

Our examination was made for the purpose of forming an opinion on the basic financial statements taken as a whole. The information on pages xx-yy is presented for purposes of additional analysis and is not a required part of the basic financial statements. Such information, except for that portion marked "unaudited" on which we express no opinion, has been subjected to the auditing procedures applied in the examination of the basic financial statements and, in our opinion, such information is fairly stated in all material respects in relation to the basic financial statements taken as a whole.

Disclaimer on FASB-Required Supplementary Information

The (identify supplementary information) on page xx is not a required part of the basic financial statements, but is supplementary information required by the Financial Accounting Standards Board. We have applied certain limited procedures which consisted principally of inquiries of management regarding the methods of measurement and presentation of the supplementary information. However, we did not audit such information and express no opinion on it.

Figure 6-41
Reporting on Information Accompanying the Basic Financial Statements In Auditor-Submitted Documents: Consolidating Information—Unqualified Opinion (SAS 29)

Our examination was made for the purpose of expressing an opinion on the consolidated financial statements taken as a whole. The consolidating information is presented for the purpose of additional analysis of the consolidated financial statements rather than to present the financial position, results of operations, and changes in financial position of the individual companies.

The consolidating information has been subjected to the auditing procedures applied in the examination of the consolidated financial statements and, in our opinion, is stated fairly in all material respects in relation to the consolidated financial statements taken as a whole.

Comment. The above report is applicable when the consolidated financial statements include consolidating information that has not been separately examined.

REPORTING ON SEGMENT INFORMATION

Certain segment information (specially defined as relating to operations in different industries, foreign operations and export sales, and major customers) is required to be disclosed by FASB Statement No. 14 (AC 2081); but this requirement is suspended by FASB Statement No. 21 (AC 2083) for nonpublic enterprises. According to AU 435, it is one of the disclosures that should be made if the statements are to be considered as being in conformity with GAAP.

The effect on the auditor's report of inadequate disclosures or the absence of required disclosures pertaining to segment information is basically the same as that for other types of informative disclosure. Misstatements or omissions that are material in relation to the financial statements taken as a whole would result in a modified opinion—usually qualified, but conceivably adverse. The auditor is not, however, required to provide the *details* of segment information that the client declines to include in the financial statements, but he should describe the *type* of information omitted.

No special mention of segment information need be made in the auditor's report unless questions of GAAP departure, scope limitation, or consistency arise, as indicated in the illustrative reports that follow and in the accompanying comments.

Figure 6-42
Reporting on Segment Information

Misstatement of Segment Information—Qualified
Opinion (AU 435)

(EXPLANATORY PARAGRAPH)

With respect to the segment information in Note X, $_____ of the operating expenses of Industry A were incurred jointly by Industries A and B. In our opinion, Statement No. 14 of the Financial Accounting Standards Board requires that those operating expenses be allocated between Industries A and B. The effect of the failure to allocate those operating expenses has been to understate the operating profit of Industry A and to overstate the operating profit of Industry B by an amount that has not been determined.

(OPINION PARAGRAPH)

In our opinion, except for the effects of not allocating certain common operating expenses between Industries A and B, as discussed in the preceding paragraph, the financial statements referred to above present fairly . . .

Figure 6-43
Reporting on Segment Information

Segment Information Omitted—Qualified
Opinion (AU 435)

(EXPLANATORY PARAGRAPH)

The Company declined to present segment information for the year ended December 31, 198Y. In our opinion, presentation of segment information concerning the Company's operations in different industries, its foreign operations and export sales, and its major customers is required by Statement No. 14 of the Financial Accounting Standards Board. The omission of segment information results in an incomplete presentation of the Company's financial statements.

(OPINION PARAGRAPH)

In our opinion, except for the omission of segment information, as discussed in the preceding paragraph, the financial statements referred to above present fairly . . .

Figure 6-44
Reporting on Segment Information

Inconsistency in Segment Information; Effect
Not Disclosed—Qualified Opinion (AU 435)

(EXPLANATORY PARAGRAPH)

In 198Y, the Company changed the basis of accounting for sales between its industry segments from the market price method to the negotiated price method, but declined to disclose the nature and effect of this change on its segment information. In our opinion, disclosure of the nature and effect of this change, which has not been determined, is required by Statement No. 14 of the Financial Accounting Standards Board.

(OPINION PARAGRAPH)

In our opinion, except for the omission of the information discussed in the preceding paragraph, the financial statements referred to above present fairly . . .

Comment. AU 435 refers to the requirement of FASB No. 14 that the nature and effect of specified inconsistencies in the preparation and presentation of segment information be disclosed in the period of change and, for certain changes, that the segment information for prior periods in comparative statements be retroactively restated. AU 435 then states that a deviation from these requirements would cause the auditor to qualify his opinion because of the departure from GAAP (i.e., failure to meet the FASB requirements), but no qualification as to consistency would be expressed, unless, of course, the change in segment information is tied in with a change in accounting principles affecting the financial statements as a whole.

Figure 6-45
Reporting on Segment Information

Segment Information Not Available for Audit;
Scope Limitation—Qualified Opinion (AU 435)

(SCOPE PARAGRAPH)

. . . Except as explained in the following paragraph, our examination . . . and such other auditing procedures as we considered necessary in the circumstances.

(EXPLANATORY PARAGRAPH)

The Company has not developed the information we consider necessary to reach a conclusion as to whether the presentation of segment information concerning the Company's operations in different industries, its foreign operations and export sales, and its major customers is necessary to conform with Statement No. 14 of the Financial Accounting Standards Board.

(OPINION PARAGRAPH)

In our opinion, except for the possible omission of segment information, the financial statements referred to above present fairly . . .

Comment. The foregoing report would be issued, according to AU 435, if the auditor does not have the knowledge to conclude whether the company has segments (as defined by FASB 14) and the client declines to develop the information needed to form a conclusion.

Figure 6-46
Reporting on Segment Information

Audit Scope Restricted; Qualified
Opinion (AU 435)

(SCOPE PARAGRAPH)

. . . Except as explained in the following paragraph, our examination . . . and such other auditing procedures as we considered necessary in the circumstances.

(EXPLANATORY PARAGRAPH)

In accordance with the Company's request, our examination of the financial statements did not include the segment information presented in Note X concerning the Company's operations in different industries, its foreign operations and export sales, and its major customers.

(OPINION PARAGRAPH)

In our opinion, except for the effects of such adjustments or disclosures, if any, as might have been determined to be necessary had we applied to the segment information the procedures we considered necessary in the circumstances, the financial statements referred to above present fairly . . .

SPECIAL REPORTS

AU 621 (as expanded on in AU 9621 interpretations) covers the auditor's reporting responsibilities applicable to special reports (sometimes referred to as special-purpose reports) of the following type.

1. Financial statements prepared in accordance with a comprehensive basis of accounting other than generally accepted accounting principles (e.g., cash basis, income tax basis, or basis prescribed by a regulatory agency solely for filing with it).

2. Specified elements, accounts, or items of a financial statement and compliance with aspects of contractual agreements or regulatory requirements related to audited financial statements.

3. Special-purpose financial presentations.

4. Financial information presented in prescribed forms or schedules requiring a prescribed form of auditor's report.

For obvious reasons, illustrations of prescribed forms to be filed with government or other bodies are not included in this chapter. AU 621 states that the auditor should reword a preprinted prescribed form or attach a separate report if the prescribed wording is not acceptable.

Figure 6-47
Special Reports

Statements Prepared on Cash Basis
(AU 621)

We have examined the statement of assets and liabilities arising from cash transactions of XYZ Company as of December 31, 198Y, and the related statement of revenue collected and expenses paid for the year then ended. Our examination was made in accordance with generally accepted auditing standards and, accordingly, included such tests of the accounting records and such other auditing procedures as we considered necessary in the circumstances.

As described in Note X, the Company's policy is to prepare its financial statements on the basis of cash receipts and disbursements; consequently, certain revenue and related assets are recognized when received rather than when earned, and certain expenses are recognized when paid rather than when the obligation is incurred. Accordingly, the accompanying financial statements are not intended to present financial position and results of operations in conformity with generally accepted accounting principles.

In our opinion, the financial statements referred to above present fairly the assets and liabilities arising from cash transactions of XYZ Company as of December 31, 198Y, and the revenue collected and expenses paid during the year then ended, on the basis of accounting described in Note X, which basis has been applied in a manner consistent with that of the preceding year.

Comment. Reports on audited financial statements prepared on a comprehensive basis other than GAAP (e.g., cash basis or income tax basis) must include the usual scope of examination paragraph (modified as necessary); a description of the basis used and its variation from GAAP; and an opinion paragraph that reflects the usual reporting standards except, of course, that the opinion (or disclaimer) is expressed with reference to the accounting basis used.

Not to be overlooked are the usual disclosure requirements with respect to material matters. AU 410 states (and so repeated in AU 621) that: "When an auditor reports on financial statements prepared in accordance with a comprehensive basis of accounting other than generally accepted principles, the first standard of reporting is satisfied by disclosing in the auditor's report that the statements are not intended to conform with generally accepted accounting principles and by expressing an opinion (or disclaiming an opinion) on whether the financial statements are presented in conformity with the comprehensive basis of accounting used."

It should be emphasized that, for purposes of AU 621, the category of "comprehensive basis of accounting other than GAAP" encompasses any one of only the following bases: (1) basis of accounting required by a government regulatory agency,and the report is to be filed with the agency; (2) income tax basis; (3) cash basis; (4) basis reflecting definite principles having substantial support (AU 621 mentions price-level basis as an example).

Figure 6-48
Special Reports

Statements Prepared on Income Tax Basis
(AU 621)

We have examined the statement of assets, liabilities, and capital-income tax basis of ABC Partnership as of December 31, 198Y, and the related statements of revenue and expenses—income tax basis and of changes in partner's capital accounts—income basis for the year then ended. Our examination was made in accordance with generally accepted auditing standards and, accordingly, included such tests of the accounting records and such other auditing procedures as we considered necessary in the circumstances.

As described in Note X, the Partnership's policy is to prepare its financial statements on the accounting basis used for income tax purposes; consequently, certain revenue and the related assets are recognized when received rather than when earned, and certain expenses are recognized when paid rather then when the obligation is incurred. Accordingly, the accompanying financial statements are not intended to present financial position and results of operations in conformity with generally accepted accounting principles.

In our opinion, the financial statements referred to above present fairly the assets, liabilities, and capital of ABC Partnership as of December 31, 198Y, and its revenue and expenses and changes in its partners' capital accounts for the year then ended, on the basis of accounting described in Note X, which basis has been applied in a manner consistent with that of the preceding year.

Figure 6-49
Special Reports

Statements on Basis Prescribed By Regulatory
Agency Solely for Filing With the
Agency (AU 621)

We have examined the statement of admitted assets, liabilities, and surplus—statutory basis of XYZ Insurance Company as of December 31, 198Y, and the related statements of income—statutory basis and changes in surplus—statutory basis for the year then ended. Our examination was made in accordance with generally accepted auditing standards and, accordingly, included such tests of the accounting records and such other auditing procedures as we considered necessary in the circumstances.

As described in Note X, the Company's policy is to prepare its financial statements on the basis of accounting practices prescribed or permitted by the Insurance Department of (State). These practices differ in some respects from generally accepted accounting principles. Accordingly, the accompanying financial statements are not intended to present financial position and results of operations in conformity with generally accepted accounting principles. This report is intended solely for filing with regulatory agencies and is not intended for any other purpose.

In our opinion, the financial statements referred to above present fairly the admitted assets, liabilities and surplus of XYZ Insurance Company as of December 31, 198Y, and the results of its operations and changes in its surplus for the year then ended, on the basis of accounting described in Note X, which basis has been applied in a manner consistent with that of the preceding year.

Comment. This form of reporting may be used only if the financial statements are prepared solely for filing with the regulatory agency or if additional distribution is recognized by an auditing interpretation or other such pronouncement of the AICPA. However, if the auditor is requested to report on statements presented on a prescribed basis other than GAAP in presentations other than filings with the regulatory body, he must use the standard form of auditor's report suitably modified to express a qualified opinion or adverse opinion. The reasons for the type of opinion expressed—that is, the departures from GAAP—must of course be given. AU 544 permits the auditor, in this circumstance, to follow the opinion paragraph with an additional paragraph in which an opinion is expressed on the conformity of the financial statements with the prescribed basis of accounting.

Figure 6-50
Special Reports

Reporting Under ERISA (AU 9621)

To XYZ Pension Plan:

We have examined the financial statements and schedules of XYZ Pension Plan as of December 31, 198Y, and for the year then ended, as listed in the accompanying index. Except as stated in the following paragraph, our examination was made in accordance with generally accepted auditing standards and, accordingly, included such tests of the accounting records and such other auditing procedures as we considered necessary in the circumstances.

The plan administrator has elected the method of compliance permitted by section 2520.103-8 of the Department of Labor Rules and Regulations for Reporting and Disclosure under the Employee Retirement Income Security Act of 1974. Accordingly, as permitted under such election, the plan administrator instructed us not to perfom, and we did not perform, any auditing procedures with respect to the information certified by the ABC Bank, the trustee of the plan, except for comparing such information, which is summarized in note X, to the related information included in the financial statements and schedules. We have been informed by the plan administrator that the trustee holds the plan's investment assets and executes transactions therein. The plan administrator has obtained a certification from the trustee that the information provided to the plan administrator by the trustee is complete and accurate.

Because of the significance of the information that we did not audit, we are unable to, and do not, express an opinion on the accompanying financial statements and schedules taken as a whole. The form and content of the information included in the financial statements and schedules, other than that derived from the information certified by the trustee, has been examined by us and, in our opinion, is presented in compliance with the Department of Labor Rules and Regulations for Reporting and Disclosure under the Employee Retirement Income Security Act of 1974.

Comment. The AU 9621 auditing interpretation states that the above report may be issued to third parties, such as plan participants, provided it is accompanied by the financial statements and the schedules referred to. See comment on preceding report regarding distribution restrictions.

Figure 6-51
Special Reports

Specified Item: Sales for Purposes
of Rental Computation (AU 621)

We have examined the schedule of gross sales (as defined in the lease agreement dated (date) between ABC Company, as lessor, and XYZ Stores Corporation, as lessee) of XYZ Stores Corporation at its Main Street store, (City), (State), for the year ended December 31, 198Y. Our examination was made in accordance with generally accepted auditing standards and, accordingly, included such tests of the accounting records and such other auditing procedures as we considered necessary in the circumstances.

In our opinion, the schedule of gross sales referred to above presents fairly the gross sales of XYZ Stores Corporation at its Main Street store, (City), (State), for the year ended December 31, 198Y, on the basis specified in the lease agreement referred to above.

Comment. Except for the first and second reporting standards, the auditing standards apply to reports on specified elements, accounts or items of a financial statement. However, the second (consistency) standard is applicable if the item reported on is in conformity with GAAP.

The auditor may not report on specified elements, etc., if they have been included in financial statements on which an adverse opinion or disclaimer is expressed if such reporting would be tantamount to a piecemeal opinion; but if those elements, accounts or items represent only a minor portion of the statements, the report on them may be issued but not as part of the regular report on the financial statements.

The special report should indicate the character of the examination, identify the item, describe the basis of presentation, and express an appropriate opinion as to fairness and consistency on the indicated basis.

It should be emphasized that when an opinion is expressed as to a specific item standing alone, the materiality standards relative to that item are more exacting, and the examination more extensive, than would be the case if the item were being considered in relation to the financial statements taken as a whole.

Figure 6-52
Special Reports

Specified Item: Production As
Related to Royalties (AU 621)

We have examined the schedule of royalties applicable to engine production of the Q Division of XYZ Corporation for the year ended December 31, 198Y, under the terms of a license agreement dated (date), between ABC Company and XYZ Corporation. Our examination was made in accordance with generally accepted auditing standards and, accordingly, included such tests of the accounting records and such other auditing procedures as we considered necessary in the circumstances.

We have been informed that, under XYZ Corporation's interpretation of the agreement referred to above, royalties were based on the number of engines produced after giving effect to a reduction for production retirements that were scrapped, but without a reduction for field returns that were scrapped, even though the field returns were replaced with new engines without charge to customers. This treatment is consistent with that followed in prior years.

In our opinion, the schedule of royalties referred to above presents fairly the number of engines produced by the Q Division of XYZ Corporation during the year ended December 31, 198Y, and the amount of royalties applicable thereto under the license agreement referred to above, on the basis indicated in the preceding paragraph.

Figure 6-53
Special Reports

Specified Item: Profit Participation (AU 621)

We have examined XYZ Company's schedule of John Smith's profit participation for the year ended December 31, 198Y. Our examination was made in accordance with generally accepted auditing standards and, accordingly, included such tests of the accounting records and such other auditing procedures as we considered necessary in the circumstances. We have examined the financial statements of XYZ Company for the year ended December 31, 198Y, and have issued our report thereon dated March 10, 198Z.

We have been informed that the documents that govern the determination of John Smith's profit participation are (a) the employment agreement between John Smith and XYZ Company dated (date), (b) the production and distribution agreement between XYZ Company and Television Network Incorporated dated (date), and (c) the studio facilities agreement between XYZ Company and QRX Studios dated (date), as amended (date).

In our opinion, the schedule of profit participation referred to above presents fairly John Smith's participation in the profits of XYZ Company for the year ended December 31, 198Y, in accordance with the provisions of the agreements referred to in the preceding paragraph.

Comment. AU 610 cautions that a report on profit participation should not be issued unless the auditor has examined the financial statements on which the participation is based.

Figure 6-54
Special Reports

Specified Item: Adequacy of
Income Tax Provision (AU 621)

We have examined the financial statements of XYZ Company, Inc., for the year ended June 30, 198Y, and have issued our report thereon dated August 15, 198Y. Our examination was made in accordance with generally accepted auditing standards and, accordingly, included such tests of the accounting records and such other auditing procedures as we considered necessary in the circumstances.

In the course of our examination, we examined the provision for Federal and state income taxes for the year ended June 30, 198Y, included in the Company's financial statements referred to in the preceding paragraph. We also reviewed the Federal and state income tax returns filed by the Company that are subject to examination by the respective taxing authorities.

In our opinion, the Company has paid or has provided adequate accruals in the financial statements referred to above for the payment of all Federal and state income taxes, and has provided for related deferred income taxes, applicable to fiscal 198Y and prior fiscal years, that could be reasonably estimated at the time of our examination of the financial statements of XYZ Company, Inc., for the year ended June 30, 198Y.

Comment. AU 610 cautions that a report on the adequacy of a provision for income taxes should not be issued unless the auditor has examined the financial statements in which the provision appears. It also states that if a considerable period of time has elapsed between the date of the report on the financial statements and the date of the special report, the auditor may wish to include in the latter a paragraph similar to the following:

"Because we have not examined any financial statements of XYZ Company, Inc., as of any date or for any period subsequent to June 30, 198Y, we have no knowledge of the effects, if any, on the income tax provision of events that may have occurred subsequent to the date of our examination."

Figure 6-55
Special Reports

Agreed-Upon Procedures Applied to Specified
Item: Proposed Acquisition (AU 621)

To Board of Directors, X Company:

We have applied certain agreed-upon procedures, as discussed below, to accounting records of Y Company, Inc., as of December 31, 198Y, solely to assist you in connection with the proposed acquisition of Y Company, Inc. It is understood that this report is solely for your information and is not to be referred to or distributed to anyone not a member of management of X Company for any purpose. Our procedures and findings are as follows:

(a) We reconciled cash on deposit with the following banks to the balances in the respective general ledger accounts and obtained confirmation of the related balances from the banks.

(Banks and balances listed)

(b) We obtained an aged trial balance of the accounts receivable subsidiary records; traced the age and amounts of approximately _____ percent of the accounts to the accounts receivable ledger; added the trial balance and compared the total with the balance in the general ledger control account. We mailed requests for positive confirmation of balances to _____ customers; differences disclosed in confirmation replies were minor in amount and nature, and we reconciled them to our satisfaction. The results are summarized as follows:

(Results summarized)

Because the above procedures were not sufficient to constitute an examination made in accordance with generally accepted auditing standards, we do not express an opinion on any of the specific amounts referred to above. In connection with the procedures referred to above, no matters came to our attention that caused us to believe that the (specified elements, accounts, or items) should be adjusted. Had we performed additional procedures or had we made an examination of the financial statements in accordance with generally accepted auditing standards, matters might have come to our attention that would have been reported to you. This report should not be associated with the financial statements of Y Company, Inc., for the year ended December 31, 198Y.

Comment. The foregoing report, as well as the one that follows, dealing with creditors' claims, are illustrative of reports applicable to engagements that are limited to applying agreed-upon procedures—as contrasted with an examination made in accordance with generally accepted auditing standards—to one or more specified elements, accounts, or items of a financial statement. As explained in AU 621, such reports are to be restricted to the named parties involved and are not to be accompanied by the company's financial statements. Among other requirements specified in AU 621, a disclaimer should be expressed and the report should also state that it is not to be associated with the financial statements. The expression of a form of negative assurance for reports of this type is also permitted (contrary to the general rule restricting the use of negative assurance) by AU 518 and 621.

Figure 6-56
Special Reports

Agreed-Upon Procedures Applied to Specified Item:
Creditors' Claims (AU 621)

To Trustee, XYZ Company:

At your request, we have performed the procedures enumerated below with respect to the claims of creditors of XYZ Company as of May 31, 198Y, set forth in the accompanying schedules. Our review was made solely to assist you in evaluating the reasonableness of those claims, and our report is not to be used for any other purpose. The procedures we performed are summarized as follows:

(a) We compared the total of the trial balance of accounts payable at May 31, 198Y, prepared by the Company, to the balance in the Company's related general ledger account.

(b) We compared the claims received from creditors to the trial balance of accounts payable.

(c) We examined documentation submitted by the creditors in support of their claims and compared it to documentation in the Company's files, including invoices, receiving records, and other evidence of receipt of goods or services.

Except as set forth in Schedule B, we found that amounts claimed by creditors and amounts shown in the Company's records were the same. Our findings are presented in the accompanying schedules. Schedule A lists claims that are in agreement with the Company's records. Schedule B lists claims that are not in agreement with the Company's records and sets forth the differences in amounts.

Because the above procedures were not sufficient to constitute an examination made in accordance with generally accepted auditing standards, we do not express an opinion on the accounts payable balance as of May 31, 198Y. In connection with the procedures referred to above, except as set forth in Schedule B, no matters came to our attention that caused us to believe that the accounts payable might require adjustment. Had we performed additional procedures or had we made an examination of the financial statements in accordance with generally accepted auditing standards, other matters might have come to our attention that would have been reported to you. This report should not be associated with the financial statements of XYZ Company for the year ended May 31, 198Y.

Figure 6-57
Special Reports

Compliance With Contractual Agreements
Related to Audited Financial Statements:
Reporting in Separate Report on Compliance
With Indenture Provisions (AU 621)

We have examined the balance sheet of XYZ Company as of December 31, 198Y, and the related statements of income, retained earnings, and changes in financial position for the year then ended, and have issued our report thereon dated February 16, 198Z. Our examination was made in accordance with generally accepted auditing standards and, accordingly, included such tests of the accounting records and such other auditing procedures as we considered necessary in the circumstances.

In connection with our examination, nothing came to our attention that caused us to believe that the Company was not in compliance with any of the terms, covenants, provisions, or conditions of sections XX to XX, inclusive, of the Indenture dated (date), with ABC Bank. However, it should be noted that our examination was not directed primarily toward obtaining knowledge of such noncompliance.

Comment. For reports on compliance with contractual agreements or regulatory requirements related to audited financial statements, contrary to the general rule restricting the use of negative assurance, a form of negative assurance is permitted by AU 518 and 621, but only if the related financial statements have been audited. This assurance may be given by including an additional paragraph in the auditor's regular report on the financial statements or in a separate report. In the latter case, the report must state that the financial statements have been audited, give the date of that report, and indicate whether the examination was made in accordance with generally accepted auditing standards.

Figure 6-58
Special Reports

Compliance With Contractual Agreements
Related to Audited Financial Statements:
Reporting in Regular Audit Report on Compliance
With Indenture Provisions (AU 621)

We have examined the balance sheet of XYZ Company as of December 31, 198Y, and the related statements of income, retained earnings, and changes in financial position for the year ended. Our examination was made in accordance with generally accepted auditing standards and, accordingly, included such tests of the accounting records and such other auditing procedures as we considered necessary in the circumstances.

In our opinion, the financial statements referred to above present fairly the financial position of XYZ Company as of December 31, 198Y, and the results of its operations and changes in its financial position for the year then ended, in conformity with generally accepted accounting principles applied on a basis consistent with that of the preceding year.

In connection with our examination, nothing came to our attention that caused us to believe that the Company was not in compliance with any of the terms, covenants, provisions, or conditions of sections XX to XX, inclusive, of the Indenture dated (date), with ABC Bank. However, it should be noted that our examination was not directed primarily toward obtaining knowledge of such noncompliance.

Note. See comment on Figure 6-57.

Figure 6-59
Special Reports

Compliance With Regulatory Requirements
Related to Audited Financial Statements—
Separate Report (AU 621)

We have examined the balance sheet of XYZ Company as of December 31, 198Y, and the related statements of income, retained earnings, and changes in financial position for the year then ended, and have issued our report thereon dated March 5, 198Z. Our examination was made in accordance with generally accepted auditing standards and, accordingly, included such tests of the accounting records and such other auditing procedures as we considered necessary in the circumstances.

In connection with our examination, nothing came to our attention that caused us to believe that the Company had failed to comply with the limitation and increased investment requirement in section 993 (d)(2) and (3) of the Internal Revenue Code of _____. However, it should be noted that our examination was not directed primarily toward obtaining knowledge of noncompliance with such requirements.

Note. See comment on Figure 6-57, similarly applicable.

Figure 6-60
Special Reports
Statements Prepared in Accordance with
Accounting Practices Specified in an
Agreement: Departures from GAAP (AU 9621)

We have examined the special-purpose balance sheet of ABC Company as of December 31, 198X, and the related special-purpose statements of income, retained earnings, and changes in financial position for the year then ended. Our examination was made in accordance with generally accepted auditing standards and, accordingly, included such tests of the accounting records and such other auditing procedures as we considered necessary in the circumstances.

The accompanying special-purpose financial statements have been prepared for the purpose of complying with, and on the basis of accounting practices specified in, Section 4 of a loan agreement between DEF Bank and the Company dated (date). These practices differ, as described in Note X, from generally accepted accounting principles. Accordingly, the financial statements are not intended to present and, in our opinion, do not present fairly the financial position, results of operations and changes in financial position of ABC Company in conformity with generally accepted accounting principles.

In our opinion, however, the accompanying special-purpose financial statements of ABC Company are presented fairly on the basis of accounting described in Note X, which basis has been applied in a manner consistent with that of the preceding year.

Comment. The AICPA interpretation expressed in AU 9621 permits the auditor, in submitting a report on special-purpose financial statements prepared in accordance with non-GAAP accounting practices specified in an agreement, to follow the opinion paragraph (expressing a qualified opinion or an adverse opinion in view of the GAAP departures) with a paragraph in which an opinion is expressed on whether the financial statements are presented fairly on the prescribed basis. This ruling is similar to (and such reference is explicitly made in AU 9621) the reporting principles applicable to reports on audited statements prepared on a basis prescribed by a regulatory body but included in presentations other than filings with that body. See comment following Figure 6-49.

Figure 6-61
Special Reports

Special-Purpose Financial Presentations (AU 9621)

Report on Schedule of Gross Income and Certain Expenses

We have examined the accompanying Historical Summary of Gross Income and Direct Operating Expenses of ABC Apartments, City, State, for each of the three years in the period ended December 31, 198X. Our examinations were made in accordance with generally accepted auditing standards and, accordingly, included such tests of the accounting records and such other auditing procedures as we considered necessary in the circumstances.

The accompanying historical summary was prepared for the purpose of complying with the rules and regulations of the Securities and Exchange Commission (for inclusion in the registration statement on Form S-11 of DEF Corporation) and excludes certain material expenses, described in Note X, that would not be comparable to those resulting from the proposed future operations of the property.

In our opinion, the historical summary referred to above presents fairly the gross income and direct operating expenses described in Note X of ABC Apartments for each of the three years in the period ended December 31, 198X, in conformity with generally accepted accounting principles applied on a consistent basis.

Report on Statement of Assets Sold and Liabilities Transferred

We have examined the statement of net assets of ABC Company as of June 8, 198X, sold pursuant to the Purchase Agreement as described in Note X, between ABC Company and XYZ Corporation dated May 8, 198X. Our examination was made in accordance with generally accepted auditing standards, and, accordingly, included such tests of the accounting records and such other auditing procedures as we considered necessary in the circumstances.

In our opinion, the accompanying statement presents fairly the net assets of ABC Company as of June 8, 198X, sold pursuant to the purchase agreement referred to above, in conformity with generally accepted accounting principles.

Comment. The foregoing reports are identified in AU 9621 as special-purpose financial presentations that do not constitute complete financial presentations of historical position or results of operations.

Reports on such statements are to be distinguished from reports on specified elements, accounts, or items of a financial statement discussed and illustrated earlier in this chapter. Reports on special-purpose financial presentations, as in the above illustrations, should indicate clearly the character of the examination and should contain an opinion (or disclaimer) on the fairness of the presentation in conformity with generally accepted accounting principles. Further, to preclude any misunderstanding as to the nature of the presentation, and to make clear that it does not purport to be a complete presentation of financial condition, operating results, or changes in financial position, the statement should be suitably titled and appropriately described in the report.

REPORTING ON SUPPLEMENTARY INFORMATION REQUIRED BY THE FASB

Guidance is provided in SAS 27 for the independent auditor in reporting on supplementary information required by the Financial Accounting Standards Board. SAS 28, which provides additional guidance in the specific case of FASB-required (FASB 33) supplementary information on the effects of changing prices, should be applied in conjunction with SAS 27. The following is a summary and analysis of applicable principles.

1. SAS 27 is applicable when audited financial statements are included in a document that should include supplementary information required by the FASB.

2. The type of supplementary information applicable here, however, should not be confused with the usual informative disclosures required by generally accepted accounting principles which accompany and are an integral part of the financial statements. Reporting principles for GAAP-related informative disclosures are covered by the reporting segment of the generally accepted auditing standards and especially by the third reporting standard.

3. Nor should the FASB-required supplementary information dealt with in SAS 27 be confused with other supplementary information accompanying the basic financial statements in auditor-submitted documents for which guidance is provided in SAS 29, a topic dealt with earlier in this chapter.

4. SAS 27 also applies when an entity voluntarily includes in its document containing audited financial statements, supplementary information required by the FASB of other entities unless the entity indicates that the auditor has not applied the SAS 27-prescribed procedures, or the auditor expands his report on the audited financial statements to include a disclaimer on the supplementary information. The provisions of AU 550 apply when, in the case of the entity's voluntary presentation of such information, the auditor has not applied the SAS 27 procedures.

5. The auditor's responsibilities dealt with in AU 550 (SAS 8) relate to client-published documents (such as annual reports) containing "other information" in addition to the audited financial statements and the auditor's report on those statements. In general, AU 550 specifies that the auditor's responsibility is limited to the financial information identified in, and encompassed by, his report, and that the auditor is not obligated to corroborate or to report upon the supplementary information. He should, however, read that information and consider whether it is consistent with information appearing in the financial statements. If the other information is found to be materially inconsistent with information contained in

the financial statements or materially misstated, the auditor should undertake certain appropriate steps as outlined in AU 550. It should also be noted that if the auditor has been engaged to examine and express an opinion on the other information, the provisions of AU 550 do not apply.

6. SAS 27 is not applicable if the auditor has been engaged to *audit* (in contrast to undertaking the limited procedures specified below) the supplementary information in accordance with generally accepted auditing standards.

7. The auditor has no responsibility to examine in accordance with generally accepted auditing standards information that is outside the basic financial statements (which statements, of course, include the notes to financial statements). The following limited procedures, however, are spelled out in SAS 27 for FASB-required supplementary information because of the importance of such information when so prescribed by the FASB. The auditor should:

(a) Consider whether the additional information does in fact fall within the category of supplementary information required by the FASB.

(b) Review applicable FASB pronouncements.

(c) Inquire of management to learn whether the information has been prepared and presented in accordance with FASB requirements and on a basis consistent with the prior period, and determine reasons for changes, if any, in method of preparation or presentation.

(d) Ascertain the assumptions underlying the preparation and presentation.

(e) Consider obtaining a written representation from management covering the supplementary information.

(f) Undertake additional procedures that may be prescribed in other statements on auditing standards (for example, in SAS 28) with respect to specific types of FASB-required supplementary information.

(g) Compare supplementary information for consistency, correspondence, and presumptive reliability, with the audited financial statements and with the data gathered by the foregoing limited procedures. Make additional inquiries to resolve any significant discrepancies or questions.

8. The FASB-required supplementary information should be clearly distinguished in the document from the audited financial statements and from other outside supplementary financial information not required by the FASB.

9. Inasmuch as the supplementary information has not been audited and is not part of the audited financial statements, the auditor need not refer in his report to the supplementary information or to the limited procedures undertaken, except that the auditor's report should be expanded by an additional paragraph, as illustrated in Figure 6-62, in any of the following circumstances:

(a) The required supplementary information has been omitted by the client (but the auditor is not obligated to include the omitted information).

(b) The information differs materially from that prescribed by the FASB.

(c) The auditor has been unable to undertake the limited procedures noted above. But if the auditor nevertheless has reason to believe that the information departs materially from FASB guidelines and the company does not revise the data, he should describe the departures in his report.

10. The foregoing circumstances do not affect the auditor's opinion on the fairness of the financial statements.

11. The auditor's standard report should also be expanded to include a disclaimer on the supplementary information in the following circumstances:

(a) The company, in presenting supplementary information, indicates that the auditor undertook corroborating procedures and does not specify that the auditor does not express an opinion on the information.

(b) Management does not place the supplementary information outside the basic financial statements and, at the same time, does not clearly mark the information as unaudited.

12. SAS 28 requires the auditor to expand his report on the audited financial statements to describe the situation if he concludes that the entity's narrative discussion of the required supplementary information on the effects of changing prices is materially inconsistent with the audited financial statements or contains a material misstatement of fact.

When the basic financial statements are accompanied by FASB-required supplementary information in an *auditor-submitted* document, SAS 29 requires that the auditor disclaim an opinion on such information unless he has been engaged to examine and express an opinion on it. An illustration of such a disclaimer is presented as part of Figure 6-40. Moreover, the auditor's report in an auditor-submitted document should be expanded along the lines required by SAS 27 in the three circumstances noted in Figure 6-62. In this connection, reference should be made to the earlier section of this chapter dealing with reporting on information accompanying the basic financial statements in auditor-submitted documents.

Figure 6-62
Supplementary Information Required
by the FASB (SAS 27)

(The following are illustrative paragraphs to be added to the auditor's standard report in each of the indicated circumstances.)

Omission of Supplementary Information Required by the FASB

The Company has not presented (describe the supplementary information required by the FASB in the circumstances) that the Financial Accounting Standards Board has determined is necessary to supplement, although not required to be part of, the basic financial statements.

Material Departures from FASB Guidelines

The (specifically identify the supplementary information) on page xx is not a required part of the basic financial statements, and we did audit and do not express an opinion on such information. However, we have applied certain limited procedures, which consisted principally of inquiries of management regarding the methods of measurement and presentation of the supplementary information. As a result of such limited procedures, we believe that the (specifically identify the supplementary information) is not in conformity with guidelines established by the Financial Accounting Standards Board because (describe the material departure(s) from the FASB guidelines).

Prescribed Procedures Not Completed

The (specifically identify the supplementary information) on page xx is not a required part of the basic financial statements, and we did not audit and do not express an opinion on such information. Further we were unable to apply to the information certain procedures prescribed by professional standards because (state the reasons).

REPORTING ON INTERNAL ACCOUNTING CONTROL

Presented in chapter 2 are commentaries and forms relating to the requirement established in AU 323 that the auditor communicate to senior management and the board of directors or its audit committee material weaknesses in the system of internal accounting control that come to his attention during an examination of financial statements conducted in accordance with generally accepted auditing standards. A checklist guide on the subject is provided in Figure 2-16, and an illustrative report is shown as Figure 2-17.

SAS 30, which leaves intact the AU 323 requirement, provides guidance for the auditor who has been engaged to report on whether the internal accounting control system as a whole was adequate to meet the objectives of internal accounting control. The likelihood of a demand for such engagements has been increased by a combination of circumstances tending to focus on the significance of a sound system of internal accounting control, on management's responsibility therefor, and on the public interest in the subject—recommendations of the Commission on Auditors' Responsibilities, provisions of the Foreign Corrupt Practices Act of 1977 pertaining to internal accounting control for companies subject to SEC regulations, and urging by the SEC (originally advanced as proposals but later withdrawn pending further review) that companies include in annual reports a management statement with respect to the system of internal accounting control, as well as the independent accoutant's report on that statement. It was in recognition of these developments that the AICPA in 1979 issued its "Report of the Special Advisory Committee on Internal Accounting Control" to provide helpful guidance for management in its review, evaluation, and monitoring of an entity's internal accounting control.

The following is a selective summary and analysis of the guidelines in SAS 30 for each of four types of reports—reports expressing an opinion on the system of internal accounting control; reports based solely on the regular audit; reports based on criteria set by regulatory agencies; and other special-purpose reports.

Report Expressing An Opinion on the System of Internal Accounting Control

1. The auditor's report on audited financial statements and his report in which an opinion is expressed on an entity's system of internal accounting control are two distinct engagements. The purpose and scope of the auditor's study and evaluation of the system of internal accounting control are different in each case. For example, in an audit, the auditor may decide to rely exclusively on

substantive tests in certain areas and forgo compliance testing of the system of internal accounting control where he does not intend to rely on the system in determining (in the words of the second standard of field work) "the resultant extent of the tests to which auditing procedures are to be restricted." In the other type of engagement, the full and exclusive focus is on the internal accounting control system and, hence, its study is generally less limited.

2. The procedures for studying and evaluating the system of internal accounting control are similar, however, in the two types of engagements, as are such concepts as: objectives and limitations of internal accounting control; the nature of material weaknesses; and compliance testing design and methodology. In fact, the procedures employed in an internal accounting control engagement may be taken into account in an audit engagement for the same client if concurrence of the engagements, timeliness, and other such considerations make it appropriate in the circumstances of the two engagements. (The materials and forms dealing with internal accounting control contained in this book, especially in Chapters 2 and 3, while designed for use on audit engagements are also relevant to engagements for reporting on an entity's system of internal accounting control.)

3. A written representation should be obtained in which management:

(a) Acknowledges its responsibility for establishing, maintaining, monitoring, and improving the system.

(b) Discloses all material weaknesses in the system, whether or not it is impracticable to correct any of them. (The written representation should include a definition of *material weakness*.)

(c) Provides details of irregularities, if any, involving personnel having key functions within the internal accounting control system.

(d) States whether any changes took place subsequent to the date as of which the system is being reported on that materially affect the system, including corrective action taken by management to overcome material weaknesses.

4. The accountant's report, to be addressed to the entity or its board of directors or stockholders, should be dated as of the completion of the field work and should include:

(b) A statement that the system is management's responsbility.

(c) An indication of the broad objectives and limitations of internal accounting control.

(d) The accountant's opinion on whether the system has met those objectives.

(e) In the event of material weaknesses, a modified opinion paragraph containing a description of the weaknesses, a statement on whether they result from absence of controls or degree of compliance with them, and a general indication of errors or irregularities that may occur as a result. If management has initiated procedures to correct the weaknesses, the accountant should not refer to such actions unless he has satisfied himself that the procedures are appropriate and are being applied. If a document (containing an auditor's opinion) includes a statement by management that the cost of correcting material weaknesses—referred to in the opinion—would exceed the resultant benefits, the auditor should not express (but may disclaim) an opinion on such statement. (An authoritative definition of material weakness—noted in Figure 2-15—is incorporated in the reports shown in Figures 6-63 and 6-64.)

5. The accountant need not place any restrictions on the distribution of the report, unlike the other types of reports on internal accounting control, as later described.

6. Restrictions on the scope of his examination of the system may preclude the accountant from expresing an unqualified opinion on the system and call for a qualified opinion or a disclaimer.

The standard form of accountant's report on internal accounting control as well as a modification of the report when material weaknesses exist are illustrated in Figure 6-63.

Reports on Internal Accounting Control
Based Solely on Audit

An auditor may be asked by a client to submit a report on the system of internal accounting control to be based solely on the study and evaluation of the system made in the examination of the financial statements. If that study and evaluation are not adequate for the expression of an opinion on the system taken as a whole (see preceding discussion on opinion reports on internal accounting control), the following rules apply:

1. A report may be issued by the auditor despite the insufficiency of his study and evaluation of the system.

2. The limited purpose of the study should be noted.

3. A disclaimer of opinion should be expressed on the system of internal accounting control taken as a whole.

4. The report should specify that its use is restricted to management, a specified regulatory agency, or a specified third party.

5. The report should describe material weaknesses in the system, if any, and state that they were taken into account in the examination of the financial statements.

Figure 6-64 provides an illustration of a report on internal accounting control based solely on an audit, as well as a modification of the report to cover an engagement in which material weaknesses in the system have been disclosed.

Report Based on Criteria Set by Regulatory Agency

The following rules apply if the auditor is requested to submit a report on internal accounting control based on criteria established by a regulatory agency to which the entity may be subject.

1. The accountant should be satisfied that the criteria are sufficiently definite and capable of application.

2. The accountant's report should include the features and references reflected in Figure 6-65, including compliance testing, criteria established by the agency, the accountant's conclusions, and material weaknesses whether or not covered by those criteria. The accountant may also report on weaknesses that are not material and, in general, may describe corrective action taken or make appropriate recommendations.

3. A material weakness for purpose of such reports is defined as either of the following:

"(a) A condition that results in more than a relatively low risk that errors or irregularities in amounts that would be material in relation to the applicable grant or program may occur and not be detected within a timely period by employees in the normal course of performing their assigned functions.

"(b) A condition in which the lack of conformity with the agency's criteria is material in accordance with any guidelines for determining materiality that are included in such criteria."

4. The report should specify that its use is restricted to the client and the regulatory agency.

Figure 6-65 illustrates the type of accountant's report on internal accounting control based on criteria established by a regulatory body.

Other Special-Purpose Reports

The accountant may be requested to submit a special report on all or a part of a present or proposed system of internal accounting control—for example, after applying agreed-upon procedures insufficient for the expression of an opinion on the system—for the restricted use of management, another independent accountant, or specified third parties. In that event, the report should:

1. Describe the scope of the study and the procedures used.
2. State the findings.
3. Disclaim an opinion on the system as a whole.
4. Specify that the report is for the sole use of management or specified third party.

Appropriate phraseology provided in Figures 6-63, 6-64, and 6-65, including explanatory paragraphs on management's responsibility, objectives and limitations of internal accounting control, and so on, may be drawn upon in fashioning a satisfactory special-purpose report.

Figure 6-63
Reporting on Internal Accounting Control

Standard Form: Expression of Opinion
(SAS 30)

(Date)

To the Board of Directors and
Shareholders of XYZ Company:

We have made a study and evaluation of the system of internal accounting control of XYZ Company and subsidiaries in effect at December 31, 198X. Our study and evaluation was conducted in accordance with standards established by the American Institute of Certified Public Accountants.

The management of XYZ Company is responsible for establishing and maintaining a system of internal accounting control. In fulfilling this responsibility, estimates and judgments by management are required to assess the expected benefits and related costs of control procedures. The objectives of a system are to provide management with reasonable, but not absolute, assurance that assets are safeguarded against loss from unauthorized use or disposition and that transactions are executed in accordance with management's authorization and recorded properly to permit the preparation of financial statements in accordance with generally accepted accounting principles.

Because of inherent limitations in any system of internal accounting control, errors or irregularities may occur and not be detected. Also projection of any evaluation of the system to future periods is subject to the risk that procedures may become inadequate because of changes in conditions or that the degree of compliance with the procedures may deteriorate.

In our opinion, the system of internal accounting control of XYZ Company and subsidiaries in effect at December 31, 198X, taken as a whole, was sufficient to meet the objectives stated above insofar as those objectives pertain to the prevention or detection of errors or irregularities in amounts that would be material in relation to the consolidated financial statements.

Reporting Material Weaknesses—Modification
of Foregoing Opinion Paragraph

Our study and evaluation disclosed the following conditions in the system of internal accounting control of XYZ Company and subsidiaries in effect at December 31, 198X, which, in our opinion, result in more than a relatively low risk that errors or irregularities in amounts that would be material in relation to the consolidated financial statements may occur and not be detected within a timely period.

Comment. The modified opinion paragraph should be followed by a description of the material weaknesses. Moreover, if the report is being issued in conjunction with an examination of the financial statements, the paragraph describing the material weaknesses should include the following sentence:

"These conditions were considered in determining the nature, timing, and extent of audit tests to be applied in our examination of the 198X financial statements, and this report does not affect our report on these financial statements dated. . . ."

Figure 6-64
Reporting on Internal Accounting Control

Report Based Solely on Audit (SAS 30)

(Date)

To the Board of Directors of
XYZ Company:

We have examined the financial statements of XYZ Company for the year ended December 31, 198X, and have issued our report thereon dated February 23, 198Y. As part of our examination, we made a study and evaluation of the Company's system of internal accounting control to the extent we considered necessary to evaluate the system as required by generally accepted auditing standards. The purpose of our study and evaluation was to determine the nature, timing, and extent of the auditing procedures necessary for expressing an opinion on the company's financial statements. Our study and evaluation was more limited than would be necessary to express an opinion on the system of internal accounting control taken as a whole.

The management of XYZ Company is responsible for establishing and maintaining a system of internal accounting control. In fulfilling this responsibility, estimates and judgments by management are required to assess the expected benefits and related costs of control procedures. The objectives of a system are to provide management with reasonable, but not absolute, assurance that assets are safeguarded against loss from unauthorized use or disposition, and that transactions are executed in accordance with management's authorization and recorded properly to permit the preparation of financial statements in accordance with generally accepted accounting principles.

Because of inherent limitations in any system of internal accounting control, errors or irregularities may nevertheless occur and not be detected. Also projection of any evaluation of the system to future periods is subject to the risk that procedures may become inadequate because of changes in conditions or that the degree of compliance with the procedures may deteriorate.

Our study and evaluation made for the limited purpose described in the first paragraph would not necessarily disclose all material weaknesses in the system. Accordingly, we do not express an opinion on the system of internal accounting control of XYZ Company taken as a whole. However, our study and evaluation disclosed no condition that we believed to be a material weakness.

This report is intended solely for the use of management (or specified third party) and should not be used for any other purpose.

Reporting Material Weaknesses

(*Note*:   If material weaknesses have come to the auditor's attention, the concluding paragraphs of the foregoing report would be modified as follows: (a) The last sentence of the disclaimer (fourth) paragraph would be revised as shown below; (b) That paragraph would be followed by a description of material weaknesses; (c) A new paragraph would be introduced as shown below; (d) The final paragraph of the above report would remain intact.)

(MODIFICATION OF DISCLAIMER PARAGRAPH)

. . . as a whole. However, our study and evaluation disclosed the following conditions that we believe result in more than a relatively low risk that errors or irregularities in amounts that would be material in relation to the financial statements of XYZ Company may occur and not be detected within a timely period.

(NEW PARAGRAPH FOLLOWING DESCRIPTION OF MATERIAL WEAKNESSES)

These conditions were considered in determining the nature, timing, and extent of the audit tests to be applied in our examination of the financial statements, and this report does not affect our report, dated February 23, 198Y, on the financial statements.

Comment.   If the report on the financial statements was qualified because of a scope restriction, the effect of the restriction on the evaluation of the system should be noted in the report on internal accounting control. The above report, appropriately modified, may also be used on an audit engagement to report material weaknesses in internal accounting control as required by AU 323.

Figure 6-65
Reporting on Internal Accounting Control

Report Based on Criteria Established by
Regulatory Agencies (SAS 30)

(SCOPE PARAGRAPH)

We understand that (*entity*) has been awarded a grant of (*amount*) from (*agency*) for the period from (*date*) through (*date*) for use in accordance with the (*title or description of program*). We have made a study of those internal accounting control procedures [and administrative control procedures, if applicable] of (*entity*) that we considered relevant to the criteria established by (*agency*), as set forth in (*section*) of its audit guide, issued (*date*). Our study included tests of compliance with such procedures during the period from (*date*) through (*date*). Our study did not consitute an audit of any financial statements prepared by (*entity*).

(EXPLANATORY PARAGRAPHS)

(See second and third paragraphs of standard report in Figure 6-63.)

(CONCLUDING PARAGRAPHS)

We understand that procedures in conformity with the criteria referred to in the first paragraph of this report are considered by the (*agency*) to be adequate for its purpose in accordance with (*name of act*) and related regulations, and that procedures not in conformity with those criteria indicate some inadequacy for such purposes. Based on this understanding and on our study, we believe (*entity's*) procedures were adequate for the agency's purposes, except for the conditions described (*reference to appropriate section of report*), which we believe are material weaknesses in relation to the grant to which this report refers. In addition to these weaknesses, other conditions that we believe are not in conformity with the criteria referred to above are described (*reference to appropriate section of report*).

This report is intended for the information of (*entity*) and (*agency*) and should not be used for any other purpose.

Comment. The foregoing report would be modified, of course, to omit reference to material weaknesses if none had come to the accountant's attention.

Figure 6-66
Reporting on Sundry Other Matters

Unaudited Replacement Cost Information: Inability to Apply Limited Procedures— Wording of Explanatory Paragraph in Audit Report (AU 730)

(EXPLANATORY PARAGRAPH)

Note X, "Unaudited Information", contains replacement cost information that we did not audit and, accordingly, we do not express an opinon on such information. Further, we have been unable to apply certain limited procedures, consisting of inquiries concerning the replacement cost information, in accordance with standards established by the American Institute of Ceritified Public Accountants because (state reasons).

Comment. As discussed in AU 730, the SEC's Regulation S-X requires certain companies to include replacement cost information in a note or separate section of audited financial statements filed with the SEC. Ordinarily, the auditor's report need make no reference to the information presented providing: it is clearly marked as unaudited; the auditor has applied certain limited procedures required by AU 730; and the information has been presented in conformity with Regulation S-X requirements. Absent those conditions, appropriate disclosures should be made in the auditor's report.

Figure 6-67
Reporting on Sundry Other Matters

Unaudited Replacement Cost Information: Not Prepared (Not Presented) In Accordance With Regulation S-X—Wording of Explanatory Paragraph in Audit Report (AU 730)

(EXPLANATORY PARAGRAPH)

Note X, "Unaudited Information," contains replacement cost information that we did not audit and, accordingly, we do not express an opinion on such information. However, we have applied certain limited procedures, which consisted of inquiries concerning the replacement cost information, in accordance with standards established by the American Institute of Certified Public Accountants. As a result of such procedures, we do not believe that (describe applicable information) has been prepared (presented) in accordance with Regulation S-X of the Securities and Exchange Commission because (state reasons).

Figure 6-68
Report on Financial Forecast—
Standard Form (AICPA Proposed Guide)

We have reviewed the accompanying financial forecast of XYZ Company, which includes the following presentations: forecasted balance sheet as of December 31, 198Y, forecasted statements of income, retained earnings and changes in financial position for the year then ending, and the related summary of significant assumptions. Our review was made in accordance with applicable guidelines of the American Institute of Certified Public Accountants for reviews of financial forecasts and, accordingly, included procedures to evaluate the assumptions used by management as a basis for the financial forecast and to evaluate the preparation and presentation of the financial forecast.

A financial forecast is management's estimate of the most probable financial position, results of operations and changes in financial position for one or more future periods, and reflects management's judgment based on present circumstances of the most likely set of conditions and its most likely course of action. Forecasts are based on assumptions about circumstances and events that have not yet taken place and are subject to variations, and there is no assurance that the forecasted results will be attained.

We have no responsibility to update this report for events and circumstances occurring after the date of this report.

Based on our review, we believe that the accompanying financial forecast has been prepared using assumptions which are reasonable as a basis for management's forecast, and is presented in conformity with applicable guidelines established by the American Institute of Certified Public Accountants for presentation of a financial forecast.

Comment. A proposed guide for the independent accountant entitled "Review of a Financial Forecast" (dated November 23, 1979) issued by an AICPA task force is a voluminous document. It contains detailed information and guidance on the scope of a review, procedures to evaluate forecast assumptions and to evaluate the preparation and presentation of the forecast, illustrative engagement and representation letters, and illustrative reports containing qualified opinions, adverse opinions and disclaimers. It is important to stress that the AICPA Code of Professional Ethics prohibits an accountant from permitting his name to be used in conjunction with a forecast in a manner that may lead to a belief that he vouches for the achievability of the forecast. The report shown above conforms with this requirement in stating, among other things, that "there is no assurance that the forecasted results will be attained.

Figure 6-69
Report by Management on the Financial Statements

(*Note*: The following is not an auditor's report. It is a report by management containing its representations regarding the financial statements and related matters. See comment below.)

The management of XYZ Corporation is responsible for all information presented in this annual report, whether audited or unaudited, including the financial statements and the accompanying notes to financial statements. These statements, which were prepared by us in conformity with generally accepted accounting principles, include amounts that are based on our best estimates and judgments. The financial information presented elsewhere in this annual report is consistent with that in the financial statements.

The Company maintains a system of internal accounting control, including a staff of trained internal auditors, designed to provide reasonable assurance that assets are safeguarded, that transactions are executed in accordance with management's authorization, and that transactions are recorded and reported properly in the books, records, and financial statements.

The financial statements of the Company have been examined by our independent accountants, (*name*), and their independent report and opinion thereon appearing on page (*indicate page number*) are based on an examination conducted in accordance with generally accepted auditing standards. The Audit Committee (composed entirely of outside directors) of the Board of Directors meets periodically with the independent auditors and with management and the internal auditors to determine whether responsibilities are being properly carried out and to assure adequate discussion of auditing, internal accounting control, and financial accounting and reporting matters.

Comment. The foregoing illustrative report contains features whose inclusion is recommended in the AICPA publication (1979) entitled "Conclusions and Recommendations of the Special Advisory Committee on Reports by Management." The committee recommends, but does not mandate, that companies that issue annual reports include such a management report therein in order to make clear to the reader management's responsibilities for the financial statements, the system of internal accounting control, and related matters. Comments on other matters may be included in the report, including qualifcation, if any, in an auditor's report, controls to assure ethical business conduct of corporate officers and other personnel, and reasons for change of auditors.

CHAPTER 7

Completing the Engagement

INTRODUCTION

It is in the concluding phase of the audit engagement that overall and final judgments by the auditor must be made and actions taken to ensure the cohesiveness, completeness, and adequacy of the entire engagement. To that end, the engagement completion checklist guide presented in Figure 7-1 has several important uses: as a reminder checklist, as an integrative tool designed to provide a unifying focus on the engagement as a whole, as a control to ensure proper review, as a record of supervisory and review personnel having major responsibilities for the engagement, and as an additional means of fixing such responsibilities.

The guide makes reference to the engagement partner, and to a pre-issuance reviewing partner not otherwise associated with the engagement, in connection with final review responsibilities. For many accounting firms, and particularly for those of smaller size, it may be more practicable to adopt other types of review arrangements that nevertheless retain appropriate quality control safeguards. It is fundamental, however, that a principal of partnership-equivalent status must assume the responsibilities corresponding to that of an engagement partner, and that whenever practicable, the independent reviewing function corresponding to that performed by a pre-issuance reviewing partner in a larger accounting firm, should be undertaken and assigned to personnel having the proper status and qualifications.

Figure 7-1
Engagement Completion Checklist Guide

_____   _____

Client   Period of financial statements

_____   _____   _____
Prepared by   Date   Reviewed by   Date   Reviewed by   Date
(In-charge   (Engagement   (Pre-issuance
accountant)   partner)   reviewer)

INSTRUCTIONS

1.   The auditor in charge of the engagement, the engagement partner, and the pre-issuance reviewer should sign in the indicated spaces above to affirm their approval and the fulfillment of their separate review or other responsibilities relative to the matters covered in this guide.

2.   Each item is to be signed in the _Yes_, _No_, or _NA_ column as appropriate for the specific item by the in-charge auditor who is responsible for the initial preparation and completion of the guide, except that items that specifically refer to the engagement partner or the pre-issuance reviewer are to be signed by them.

3.   For every item recorded as _No_ or _NA_, an appropriate explanation should be noted in the comment section at the end of the guide and initialed by the engagement partner as indication of approval.

4.   Any problems and unresolved matters pertaining to this guide, as well as their subsequent resolution, should similarly be noted in the comment section together with the signature of the engagement partner as indication of final approval.

CHECKLIST

	Yes	No	NA

Items numbered 1 to 10 below have been obtained or completed, and reviewed for contents and completeness, and appropriate cognizance or action has been taken as required by the circumstances.

1. Auditor's report checklist review guide (Figure 7-3).
2. Financial statements checklist review guide (Figure 7-4).
3. Financial statement disclosures checklist reminder and review guide (Figure 7-5).
4. Working papers checklist review guide (Figure 7-6).
5. Client representation letters.
6. Updated client representation letter where an undue time lag exists.
7. Attorney letters.
8. Updated attorney responses, if such updating is required.
9. Updated *subsequent events* section of the audit program guide or, as appropriate, last-minute inquiries of management regarding significant subsequent events.
10. Updated representation from corporate secretary regarding completeness of the minutes to ensure that recent directors' or other important corporate committee meetings are not overlooked.
11. Memorandum on unresolved questions and problems for consultation with engagement partner:
(a) Has been prepared by in-charge auditor.
(b) Has been reviewed by engagement partner and questions and problems satisfactorily resolved and so noted on memorandum.

12. Letter communicating material weaknesses in internal accounting control has been prepared and approved.

13. The adjusting journal entries developed during the examination have been reviewed and approved by the:

(a) Comptroller, whose signature has been obtained as indication that they have been approved and accepted and are to be recorded in the accounts.

(b) In-charge accountant.

(c) Engagement partner.

14. The form for *bypassed adjusting journal entries* has been completed and approved.

15. The memorandum prepared by the tax department upon completion of its review of the income tax accounts—provisions, accruals and deferred amounts—has been reviewed.

16. The draft of the auditor's report and of the financial statements including notes to financial statements has been reviewed by:

(a) Review department.

(b) Industry or other specialists within the firm, where indicated.

(c) In-charge accountant.

(d) Engagement partner.

(e) Pre-issuance reviewer.

17. Final meetings have been held with client management and/or the audit committee at which the following documents were reviewed:

(a) Draft of auditor's report and financial statements.

(b) Draft of letter communicating material weaknesses in internal accounting control.

(c) Management letter (if other than item (b) above).

(d) _____

(e) _____

18. In accordance with the responsibilities attached to their individual status and assignment, the individuals noted below express the following conclusions with respect to this engagement:

(a) The engagement was carried out in conformity with the firm's policies and procedures.

(b) The examination was conducted in accordance with generally accepted auditing standards and included all procedures considered necessary in the circumstances.

(c) The auditor's report conforms with generally accepted auditing standards.

(d) The financial statements, in their opinion, are fair presentations in conformity with generally accepted accounting principles.

(e) Except as noted in the auditor's report, it is their opinion that the accounting principles have been applied on a basis consistent with that of the preceding period, and that all material informative disclosures have been made in the financial statements whose disclosure is necessary to make the statements fair and not misleading.

    (i)   In-charge accountant.

    (ii) Engagement partner.

    (iii) Pre-issuance reviewer.

19.   The following services in addition to the audit examination and report have been satisfactorily rendered and completed.

    (a) _____

    (b) _____

20.   A summary memorandum has been prepared by the engagement partner on the basic overall relationship with the client covering such matters as the desirability of retaining the client, additional services, arrangements regarding future engagements, fees, and special problems or considerations.

21.   The following have been processed and issued on the date indicated.

Document	No. of Copies	Date Issued
(a) Auditor's report	_____	_____
(b) Report letter communicating material weaknesses in internal accounting control	_____	_____
(c) Management letter	_____	_____
(d) _____	_____	_____
(e) _____	_____	_____

22.   Note has been taken of the guidelines, described in AU 561, to be followed by an auditor who, subsequent to the date of issuance of his report, becomes aware that facts may have existed at that date which might have affected his report if he had then been aware of such facts.

Comments on Items Listed Above

(Record below a description of any problems and unresolved matters pertaining to the guide, and explanations of any items recorded as *No* or *NA*. The subsequent resolution of such matters or explanations should also be noted along with the signature of the engagement partner as indication of final approval.)

_____

_____

IMMATERIAL ADJUSTING ENTRIES

A control form for Bypassed Adjusting Journal Entries is shown in Figure 7-2. The instructions should be read with due care and with special reference to the comments on the concept of materiality noted therein. The financial statements would be unfairly stated if certain adjustments that ordinarily would have been made have been improperly bypassed because of faulty judgment as to their materiality individually or in the aggregate.

Figure 7-2
Bypassed Adjusting Journal Entries

Client   Period

Prepared by   Reviewed by

INSTRUCTIONS

1.   Signatures of the auditor in charge and the engagement partner are to be recorded above.

2.   The client's agreement to waive the adjustments noted below would be obtained. To indicate approval, the comptroller's signature should be recorded on a copy of this form or on a working paper containing the same listing of bypassed entries.

3.   Only entries waived on the ground of their immateriality are to be listed. Any other adjustments not as yet recorded in whole or in part because of uncertainty, unresolved matters, disagreement with the client, or other considerations, fall into an entirely different but highly important category and are to be discussed with the engagement partner in accordance with firm policy and procedures.

4.   The listing below is to be scrutinized and carefully reviewed to ascertain whether the adjustments are in fact immaterial:

(a)   Standing by themselves.

(b)   In relationship to such significant bases for the current and prior years, as revenue, operating income, net income, current assets, and so on.

(c)   Considering the nature of the item (e.g., transactions with related parties are ordinarily associated with a lower threshold of materiality).

(d)   Taking into account the multiple impact of the adjustment (e.g., an inventory adjustment otherwise considered immaterial in amount will affect current assets, costs of sales, net income, and so on, and thus have a more material cumulative impact).

(e)   In the aggregate, bearing in mind that immaterial items may add up to a total that is material.

BYPASSED ENTRIES

(Note: number the entries and, below each entry, record an explanation of the entry as well as any pertinent comments such as reference to client discussion, if any.)

CHECKLIST REVIEW GUIDES

Four review guides covering the several aspects of the report and examination are presented in this chapter. They appear in the following order:

1. Auditor's Report Checklist Review Guide (Figure 7-3).
2. Financial Statements Checklist Review Guide (Figure 7-4).
3. Financial Statement Disclosures Checklist Reminder and Review Guide (Figure 7-5).
4. Working Papers Checklist Review Guide (Figure 7-6).

While they are presented as separate guides for convenience in use or reference, in their totality they provide a comprehensive focus on the vital questions that reviewers of the auditor's report, financial statements, and working papers are expected to ask and to find underlying support for.

The review process varies greatly in practice. The number of personnel, the status of those involved in the process, and the review methods followed, will depend upon the size of an accounting firm, number of partners, type of practice, individual preferences, and other factors. In some firms, an engagement partner may be assisted in his review by a manager or supervisor other than the one in charge of the audit engagement; in other firms, certain review responsibilities are assigned by the engagement partner to a review department. The matters covered in the review guides must be considered by all persons who should be participating in the review at the various levels—auditor in charge of the engagement, engagement manager (if any), review department (if any), engagement partner, and a pre-issuance reviewing partner or other qualified reviewer who has not participated in the particular engagement and can therefore provide a final independent overall review. The type of review, and the extent of involvement with supporting detail, will depend on the approach appropriate for the level and status of the particular reviewer.

The review guides presented in this chapter are of the questionnaire type in which each item to be reviewed is expressed as an affirmative statement calling in general for a *Yes*, *No*, or *NA* (i.e., not applicable) response. A check in the *No* column signifies an unsatisfactory condition that must be properly dealt with by the reviewers. As provided for in the introductory instructions to each guide, such conditions as well as any other questions or unresolved matters arising during the review process, as well as their ultimate disposition, are required to be written up in a comment section appended to each of the guides.

It is important to note too that while they are presented last, the financial statement disclosures review guide and the working papers review guide should have been completed and relevant problems resolved before the auditor's report and financial statements review guides can be fully and definitively completed. The ultimate focus in the auditor's examination and in the review process is, of course, on the auditor's report and the financial statements.

Figure 7-3
Auditor's Report Checklist Review Guide

Client	Period

Prepared by Date	Reviewed by (Date)	Reviewed by (Date)
(in-charge	(engagement	(Pre-issuance
accountant)	partner)	reviewer)

INSTRUCTIONS

See instructions for Figure 7-1, which similarly apply here.

CHECKLIST

	Yes	No	NA

1. The date of the auditor's report conforms with the dating principles expressed in the Statements on Auditing Standards and, in particular, AU 505 and 530.

2. The report has been addressed to the proper party as appropriate for this engagement, and the form of address is in conformity with AU 509.08.

3. The report contains:

(a) Either an expression of opinion (which may be an unqualified, qualified, or adverse opinion) regarding the financial statements taken as a whole, or a disclaimer in which it is stated that an opinion cannot be expressed along with reasons therefor.

(b) A clear-cut indication of the character of the examination, if any.

4. The working papers contain adequate support for all matters mentioned

in the auditor's report—scope of examination, explanatory comments, opinion or disclaimer of opinion.

5. Any comments or expression of opinion by the auditor on the scope of examination or on the financial statements are made in the auditor's report and not in the financial statements or accompanying notes to financial statements.

6. If an unqualified opinion is being expressed:

(a) The wording conforms to the standard form of report for an unqualified opinion.

(b) The examination has been made in accordance with generally accepted auditing standards and, moreover, included all procedures considered necessary in the circumstances of the specific engagement in addition to those procedures normally and generally employed.

(c) There are no reservations and exceptions relating to scope and character of examination, fairness of the financial statements, consistency in application of accounting principles, uncertainties, examination by other auditors, or otherwise that would require a qualified or adverse opinion or a disclaimer.

(d) Consideration has been given to introducing a permissible separate paragraph (usually as a middle paragraph) in the auditor's report to emphasize a matter of importance regarding the financial statements.

(e) If a separate paragraph is used to emphasize an important matter, such comments are not made because of reservations or qualifications that preclude an unqualified opinion.

(f) The disclosures required by Rule 203 of the AICPA's Code of Professional Ethics and by AU 509.18–19 with respect to justified departures from an officially promulgated accounting principle, are properly made in the report.

7. If a qualified opinion is being expressed:

(a) *All* substantive reasons for the qualified opinion are expressed in a separate explanatory paragraph of the report, which also sets forth the effects of the matters involved on the financial statements if determinable.

(b) The opinion paragraph makes reference to the foregoing explanatory paragraph.

(c) The opinion paragraph properly uses such phrases as "except for" or, as in the case of qualifications based on uncertainties, "subject to".

(d) The reasons for the qualified opinion have been carefully analyzed and it has been determined that the qualifications are not so material or pervasive, individually or in the aggregate, as to require an adverse opinion or a disclaimer.

(e) Disclosures of essential information that have not been made in the financial statements as required by GAAP have been made in the auditor's report.

8.   If a disclaimer of opinion is being expressed:

(a)   All substantive reasons for disclaiming an opinion are set forth in a separate paragraph of the report.

(b)   Where scope limitation is the reason for the disclaimer:

(i)   The report indicates the nature of the departure from generally accepted auditing standards.

(ii)   The disclaimer paragraph clearly states that the scope of examination was not sufficient to warrant the expression of an opinion, and an opinion is not being expressed.

(iii)   The procedures actually performed are not mentioned.

(c)   All reservations regarding the fairness of the financial statements or the consistency of their application are presented in the report.

(d)   The report does not express either negative assurances on the fairness of the financial statements or piecemeal opinions.

9.   If an adverse opinion is being expressed:

(a)   All substantive reasons and the principal effects on the financial statements are disclosed in a separate paragraph and referred to in the opinion paragraph.

(b)   Any reservations regarding the fairness of the financial statements apart from those giving rise to the adverse opinion are also stated in the report.

10.   Material uncertainties whose outcome and impact on the financial statements cannot be reasonably estimated:

(a)   Have been reported in a separate paragraph of the report.

(b)   And either a qualified opinion ("subject to") or a disclaimer has been expressed.

11.   The reporting principles applied in the following areas are in conformity with auditing standards and the specific requirements set forth in the indicated references:

(a)   Consistency in application of accounting principles (AU 546).

(b)   Comparative financial statements (AU 505).

(c)   Segment information (AU 435).

(d)   Unaudited replacement cost information (AU 730).

(e)   Special reports (AU 621).

12.   With respect to related party transactions of a significant nature:

(a)   If appropriate disclosures have not been made in the financial statements, a qualified opinion or an adverse opinion has been expressed.

(b)   If representations are made in the financial statements that the transaction(s) has been consummated on terms equivalent to an arms-length transaction and the correctness of the representation cannot be determined, then a qualified opinion or a disclaimer has been expressed; or if the representation is misleading, a qualified opinion or an adverse opinion has been expressed.

13.   If additional information accompanies the basic financial state-

ments, it has been prepared and reported on in accordance with SAS requirements.

Comments on Items Listed Above

_____

_____

Figure 7-4
Financial Statements Checklist Review Guide

Client _____ Statement period_____

Prepared by _____ Date_____
        (in-charge accountant)

Reviewed by _____ Date_____
        (engagement partner)

Reviewed by _____ Date_____
        (pre-issuance reviewer)

INSTRUCTIONS

See instructions for Figure 7-1 which similarly apply here.

CHECKLIST

	Yes	No	NA
1. The financial statements reflect:			
(a) The precise legal name of the entity.			
(b) Clear identification of the several financial statements.			
(c) Correct dates and periods covered.			
(d) Proper form, classification, content, and terminology			
(e) Clear and adequate notes and terminology appropriately referenced to the basic financial statements.			
2. The financial statements accounts and balances have been traced to and correspond to the adjusted balances per the working trial balance, the lead schedules, and the underlying working papers.			

3.   The unadjusted balances per the working trial balance have been reconciled with the adjusted balances and are in agreement with unadjusted balances as reflected in the underlying working papers.

4.   The financial statements and accompanying notes have been doublechecked for intra- and interstatement consistency and for mathematical accuracy.

5.   An analytical review of the financial statements:

(a)   Has been made and has been written up in a memorandum that has been reviewed by the engagement partner.

(b)   Significant variations in account balances, relationships, trends, and other important factors as between current year and prior years, industry data, and budgets and forecasts have been satisfactorily explained in the memorandum and in the working papers.

6.   The financial statements are presented fairly in conformity with generally accepted accounting principles unless otherwise noted in the auditor's report.

7.   Any departures with respect to the consistency in application of these accounting principles have been disclosed in the financial statements in accordance with GAAP.

8.   The financial statements, including accompanying notes, disclose all information whose disclosure is necesaary to make the statements fair and not misleading, and to conform with the GAAP disclosure requirements.

9.   The financial statement disclosures reminder and review checklist guide:

(a)   Has been prepared and reviewed.

(b)   All applicable matters specified in the guide as requiring disclosure in the financial statements have in fact been disclosed.

(c)   All questions and initially unresolved matters commented on in the guide have been satisfactory resolved and the pertinent facts and judgments are there clearly set forth.

10.   The financial statements including the accompanying notes to financial statements are consistent with and supported by:

(a)   The findings and conclusions set forth in the financial statement disclosures checklist reminder and review.

(b)   The underlying working papers and supporting evidential matter as indicated therein.

(c)   Pertinent authoritative pronouncements.

Comments on Items Listed Above

Figure 7-5
Financial Statement Disclosures
Checklist Reminder and Review Guide

Client _____ Statement period_____

Prepared by _____ Date_____
      (in-charge accountant)

Reviewed by _____ Date_____
      (engagement partner)

Reviewed by _____ Date_____
      (pre-issuance reviewer)

INSTRUCTIONS

1. This Guide is to be used in connection with annual reports containing financial statements prepared in conformity with generally accepted accounting principles or, in the case of certain types of special reports, on a comprehensive basis of accounting other than generally accepted accounting principles.

2. These instructions, as well as the other two sections of the Guide preceding the actual checklist—Some Basic Principles, and General Areas and Types of Disclosure—should be read with due care.

3. For each checklist item, check the appropriate response to signify the following:

(a) *Yes*: adequate disclosure has been made either in the body of the financial statements or in the accompanying notes, as appropriate.

(b) *No*: adequate disclosure has *not* been made of matters whose disclosure is necessary to make the statements fair and not misleading. A substantive explanation giving the nature of the matter, its significance, the reasons for the client's refusal to permit the disclosure, and the effect on the auditor's report, should be recorded in the comment section at the end of the guide.

(c) *NM*: the matter is not sufficiently material to warrant disclosure. The nature of the matter involved, the degree of materiality, and a substantive explanation and justification for the judgment should be recorded in the comment section. In this connection, note carefully the comments below, under the caption *Some Basic Principles*, on materiality, and especially the point that an accumulation of immaterial matters may, in the aggregate, have a material impact on the financial statements.

(d) *NA*: the matter(s) is not present and, therefore, does not apply.

(e) *WP*: the working paper reference number should be noted for all items checked including NA items, although for some *NA* checks the inapplicability of the matter may be so clear-cut and obvious that working paper documentation would ordinarily be unreasonable or meaningless. The working papers pertinent to the informative disclosure items in question should fully describe their nature, impact, degree of materiality, relevant auditing procedures and supporting evidence. A disagreement with the client on any important matter should be described and documented.

4. The checklist is not intended to be a fully comprehensive listing of all disclosures required by professional pronouncements and by GAAP in general. Those responsible for completing and reviewing the guide should:

(a) Consider the circumstances and practices peculiar to the individual company or its industry.

(b) Take into account the general areas and types of disclosure that are listed in the section preceding the checklist. Such disclosures generally apply even in the absence of specific mention in authoritative pronouncements.

(c) With respect to matters that are disclosed in the financial statements or would seem to call for such disclosure, read carefully pertinent provisions in professional pronouncements to ensure comprehensiveness of coverage of details that are required to be disclosed.

5. References used in this Guide are as follows:

(a) AU: AICPA, Professional Standards Volume 1, Auditing.

(b) AC: AICPA, Professional Standards Volume 3, Accounting. (AC sections are usually preceded by reference to the related ARB, APB, or FASB pronouncement.)

(c) S-X: U.S. Securities and Exchange Commission, Regulation S-X. (The references to Regulation S-X have been included because of their relevance even for non-SEC engagements, but, as with the other authoritative reference, they are not intended to be all-encompassing.)

Some disclosure items may be unsupported by specific provision in authoritative pronouncements but they are nevertheless included because of their general acceptability as matters to be disclosed.

SOME BASIC DISCLOSURE PRINCIPLES

1. All material matters must be disclosed in the body of the financial statements or in the appended notes, the disclosure of which is necessary to achieve a fair presentation in conformity with generally accepted

accounting principles, and to make the financial statements not misleading.

2. The financial statements and the appended notes are the representations of management, and it is management's responsibility to make the necessary disclosures. This principle applies even though the auditor may prepare, or assist the client in preparing, the financial statements.

3. Any comments of the auditor on the scope of his examination or any opinion on the fairness of the financial statements belong in his report and should not appear in notes to the financial statements.

4. If essential information is not disclosed in the financial statements, including the accompanying notes, the auditor should provide the information in his report (unless, as in the case of failure to include a statement of changes in financial position, the omission, in certain circumstances, is recognized as appropriate) and proceed to express a qualified opinion or an adverse opinion. This proposition reflects the third and fourth standard of reporting.

5. The purpose of informative disclosures is to enhance the basic fairness of the financial statements. If the statements contain departures from generally accepted accounting principles, mere disclosure of that fact cannot cure the deficiency. The statements must either be revised or the auditor would be required to express either a qualified opinion or an adverse opinion.

6. The auditor may wish to emphasize some matter relating to the financial statements even though he intends to issue an unqualified opinion. He may do so in a separate paragraph of his report even though the information may already have been provided in the financial statements or accompanying notes.

7. Financial reporting is only concerned with significant information. Hence, the concept of adequacy of informative disclosures and the third standard of reporting apply to matters that are considered to be material. Materiality itself is a complex concept and may be evaluated in a variety of ways: the absolute amount of an item standing alone; the aggregate of a group of otherwise immaterial items; in relationship to other important accounts; relative to various bases of the current or prior years, such as total assets, current assets, revenue, income before extraordinary items, net income; as indicative of future trends; normality or abnormality; expectedness or unexpectedness; relatedness of parties involved; involvement of officers; state of solvency.

Materiality may encompass quantitative as well as qualitative elements. In general, the more sensitive an item is (e.g., illegal acts or transactions among related parties), the less is the dependence placed on any given quantitative materiality standard. The fundamental consideration in forming a judgement as to whether a matter is sufficiently material to require disclosure is whether the information is significant enough to affect the evaluations, judgments, and decisions of readers of the financial statements, especially of credit-grantors and present or prospective stockholders or other investors. In addition to exercising his independent and objective judgment of the significance of the matter in question, the auditor must also perceive it as though through the eyes of the readers of the financial statements and with their lay conception of the significance of the item.

8.   Where a reasonable doubt exists as to whether a matter should be disclosed, it should be resolved in favor of disclosure. However, it should not be considered necessary to make disclosures that may be harmful to the company or its stockholders but unnecessary to ensure the fairness of the financial statements. Further, excessive verbiage in making disclosures can be confusing to the reader and should be avoided. Disclosure comments should be clear and complete but also brief and to the point.

GENERAL AREAS AND TYPES OF DISCLOSURE

The following is a succinct listing of some of the important general areas and types of informative disclosures which conform with current reporting theory and practice. The listing can be used as a checklist of broad disclosure categories, and can serve as a framework of reference in judging whether matters relating to an individual client are of the type that should be disclosed, assuming, of course, that they are material. It will also help to ensure that informative disclosures are made even in the absence of specific pronouncements mandating disclosure, or in the event any such pronouncement might inadvertently have been overlooked. But again, it should be cautioned that the categories listed are broad in scope and, moreover, do not necessarily constitute a definitively comprehensive presentation. The areas mentioned will, of course, be expanded on in the checklist section of the guide.

1.   Meaningful, informative, logical, and clear classification and description of items in the financial statements, and designation of totals of subordinate groupings as well as of major classifications.

2.   Clear and precise terminology.

3.   Avoidance of improper offset of assets and liabilities or, in general, of any account categories; hence, disclosure of valuation accounts.

4.   Accounting policies followed—accounting principles and methods of applying them.

5.   Market value for certain assets.

6.   Conditions, restrictions, and special obligations affecting assets, liabilities, and stockholders' equity.

7.   Assets subject to mortgages, liens, and restrictions on use or disposition.

8.   Creditor or stockholder preferences.

9.   Major commitments including leasing or other contractual arrangements, and pension and other compensation plans.

10. Contingencies, including present or potential threats and vulnerabilities relating to the entity's assets, operations, solvency, and existence; includes contingencies arising from government regulations.

11. Unusual, infrequently occurring, or extraordinary items relating to either operating results or financial condition.

12. Certain types of events occurring subsequent to the statement date.

13. Transactions and account balances with key employees, officers, directors, stockholders, related companies, and other related parties.

14. Illegal acts.

15. Segment information.

16. Per share and other such data of special interest to stockholders.

17. Accounting changes.

18. Matters affecting comparability.

DISCLOSURE CHECKLIST

	Yes	No	NM	NA	WP

General and Overlapping Items

1. All material matters whose disclosure is necessary to make the statements fair and not misleading. (APB Statement 4, AC 1024.34; AU 430; S-X 3.06)

2. Comparative financial statements: presentation; reference to prior years' footnotes; explanations and auditor's qualifications; exceptions to comparability. (ARB 43, Chapt. 2A, AC 2041)

3. Clear-cut captions and/or totals for such items as current assets, current liabilities, total assets, total liabilities, stockholders' equity, revenue, costs and expenses, income from continuing operations, income taxes, income before extraordinary items, extraordinary items, net income. (ARB 43, Chapt. 3A, AC 2031; FASB 6, AC 2033.15; APB Statement 4, AC 1027.18, .25; APB 30, AC 2012)

4. Summarization of accounting policies to be presented under a caption like Summary of Significant Accounting Policies preceding the notes to financial

statements or as the initial note. The summary may also refer to details presented in the subsequent notes. Some examples of accounting policies described in the summary: accounting principles followed; methods of applying them, especially when acceptable alternatives are available; principles and methods peculiar to the industry; unusual or innovative applications of GAAP; basis of consolidation; depreciation methods; amortization of intangibles; inventory pricing; recognition of profit on long-term construction-type contracts; revenue recognition (APB 22, AC 2045, 12–.15; S-X 3.08).

5. Basis of presentation and nature of differences with GAAP, where financial statements are prepared in accordance with a comprehensive basis of accounting other than GAAP (AU 621.05).

6. Departures from accounting principles promulgated by the body (currently FASB) designated by AICPA Council to establish such principles, with explanation of reasons that adherence to promulgated principles would have caused the financial statements to be misleading, and indication of effect upon the statements. (Rule 203 of AICPA Code of Professional Ethics; AC 520; applicable to auditor's reporting responsibilities, but appropriate disclosure is basically the company's responsibility.)

7. Assets and liabilities separately stated without offset, except for legal right of offset. (APB Statement 4, AC 1027.25; APB 10, AC 2032; ARB 43, Chapt. 11A, AC 4041.22)

8. Accounting changes:

(a) The nature of and justification for a change in accounting principle and its effect on income. (APB 20, AC 1051.17, .19, .28, .30; S-X 3.07)

(b) "For cumulative effect" type of change, income before extraordinary items and net income on pro forma basis, as well as per share amounts, for all periods presented as if newly adopted principle had been applied. (APB 20, AC 1051.19, .21, .25)

(c) Effect of change in accounting estimate on income before extraordinary items, net income, and related per share amounts. (APB 20, AC 1051.33)

(d) Nature and reason for change in reporting entity and effect of change. (APB 20, AC 1051.35)

(e) Nature of error in previously issued financial statements and effect of correction. (APB 20, AC 1051.37)

(f) Prior period adjustments. (FASB 16, AC 2014, S-X 3.07)

(g) Per share effects of restatement of prior periods. (APB 15, AC 2011.18)

9. Comparability: any matters significantly affecting comparability of current year with prior years, or having that potential with respect to future years. (APB Statement 4, AC 1024.32)

10. Consolidated financial statements:

(a) Principles of consolidation. (ARB 51, AC 2051.06; APB 22, AC 2045.13; S-X Rule 4.04)

(b) Effect of material intervening transactions where fiscal years of parent and subsidiary differ. (ARB 51, AC 2051.05)

(c) Undistributed earnings of a subsidiary for which income taxes have not been accrued. (ARB 23, AC 4095.14)

(d) Intercompany balances, transactions, and profits or losses eliminated; or disclosures made if not determinable. (ARB 51, AC 2051.07; S-X 3.16, 4.06)

(e) Foreign subsidiaries. (ARB 43, Chapt. 12, AC 1081.08-.09)

(f) Aggregate foreign exchange gain or loss. (FASB 8, AC 1083.032)

(g) Effects of exchange rate changes on reported results of operations. (FASB 8, AC 1083.033-.034)

(h) Unconsolidated subsidiaries. (ARB 51, AC 2051.18-.20; also see section on Investments.)

11. Contingencies and uncertainties:

(a) Nature and amount of accrual for loss contingency. (FASB 5, AC 4311.09) Some examples of loss contingencies are: collectibility of receivables; product warranties; casualty risks; threat of expropriation of assets; pending or threatened litigation; and claims and assessments. (FASB 5, AC 4311.03)

(b) Nature of contingency and estimate of possible loss or range of loss where criteria have not been met for actual accrual or loss, or state that an estimate cannot be made. (FASB 5, AC 4311.10; S-X 3.16)

(c) Nature of loss or loss contingency arising after the date of the financial statements, and estimate of amount or range of loss or possible loss, or state that estimate cannot be made. (FASB 5, AC 4311.11)

(d) Contingencies that may result in gains, but avoid misleading implications on likelihood of realization. (FASB 5, AC 4311.17)

12. Development stage enterprises. (FASB 7, AC 2062.10-.13)

13. Commitments, obligations, and restrictions:

(a) Nature and amount of guarantees and, if estimable, value of possible recovery from outside party. Some examples are guarantees of indebtedness of others and guarantees to repurchase receivables or other property. (FASB 5, AC 4311.12)

(b) Assets pledged as security for loans. (FASB 5, AC 4311.18-.19)

(c) Unutilized letters of credit. (FASB 5, AC 4311.18-.19)

(d) Obligations to reduce debts, maintain working capital, or restrict dividends. (FASB 5, AC 4311.18-.19)

(e) Commitments such as for plant expansion, permanent or long-term investments, asset leasing. (FASB 5, AC 4311.18-.19; S-X 3.16)

(f) Restrictions on acquisition of treasury stock.

(g) Bonus, profit-sharing, and special compensation agreements. (S-X 3.16)

14. Leases:

(a)   Lessee disclosures. (FASB 13, AC 4053.013, .016; S-X 3.16)

(b)   Lessor disclosures. (FASB 13, AC 4053.023. 047)

15.   Pension plans: existence; description of employee groups covered; accounting and funding policies; pension cost provision for the period; excess of actuarially computed value of vested benefits over a specified base; nature and effect of significant matters affecting comparability. (APB 8, AC 4063.46; S-X 3.16) For defined benefit pension plans, additional data including actuarial present value of vested and nonvested accumulated plan benefits. (FASB 36)

16.   Stock option and stock purchase plans, warrants and rights; status of option or plan at close of reporting period; number of shares under option; option price; number of shares as to which options were exercisable; number of shares exercised during reporting period and option price; (ARB 43, Chapt. 13B, AC 4061.15) warrants or rights outstanding. (S-X 3.16)

17.   Income taxes:

(a)   Differentiation of income tax expense as between amounts currently payable and amounts reflecting tax allocation; and classification of deferred taxes by net current amount and net noncurrent amount. (APB 11, AC 4091.11e, .56, .59; S-X 3.16)

(b)   Allocation of income tax expense, as appropriate, to income before extraordinary items and to extraordinary items. (APB 11, AC 4091.59)

(c)   Amounts of operating loss carryforwards not recognized in the loss period, together with expiration dates and significant amounts of any other unused deductions or credits and their expiration dates. (APB 11, AC 4091.62)

(d)   Status of IRS reviews of prior years' returns.

(e)   Reasons for significant variations in customary relationship between income tax expense and accounting income if not otherwise apparent; and significant differences between pretax accounting income and taxable income. (APB 11, AC 4091.62)

(f)   Method of accounting for the investment credit, and amounts involved. (APB 2, 4, AC 4094.18)

18.   Business combinations:

(a)   Pooling of interests method. (APB 16, AC 1091.63–.65)

(b)   Purchase method. (APB 16, AC 1091.95–.96)

19.   Long-term construction-type contracts. (ARB 45, AC 4031)

20.   Subsequent events. Some events occurring subsequent to the date of the financial statements but prior to their issuance may require adjustment of the financial statements while other such events may require disclosure. Some examples of the latter are: issuance of bonds or capital stock; purchase of a business; litigation; and casualty losses. (AU 560.06)

21.   Related parties: nature of relationship, description and dollar volume of transactions, effects of change in method of establishing terms, and amounts due from or to related parties. (AU 335.16–.18; FASB 21, AC 2083.09; ARB 43, AC 5111.01) Capital stock optioned, sold or offered for sale to directors, officers and key employees. (S-X 3.16)

22.   Illegal acts. (AU 328.15)

23.   Segments of a business enterprise—industry segments, foreign operations and export sales, major customers. (FASB 14, AC 2081; disclosures not required for nonpublic companies—FASB 21, AC 2083)

24.   Current replacement cost information; for certain companies required to disclose such data by the SEC's Regulation S-X. (S-X Rule 3.17; AU 730)

25.   Interim (quarterly) financial information included in notes to annual financial statements (S-X Rule 3.16t; APB 28, AC 2071; SAS 24, AU 721; AU 9516; for disclosures applicable to interim financial statements, see APB 28, AC 2071.)

Assets

26.   Valuation accounts shown separately as deductions from related assets. (APB 12, 2044.02; S-X 3.09)

27.   Assets mortgaged, pledged, assigned, subject to liens, or restricted as to use. (AU 430.02; FASB 5, AC 4311.18–.19; S-X 3.16)

28.   Current assets classified as such in accordance with authoritative definition, with appropriate explanation where normal operating cycle is longer than one year. (ARB 43, Chapt. 3A, AC 2031; S-X 3.11)

29.   Cash:

(a)   Withdrawal or usage restrictions. (ARB 43, Chapt. 3A, AC 2031.06; S-X 5.02)

(b)   Compensating balance arrangements. (S-X 5.02-1, ASR 148)

30.   Accounts and notes receivable.

(a)   Related parties including officers and employees. (ARB 43, Chapt. 1A; AC 5111.01; SAS 6, AU 335; S-X 5.02)

(b)   Unusual receivables such as tax refunds and contract termination claims. (APB 11, AC 4091.57; ARB 43, Chapt. 11C, AC 4043.05)

(c)   Installment receivables; also amounts not due in one year but reflected as current in accordance with trade practice. (S-X 3.11 and 5.02-3b)

(d)   Allowance for doubtful accounts. (APB 12, AC 2044.01–.02; S-X 5.02-4)

(e)   Unearned discounts, finance charges and interest, or deduction from face amount of receivables if so included. (APB 6, AC 2031.10; S-X 5.02)

(f)   For notes carried at "present value": description of note, face amount, effective interest rate, and application of discount or premium to face amount of note. (APB 21, AC 4111.15)

(g)   Pledged, assigned, or sold with recourse.

(h)   From sale of capital stock, as deduction from stockholders' equity.

31.   Inventories:

(a)   Basis of stating inventories and method of computing cost. (ARB 43, Chap. 3A, AC 2031.09; S-X 5.02; APB 22, AC 2045.13)

(b)   Relationship of standard costs (if used) to recognized costing method. (ARB 43, Chapt. 4, AC 5121.06)

(c)   Inventory classification—e.g., finished goods, work-in-process, raw materials, supplies. (ARB 43, Chapt. 3A, AC 2031; S-X 5.02–6a)

(d)   Excess of replacement cost over LIFO inventories. (S-X 5.02–6c)

(e)   Substantial and unusual losses in applying the rule of lower of cost or market. (ARB 43, Chapt. 4, AC 5121.14)

(f)   Material losses on purchase commitments. (ARB 43, Chapt. 4, AC 5121.17)

32.   Investments:

(a)   In general, basis at which stated; market value if determinable (but not required for investments in common stock of subsidiaries); distinction between current and noncurrent; and disclosures on pledging of assets or other restrictions or encumbrances. (APB 22, AC 2045.12; ARB 43, Chapt. 3A, AC 2031.06, .09; APB 18, AC 5131.20b; FASB 12, AC 5132; FASB 5, AC 4311.18; S-X 5.02)

(b)   Marketable equity securities (not accounted for by the equity method) appropriately segregated as between current and noncurrent assets, with disclosure of aggregate cost and market value, realized and unrealized gains or losses, and other data as detailed in FASB 12. (FASB 12, AC 5132)

(c)   Other marketable securities, appropriately segregated between current and noncurrent, with disclosure of cost or other basis at which stated, and market value. (ARB, Chapt. 3A, AC 2031.09; APB 18, AC 5131; S-X 5.02–2)

(d)   Investments in common stock—equity method. (APB 18, AC 5131.11, .19, .20)

33.   Property, plant and equipment:

(a)   Basis on which stated. (APB 22, AC 2045.12; S-X 5.02)

(b)   Balances of major classes. (APB 12, AC 2043.02)

(c)   Depreciation expense and accumulated depreciation. (APB 12, AC 2043.02)

(d)   Method or methods used in computing depreciation with respect to major classes of depreciable assets. (APB 12, AC 2043.02; S-X 3.16)

(e)   Mortgages or other liens.

34.   Intangible assets:

(a)   Basis on which stated. (APB 22, AC 2045.12; S-X 5.02)

(b)   Classification and description by type.
(c)   Method and period of amortization. (APB 17, AC 5141.30)

Liabilities

35.   Current liabilities:
(a)   Criteria for classification as current or noncurrent, with appropriate explanation where operating cycle is longer than one year. (ARB 43, Chapt. 3A, AC 2031; FASB 6, AC 2033; S-X 3.12)
(b)   Appropriate classification—for example, trade, banks, accruals, and so on. (S-X 5.02)
(c)   Liabilities to related parties. (AU 335; S-X 5.02)
(d)   Guarantees by other parties.
(e)   Stating the total for current liabilities. (FASB 6, AC 2033.15)
(f)   Classification as noncurrent liability of short-term obligations expected to be refinanced. (FASB 6, AC 2033)
(g)   Inclusion of portion of long-term debt due within one year.
36.   Noncurrent liabilities:
(a)   Description, amortization, interest, and other significant provisions; conversion features; subordination agreement; assets pledged or mortgaged; current portion as current liability; indenture commitments and restrictions; and premium and discount. (FASB 5, AC 4311.18–.19; S-X 5.02)
(b)   Defaults in principal, interest or other required payments, or breach of covenant of indenture or other agreement. (S-X 3.16)
(c)   For notes carried at "present value": description of note, face amount, effective interest rate, and application of discount or premium to face amount of note. (APB 21, AC 4111.15)

Stockholders' Equity

37.   Pertinent rights and privileges of the various securities outstanding, including the following: dividend and liquidation preferences; participation rights; call prices and dates; conversion or exercise prices or rates and pertinent dates; sinking fund requirements; and unusual voting rights. (APB 15, AC 2011.19; APB 10, AC 5515.01–.02; S-X 3.16, 5.02)
38.   Elements of stockholders' equity clearly differentiated: capital stock, additional paid-in capital, retained earnings (S-X 5.02)
39.   Changes in separate accounts comprising stockholders' equity (in addition to retained earnings), and of changes in the number of shares of equity securities during at least the most recent annual fiscal period and any subsequent interim period. (APB 12, AC 2042.02)

40.   Cumulative preferred stock dividends in arrears. (FASB 5, AC 4311.18–.19; APB 10, AC 5515.01–.02; S-X 3.16)

41.   Appropriation of retained earnings clearly identified as such. (FASB 5, AC 4311.15)

42.   Dividends in cash or in kind or other distributions to shareholders. (APB 19, AC 2021.14)

43.   Restrictions on dividend payments based on working capital or other requirements or conditions. (FASB 5, AC 4311.18–.19; S-X 3.16)

44.   Restrictions on acquisition of treasury stock.

45.   Carrying basis of treasury stock. (ARB 43, Chapt. 1B, AC 5542.13; S-X 3.14)

Statement of Income

46.   Disclosure of significant elements, for example: revenue (sales); costs and expenses; income (or loss) before extraordinary items; extraordinary items; provision for income taxes; if applicable, income (or loss) from continuing operations and from discontinued operation of a segment of the business; and net income. (APB 9, AC 2010.28; APB 30, AC 2012.09–.11; S-X 5.03)

47.   Unusual or infrequently occurring items that do not meet criteria for classification as extraordinary items. (APB 30, AC 2012.26)

48.   Total research and development costs charged to expense in each period for which an income statement is presented. (FASB 2, AC 4211.13)

49.   Basis of revenue recognition, especially with respect to installment sales, long-term contracts, or unusual transactions, or if alternative methods can be applied. (APB Statement 4, AC 2045.12; S-X 3.16)

50.   Gains and losses from extinguishment of debt as extraordinary items, net of related income tax effect; but disclose as separate item gains or losses from cash purchases of debt made to satisfy current or future sinking fund requirements. (FASB 4, AC 2013.08)

51.   The nature of non-monetary transactions, basis of accounting for assets transferred, and recognized gains or losses. (APB 29, AC 1041.28)

52.   Results of discontinued operations including identity of segment involved, manner of disposal, dates, segment assets and liabilities remaining, income taxes, revenues, and gains or losses on disposal of the business segment. (APB 30, AC 2012.08, .18)

53.   For marketable equity securities: net realized gain or loss; basis on which cost was determined in computing realized gain or loss; and amount of change in valuation allowances included in income. (FASB 12, AC 5132.12)

54.   Per share data (not applicable to nonpublic enterprises—FASB 21, AC 2083): earnings or net loss per share; primary and fully diluted; assumptions and adjustments involved in computation; earnings per

share for continuing operations; per share effect of discontinued operations; conversions during or after period under examination. (APB 15, AC 2011; APB 30, AC 2012.09)

Statement of Changes in Financial Position

55. A required statement. (APB 19, AC 2021.07)

56. All important aspects of financing and investing activities whether or not cash or other working capital elements are directly affected. (APB 19, AC 2021.08)

57. Income or loss for the period before extraordinary items as the beginning caption. (ABP 19, AC 2021.10)

58. Net changes in each element of working capital at least for the current period. (APB 19, AC 2021.12)

59. Other disclosures, such as outlays for long-term assets with separate identification of items like investments and property; conversions to common stock; issuance, redemption or purchase of capital stock. (APB 19, AC 2021.14)

Financial Reporting and Changing Prices

60. Supplementary information to be presented in published annual reports as required for public enterprises meeting specified criteria: income from continuing operations adjusted for the effects of general inflation; purchasing power gain or loss on net monetary items; also: income from continuing operations on a current cost basis; current cost amounts of inventory and property, plant and equipment at end of fiscal year; increases or decreases in current cost amounts of inventory and property, plant and equipment, net of inflation; also, a five-year summary of selected specified financial data. (FASB 33; SAS 27, 28)

Figure 7-6
Working Papers Checklist Review Guide

_____   _____
Client   Period

_____   _____   _____
Prepared by   Date   Reviewed by   Date   Reviewed by   Date
(in-charge   (engagement   (pre-issuance
accountant)   partner)   reviewer)

INSTRUCTIONS

See instructions for Figure 7-1 which similarly apply here.

CHECKLIST

	Yes	No	NA

1.   All working papers are clearly identified as to the client, title and purpose,
and financial statement date or period.

2.   Working papers are properly indexed.

3.   Clear explanations are provided of
tickmarks or other symbols.

4.   Initials or signatures of both preparer and reviewer, as well as dates of
such preparation and review, appear on
all working papers including all sections
of the internal accounting control guide
and the audit program guide.

5.   The basis for, and approval of (at
the appropriate supervisory level), significant modifications of the audit program
and auditing procedures are noted and
documented in the working papers.

6.   Mathematical accuracy of working
papers prepared by the client has been
independently checked.

7. Evidential matter examined and sources of information are clearly indicated.

8. The financial statement balances are in agreement with the adjusted balances per the working trial balance.

9. The unadjusted and adjusted balances per the working trial balance are in agreement with and supported by the underlying working papers.

10. Financial statement balances, notes to financial statements, comments in the auditor's report, and the auditor's opinion, are all supported by the working papers and by sufficient competent evidential matter contained in or described in the working papers.

11. There are no indications in the working papers of:

(a) Any client restrictions on the scope of examination.

(b) Any other limitations on the ability of the auditors to gain satisfaction as to the validity and fairness of the accounts.

12. The permanent file working papers are properly indexed, updated, cross referenced to current working papers, subjected to verification and auditing procedures as indicated in the circumstances, and reflected, as appropriate, in the financial statements and auditor's report. Specifically, the foregoing applies to the following items, copies or excerpts of which are contained in the permanent file working papers:

(a) Minutes of stockholder meetings.

(b) Minutes of directors meetings.

(c) Minutes of executive committee meetings.

(d) Important contracts.

(e) Lease and other agreements.

(f) Pension, profit-sharing, and other compensation plans.

(g) Cumulative (summary or otherwise) analyses and schedules for property, plant and equipment, depreciation, stockholder equity accounts, and the like.

(h) Background information regarding the company, its organization, accounting system, industry practices and data, etc.

(i) Historical summary regarding income tax returns and examinations.

13. Statistical sampling or other sampling plans and procedures are adequately described.

14. For each segment of the examination, as well as overall, evaluations are made and conclusions are expressed and documented regarding:

(a) Adequacy of the system of internal accounting control, with specification of strengths and weaknesses.

(b) Extent of reliance on the system of internal accounting control in undertaking substantive tests.

(c) Sufficiency of competent evidential matter examined.

(d) Analytical reviews.

(e) Impact, where relevant, of the client's EDP system.

14. The following items or areas of audit concern are contained in or covered in the working papers, properly signed as required, and acceptable and complete in form and content. Moreover, there is satisfactory indication that additional and sufficient corroborative evidence was obtained as required by the circumstances; that appropriate reviews were made at the various audit supervisory levels; and that relevant data have been reflected, as appropriate, in the financial statements and accompanying notes:

(a) Audit plans.

(b) Audit programs for all significant accounts or account groupings tailored to the specific engagement.

(c) Internal accounting control questionnaires and working papers tailored to the specific engagement.

(d) Audit programs and related working papers dealing with subsequent events review; illegal acts; related party transactions; disclosure of unrecorded, understated, or previously unrevealed liabilities and contingencies; errors or irregularities; and risk areas.

(e) Management representation letters.

(f) Responses from client's attorneys.

15. The working papers describe adequately, with respect to internal auditors, outside specialists, and the use of other independent auditors, if applicable, the audit services provided by them, their qualifications, and our evaluation and extent of reliance upon those services.

16. The working papers contain evidence that adequate tests have been made and sufficient supporting evidence obtained (and adjusting entries recorded as necessary) with respect to:

(a) Cutoff of sales, purchases, inventories; cutoff of cash receipts and disbursements.

(b) Collectibility of accounts receivable and adequacy of the allowance for doubtful accounts, and the write-off of uncollectible accounts whether or not offset by an allowance account.

(c) Intervening inventory transactions if observation of physical inventory count was made at interim dates.

(d) Bases on which assets are stated.

(e) Market values of assets where relevant (inventories, securities, other investments, etc.) with market value being properly defined and applied as appropriate for the given asset and circumstance (e.g., replacement cost, realizable value, realizable value reduced by costs of disposal and by a normal profit margin; lower of cost or market item by item or in the aggregate; etc.).

17. The working papers show that oral or written representations or

explanations of the client are followed up and adequate corroborative evidence obtained, as appropriate in the circumstances.

18. Sufficient competent evidential matter in the form of physical observation, physical count, inspection and confirmation, has been obtained for the following accounts, and appropriate summaries of the results of these procedures and conclusions regarding their adequacy, are contained in the working papers: cash; receivables; iventories; securities and other investments; and so on.

19. The working papers clearly show that all confirmation replies (from banks, receivables, credit-grantors, etc.) have been carefully scrutinized and reconciled with the corresponding accounts, and cognizance taken of indications of assets pledged, mortgaged, assigned or restricted, or of the existence of unrecorded or previously undisclosed liabilities or contingencies.

20. A tax review memorandum has been prepared by the (auditor's) tax department on the adequacy of the income tax provisions, accruals, and deferred accounts.

21. The working papers contain evidence that adequate consultations occurred at appropriate supervisory and partner levels on difficult or questionable matters of a material nature, and that decisions made are supported by adequate documentation.

22. The working papers contain evidence that the adjusting journal entries:

(a) Are adequately supported by evidential matter.

(b) Have been approved by the engagement partner.

(c) Have been approved by the client.

23. The control form for bypassed adjusting journal entries has been properly completed and approved.

24. All "to do" notes, points to be cleared, and matters noted for further consultation and discussion with client or audit supervisors have been satisfactorily cleared and resolved and disposition clearly recorded and documented.

25. The working papers contain a copy of a letter reporting material weaknesses in internal accounting control:

(a) In satisfactory form, with conclusions supported by findings noted in the working papers.

(b) With indication that the contents have been discussed with management and the board of directors or its audit committee.

26. Time budgets have been prepared, completed, and reviewed for each phase of the engagement, and significant differences between actual and budgeted data have been investigated and explained.

27. A memorandum has been prepared, approved, and included in the working papers on helpful suggestions for use on the next engagement.

28.   A signed engagement letter covering the specific engagement is contained in the working papers.

29.   The actual engagement has been carried out in conformity with the provisions of the engagement letter.

Comments on Items Listed Above

_____

_____

CHAPTER 8

Compilation and Review of Financial Statements; Unaudited Financial Statements

INTRODUCTION: TYPES OF UNAUDITED FINANCIAL STATEMENTS

Financial statements are audited if the accountant has—and are unaudited if he has not—performed an examination in accordance with generally accepted auditing standards with the objective of expressing an opinion regarding the financial statements taken as a whole and has applied auditing procedures sufficient in scope to permit him to report on the financial statements in the manner described in Statement on Auditing Standards No. 2 (AU 509).

The accountant may be associated with unaudited financial statements in the following ways that are differentiated in authoritative AICPA pronouncements, noted parenthetically below, that provide general guidance applicable to each category.

1. *Compilation of financial statements of a nonpublic entity.* (Statements on Standards for Accounting and Review Services [SSARS] Nos. 1 and 2)

2. *Review of financial statements of a nonpublic entity.* (SSARS Nos. 1 and 2)

3. *Review of interim financial statements of public entity, and review of interim financial information included in a note to audited financial statements of a public or nonpublic entity.* (SAS No. 24)

4. *Association with financial statements of a public entity* that have been neither audited nor reviewed. (SAS No. 26)

In reporting on unaudited financial statements for either public or nonpublic companies, the accountant must of course express a disclaimer of opinion, but the wording of the report will vary with the type of engagement.

The foregoing AICPA references reflect a recent development in which the AICPA instituted a division of responsibility between the AICPA Auditing Standards Board and the recently established AICPA Accounting and Review Services Committee. The former has responsibility, as heretofore, for the promulgation of standards relating to audit engagements for both public and nonpublic entities and to reporting on unaudited financial statements of public entities; its pronouncements appear usually as Statements on Auditing Standards (SAS) which are reproduced in the AU sections of *AICPA Professional Standards,* Volume 1. The Accounting and Review Services Committee is the Institute's senior technical committee designated to develop standards of reporting in connection with the unaudited financial statements of a nonpublic entity. Its pronouncements are issued as Statements on Standards for Accounting and Review Services which are reproduced in AR sections of *AICPA Professional Standards,* Volume 1. For nonpublic companies, reports on unaudited financial statements may not be issued unless the accountant has either *compiled* the financial statements or *reviewed* the financial statements in accordance with the SSARS standards and procedures.

In this context, both SSARS No. 2 (amending the definition in SSARS No. 1) and SAS No. 26 define a nonpublic entity as any entity other than (*a*) one whose securities are traded on a public market, or (*b*) one that files with a regulatory agency preparatory to a public sale of its securities, or (*c*) a subsidiary, corporate joint venture, or other entity controlled by an entity covered by (*a*) or (*b*).

Planning and program guides, engagement letters, representation letters, accountants' reports, review guides, and interpretive commentary are presented in this chapter for the several types of engagements in which an accountant may be associated with unaudited financial statements. On occasion, reference will be made to comparable materials included in this book applicable to audit engagements in order to avoid duplication where use of substantially the same material would be appropriate, even if only in part and in different ways. In general, moreover, basic audit materials may often provide a richer context and understanding of certain matters that are also dealt with on unaudited engagements although in a quite different manner. For example, a guide for acquiring a knowledge of the client's business for use on audits can be drawn on quite easily for the design of a much simpler and less demanding guide for use, say, in a compilation or review of financial statements.

The term *accountant* rather than *auditor* is used deliberately in this chapter inasmuch as the professional services rendered in connection with such non-audit engagements as compilation or review of financial statements are referred to in AICPA pronouncements as *accounting services*. On such engagements, moreover, the use of the term like *audit, auditor* or *examination* are not only misleading but may result quite unnecessarily in burdensome professional and other consequences.

COMPILATION OF FINANCIAL STATEMENTS

A *compilation of financial statements* is the term used to describe the service rendered by the accountant for a nonpublic entity in presenting in the form of financial statements information made available by the management (owners) as the entity's representation, but without any expression by the accountant of any assurance on the statements. A compilation is in the nature of an *accounting* service and should not be identified in any way as an *audit* service.

A compilation engagement would most often be undertaken for a smaller size company. Sometimes, it may be necessary for the accountant to undertake other accounting services to enable him to compile the financial statements, such as consultation on accounting or tax matters, assistance in recordkeeping and in adjusting the books of account, and preparing a working trial balance. But ultimately and fundamentally, the financial statements compiled and the information on which they are based are the client's representations, and that should be explicitly emphasized by the accountant and recognized by management.

A planning and program guide for use on a compilation engagement is shown as Figure 8-1. The guide is made up of three segments, each setting forth the procedures pertinent to the corresponding stages of the engagement—(1) before accepting the engagement; (2) subsequent to acceptance; and (3) completing the engagement.

Figure 8-1
Compilation of Financial Statements
Engagement Planning and Program Guide

_____   _____
(Client)   (Period of financial statements)

_____   _____
(Prepared by)   (Date)   (Reviewed by)   (Date)

INSTRUCTIONS

1. Signatures of the accountant responsible for preparing the guide and of the reviewer should be recorded in the spaces provided for above.

2. The column "Performed by" should be initialed by the accountant who undertakes the procedure.

3. The comment section at the end of the guide should be used for comments on any difficulties encountered, questions raised, or matters to be clarified. Comments should be keyed to the specific item. The disposition of matters commented on should be clearly noted along with indication, where appropriate, of supervisory approval.

4. Items considered to be not applicable are to be initialed in the NA column.

5. Fill in, where appropriate, the working paper reference number in the "W/P Ref." column. It is important to maintain adequate working papers in support of work done in carrying out the engagement.

GUIDE

Performed By	NA	W/P Ref.

I. Before Accepting the Engagement for the Compilation of Financial Statements

1. Review AICPA's Statements on Standards for Accounting and Review Services (SSARS) for guidance as to procedural and reporting standards and requirements.

2. Note the reference in Appendix E of SSARS No. 1 to Rule 201 of the rules of conduct of the AICPA's Code of Professional Ethics. Even though this is not an audit engagement, standards of professional competence, due professional care, adequate engagement planning and supervision, and other such standards must be thoroughly observed.

3. Discuss with management, and determine in specific terms, the nature of the services to be performed, including any accounting services in addition to those pertaining to the compilation of financial statements.

4. Discuss with management:

(a) The meaning and nature of a compilation engagement.

(b) Its differentiation from a review of financial statements or an audit of financial statements.

(c) Type of report to be issued, and the inclusion of a disclaimer.

(d) The reasons a compilation is desired rather than a review or an audit, and the appropriateness of a compilation report in satisfying the needs of the entity.

(e) Planned distribution of the report including any to banks, other credit-grantors, and other outside parties.

5. Explain to management that the financial statements and the information on which the compilation is based are

the entity's responsibility as its representations even though additional accounting services may be performed, such as recordkeeping assistance and help in adjusting the books of account. Also, discuss the contents of a representation letter (if one is to be obtained) to be later signed by the company's president.

6. Inquire as to predecessor accountant, if any, the type of services rendered, and reason for the change in accountants, and obtain permission to communicate with him.

7. Consider communicating with predecessor accountant to ascertain his explanation of the change and to inquire, among other matters, as to the client's reputation and any circumstances that would militate against accepting the engagement or might later present problems.

8. Consider obtaining permission to inquire of business and banking references as to the reputation of the entity and its top management, and make such inquiries if desirable.

9. Point out to management that the engagement cannot be relied upon to disclose errors, irregularities, fraud, defalcations or illegal acts that may exist but that management and/or the board of directors will be informed of any such matters that come to our attention.

10. By inquiries of management, selected company personnel, and observation, develop a general understanding of:

(a) Nature of the company's business, business transactions, and general financial condition.

(b) Type and condition of the accounting records.

(c) Qualifications of accounting personnel.

(d) Accounting basis on which financial statements are to be presented.

(e) The extent to which disclosures required by generally accepted accounting principles (including those that might appear in the body of the financial statements) are to be omitted.

(f) The form and content of the financial statements to be compiled. In this connection, note the type of reports and the form and content of financial statements previously issued by the company.

11. If there is a lack of familiarity with the industry in which the entity operates, gain an understanding of the industry's accounting principles and practices sufficient to permit the compilation of financial statements in appropriate form. Such understanding may be obtained by consulting AICPA guides, industry and other publications, published financial statements, and knowledgeable accountants and other persons.

12. Based on information gathered, consider whether it would be proper or desirable to accept the engagement. In making this judgment, take into account:

(a) Any factors or knowledge gained that might suggest that the information upon which the compiled statements would be based might be false and misleading.

(b) The existence, if applicable, of a troubled and complex financial condition, including substantial indebtedness to credit-grantors that would ordinarily suggest the need for either an audit or a review of financial statements rather than simply a compilation of financial statements.

(c) Any other questionable or negative indications such as an unexplained change from previously audited or reviewed financial statements to a compilation engagement.

13. Discuss the contents of the engagement letter with management.

14. Obtain an engagement letter signed by the president of the company. This letter should incorporate the following understanding:

(a) Services to be performed; their nature and limitations; and fees.

(b) Description of report expected to be issued.

(c) That the engagement cannot be relied upon to disclose errors, irregularities, or illegal acts, but the entity will be informed of any such matters that come to the accountant's attention.

II. Subsequent to Acceptance of Engagement

15. Bear in mind that the following actions are to be avoided during the engagement:

(a) Using in the working papers, financial statements, report, or any communications with the client or outside parties, any words, phrases, or terms like *audit, auditor, audit fees, examination,* or *review* that may suggest that an audit or a review is being or has been conducted. This prohibition also applies to a description of any procedures that might have been undertaken as supplementary services at the request of the client, even though they may appear to be similar to the type of procedures undertaken in a regular audit engagement. Any such procedures are to be identified as accounting services and not as audit or review services.

(b) Changing the character of the engagement to an audit or review, or undertaking any audit or review procedures even as supplementary measures if not previously provided for in the engagement letter, without consultation with and approval of the engagement partner.

(c) Making inquiries or performing other procedures to verify, corroborate, or review information supplied by the client. Such actions are not required in a compilation engagement. They may be undertaken, however, if originally agreed upon with the client in specific terms, or later as requested by the client and as warranted by the circumstances, but only after consultation with and approval of the engagement partner.

16. If the knowledge gained prior to accepting the engagement regarding the business, the accounting records, and industry accounting practices is incomplete, make further inquiries to the extent necessary.

17. Review provisions of the signed engagement letter.

18. Review prior period working papers, correspondence and tax files

in our office noting significant matters covered in all correspondence pertaining to the client.

19.   Perform accounting services that are prerequisites to the compilation of financial statements. But first consult with and obtain approval of engagement partner regarding any accounting services not originally explicitly agreed to with the client. Those prerequisite accounting services are (*Performed by* column to be initiated upon completion of the service):

(a)   _____
(b)   _____
(c)   _____
(d)   _____

20.   Obtain the information required to permit the compilation to be made. Describe precisely in the working papers the nature and source of the information obtained. (The information is usually the general ledger if, in fact, one is kept.)

21.   Prepare from the information so obtained a working trial balance.

22.   If the trial balance is prepared by the client, compare account titles and balances with general ledger account balances or, in the absence of a general ledger, with the other information used in preparing the trial balance.

(Note: Although this step is not mentioned in SSARS No. 1, it would appear to be an essential procedure to guard against the possibility that the client may have submitted a trial balance with fictitious figures having no or little correspondence to balances in the general ledger or comparable source. However, it is not to be considered as an *auditing* procedure but rather as an accounting service in which the information required for the compilation is properly identified.)

23.   Provide assistance, if required or arranged for, in adjusting the books of account, but explain to the client that the adjustments are the responsibility of the entity and any assistance given was simply in the nature of a requested accounting service.

24.   Request client to furnish information so that disclosures may be made in the body of the financial statements or accompanying notes, as required by generally accepted accounting principles. This request is not necessary if it is understood that substantially all disclosures are to be omitted, and it is so noted in the report.

25.   Compile the financial statements.

26.   Check the mathematical accuracy and internal consistency of the financial statements.

III.   Completing the Engagement

27.   Read the compiled financial statements.

28.   Consider whether the financial statements, including disclosures if any, appear to be:

(a) Appropriate in form.

(b) Free from obvious errors of the following nature: mistakes in compilation; arithmetical or clerical mistakes; mistakes in application of accounting principles including inadequate disclosure.

29. Although the engagement does not call for undertaking any inquiries or other procedures to corroborate or review the information supplied by management, be aware of the possibility that the information so supplied for use in compiling the financial statements may be incorrect, incomplete, or otherwise unsatisfactory for that purpose.

30. In exercising such awareness, take into account knowledge gained from prior engagements for the company, the results of the usual inquiries made prior to and subsequent to acceptance of the engagement, the results of other accounting services performed, and a reading of the financial statements on their face.

31. If the information obtained as a basis for compilation and the compiled financial statements are incorrect, incomplete, or otherwise unsatisfactory:

(a) Discuss with the client.

(b) Obtain additional or revised information, and compile corrected financial statements.

(c) If management refuses to furnish such information, withdraw from the engagement.

(d) If the information has been deliberately falsified by the client, withdraw from the engagement.

32. Perform and complete other accounting services contemplated by the engagement (list below):

(a) Preparation of tax returns.

(b) Special bookkeeping services.

(c) Consultation on _____.

(d) _____.

(e) _____.

33. Inquire as to whether material events have occurred after the statement date of a type required by GAAP to be disclosed or otherwise reflected in the financial statements.

34. Prepare the report in accordance with the standards laid down in Statements on Standards for Accounting and Review Services.

35. Present to and discuss with the client a draft copy of the report and the financial statements.

36. Obtain a signed representation letter from the client.

37. Prepare a memorandum for submission to and discussion with the engagement partner containing:

(a) Description of unresolved questions and problems. The disposition of such matters is to be later noted and initialed by the engagement partner.

(b) Suggestions for use on subsequent engagements.

38. Prepare a memorandum for review by the engagement partner in which an evaluation of the conduct of the engagement is made in terms of its conformity with the standards and requirements of the Statements on Standards for Accounting and Review Services.

39. After supervisory and partner review procedures have been followed and review guides have been completed, arrange for typing of report and submission to client.

Comments on Items Listed Above

(Use this section of the guide for comments on any difficulties encountered or matters to be clarified. Comments are to be keyed to the specific item. Their disposition is to be clearly noted, along with indications, where appropriate, of supervisory approval.)

_____

_____

538 FORMS MANUAL FOR THE CPA

with the standards and requirements of the AICPA's SSARS, and the review report may be processed and issued.

Comments on Items Listed Above

(Record below comments on *No* responses or on any other matters to be clarified or resolved. A clear indication of how the matter was resolved should also be noted. Comments are to be keyed to the pertinent checklist item, dated, and initialed by the person recording the comment; notations as to their disposition are to be initialed and dated by the engagement partner.)

_____

_____

COMPILATION ENGAGEMENT LETTER

The subject of engagement letters in general and also for audit engagements is discussed and illustrated in Chapter 1. See particularly Figures 1-3 and 1-4 and associated commentary.

Figure 8-2 is an illustrative engagement letter for a compilation engagement drawn from SSARS No. 1. This letter has been modified, however, in Figure 8-3 to include additional provisions in order to highlight such important considerations as the statements being the client's representation and the possibility of additional services being required to complete the compilation.

Figure 8-2
Engagement Letter for a Compilation
of Financial Statements (SSARS No. 1)

(Accountant's Letterhead)

(Date)

(Appropriate Salutation)

This letter is to confirm our understanding of the terms and objectives of our engagement and the nature and limitations of the services we will provide.

We will perform the following services:

1. We will compile, from information you provide, the annual and interim balance sheets and related statements of income, retained earnings, and changes in financial position of XYZ Company for the year 19XX. We will not audit or review such financial statements. Our report on the annual financial statements of XYZ Company is presently expected to read as follows:

"The accompanying balance sheet of XYZ Company as of December 31, 19XX, and the related statements of income, retained earnings, and changes in financial position for the year then ended have been compiled by us.

A compilation is limited to presenting in the form of financial statements information that is the representation of management. We have not audited or reviewed the accompanying financial statements and, accordingly, do not express an opinion or any other form of assurance on them."

Our report on your interim financial statements, which statements will omit substantially all disclosures, will include an additional paragraph that will read as follows:

"Management has elected to omit substantially all of the disclosures required by generally accepted accounting principles. If the omitted disclosures were included in the financial statements, they might influence the user's conclusions about the company's financial position, results of operations, and changes in financial position. Accordingly, these financial statements are not designed for those who are not informed about such matters."

If, for any reason, we are unable to complete the compilation of your financial statements, we will not issue a report on such statements as a result of this engagement.

2. We will also . . . (discussion of other services).

Our engagement cannot be relied upon to disclose errors, irregularities, or illegal acts, including fraud or defalcations, that may exist. However, we will inform you of any such matters that come to our attention.

Our fees for these services . . . .

We shall be pleased to discuss this letter with you at any time.

If the foregoing is in accordance with your understanding, please sign the copy of this letter in the space provided and return it to us.

Sincerely yours,

_____

(Signature of accountant)

Acknowledge:

XYZ Company

_____

President

_____

Date

_____

Comment. Some accountants prefer not to obtain an acknowledgment, in which case their letter would omit the paragraph beginning "If the foregoing . . . " and the spaces for the acknowledgment. The first paragraph of their letter might begin as follows: "This letter sets forth our understanding of the terms and objectives of our engagement . . . " (SSARS No. 1)

Figure 8-3
Expanded Engagement Letter for
Compilation of Financial Statements

(Accountant's Letterhead)

(Date)

(Appropriate Salutation)

It is a source of satisfaction to us that you have engaged our firm to perform certain accounting services for the Client Corporation, with office at the address noted above. This letter will confirm our mutual understanding of the terms of the engagement and the nature and limitations of the services to be provided.

The following accounting services are to be performed by us:

1. Compilation, from information you provide, of the annual and quarterly balance sheets and related statements of income, retained earnings, and changes in financial position of the Client Corporation for the year 198X. We will not audit or review these financial statements or the information provided by you on which the compilations of the financial statements are based.

2. Submission to you of a report on the annual financial statements that is expected to read as follows:

"The accompanying balance sheet of XYZ Company as of December 31, 198X and the related statements of income, retained earnings, and changes in financial position for the year then ended have been compiled by us.

A compilation is limited to presenting in the form of financial statements information that is the representation of management. We have not audited or reviewed the accompanying financial statements and, accordingly, do not express an opinion or any other form of assurance on them."

3. Submission to you of reports on your quarterly interim financial statements that will include the following additional paragraph inasmuch as those financial statements will omit substantially all disclosures required by generally accepted accounting principles:

"Management has elected to omit substantially all of the disclosures required by generally accepted accounting principles. If the omitted disclosures were included in the financial statements, they might influence the user's conclusions about the company's financial position, results of operations, and changes in financial position. Accordingly, these financial statements are not designed for those who are not informed about such matters."

4.   Other services to enable us to compile the financial statements. They include:

(a)   _____

(b)   _____

(c)   _____

5.   Preparation of the following income and business tax returns:

_____

_____

_____

6.   _____

If, for any reason, we are unable to complete the compilation of the financial statements, we will not issue the report or submit to you the financial statements in any form.

We will request, and you will submit to us during the engagement, a signed representation letter acknowledging that the information submitted by you and the financial statements from which they are compiled are the representations of the company which is responsible for their fairness.

Our engagement is not intended to and cannot be relied upon to uncover or disclose errors, irregularities, fraud, defalcations, or illegal acts that may exist. However, we will inform you of any such matters that come to our attention.

Our fees for these services are as follows:

_____

_____

If the terms of this letter meet with your approval, please sign one copy in the space provided and return it for our files. We look forward to a pleasant association and the opportunity to render the services contemplated by this engagement.

Sincerely yours,

John A. Accountant & Co.

_____

Walter B. Brown, Partner

Date _____

We are in agreement with the terms of this letter.

Client Corporation

_____

William E. Smith, President

REPRESENTATION LETTER FOR COMPILATION ENGAGEMENTS

A representation letter of the type that might be used on compilation engagements is shown in Figure 8-4. SSARS No. 1 does contain an illustrative representation letter, shown later as Figure 8-20, but only for use in a review of financial statements. It is also indicated in SSARS No. 1 that obtaining such a letter for a review engagement is advisable rather than mandatory. It would seem, however, that it would be equally advisable for the accountant to obtain a representation letter for compilation engagements to emphasize the client's responsibility for the fairness of the information submitted for use in the compilation.

A broader discussion of the subject of representation letters in general as well as illustrative letters for use on audit engagements are contained in Chapter 2.

Figure 8-4
Representation Letter for Compilation Engagements

(Client Letterhead)

(Date of accountant's report)

(Addressed to accountant)

Gentlemen:

In connection with your compilation of the (identification of financial statements) of (name of client), we confirm, to the best of our knowledge and belief, the representations recorded below made to you during the engagement. Exceptions or supplementary comments, if any, will be stated at the end of this letter in the section captioned *Exceptions* and will be appropriately numbered to correspond with the related item.

1. We have provided you with the information needed for the compilation of the financial statements including related notes to financial statements. Such information and the financial statements on which they are based are our responsibility as our representations.

2. The information submitted for purposes of compilation is fair and accurate in all material aspects and provide a proper and sufficient basis for the compilation of financial statements that conform with generally accepted accounting principles.

3. The financial statements are in conformity with generally accepted accounting principles. (Or, if applicable, in conformity with a comprehensive basis of accounting other than generally accepted accounting principles, which should be described; e.g., cash basis or income tax basis.)

4. All material disclosures that are required to be made by generally accepted accounting principles have been communicated to you and are reflected in the financial statements. (Not pertinent if substantially all disclosures are omitted; see discussion on this subject in later section covering compilation reports.)

EXCEPTIONS (Note exceptions, if any, to the foregoing representations.)

_____

_____

Very truly yours,

_____

(Signature of chief
executive officer and title)

_____

(Signature of chief financial
officer and title,
where applicable)

REPORTING ON COMPILED OR REVIEWED FINANCIAL
STATEMENTS OF NONPUBLIC ENTITIES

A guide to reporting standards, principles, and rules for compilation and review engagements is provided in Figure 8-5. The guide reflects both the letter and spirit of the provisions of Statements on Standards for Accounting and Review Services Nos. 1 and 2 but it does not purport to be a complete summary of the reporting standards set forth in those statements.

These standards and the applicable rules are reflected in the illustrative compilation and review reports that are later presented, in the comments appended to those reports, and in the checklist review guides for compilation and review engagements shown as Figures 8-16 and 8-33, respectively.

Figure 8-5
Reporting Standards Guide for Compilation and Review Engagements

This guide should be used in conjunction with careful reference to, and a close reading of, the provisions of Statements on Standards for Accounting and Review Services (SSARS) No. 1, which covers the general reporting standards, and No. 2, which deals with reporting on comparative financial statements. While the guide reflects both the letter and spirit of these statements, it does not purport to provide a complete summary of the reporting standards, principles and rules contained therein. When reference is made to those statements, a citation that is recorded as, for example, SSARS 2.5, should be read as Statement No. 2, paragraph 5.

When the recorded standard or explanatory comment applies only to a compilation or only to a review, it will be so indicated; absent such indication, the item should be read as applying to both. For convenience of reference, the guide consists of two segments, the first covering general standards and the second those pertaining to reports on comparative statements.

General Standards

1. A report must be issued whenever a compilation or review engagement for a nonpublic entity is completed in compliance with the requirements of SSARS No. 1; but neither a report nor the financial statements may be issued unless the standards of SSARS No. 1 are complied with. Hence, the accountant may not provide merely the service of typing or reproducing financial statements as an accommodation to the client. (SSARS 1.7)

2. The accountant should not consent to the use of his name in client-prepared documents or communications containing unaudited financial statements of nonpublic entities, unless he has compiled or reviewed the statements and his report accompanies them, or the client has noted that the accountant has not compiled or reviewed them and that he is not responsible for them; if he learns of any improper use of his name in a client-prepared document, the accountant should consider appropriate action. (SSARS 1.6)

3. A review report may not be issued if the accountant is not independent with respect to the entity. But a compilation report may be submitted in the absence of independence provided the standards are met for a compilation engagement. (SSARS 1.38)

4. The report should be dated as of the date of completion of the compilation or of the review procedures. (SSARS 1.15, .33)

5. The spirit and essence of the fourth reporting standard of the generally accepted auditing standards (a standard applicable to public company engagements and to audit engagements for nonpublic companies, and not specifically mentioned as a standard in SSARS No. 1) also applies to both compilation and review engagements. The standard requires that the accountant indicate clearly in his report the character of the work done by him and the degree of responsibility he is assuming. A disclaimer of opinion must therefore be expressed in either compilation or review reports.

6. In addition to the disclaimer, in a review report limited assurance is expressed that the accountant is not aware of any material modification that must be made to the financial statements for them to conform with GAAP other than disclosed departures, if any, from GAAP. (SSARS 1.32) But in a compilation report, the statement is made that no form of assurance is expressed.

7. Each page of the financial statements should carry a warning such as, depending on the type of report, "See Accountant's Compilation Report"; "See Accountant's Review Report"; or "See Accountant's Report". (SSARS 1.16, .34) While not mentioned in SSARS, it would seem that an accountant may, if he wishes, add the word *unaudited*, so that the phrase would read: "Unaudited—See Accountant's Compilation (or Review) Report".

8. The compilation report should (SSARS 1.14):

(a) State that a compilation was performed.

(b) Explain what is meant by a compilation.

(c) Emphasize that the financial statements have not been audited or reviewed.

(d) Express a disclaimer of opinion.

(e) State that no assurance is expressed as to the financial statements.

9. In addition to expressing the disclaimer and limited assurance, the review report should (SSARS 1.32):

(a) State that a review was performed in accordance with AICPA standards.

(b) Explain what is meant by a review and that it is not an audit.

(c) Note that the financial statements are the representations of management.

10. The report should not describe any audit or other procedures (except for the brief reference to inquiries and analytical procedures when explaining the nature of a review) that the accountant may have performed before or during the compilation or review engagement. (SSARS 1.32) Any such description of procedures performed would blur the distinction that the accounting profession has drawn between an

audit and a *review* and would be both misleading and confusing to the readers of the accountant's report. They could easily misinterpret a description of procedures as signifying that an audit was actually performed, despite the wording of the report. But SSARS does not prohibit an accountant from undertaking auditing or other procedures that go beyond the (minimum) standards and procedures applicable to a compilation or review engagement. But see SSARS 1.44–.49 for rules that pertain for a change in engagement from audit to review or compilation.

11. An accountant may compile financial statements that omit substantially all disclosures required by GAAP provided the omission is disclosed in his report and is not the result of an intention by management to mislead the user. (SSARS 1.10–.21) However, a review report may not be issued under such circumstances. Such substantial omissions would preclude the expression of limited assurance and would negate the *review* character of the engagement.

12. If the accountant is aware that the financial statements reflect a material departure from GAAP and the statements are not revised, the standard report must be modified to make the necessary disclosures. But if modification of the standard report is not adequate to deal with the deficiencies, the accountant should withdraw from the engagement and provide no further services in connection with the financial statements. (SSARS 1.41) But see item above relating to compilation reports and the omission of substantially all disclosures required by GAAP. The standard report need not normally be modified to disclose a material uncertainty or an inconsistency in the application of accounting principles if such disclosures are made in the financial statements. But the accountant, if he wishes, may report in a separate paragraph of his report on these or any other matter relating to the financial statements that he may wish to emphasize. (SSARS 1.40)

Standards for Reports on Comparative Financial Statements

(Note: Paragraph references are to SSARS No. 2)

13. Each period presented should be covered in an appropriate report or reports (para. 2).

14. Reports for prior periods may be modified (para. 4).

15. Reports on comparative financial statements may not be issued when one or more—but not all—statements omit substantially all disclosures required by GAAP (para. 5). The reason is that the comparative financial statements would not be comparable. But a report is permitted on comparative financial statements that omit such disclosures, provided the report is a *compilation* and not a *review* report and is modified to reveal that for one of the prior included periods the previous report did not omit substantially all disclosures (para. 29, 30).

16. As stated earlier, a reference such as "See Accountant's Report" should appear on each page of the comparative financial statements compiled or reviewed (para. 6).

17. A continuing accountant performing the same or higher level of service for the current period should update his report on the prior period statements presented with the current period.

(a) A continuing accountant is defined as one who has audited, reviewed, or compiled the statements of the current period and one or more consecutive periods immediately prior to the current one (para. 8).

(b) An updated report is defined as a report by a continuing accountant who takes account of information developed during the current engagement relative to the prior year and, as a result, expresses, as of the date of the current report, conclusions on the prior period statements that are either the same or different from the original report, depending on the circumstances.

(c) In interpreting the phrase *higher level of service*, starting with the highest, the order is: audit, review, compilation.

18. A continuing accountant performing a lower level of service for the current period should either include a separate paragraph in his report describing the responsibility (i.e., type of report) assumed by him for the prior period, or reissue his report on the prior period. A reissued report may be defined as one that has the same date as the original report; if revised to reflect certain events, the reissued report should be dated as in the original report but dual-dated with a separate date relating to the specific event, if any, that subsequently arose. See also SSARS 2.29 for restatement of this principle when financial statements have been compiled or reviewed for the current period but audited—by either continuing or predecessor accountant—in the prior period. Note, too, that the principles of reporting on comparative financial statements when the current period has been audited but a prior period compiled or reviewed, are covered in SAS No. 26 and are summarized in a later section of this chapter.

19. A predecessor accountant may, but is not obligated to, arrange with the client for reissuance of his compilation or review report on the financial statements of a prior period. Before the report is reissued, the predecessor should: (SSARS 2.16, .20-.24)

(a) Consider whether the report is still appropriate, taking into account the current change in form of presentation of the prior-period statements, awareness of subsequent events that affect the prior period, and the need, if any, to modify the original report.

(b) Perform the following procedures: (i) Read the successor's report and the current financial statements; (ii) Compare the prior-period statements, as included in the current report, with both prior-period statements as originally issued and current-period statements; (iii) Obtain a letter from the successor accountant advising whether the latter is aware of any material matter affecting the prior-period financial statements and not reflected therein. The reissued report, however, should make no reference to the letter or the successor's report.

(c)   If he becomes aware of information, like events subsequent to the date or his original report, that may significantly affect either the prior-period statements or his report: (i) Make inquiries and undertake procedures appropriate in the circumstances in order to gain the proper understanding of the circumstances; (ii) Use the original report date for the reissued report and, if the report on the financial statements has been revised to reflect the given circumstance or event, dual date the report to read, for example: "March 1, 198X, except for note X, as to which the date is March 15, 198Y; (iii) Obtain a written statement from the former client in which management acknowledges the newly acquired information and its effect on the prior-period statements and on the reissued report.

20.   If the predecessor accountant does not reissue his compilation or review report on the prior-period financial statements, the successor accountant should either:

(a)   Perform a compilation, review, or audit of the prior-period financial statements and issue an appropriate report on them; or

(b)   Make reference in an additional paragraph of his report on the current-period financial statements to the predecessor's report, including in such paragraph the following information with respect to the prior report: (i) the fact that the financial statements of the prior period were, as applicable, compiled or reviewed by another accountant (who should not be named); (ii) date of prior-period report; (iii) description of disclaimer or limited assurance, as applicable; (iv) description of any modification of the prior-period report.

21.   It is the current status of the client that determines whether the accountant in reporting on comparative annual or interim financial statements should look for guidance to the Statements on Auditing Standards (SAS) or the Statements on Standards for Accounting and Review Services (SSARS). The former should be referred to (especially SAS No. 26) when the current status is that of a public company (or nonpublic entity with currently audited statements) and the latter for a currently nonpublic entity whose current-period statements have been compiled or reviewed. (SSARS 2.31-.32) Thus:

(a)   If the entity is one that is public in the current period and nonpublic in the prior period, the previous compilation or review report should not be reissued or referred to in the current report (since it would be inappropriate for the entity's current status) and SAS No. 26 should be looked to for guidance. This point is expanded upon in Figure 8-40 later in this chapter in the summary of reporting principles that apply under SAS when audited and unaudited financial statements are presented in comparative form.

(b)   If the entity is one that is nonpublic in the current period but public in the prior period and the latter had been audited, the compilation or review report of the current period should make reference to the prior-period report, or the report on the prior period should be reissued.

Figure 8-6
Compilation Report

Standard Report—Single Year (SSARS 1)

The accompanying balance sheet of XYZ Company as of December 1, 198Y, and the related statements of income, retained earnings, and changes in financial position for the year then ended have been compiled by me (us).

A compilation is limited to presenting in the form of financial statements information that is the representation of management (owners). I (we) have not audited or reviewed the accompanying financial statements and, accordingly, do not express an opinion or any other form of assurance on them.

Comments:

1.   The customary reporting principles apply with respect to signing the report and using the appropriate salutation. See Figure 8-5.

2.   See prior discussion in this chapter on the reporting principles applicable to compilation engagements and note that the listing therein of matters to be covered in the report are reflected in the above illustration. Additionally, each page of the financial statements should carry a warning such as: "See Accountant's Compilation Report."

Figure 8-7
Compilation Report

Standard Report—Comparative Financial Statements; Compilation for Each Period (SSARS 2)

The accompanying balance sheets of XYZ Company as of December 31, 198Y and 198X, and the related statements of income, retained earnings, and changes in financial position for the years then ended have been compiled by me (us).

A compilation is limited to presenting in the form of financial statements information that is the representation of management (owners). I (we) have not audited or reviewed the accompanying financial statements and, accordingly, do not express an opinion or any other form of assurance on them.

Comment. See prior discussion in this chapter on reporting principles relating to compilation report by continuing accountant on comparative financial statements.

Figure 8-8
Compilation Report

Substantially All Disclosures Required by GAAP
Omitted (SSARS 1)

The accompanying balance sheet of XYZ Company as of December 31, 198Y, and the related statements of income, retained earnings, and changes in financial position for the year then ended have been compiled by me (us).

A compilation is limited to presenting in the form of financial statements information that is the representation of management (owners). I (we) have not audited or reviewed the accompanying financial statements and, accordingly, do not express an opinion or any other form of assurance on them.

Management has elected to omit substantially all of the disclosures required by generally accepted accounting principles. If the omitted disclosures were included in the financial statements, they might influence the user's conclusions about the company's financial position, results of operations, and changes in financial position. Accordingly, these financial statements are not designed for those who are not informed about such matters.

Comments:

1.   If the statement of changes in financial position has also been omitted, the first paragraph should be modified accordingly, and the last paragraph should be modified somewhat as follows:

". . . substantially all of the disclosures (and the statement of changes in financial position) required by . . . "

2.   Accountants are permitted to compile and report on such statements if the omission is disclosed in the report but only if he has no knowledge that the client wishes to omit substantially all disclosures required by GAAP in order to mislead users of the financial statements.

3.   Absent such improper intentions, if the client wishes to disclose only a few matters in notes to the financial statements, the above report would still be appropriate and required, but the disclosure notes should be labeled: "Selective Information—Substantially all Disclosures Required by Generally Accepted Accounting Principles Are Not Included." (SSARS 1.19)

4.   Disclosure must, however, be made either in the financial statements or the accountant's report, of the basis of accounting if a comprehensive basis of accounting other than GAAP (such as a cash basis or tax accounting basis) has been used in compiling the financial statements. (SSARS 1.20)

Figure 8-9
Compilation Report

Substantially All Disclosures Required by GAAP Not Omitted in Prior Year But Omitted in Comparative Financial Statements (SSARS 2)

The accompanying balance sheets of XYZ Company as of December 31, 198Y and 198X, and the related statements of income, retained earnings, and changes in financial position for the years then ended have been compiled by me (us).

A compilation is limited to presenting in the form of financial statements information that is the representation of management (owners). I (we) have not audited or reviewed the accompanying financial statements and, accordingly, do not express an opinion or any other form of assurance on them.

Management has elected to omit substantially all of the disclosures required by generally accepted accounting principles. If the omitted disclosures were included in the financial statements, they might influence the user's conclusions about the company's financial position, results of operations, and changes in financial position. Accordingly, these financial statements are not designed for those who are not informed about such matters.

The accompanying 198X financial statements were compiled by me (us) from financial statements that did not omit substantially all of the disclosures required by generally accepted accounting principles and that I (we) previously reviewed as indicated in my (our) report dated March 1, 198Y.

Comments:

1.   If prior year statements previously compiled, reviewed, or audited by an accountant did not originally omit substantially all GAAP-required disclosures, and the accountant is later requested to compile the prior year statements with the omission of those disclosures, he may do so and include those statements in a comparative compilation report. An appropriate explanation, however, must be given, as shown in the last paragraph of the foregoing report. (SSARS 2.29)

2.   The foregoing report without the last paragraph would be appropriate for comparative compiled financial statements that include a prior period for which a compilation report had originally been issued in which the financial statements omitted substantially all GAAP-required disclosures.

Figure 8-10
Compilation Report

Departure from GAAP Disclosed (SSARS 1)

The accompanying balance sheet of XYZ Company as of December 31, 198Y, and the related statements of income, retained earnings, and changes in financial position for the year then ended have been compiled by me (us).

A compilation is limited to presenting in the form of financial statements information that is the representation of management (owners). I (we) have not audited or reviewed the accompanying financial statements and, accordingly, do not express an opinion or any other form of assurance on them. However, I (we) did become aware of a departure (certain departures) from generally accepted accounting principles that is (are) described in the following paragraph(s).

(SEPARATE PARAGRAPH)

As disclosed in note X to the financial statements, generally accepted accounting principles require that land be stated at cost. Management has informed me (us) that the company has stated its land at appraised value and that, if generally accepted accounting principles had been followed, the land account and stockholders' equity would have been decreased by ($ amount).

(OR)

A statement of changes in financial position for the year ended December 31, 198Y, has not been presented. Generally accepted accounting principles require that such a statement be presented when financial statements purport to present financial position and results of operations.

Comments:

1. If the statement of changes in financial position has been omitted, the first paragraph should be modified accordingly.

2. The client should, of course, be encouraged to agree to a revision of the financial statements so that they conform with GAAP.

3. In the absence of such revision, the accountant should consider whether it is appropriate and not misleading to issue a compilation report even if it is modified to reflect the situation.

4. If it is concluded that it would be proper to issue a report, the departure from GAAP must be disclosed in a separate paragraph of the report.

5. The impact of the departure must be disclosed in the report if determined by management, but if not so determined, the accountant is not required to do so provided he states in his report that a determination of the effects of the departure from GAAP has not been made. (SSARS 1.39, .40)

Figure 8-11
Compilation Report

Changed Reference in Comparative Financial Statements to Prior Period Departure from GAAP

The accompanying balance sheets of XYZ Company as of December 31, 198Y and 198X, and the related statements of income, retained earnings, and changes in financial position for the years then ended have been compiled by me (us).

A compilation is limited to presenting in the form of financial statements information that is the representation of managers (owners). I (we) have not audited or reviewed the accompanying financial statements and, accordingly, do not express an opinion or any other form of assurance on them.

In my (our) previous compilation report dated March 1, 198Y on the 198X financial statements, I (we) referred to a departure from generally accepted accounting principles because the company carried its land at appraised values. However, as disclosed in note X, the company has restated its 198X financial statements to reflect its land at cost in accordance with generally accepted accounting principles.

Comments:

1.   In discussing the issue, SSARS 2.13–.15 provides as an illustration only the last paragraph of the foregoing report, but it has been combined with the standard form in order to present a complete report.

2.   A *changed reference* may be either a new reference to or the removal of a prior reference to a departure from GAAP. Circumstances may subsequently arise, and become known to the accountant, that suggest the need for a changed reference when comparative financial statements are reported on that include the prior year in question. In that event, a separate explanatory paragraph should be added, as in the last paragraph of the foregoing report, disclosing: (*a*) date of prior report; (*b*) circumstances causing the changed reference; and (*c*) if applicable, that the financial statements of the prior period have been changed.

Figure 8-12
Compilation Report

Supplementary Information Accompanying
Basic Financial Statements

The accompanying balance sheet of XYZ Company as of December 31, 198Y, and the related statements of income, retained earnings, and changes in financial position for the year then ended have been compiled by me (us). The other data accompanying the financial statements are presented only for supplementary analysis purposes and have also been compiled by me (us).

A compilation is limited to presenting in the form of financial statements information that is the representation of management (owners). I (we) have not audited or reviewed the accompanying financial statements or the supplementary data and, accordingly, do not express an opinion or any other form of assurance on them.

Comment. The above report would appear to meet the reporting standards of SSARS, para. 43, if the compiled basic financial statements are accompanied by information presented only for supplementary analysis purposes, and such other data have also been compiled by the accountant.

Figure 8-13
Compilation Report

Statements Prepared on Cash Basis

The accompanying statement of assets and liabilities arising from cash transactions of XYZ Company as of December 31, 198Y, and the related statement of revenue collected and expenses paid for the year then ended have been compiled by me (us).

A compilation is limited to presenting in the form of financial statements information that is the representation of management (owners). I (we) have not audited or reviewed the accompanying financial statements and, accordingly, do not express an opinion or any other form of assurance on them.

As described in Note X, the Company's policy is to prepare its financial statements on the basis of cash receipts and disbursements; consequently, certain revenue and the related assets are recognized when received rather than when earned, and certain expenses are recognized when paid rather than when the obligation is incurred. Accordingly, the accompanying financial statements are not intended to present financial position and results of operations in conformity with generally accepted accounting principles.

_____

Comment. This report was prepared on an informal and unofficial basis by the AICPA technical information service. The report adapts and combines the report format for audited financial statements prepared on a cash basis, as illustrated in AU 621.08, with the standard compilation report.

Figure 8-14
Compilation Report

Statements Prepared on Income Tax Basis

The accompanying statement of assets, liabilities, and capital—income tax basis—of XYZ Company as of December 31, 198Y, and the related statements of revenue and expenses—income tax basis—for the year then ended have been compiled by me (us).

A compilation is limited to presenting in the form of financial statements information that is the representation of management (owners). I (we) have not audited or reviewed the accompanying financial statements and, accordingly, do not express an opinion or any other form of assurance on them.

As described in Note X, the Company's policy is to prepare its financial statements on the accounting basis used for income tax purposes; consequently, certain revenue and the related assets are recognized when received rather than when earned, and certain expenses are recognized when paid rather than when the obligation is incurred. Accordingly, the accompanying financial statements are not intended to present financial position and results of operations in conformity with generally accepted accounting principles.

Comment.   This report was prepared on an informal and unofficial basis by the AICPA technical information service. The report adapts and combines the report format for audited financial statements prepared on an income tax basis, as illustrated in AU 621.08, with the standard compilation report.

Figure 8-15
Compilation Report

Accountant Not Independent

(The wording of the compilation report should be the same as would ordinarily have been issued in the circumstances of the particular engagement, except for the added last paragraph of the report, as shown below.)

(WORDING OF LAST PARAGRAPH)

I (we) are not independent with respect to the XYZ Company.

Comments:

1.   An accountant who is not independent with respect to the client may nevertheless issue a compilation report. (SSARS 1.22)

2.   He must, however, disclose in the last paragraph of his report the fact that he is not independent, but he should not give the reasons for the lack of independence.

3.   A footnote to SSARS 1.22 suggests that, in judging whether he is or is not independent, the accountant should refer to the AICPA Code of Professional Ethics and should be aware that independence is not necessarily impaired, under Code Rule Interpretation 101.3, if bookkeeping services are rendered to a nonpublic client.

CHECKLIST REVIEW GUIDE FOR COMPILATION ENGAGEMENTS

A checklist review guide for use on compilation engagements is shown as Figure 8-16. It is made up of three segments covering the accountant's report, the financial statements, and working papers and other matters. Some accountants may believe that the simplicity of a compilation engagement normally would not warrant the use of a review guide in addition to the planning and program guide shown in Figure 8-1. They may feel that the use of both guides on such an engagement especially for, as would probably often be the case, a small-size company would be too cumbersome and unnecessarily time consuming.

Conceivably the program guide, in the judgment of the accountant and in the individual circumstances of a particular engagement, may also serve as a review guide, especially if it is also perceived as such and its review is undertaken in the proper manner by the engagement partner or an assigned qualified reviewer. However, the review guide does provide inherently an orderly, distinctive and direct focus on the top-level review phase of the engagement and the responsibilities that relate to it, and its use, therefore, yields significant benefits to the accountant in ensuring satisfaction with the proper professional execution of the engagement.

Figure 8-16
Checklist Review Guide for Use on
Compilation Engagements

_____   _____
(Client)   (Period of financial statements)

_____   _____
(Prepared by)   (Date)   (Reviewed by)   (Date)

INSTRUCTIONS

1. This guide, whose proper use and completion is the responsibility of the engagement partner, is designed to assist those persons participating in a final review of the accountant's compilation report, the compiled financial statements, and the working papers. All persons so involved—the preparer responsible for the initial completion of the checklist and any other reviewers including the engagement partner—are expected to undertake a careful review adequate in scope to support the reponses and conclusions set forth in this guide.

2. A _No_ response is presumed to signify an unsatisfactory condition, and all such responses should be fully explained, substantiated, and commented upon in the comment section at the end of the guide. The manner in which the matter has been remedied or resolved, the basis for the decision, and partner approval of the action taken, should similarly be recorded in the comment section and keyed to the item in question.

3. The comment section may also be used for any other comments that may be needed or helpful in accomplishing a proper review, but the details and approvals relative to the disposition of any questions and problems must be clearly noted.

4. If a standard or guide relating to a listed item has been provided in the AICPA's Statements on Standards for Accounting and Review Services (SSARS), appropriate parenthetical reference to the statement will be made; for example, the reference _SSARS 2.12_ would signify Statement No. 2, para. 12. Where the accountant using the guide has any doubt as to the full range of responsibilities in a particular area, the original reference sources should be consulted.

REVIEW GUIDE

	Yes	No	NA

Accountant's Report

1. Cognizance has been taken of the following basic principles applicable to reporting on unaudited financial statements of a nonpublic entity: (SSARS 1.1)

(a) The report can only be based on either a compilation or a review of financial statements.

(b) A report must be issued whenever a compilation or review engagement is completed in accordance with requirements and provisions of SSARS.

(c) Niether a report nor the financial statements may be submitted unless the compilation or review engagement is completed in accordance with the requirements and provisions of SSARS.

2. The date of the accountant's report is the same as the date of completion of the compilation. (SSARS 1.15)

3. The report has been addressed to the proper party (e.g., company, board of directors, or stockholders) as indicated by the individual engagement.

4. The report states that:

(a) A compilation has been performed and identifies the financial statements compiled. (SSARS 1.14) It is permissible to issue a compilation report on one financial statement like the balance sheet, and not on, say, related income and other statements. (SSARS 1.18)

(b) A compilation is limited to presenting in the form of financial statements information that is the representation of management (owners). (SSARS 1.14)

(c) The financial statements have not been audited or reviewed. (SSARS 1.14)

(d) An opinion or any other form of assurance on the financial statements is not being expressed. (SSARS 1.14) In effect, this is a disclaimer of opinion.

5. The report does not describe any procedures the accountant might have performed either before or during the compilation engagement. (SSARS 1.14)

6. Each page of the financial statements contains a reference such as "See Accountant's Compilation Report." (SSARS 1.16)

7. The report has been prepared in accordance with the standards and provisions of SSARS. Note should be taken of the injunction that if an accountant performs more than one service, for example, compilation and audit or compilation and review, he should issue a report appropriate for the highest level of service. (SSARS 1.5) Starting with the highest level, the order is: audit, review, compilation.

8. If the compilation report covers comparative financial statements, the reporting standards set forth in SSARS No. 2 have been complied with.

9. No words or phrases appear in the accountant's report, in the financial statements, or in the working papers that might indicate or suggest that an audit or review was performed. Examples of such expressions to be avoided are: audit, auditing, auditor, review, examination, auditing procedure, audit fees, and accrued auditing expense.

10. The accountant is independent with respect to the client. (In making this judgment, which takes in the accounting firm and the personnel assigned to the engagement, all pertinent facts and circumstances are considered as well as the specific criteria set forth in the AICPA Code of Professional Ethics. (SSARS 1.22)

11. If the accountant is not independent, the compilation report may nevertheless be issued. In that event, it:

(a) Discloses the lack of independence. (SSARS 1.22)

(b) Does not describe the reasons for the lack of independence. (SSARS 1.22)

12. The financial statements have been compiled, and the engagement conducted, in accordance with the standards, requirements, and provisions of SSARS.

13. If the client has requested that the compiled financial statements omit, and they do omit, substantially all of the disclosures required by GAAP (or by other comprehensive basis of accounting) including disclosures that might ordinarily appear in the body of the financial statements:

(a) The omission is clearly indicated in the accountant's report. (SSARS 1.19–.21)

(b) The client's request has not been made, to the best of the accountant's knowledge, with the intention of misleading any parties who might be using the financial statements. (SSARS 1.19)

(c) If disclosures are nevertheless to be included at the client's request, but only on a few matters, they are made in notes to financial statements labeled: "Selected Information—Substantially All Disclosures

Required by Generally Accepted Accounting Principles Are Not Included." (SSARS 1.19)

14.   If the financial statements are compiled on a comprehensive basis of accounting other than GAAP, the basis used is disclosed either in the financial statements or in the accountant's report. (SSARS 1.20)

15.   If there is awareness of a material departure from generally accepted accounting principles (other than the omission of substantially all disclosures, as to which see relevant item above), and the financial statements have not been revised:

(a)   The standard compilation report has been modified to disclose the departure, including the effects on the financial statements if such effects have been determined by management or otherwise known. (SSARS 1.40) If the effects are not known, the accountant is not required to determine what they are, but his report must state that a determination was not made. (SSARS 1.40)

(b)   If such modification of the report is not adequate (perhaps because of the magnitude or quantity of deficiencies, or for any other reason), the following action is being taken: withdrawal from the engagement and withholding of any further services with respect to the financial statements. (SSARS 1.41)

16.   Consideration has been given to introducing a separate paragraph in the accountant's report to emphasize a matter of importance (apart from any accounting deficiency) regarding the financial statements. (SSARS 1.40)

17.   Material uncertainties affecting the financial statements as well as inconsistencies in the application of accounting principles, if applicable, are disclosed in the financial statements. If so disclosed, there is normally no need to modify the accountant's report. (SSARS 1.40)

18.   If the accountant was originally engaged to conduct an audit in accordance with generally accepted auditing standards but, before the completion of the examination, has been requested by the client to change the engagement to a compilation of financial statements, before agreeing to the change consideration has been given to:

(a)   The reason given for the request. A change in circumstances so that an audit is no longer needed, or an honest misunderstanding by the client of the nature of an audit, may be acceptable reasons. (SSARS 1.45, .46)

(b)   The possibility that a change because of restriction(s) in the audit scope by the client or by circumstances may signify that information in question may be incorrect, imcomplete, or otherwise unsatisfactory. (SSARS 1.47)

(c)   The fact that a compilation should not ordinarily be issued if the client, during the original audit engagement, has prohibited the accountant from corresponding with the entity's legal counsel, or has refused to sign a representation letter. (SSARS 1.47)

(d) The propriety of accepting a change in the engagement if the auditing procedures are substantially complete or the cost to complete the audit engagement is relatively insignificant. (SSARS 1.48)

(e) The requirement that, if the change to a compilation engagement is justified and the standards applicable to such an engagement are adhered to, the compilation report should not make reference to the original engagement, the auditing procedures performed, or the scope limitations, if any, that resulted in changing the engagement. (SSARS 1.49)

19. If the accountant was originally engaged to conduct a review of the financial statements but is unable to perform the inquiry and analytical procedures necessary to achieve the limited assurance that a proper review is intended to provide; and he has been requested by the client or is otherwise planning to submit a compilation report, consideration has been given to:

(a) Whether the circumstances underlying the incomplete review also preclude the issuance of a compilation report. (SSARS 1.36)

(b) Any matters similar to those noted in the item above regarding a change from an audit to a compilation engagement. (SSARS 1.36, .44, .49)

20. If the financial statements are accompanied by information presented for supplementary analysis purposes, the compilation report should also cover such other data. (SSARS 1.43)

21. Note has been taken of the guidance in AU 561, also relevant to compilation engagements, to be followed when there is awareness, subsequent to the date of the accountant's report, that facts may have existed at that date which might have led him to believe that information supplied by the entity was incorrect, incomplete, or otherwise unsatisfactory. (SSARS 1.42)

Financial Statements

22. The financial statements reflect:
(a) The precise legal name of the entity.
(b) Clear identification of the several financial statements. (SSARS 1.4)
(c) Correct dates and periods covered.

23. The financial statements have been read and appear to be appropriate in form. (SSARS 1.13)

24. The financial statements appear to be free from obvious errors with respect to: (SSARS: 1.13)
(a) Compilation of the financial statements.
(b) Arithmetical or clerical aspects.

(c)   Application of accounting principles, including adequate disclosure.

Working Papers and Other Matters

25.   All working papers are clearly identified as to client, title and purpose, and financial statement date or period.

26.   Working papers are properly indexed and filed.

27.   Clear explanations are provided for any symbols used.

28.   Initials or signatures of both preparer and reviewer as well as dates of such preparation and review appear on all working papers including program and review guides.

29.   The working papers contain information (including sources of such information), as appropriate for a compilation engagement, covering among other subjects:

(a)   In general, matters dealt with in the engagement planning and program guide that logically and normally would be written up in an appropriate form in the working papers for a compilation engagement.

(b)   Significant discussions with the client (e.g., nature of engagement; special services to be performed; questionable or other important matters coming to the accountant's attention).

(c)   An understanding of industry accounting principles and practices.

(d)   Obtaining knowledge of the entity's business transactions and general financial condition, type and condition of accounting records, and qualifications of accounting and recordkeeping personnel.

(e)   The nature and sources of information made available by the client for compilation of the financial statements.

(f)   Any knowledge or indication that the information submitted by the client is incomplete, erroneous, false, misleading, or otherwise unsatisfactory for compilation purposes; and, in such circumstances, additional or revised information.

30.   The financial statement accounts and balances have been traced to, and correspond to, the adjusted trial balance in the working papers.

31.   The working papers indicate that adjustments have been discussed with the client and that the client has approved the adjustments as well as the compiled financial statements as its representations.

32.   A properly prepared engagement letter signed by the client is included in the working papers.

33.   The terms of the engagement letter have been complied with, and the following accounting services, in addition to the compilation and report, have been satisfactorily rendered and completed:

(a)   _____ .

(b) _____ .

(c) _____ .

34. A properly prepared representation letter signed by the client is included in the working papers, and comments, if any, recorded therein in the *Exceptions* section have been noted, appropriate action has been taken and approved, and the circumstances clearly described in the comment section below and in the working papers.

35. The following memoranda prepared by the in-charge accountant are contained in the working papers and have been reviewed by the engagement partner:

(a) Description of unresolved questions and matters. These have been satisfactorily resolved and so noted.

(b) Evaluation of the conduct of the engagement in terms of SSARS standards and requirements which, it is stated therein, have been complied with.

(c) Suggestions for use in subsequent engagements.

36. All "to do" notes, points to be cleared, and matters noted for further consultation and discussion with client or engagement supervisor and engagement partner have been satisfactorily cleared and resolved and so noted in the working papers.

37. Time budgets have been prepared, completed, and reviewed for each phase of the engagement, and signifcant differences between actual and budgeted data have been satisfactorily explained and clarified.

38. The engagement has been satisfactorily completed in conformity with the standards and requirements of the AICPA's SSARS, and the compilation report may be processed and issued.

Comments on Items Listed Above

(Record below comments on *No* responses or on any other matters to be clarified or resolved. A clear indication of how the matter was resolved should also be noted. Comments are to be keyed to the pertinent checklist item, dated, and initialed by the person recording the comment; notations as to their disposition are to be initialed and dated by the engagement partner.)

_____

_____

REVIEW OF FINANCIAL STATEMENTS OF NONPUBLIC ENTITIES—FUNDAMENTAL PRINCIPLES

A *review of financial statements* is the term used to describe the inquiry and analytical procedures undertaken by the accountant as a basis for expressing in his report on the financial statements of a nonpublic entity, *limited assurance* regarding the conformity of the statements with generally accepted accounting principles (or, if applicable, with another comprehensive basis of accounting such as the cash basis or income tax basis). However, inasmuch as the financial statements have not been audited, the report must also include a disclaimer of opinion on the financial statements taken as a whole.

The wording as to limited assurance takes the form of the accountant stating in his report that he is "not aware of any material modifications that should be made to the accompanying financial statements in order for them to be in conformity with generally accepted accounting principles."

This limited assurance is similar to what is also referred to as *negative assurance* whose use has been severely restricted (see SAS 26, para. 18-20) in the case of public companies to reviews of interim financial information, letters for underwriters, and certain types of special reports. Such limited assurance in the case of nonpublic companies may only be given for a *review of financial statements*, as mentioned above, and for a review of interim financial information included in a note to audited financial statements (SAS 24, para. 2). No assurance whatsoever may be expressed in an engagement in which the financial statements have been compiled, unless it is a review engagement in which compilation of financial statements is simply an adjunct accounting service.

It may sometimes be necessary for the accountant to compile the financial statements and to undertake other accounting services to enable him to review the financial statements. Such other accounting services may include assistance in recordkeeping, adjusting the books of account, and preparing a working trial balance. But ultimately and fundamentally, the financial statements to be reviewed, and the information on which they are based, are the client's representations and that should be explicitly emphasized by the accountant and recognized by management.

A review is to be sharply distinguished from an audit engagement in which an examination of the financial statements is made in accordance with generally accepted auditing standards as a basis for the expression of an opinion regarding the fairness of the statements taken as a whole in conformity with GAAP and on a basis consistent with the prior period. A review is not an audit and, as explained in the guide later presented, terms like *audit, auditor,* and *examination* should be strictly avoided. The following are illustrative of auditing procedures or responsibilities associated with audit engagements but not contemplated by a review: study and evaluation of internal accounting control; tests of accounting records; corroboration of responses to inquiries; obtaining audit evidence by inspection, count and observation of counts, confirmation, and gathering and evaluating documentary evidence. The accountant, however, may have to go beyond the basic inquiry and analytical review procedures contemplated by a review of financial statements when, in his judgment, additional procedures may be necessary to enable him to achieve limited assurance regarding the financial statements.

The foregoing principles are reflected explicitly, and often implicitly, in the Statements on Standards for Accounting and Review Services. Thus in its general description of the inquiry and analytical procedures appropriate for a review engagement, as well as in its listing of illustrative inquiries, SSARS No. 1 avoids mention of procedures that could be construed as being strictly *auditing* procedures in the traditional sense. In doing so, the intention is to preserve the special character of a review engagement and avoid the possibility of its confusion with an audit engagement. The accountant is not required to verify, corroborate or review information supplied; but it is also important to note that he is not precluded from doing so by the SSARS provisions.

The element of judgment, however, is also stressed in SSARS No. 1, and the accountant must therefore exercise such judgment in evaluating the adequacy and effectiveness of the review procedures in enabling him to achieve limited assurance regarding the financial statements. Some accountants may wish to interpret the scope of "inquiry and analytical procedures" somewhat broadly. For example, SSARS includes the following as inquiries or areas of inquiry: "Do the general ledger control accounts agree with subsidiary records?" and, "Have bank balances been reconciled with book balances?" An accountant may not feel satisfied unless, in addition to appropriate inquiries in these areas, he himself has actually compared the control account with the subsidiary listing, or has at least scanned the bank reconciliation. Some analytical procedures may call for inquiries regarding variations between budgets and actual financial data and some accountants may wish to see the budget documents.

Any written matter or documentation of the type mentioned should be regarded not as corroborative evidence in the usual audit sense, but rather as information that is, and should be expected to be, made available by management for mutual reference, discussion, and review purposes as a material and helpful resource in the formulation of responses to the accountant's inquiries. The accountant's act in referring to, and in reviewing written materials in this context, is part of the process of reviewing the financial statements; it is not an auditing procedure and should not be referred to as such.

These principles have been applied in the construction of the engagement planning and program guide for use in a review of financial statements, presented in Figure 8-17. When, for example, a procedure is noted that calls for the accountant to review the aged schedule of accounts receivable, such a review should be thought of as taking place within the context of the client's responding to inquiries of the accountant regarding the collectibility of receivables. Having the aged schedule at hand for mutual reference purposes then becomes an aid in formulating informative responses rather than audit evidence furnished as corroboration of information supplied. Similarly, a comparison of the sum total of a listing of accounts receivable balances with the controlling account can be seen not as an audit verification procedure but as part of the necessary process in a review engagement of being alert to whether the data in the financial statements do in fact have their source in the client's accounting records.

The SSARS standards and requirements relating to a review of financial statements of nonpublic companies apply to both interim and year-end engagements. However, when year-end financial statements of a client have been reviewed, certain procedures that would normally have been performed by the accountant in a later review of interim financial statements of the following year, may be modified or otherwise affected by the knowledge previously acquired.

Figure 8-17
Review of Financial Statements of Nonpublic Entity

Engagement Planning and Program Guide

_____   _____

(Client)   (Period of financial statements)

_____   _____

(Prepared by)   (Date)   (Reviewed by)   (Date)

INSTRUCTIONS

1.   The comment section at the end of the guide should be used for comments on any difficulties encountered, questions raised, or matters to be clarified. The disposition of matters commented on should be clearly noted, along with indication, where appropriate, of supervisory approval.

2.   Signatures of the accountant responsible for the completion of the guide and of the reviewer should be recorded in the spaces provided for above.

3.   The column "Performed by" should be initialed by the accountant who has undertaken the particular act.

4.   If it is not practicable—because of the number of client personnel involved, the complexities of the matter in question, or other considerations—to fill in, for any particular item, the name(s) of client personnel with whom the matter has been discussed, place a dash in the space provided. The applicable "W/P Ref." should be filled in, however, as an indication that that information along with other relevant data have been provided in the working papers.

5.   Items considered to be not applicable are to be initialed in the _NA_ column, but an explanation of the reasons for the inapplicability, unless quite obvious, should be stated in the comment section of the guide. Any client restriction or lack of cooperation is not a valid reason for marking an item _NA_, and the circumstances should be promptly discussed with the engagement partner.

6.   Fill in, where appropriate, the working paper reference number in the "W/P Ref." column. It is important to maintain adequate working papers in support of work done in carrying out the engagement.

7.   In undertaking the procedures set forth in the guide, bear in mind that this is a _review_ and not an _audit_ engagement, and that the procedures are essentially limited to inquiry and analytical procedures. A review of

financial statements does not contemplate procedures such as the following that are associated with audits: study and evaluation of internal accounting control; tests of accounting records; corroboration of responses to inquiries; obtaining audit evidence by inspection, count and observation of count, and confirmation; and gathering and evaluating documentary evidential matter. The engagement partner should be consulted if circumstances appear to warrant undertaking such corroborative procedures.

8.   The exercise of judgment in formulating or expanding inquiries and in performing the analytical procedures will be enhanced by taking into account, among other considerations:

(a)   Nature of the item or matter under review.

(b)   Materiality factor.

(c)   Likelihood or reasonable suspicion of misstatement, deliberate or otherwise.

(d)   Knowledge gained during the current or previous engagements.

(e)   Discernible high risk conditions or areas.

(f)   Qualifications of client's accounting personnel.

(g)   Inadequacies in the underlying accounting records and data.

(h)   Extent to which a matter having significance for the financial statements is affected by management's judgment.

GUIDE

	Performed by	Discussion with/Infor-mation Sup-plied by	NA	W/P ref.
I. Before Accepting the Engagement:				
1. Review AICPA's Statements on Standards for Accounting and Review Services (SSARS) for guidance on procedural and reporting standards and requirements.				
2. Note the reference in Appendix E of SSARS No. 1 to Rule 201 of the rules of conduct of the AICPA's Code of Professional Ethics. Even though this is not an audit				

engagement, standards of professional competence, due professional care, adequate engagement planning and supervision, and other such standards must be thoroughly observed.

3. Discuss with management, and determine in specific terms, the nature of the services to be performed, including any accounting services such as the compilation of financial statements that may be necessary to enable a review to be made.

4. Discuss with management:
ment:

(a) The meaning and nature of a review engagement.

(b) Its differentiation from a compilation of financial statements or an audit of financial statements.

(c) Type of report to be issued.

(d) The expression in the report of limited assurance and disclaimer of opinion.

(e) The reasons a *review* is desired rather than a *compilation* or an *audit*, and the appropriateness of a review in satisfying the needs of the entity.

(f) Planned distribution of the report to stockholders, banks, other credit-grantors, and other outside parties.

5. Explain to management that the financial statements and the information on which they are based are the entity's responsibility as its representations, even though accounting services may be performed by the accountant in such matters as recordkeeping assistance, help in adjusting the books of account, or compilation of the financial statements. Go over the contents of a representation letter after advising that a completed, signed representation letter or letters must be submitted by the client before the conclusion of the engagement.

6. Inquire about predecessor accountant, if any, the type of services rendered, and reason for the change in accountants, and obtain permission to communicate with him (or his firm).

7. Communicate with predecessor accountant to ascertain reasons for the change and type of services performed, and to inquire, among other matters, about client reputation and any circumstances that would militate against accepting the engagement or might later present problems.

8. Consider obtaining permission to inquire of business and banking references concerning the reputation of the entity and the reputation and integrity of top management, and make such inquiries if desirable.

9. Point out to management that the engagement cannot be relied upon to disclose errors, irregularities, fraud, defalcations, or illegal acts that may exist, but that management and/or the board of directors will be informed of any such matters that come to our attention.

10. By inquiries of management, selected company personnel, and observation, develop an initial understanding of:

(a) Nature of the company's business, business transactions, and general financial condition. An understanding of the business should include (the following are specifically mentioned in SSARS 1, para. 26):

(i) General understanding of the organization.

(ii) Operating characteristics.

(iii) Nature of the assets, liabilities, revenues, and expenses.

(iv) General knowledge of production, distribution, and compensation methods.

(v) Types of products and services.

(vi) Operating locations.

(vii) Material related-party transactions.

(b) Type and condition of the accounting records.

(c) Qualifications of accounting personnel.

(d) Form and content of the financial statements and the type of financial statements and accountants' reports previously issued.

(e) Accounting basis on which financial statements are to be presented.

(f) The availability of reliable records and data for use by management in making informed responses to the accountant's inquiries, including those pertaining to the conformity of the financial statements with GAAP consistently applied.

11. If there is a lack of familiarity with the industry in which the entity operates, gain an understanding of the industry's accounting principles and practices sufficient to provide a basis, together with the inquiry and analytical procedures, for expressing limited assurance in the report as to conformity of the statements with GAAP. Such understanding may be obtained by consulting AICPA guides, industry and other publications, published financial statements, and knowledgeable accountants and other persons.

12. Based upon information gathered, consider whether it would be proper or desirable to accept the engagement. In making this judgment, take into account:

(a) Any factors or knowledge gained that might suggest that the financial statements or the information upon which they are based (or are to be compiled) might be false and misleading.

(b) The existence, if applicable, of a troubled and complex financial condition including substantial indebtedness to credit-grantors that would ordinarily suggest the need for an *audit* and not simply a *review* of the financial statements.

(c) Any other questionable or negative indications such as an unexplained change from previously audited financial statements to a review engagement.

13. Discuss the contents of the engagement letter with management.

14. Obtain an engagement letter signed by the president of the company. This letter should incorporate the following understanding among others:

(a) Services to be performed: their nature and limitations; and fees.

(b)   Description of report expected to be issued.

(c)   That the engagement cannot be relied upon to disclose errors, irregularities, or illegal acts, but the entity will be informed of any such matters that come to the accountant's attention.

II.   Subsequent to Acceptance of the Engagement

General Matters

15.   Bear in mind that the following actions are to be avoided during the engagement:

(a)   Using in the working papers, financial statements, report, or any communications with the client or outside party, any words, phrases, or terms, like *audit, audit fees, auditor, auditing procedure,* or *examination,* that may suggest that an audit is being or has been conducted. This prohibition also applies to a description of any procedures that might have been undertaken as supplementary services at the request of the client, even though they may appear to be similar to the type of procedures undertaken in a regular audit engagement.

(b)   Changing the character of the engagement to an audit, or undertaking any procedures generally identified as auditing procedures, if not previously provided for in the engagement letter, without consultation with and approval of the engagement partner.

16.   If the knowledge gained, prior to accepting the engagement, regarding the business, the accounting records, and industry accounting practices is incomplete, make further inquiries to the extent necessary.

17.   Review correspondence and tax files in our office pertaining to the client.

18.   Review permanent file and prior period working papers and financial statements.

19.   Make further inquiries and obtain additional background information relating to:

(a)   The company's financial condition and operations, including production, distribution and compensation methods and plans, types of products and services, and operating locations.

(b)   Significant changes in important operational areas.

(c)   Sales trends and profitability of the several product lines.

(d)   Financial problems or difficulties faced by the company.

(e)   Major acquisitions or sales of plant and subsidiary companies.

(f)   Related party transactions.

(g)   Significant financial ratios.

(h)   Budgets and forecasts.

(i)   Government regulations affecting the entity.

(j)   Contingencies and commitments.

(k)   Long-term contracts and leases.

20.   Inquire about the accounting principles and methods employed, their conformity with GAAP, and their consistency with prior periods.

21.   Discuss with senior officers, including the chief accounting officer, the informative disclosures that are required to be made to ensure conformity of the financial statements with GAAP, and ascertain whether the necessary information is readily available.

22.   Inquire about matters authorized or actions taken or considered at meetings of stockholders, board of directors or executive committees that may materially affect the financial statements, and ask whether these matters are reflected, as appropriate, in the accounting records and the financial statements. Although this is a review and not an audit engagement, the minutes should be made available by the client so that they may be referred to for mutual reference as an aid in recalling significant matters that could have been overlooked or in clarifying ambiguous or complex proposals or actions.

23.   At the appropriate time, obtain reports from other accountants, if any, who have audited or reviewed for the current period the financial statements of branches, other significant components of the client company, its subsidiaries, and other investee companies. In addition:

(a)   Inquire about the reputation of these accountants.

(b)   Take note of the details of their report, character of their examination or review, and the degree of responsibility assumed by them.

(c)   Discuss these reports with the client.

(d)   Consider whether reference is to be made in the report on review of the financial statements to the work of the other accountants relative to any subsidiaries or other components included in the financial statements.

24.   Obtain information from accounting personnel regarding the accounting records maintained and the procedures followed for recording, classifying, and summarizing transactions, and accumulating information for disclosure in financial statements.

25.   Make inquiries regarding the system of internal accounting control and any changes therein—in terms of accuracy, completeness and timeliness—relating to: the accounting records; recording, classifying, and summarizing of transactions; recording of accruals and adjusting entries; and accumulation of information for disclosure in financial statements. (Note: A review does not contemplate a study and evaluation of the system of internal accounting control. The aforementioned inquiries are not to be made, as in an audit engagement, for the purpose of determining the extent of audit tests, but rather simply to gain a better understanding of the quality and reliability of the accounting system and records and, hence, of their impact on the client's preparation of financial statements—interim as well as year-end.)

26.   Perform accounting services that are prerequisites to undertaking the review of financial statements. (But first consult with and obtain approval of engagement partner regarding any accounting serv-

ices not originally explicity agreed to with the client.) These prerequisite accounting services are (*performed by* column is to be initialed upon completion of the service):

(a) _____

(b) _____

(c) _____

27.   Obtain a trial balance of general ledger accounts and compare with general ledger balances (or, in the absence of a general ledger, with comparable records). In making the comparison, scan the accounts, taking note of unusual fluctuations or entries.

28.   While inquiring as to the type of general ledger adjustments usually required to be made as of the statement date, scan adjustments recorded in the general journal during a selected prior period.

29.   Compare opening balances in general ledger with adjusted trial balance of prior engagement (or, for a new engagement, with accounting report and/or general ledger of prior period).

Cash

30.   Review bank reconciliations and take note of, or inquire as to:

(a)   Agreement of book and bank balances reflected on bank reconciliation with corresponding balances per books and bank statement.

(b)   Propriety of reconciling items and need for adjusting entries.

(c)   Long-outstanding checks and other old or unusual reconciling items.

(d)   Adequacy of cutoff of cash transactions and whether cash books have been improperly kept open.

31.   Inquire about whether cash funds have been counted and reconciled to the accounting records, and review the cash count reconciliation prepared by the client.

32.   Ascertain whether there are any restrictions on withdrawal of cash from bank accounts.

Receivables and Sales

33.   Review aged schedule of accounts receivable as well as schedule of notes receivable, and inquire about, or to take note of:

(a)   Reconciliation of totals per schedules with general ledger balances.

(b)   Collectibility of accounts that are past due.

(c)   Accounts being carried as receivables that should be written off as uncollectible.

(d)   Accounts that appear unusual or questionable in terms of their character or materiality.

(e)   Non-trade receivables including: receivables from officers, employees, and other related parties or companies; deposits; and advances to suppliers.

(f)   Credit balances.

34.   Discuss with client the collectibility of accounts and notes receivable and the adequacy of the allowance for doubtful accounts and inquire about:

(a)   Average collection period currently and in prior years.

(b)   Accounts written off during the current period.

(c)   Cash collected, credits granted, and accounts written off subsequent to the date of the financial statements.

(d)   Basis of arriving at the allowance for doubtful accounts, and comparison of the method of computation with that of prior periods, taking into account changes in sales volume, customer composition, collection problems and trends, and other relevant considerations.

35.   Determine whether receivables have been properly classified as between current and noncurrent.

36.   Inquire as to whether any of the receivables have been pledged, discounted, or factored.

37.   Ascertain whether the company engages in consignment sales in or out and, if so, whether they have been properly recorded.

38.   Obtain information regarding special sales contracts and terms of sales, including discount policy and warranties.

39.   Inquire regarding sales transactions with related parties and whether they have been conducted on a basis unfavorable to the client.

40.   Consider whether recorded cash and other discounts and warranty costs appear reasonable after application of estimated overall percentages and after comparison with comparable data for prior periods.

41.   In inquiring regarding the adequacy of the cutoff of sales transactions, ask specifically about:

(a)   Method used in ensuring a proper cutoff.

(b)   In transit items.

(c)   Sales returns.

(d)   Coordination with physical inventory count.

42.   Compare sales of current period, by product lines and in total, with prior periods and with budgets and forecasts and obtain explanations regarding variations, fluctuations, and trends that appear to be significant or questionable.

43.   Relate sales discounts and sales returns to sales and to sales and discount policy and compare data with prior periods.

44.   Consider the reasonableness of interest income recorded for notes and loans receivable taking into account outstanding receivables and interest terms.

Investments

    45.   Review schedule of investments and inquire as to, or take note of:

(a)   Agreement of schedule total with general ledger balance.

(b)   Basis of valuation of investments: whether investments are stated at cost, lower of cost or market, or on the equity basis, as appropriate in applying GAAP; whether, specifically, marketable equity securities have been properly accounted for.

(c)   Impairment in value that would require write-down below carrying amount.

(d)   Proper recording of gains and losses on sale or other disposal, and any gains or losses that appear to be especially material or unusual.

    46.   Consider the reasonableness of dividend and interest income in relationship to investments.

    47.   Discuss with client reports of subsidiary or investee companies issued by other accountants and the information contained therein for bearing on carrying value of investments.

    48.   Inquire about:

(a)   Investments that may be hypothecated, pledged, or otherwise encumbered.

(b)   Material market declines as of or subsequent to the balance sheet date.

(c)   Classification of investments as between current and noncurrent.

(d)   Investments involving related companies or other related parties.

Inventories

    49.   Obtain an inventory representation letter from the client.

    50.   Inquire regarding the following matters:

(a)   Whether and where inventories were physically counted, and the type of controls exercised during the count; or, if not counted, how inventory quantities were determined.

(b)   Reconciliation procedures used to account for transactions and inventory movements between date of the count and the statement date.

(c)   Basis of valuation and conformity with GAAP; specifically, methods of arriving at cost, market, and lower of cost or market; inclusion in cost of materials, labor and applicable overhead.

(d)   Obsolete or slow-selling merchandise and write-down to net realizable value.

(e)   Consistency with prior periods in inventory pricing.

(f)   Adequacy of inventory cutoff and coordination with cutoff of purchase and sales transactions.

    51.   Compare summary totals of inventory listings with general ledger balances.

52. Inquire as to:

(a) Inventories hypothecated, pledged, or otherwise encumbered.

(b) Material market declines or other significant events affecting the inventories that have taken place subsequent to the balance sheet date.

(c) Purchase and sales commitments and whether they are abnormal or unfavorable in any material respect.

(d) Inventory on hand owned by others and held on consignment, and owned inventory out on consignment or held by warehouses or other custodians; and discuss with client in detail how such transactions were controlled and recorded and whether the proper accounting entries were made.

53. Undertake appropriate comparison tests of inventory balances as well as gross profit percentage, inventory turnover ratio, ratio of inventories to total current assets, and other significant relationships. Comparisons should be made with prior periods, budgets, forecasts, and industry data, taking into account sales volume and trends, market conditions, and changes in product lines and in production or maketing methods.

Property, Plant and Equipment

54. Ascertain by inquiries and discussions with client whether:

(a) Property, plant and equipment are stated at cost less accumulated allowances.

(b) Cost of assets includes all pertinent elements of cost and doe not include repairs, maintenance or other expenses improperly capitalized. In that connection, ascertain policy of the company for distinguishing between capital and revenue expenditures.

(c) Fixed assets may have been improperly expensed to repairs and maintenance or other expense accounts.

(d) Depreciation methods and rates used are in conformity with GAAP and have been applied on a consistent basis.

(e) Additions, retirements, and gain or loss on sale or disposals have been properly recorded and in the proper accounting period, with elimination of applicable allowances upon disposal of assets.

(f) Assets have been mortgaged or otherwise encumbered.

(g) Material lease agreements exist and have been capitalized and/or disclosed in accordance with GAAP requirements. Roughly approximate rental income (or expense) for the period and compare with prior period and with general ledger balances.

55. Scan depreciation schedules that are being reviewed with the client, and compare summary totals with general ledger balances.

56. Ask client for information on the nature of and circumstances relating to major additions and disposals of the current year.

57.   In evaluating the overall reasonableness of property, plant and equipment and related accounts, compare the following with comparable data for prior periods: assets and related allowances, depreciation, repairs and maintenance, current additions and retirements, gains and losses on sales or other disposals, rental income.

58.   Relate amount of repairs and maintenance expense to plant assets.

59.   Relate depreciation expense to plant assets.

60.   Relate plant assets to: amount of insurance coverage; sales volume; and changes in production methods and product lines.

Prepaid Expenses, Deferred Charges, Intangibles, and Other Assets

61.   Inquire as to:

(a)   Whether these assets are stated at cost and, if related parties involved, whether cost was determined on an arms-length basis.

(b)   Period of useful life and method of amortization.

(c)   Continued usefulness of intangibles and deferred charges.

(d)   Conformity of carrying value and method and period of amortization with GAAP.

(e)   Expensing of research and development costs.

62.   Obtain schedules of significant assets in this category and compare with general ledger balances.

Purchases, Expenses, and Liabilities

63.   Review schedules of accounts and notes payable and inquire as to, or take note of:

(a)   Agreement of totals with general ledger balances.

(b)   Past-due or unusual accounts.

(c)   Accounts representing payables to officers, employees and other related parties or companies, deposits, and advances from customers.

(d)   Debit balances.

64.   Inquire as to whether assets have been pledged to secure the liabilities.

65.   Discuss with client the methods adopted to ensure that all liabilities have been recorded in full as of the balance sheet date.

66.   Inquire as to adequacy of cut-off procedures.

67.   Ascertain whether payables have been properly classified with appropriate disclosures as to:

(a)   Current and long-term.

(b)   Bank liabilities and terms.

(c)   Accrued liabilities.

(d)   Mortgage and bond indebtedness and interest and amortization terms.

(e)   Current portion of long-term debt.

68.   Relative to income taxes and other taxes, inquire regarding:

(a)   Provision for current and prior years.

(b)   The income tax situation, IRS examinations, and current and past assessments.

(c)   Timing differences and proper recording of deferred taxes.

(d)   Provision for state and local income taxes and for business taxes generally.

69.   Review client's reconciliation of taxable income with accounting income, and computation of tax liability for the current year.

70.   Inquire regarding terms of pension and profit-sharing plans or special compensation agreements.

71.   Inquire regarding restrictive covenant provisions relating to long-term debt and whether any violations have occurred or are likely to occur.

72.   In inquiring about contingencies and commitments, ask specifically about:

(a)   Litigation and other matters in the hands of the client's attorneys.

(b)   Asserted and unasserted claims.

(c)   Discounted notes, guarantees and warranties.

(d)   Obligations and commitments of a material nature relating to construction, acquisition or sale of any assets or company securities.

(e)   Other material contingencies and uncertainties.

73.   Undertake an overall review of the reasonableness of liability accounts including accrued expenses. Compare balances with prior periods and relate them to current year's operations. Request client to explain any material variations.

74.   Undertake an overall review of the reasonableness of major expense accounts by comparing current year balances and ratios with those of prior years and with budgets and forecasts. In making the comparison tests include the following relationships:

(a)   Cost of sales and gross profit to sales.

(b)   Components of cost of sales to total cost of sales and to sales.

(c)   Purchase discounts to purchases.

(d)   Freight to purchases.

(e)   Commissions to sales.

(f)   Payroll taxes to payroll.

(g)   Payroll to sales, cost of sales, and selling and administrative expense, depending on the payroll category.

(h)   Payroll totals to totals per payroll tax forms and other government forms.

(i)   Repairs and maintenance to property, plant and equipment.

Stockholders' Equity

75.   Inquire regarding classes of capital stock, capital stock preferences, amounts authorized, issued and outstanding, and treasury stock.

76.   Review listings prepared by client from subsidiary records and compare totals with equity account balances.

77.   In the process of making inquiries regarding stockholder equity accounts, review corporate charter and pertinent minutes.

78.   Inquire as to changes in the equity accounts and compare balances with prior years.

79.   Inquire regarding matters requiring disclosure such as bond indenture restrictions affecting dividends and acquisition of treasury stock.

80.   Review client's reconciliation of dividends for the period with outstanding shares.

81.   Make inquiries regarding dividends in arrears, stock option or stock repurchase plans and other matters requiring disclosure in the financial statements.

Other Matters

(See also procedures previously covered under General Matters)

82.   Inquire regarding material events occurring subsequent to the balance sheet date that may require either adjustment to the accounts as of the statement date or disclosure in the financial statements. When making such inquiries, provide the client with illustrations of the type of event that could have significance.

83.   Inquire regarding extraordinary items of profit and loss and discontinued operations.

84.   Scan monthly and quarterly financial statements prepared by the client during the current year and note unusual or questionable data and fluctuations within the current period and in comparison with prior periods and with budgets and forecasts.

III. Completing the Engagement

85.   Resolve open problems and questions recorded in audit notes, and consult with and obtain approval of engagement partner with respect to important matters still to be resolved that require his attention.

86.   Perform and complete other accounting services contemplated by the engagement (list below):

(a)   Preparation of tax returns.

(b)   _____.

(c)   _____.

87.   Inform the client (and, where appropriate, the board of directors) of any important matters coming to our attention during the review, such as irregularities, frauds, defalcations, illegal acts, and significant errors.

88.   Discuss with client the account adjustments accumulated during the review and obtain client's acceptance and approval.

89. Trace balances on adjusted trial balance to financial statements.

90. Check mathematical accuracy of the financial statements.

91. Read the financial statements analytically.

92. Consider whether the statements appear to be:

(a) Appropriate in form.

(b) Free from arithmetical errors and from improper inclusions or omissions.

(c) Properly classified.

(d) In conformity with generally accepted accounting principles including adequate disclosures.

93. Utilize the financial statement disclosures checklist reminder and review guide (shown as Figure 7-5) as an aid in ascertaining whether the financial statements and accompanying notes to financial statements contain adequate disclosures of important matters whose disclosure is required by GAAP for the statements to be fair and not misleading.

94. Compare the account balances and significant ratios pertaining to the financial statements of the current period, with comparable data as reflected in prior period financial statements and in available budgets and forecasts. Take into account trends, general business and industry conditions, and changes in operations. Discuss with client and obtain approriate explanations of significant fluctuations and variations. Comparison tests should encompass:

(a) Sales volume in quantities, if data are available, and in dollar amounts.

(b) Cost of sales, gross profit and gross profit percentage.

(c) Income before extraordinary items, income from continuing operations before income taxes, and net income; and the ratio to revenues, total assets and stockholders' equity.

(d) Income taxes in relationship to income before income taxes.

(e) Current assets, current liabilities, working capital, current ratio, and liquidity ratio.

(f) Long-term debt, stockholders' equity, fixed assets to long-term liabilities, stockholders' equity to total assets.

(g) Earnings per share.

95. Prepare a memorandum covering the results of aforementioned overall analytical review of the financial statements as well as the analytical procedures pertaining to specific accounts.

96. Prepare the accountant's report in accordance with the standards laid down in Statements on Standards for Accounting and Review Services.

97. Discuss the financial statements and the accountant's report with the client. Among matters to be discussed and considered are:

(a) Client's awareness that the financial statements are the representations of management (the entity).

(b) Client's assurance that the financial statements are in conformity with GAAP, applied on a basis consistent with the prior period, and include all disclosures required by GAAP.

(c)   Any last-minute events that may require modification of the financial statements.

(d)   The details of the accountant's report and especially any modification of the standard report for a review engagement.

98.   Obtain a signed representation letter from the client.

99.   Prepare a memorandum for review by the engagement partner in which an evaluation of the conduct of the engagement is made in terms of its conformity with the standards and requirements of the AICPA's Statements on Standards for Accounting and Review Services.

100.   Prepare a memorandum containing suggestions for use on subsequent engagements.

101.   After supervisory and partner review procedures have been followed and review guides have been completed, arrange for typing of report and submission to the client.

Comments on Items Listed Above

(Use this section of the guide for comments on any difficulties encountered or matters to be clarified. Comments are to be keyed to the specific item. Their disposition is to be clearly noted along with indication, where appropriate, of supervisory approval.)

_____

_____

ENGAGEMENT LETTER FOR REVIEW ENGAGEMENTS

The subject of engagement letters in general as well as for audit engagements is discussed in Chapter 1 and illustrations are provided in Figures 1-3 and 1-4.

Figure 8-18 is an illustrative engagement letter for a review of financial statements drawn from SSARS No. 1. Shown as Figure 8-19 is a more comprehensive engagement letter covering additional matters that an accountant may wish to include.

Figure 8-18
Engagement Letter for a Review of Financial
Statements (SSARS No. 1)

(Accountant's Letterhead)

(Date)

(Appropriate Salutation)

This letter is to confirm our understanding of the terms and objectives of our engagement and the nature and limitations of the services we will provide.

We will perform the following services:

1.   We will review the balance sheet of XYZ Company as of December 31, 19XX, and the related statements of income, retained earnings, and changes in financial position for the year then ended, in accordance with standards established by the American Institute of Certified Public Accountants. We will not perform an audit of such financial statements, the objective of which is the expression of an opinion regarding the financial statements taken as a whole, and, accordingly, we will not express such an opinion on them. Our report on the financial statements is presently expected to read as follows:

"We have reviewed the accompanying balance sheet of XYZ Company as of December 31, 19XX, and the related statements of income, retained earnings, and changes in financial position for the year then ended, in accordance with standards established by the American Institute of Certified Public Accountants. All information included in these financial statements is the representation of the management of XYZ Company.

"A review consists principally of inquiries of company personnel and analytical procedures applied to financial data. It is substantially less in scope than an examination in accordance with generally accepted auditing standards, the objective of which is the expression of an opinion regarding the financial statements taken as a whole. Accordingly, we do not express such an opinion.

"Based on our review, we are not aware of any material modifications that should be made to the accompanying financial statements in order for them to be in conformity with generally accepted accounting principles."

If, for any reason, we are unable to complete our review of your financial statements, we will not issue a report on such statements as a result of this engagement.

2. We will also . . . (discussion of other services).

Our engagement cannot be relied upon to disclose errors, irregularities, or illegal acts, including fraud or defalcations, that may exist. However, we will inform you of any such matters that come to our attention.

Our fees for these services . . .

We shall be pleased to discuss this letter with you at any time.

If the foregoing is in accordance with your understanding, please sign the copy of this letter in the space provided and return it to us.

Sincerely yours,

_____

(Signature of accountant)

Acknowledge:
XYZ Company

_____

President

_____

Date

_____

Comments:

1. Some accountants prefer not to obtain an acknowledgment, in which case their letter would omit the paragraph beginning "If the foregoing . . . " and the space for the acknowledgment. The first paragraph of their letter might begin as follows: "This letter sets forth our understanding of the terms and objectives of our engagement. . . "

2. If the engagement entails a compilation of quarterly (or other interim) financial statements and a review of annual financial statements, the engagement letters shown in Figures 8-18 and 8-19 would have to be modified by incorporating relevant sections of the compilation engagement letters represented by Figures 8-2 and 8-3.

Figure 8-19
Expanded Engagement Letter—
Review of Financial Statements

(Accountant's Letterhead)

(Date)

(Appropriate Salutation)

It is a source of satisfaction to us that you have engaged our firm to perform certain professional services for the Client Corporation whose headquarters are at the address noted above. This letter will confirm our mutual understanding of the terms of the engagement and the nature and limitations of the services to be provided.

The following services are to be performed by us:

1. We will review the balance sheet of the Client Corporation as of December 31, 198X, and the related statements of income, retained earnings, and changes in financial position for the year then ended. The review will be made in accordance with standards established by the American Institute of Certified Public Accountants pertaining to this type of review engagement. We will not perform an audit of the financial statements, the objective of which is the expression of an opinion regarding the financial statements taken as a whole, and, accordingly, we will not express such an opinion on them.

2. We will submit to you a report on the financial statements identified above that is expected to read as follows:

"We have reviewed the accompanying balance sheet of XYZ Company as of December 31, 198X, and the related statements of income, retained earnings, and changes in financial position for the year then ended, in accordance with standards established by the American Institute of Certified Public Accountants. All information included in these financial statements is the representation of the management of XYZ Company.

"A review consists principally of inquiries of company personnel and analytical procedures applied to financial data. It is substantially less in scope than an examination in accordance with generally accepted auditing standards, the objective of which is the expression of an opinion regarding the financial statements taken as a whole. Accordingly, we do not express such an opinion.

"Based on our review, we are not aware of any material modifications that should be made to the accompanying financial statements in order for them to be in conformity with generally accepted accounting principles."

3.   We will render accounting services needed to enable us to perform a review of the financial statements, as follows:

(a)   _____ .

(b)   _____ .

(Note: Some services that may be applicable are compilation of financial statements, preparing a working trial balance, assistance in adjusting the books of account, and bookkeeping services.)

4.   We will prepare the following income and business tax returns:

_____

_____

_____

If for any reason, we are unable to complete our review of your financial statements, we will not issue a report on such financial statements or submit the financial statements to you in any form.

We will request, and you will submit to us during the engagement, signed representation letters in which the company acknowledges its basic responsibility for the fairness of the financial statements (and the underlying accounting records on which they are based) and their conformity with generally accepted accounting principles including the disclosure of material matters whose disclosure is necessary for the financial statements to be fair and not misleading.

You have assured us of your cooperation in facilitating the progress of our review and of the other services to be performed.

Our engagement cannot be relied upon to uncover or disclose errors, irregularities, fraud, defalcations, or illegal acts, that may exist. However, we will inform you of any such matters that come to our attention.

Our fees for the services are as follows: _____

_____

If the terms of this letter meet with your approval, please sign one copy in the space provided and return it to us for our files. We look forward to a pleasant association and the opportunity to render the services contemplated by this engagement.

Very truly yours,

John A. Accountant & Co.

_____

Walter B. Brown, Partner

Date _____

We are in agreement with the terms of this letter.

Client Corporation

_____
William E. Smith, President

REPRESENTATION LETTER FOR REVIEW ENGAGEMENTS

A general representation letter of the type that might be used on review engagements is shown in Figure 8-20. It is a modified and expanded version of the illustrative representation letter appearing in SSARS No. 1. It is suggested in that statement that, based on the circumstances of the particular engagement, additional matters may be included or certain representations deleted. The point is also made that obtaining such a letter is advisable rather than mandatory.

It would be difficult, however, to overestimate the value of a client representation letter. Obtaining such a letter is a requirement in the case of an audit engagement (AU 333). Some accountants may wish to extend the practice routinely to compilation or review engagements and may even consider it advisable to obtain an inventory representation letter in addition to a general representation letter. The inventory letter shown in Figure 2-3 for use on an audit engagement may be used in its entirety on a review engagement, but the word *examination* in the introductory sentence should be changed to *review*.

A broader discussion of representation letters as well as illustrative letters for use in audit engagements will be found in Chapter 2.

Figure 8-20
Representation Letter for Review of Financial Statements (Modified and Expanded version of illustrative letter in SSARS 1)

(Client Letterhead)

(Date of accountant's report)

(Addressed to accountant)

Gentlemen:

In connection with your review of the (identification of financial statements) of (name of client) as of (date) and for the (period of review) for the purpose of expressing limited assurance that there are no material modifications that should be made to the statements in order for them to be in conformity with generally accepted accounting principles, we confirm, to the best of our knowledge and belief, the representations recorded below made to you during your review. Exceptions or supplementary comments, if any, will be stated at the end of this letter in the section captioned *Exceptions*.

1.   The financial statements referred to above present the financial position, results of operations, and changes in financial position of (name of client) in conformity with generally accepted accounting principles.

2.   The company's accounting principles, and the practices and methods followed in applying them, are as disclosed in the financial statements.

3.   There have been no changes during the (period reviewed) in the company's accounting principles and practices.

4.   Informative disclosures have been made in the financial statements, including footnotes, of all material matters whose disclosure is necessary to make the statements fair and not misleading.

5.   We have no plans or intentions that may materially affect the carrying value or classification of assets and liabilities.

6.   There are no material transactions that have not been properly reflected in the financial statements.

7.   There are no material losses (such as from obsolete inventory or purchase or sales commitments) that have not been properly accrued or disclosed in the financial statements.

8.   There are no violations or possible violations of laws or regulations whose effects should be considered for disclosure in the financial statements or as a basis for recording a loss.

9.   All liabilities, including accrued liabilities, have been properly recorded.

10.   All gain or loss contingencies have been properly recorded (accrued) or disclosed in the financial statements. Examples of loss contingencies include, among others: pending or threatened litigations, claims and assessments; obligations relating to product warranties and product defects; unusual risk of loss or damage of enterprise property by fire, explosion, or other hazards; guarantees of indebtedness of others; receivables sold with recourse; receivables doubtful of collection.

11.   The company has satisfactory title to all owned assets, and there are no liens or encumbrances on such assets nor has any asset been pledged.

12.   There are no related party transactions or related accounts receivable or payable that have not been properly disclosed in the financial statements.

13.   We have complied with all aspects of contractual agreements that would have a material effect on the financial statements in the event of noncompliance.

14.   No events have occurred subsequent to the balance sheet date that would require adjustment to, or disclosure in, the financial statements. Examples of such events are: loss of major customers; casualty losses; material changes in stockholders' equity or property, plant and equipment; litigation or settlement of law suits or other claims; tax assessments; material or unusual sales returns and allowances.

15.   We have advised you of all actions taken at meetings of stockholders, board of directors, and committees of the board of directors (or other similar bodies, as applicable) that may affect the financial statements.

16.   We have responded fully to all inquiries made to us by you during your review.

17.   _____.

18.   _____.

EXCEPTIONS: _____

_____

_____

Very truly yours,

_____   _____

Signature of chief   Date
executive officer and title

_____   _____

Signature of chief   Date
financial officer and title

_____

Comment. Accountants wishing to obtain an inventory representation letter in addition to a general representation letter of the type
illustrated above, may wish to refer to and use the inventory letter shown
in Figure 2-3, but the word *review* should replace *examination* in the
introductory sentence.

Figure 8-21
Review Report

Standard Report: Single Year (SSARS 1)

I (we) have reviewed the accompanying balance sheet of XYZ Company as of December 31, 198Y, and the related statements of income, retained earnings, and changes in financial position for the year then ended, in accordance with standards established by the American Institute of Certified Public Accountants. All information included in these financial statements is the representation of the management (owners) of XYZ Company.

A review consists principally of inquiries of company personnel and analytical procedures applied to financial data. It is substantially less in scope than an examination in accordance with generally accepted auditing standards, the objective of which is the expression of an opinion regarding the financial statements taken as a whole. Accordingly, I (we) do not express such an opinion.

Based on my (our) review, I am (we are) not aware of any material modifications that should be made to the accompanying financial statements in order for them to be in conformity with generally accepted accounting principles.

Comments:

1. The customary reporting principles apply with respect to signing the report and using appropriate salutation. See Figure 8-5.

2. Note the disclaimer of opinion as well as the limited assurance.

3. Additionally, each page of the financial statements should carry a warning such as: "See Accountant's Review Report."

Figure 8-22
Review Report

Comparative Financial Statements: Standard Report;
Review for Each Period (SSARS 2)

I (we) have reviewed the accompanying balance sheets of XYZ Company as of December 31, 198Y and 198X, and the related statements of income, retained earnings, and changes in financial position for the years then ended, in accordance with standards established by the American Institute of Certified Public Accountants. All information included in these financial statements is the representation of the management (owners) of XYZ Company.

A review consists principally of inquiries of company personnel and analytical procedures applied to financial data. It is substantially less in scope than an examination in accordance with generally accepted auditing standards, the objective of which is the expression of an opinion regarding the financial statements taken as a whole. Accordingly, I (we) do not express such an opinion.

Based on my (our) reviews, I am (we are) not aware of any material modifications that should be made to the accompanying financial statements in order for them to be in conformity with generally accepted accounting principles.

Comment. See Figure 8-5 for reporting standards that apply to a review report by continuing accountant on comparative financial statements.

Figure 8-23
Review Report

Comparative Financial Statements: Review for Current Period; Compilation for Prior Period (SSARS 2)

I (we) have reviewed the accompanying balance sheet of XYZ Company as of December 31, 198Y, and the related statements of income, retained earnings, and changes in financial position for the year then ended, in accordance with standards established by the American Institute of Certified Public Accountants. All information included in these financial statements is the representation of the management (owners) of XYZ Company.

A review consists principally of inquiries of company personnel and analytical procedures applied to financial data. It is substantially less in scope than an examination in accordance with generally accepted audited standards, the objective of which is the expression of an opinion regarding the financial statements taken as a whole. Accordingly, I (we) do not express such an opinion.

Based on my (our) review, I am (we are) not aware of any material modifications that should be made to the 198Y financial statements in order for them to be in conformity with generally accepted accounting principles.

The accompanying 198X financial statements of XYZ Company were compiled by me (us). A compilation is limited to presenting in the form of financial statements information that is the representation of management (owners). I (we) have not audited or reviewed the 198X financial statements and, accordingly, do not express an opinion or any other form of assurance on them.

Figure 8-24
Review Report

Comparative Financial Statements: Compilation for Current Period; Review for Prior Period (SSARS 2)

(For comparative financial statements compiled for the current year but reviewed in the prior year, the continuing accountant should either: (a) Issue a compilation report for the current period with an added paragraph, as shown below, that provides the indicated data with respect to the prior year report; or (b) Combine the compilation report with the reissued review report or present them separately, but the report should note that no review procedures were performed subsequent to the date of the review report. (SSARS 2.11)

ADDITIONAL PARAGRAPH (SSARS 2.12)

The accompanying 198X financial statements of XYZ Company were previously reviewed by me (us) and my (our) report dated March 1, 198Y, stated that I was (we were) not aware of any material modifications that should be made to those statements in order for them to be in conformity with generally accepted accounting principles. I (we) have not performed any procedures in connection with that review engagement after the date of my (our) report on the 198X financial statements.

Figure 8-25
Review Report

Departure from GAAP Disclosed (SSARS 1)

I (we) have reviewed the accompanying balance sheet of XYZ Company as of December 31, 198Y, and the related statements of income, retained earnings, and changes in financial position for the year then ended, in accordance with standards established by the American Institute of Certified Public Accountants. All information included in these financial statements is the representation of the management (owners) of XYZ Company.

A review consists principally of inquiries of company personnel and analytical procedures applied to financial data. It is substantially less in scope than an examination in accordance with generally accepted auditing standards, the objective of which is the expression of an opinion regarding the financial statements taken as a whole. Accordingly, I (we) do not express such an opinion.

Based on my (our) review, with the exception of the matter(s) described in the following paragraph(s), I am (we are) not aware of any material modifications that should be made in the accompanying financial statements in order for them to be in conformity with generally accepted accounting principles.

(SEPARATE PARAGRAPH—ILLUSTRATION I)

As disclosed in note X to the financial statements, generally accepted accounting principles require that inventory cost consist of material, labor, and overhead. Management has informed me (us) that the inventory of finished goods and work in process is stated in the accompanying financial statements at material and labor cost only, and that the effects of this departure from generally accepted accounting principles on financial position, results of operations, and changes in financial position have not been determined.

(SEPARATE PARAGRAPH—ILLUSTRATION II)

As disclosed in note X to the financial statements, the company has adopted (description of newly adopted method), whereas it previously used (description of previous method). Although the (description of newly adopted method) is in conformity with generally accepted accounting principles, the company does not appear to have reasonable justification for making a change as required by Opinion No. 20 of the Accounting Principles Board.

Comments:

1. The client should, of course, be encouraged to agree to a revision of the financial statements so that they conform with GAAP.

2. In the absence of such revision, the standard report must be modified to disclose the departure from GAAP in a separate paragraph. The impact of the deficiency on the financial statements must also be disclosed if determined by management or otherwise known to the accountant; but if the effects are not so determined, the accountant is not required to do so provided he states in his report that a determination of the effects of the departure from GAAP has not been made. (SSARS 1.39, .40)

3. But if the accountant believes that such modification of the standard report is not adequate in terms of the financial statements taken as a whole, the report should not be issued and he should withdraw from the engagement and provide no further services in connection with the financial statements. (SSARS 1.41)

Figure 8-26
Review Report

Changed Reference in Comparative Financial Statements to Prior Period Departure from GAAP

(The additional paragraph recorded below should follow the three paragraphs of the standard review report on comparative financial statements.)

(ADDITIONAL PARAGRAPH)

In my (our) previous review report dated March 1, 198Y, on the 198X financial statements, I (we) referred to a departure from generally accepted accounting principles because the company carried its land at appraised values. However, as disclosed in note X, the company has restated its 198X financial statements to reflect its land at cost in accordance with generally accepted accounting principles.

Comments:
1. The foregoing illustration is derived from SSARS 2.
2. A *changed reference* may be either a new reference to, or the removal of a prior reference to, a departure from GAAP. Circumstances may subsequently arise, and become known to the accountant, that suggest the need for a changed reference when comparative financial statements are reported on that include the prior year in question. In that event, a separate explanatory paragraph should be added, as in the last paragraph of the foregoing report, disclosing: (*a*) date of prior report; (*b*) circumstances causing the changed reference; and (*c*) if applicable, that the financial statements of the prior period have been changed.

Figure 8-27
Review Report

Comparative Financial Statements: Predecessor Accountant's Compilation or Review Report Not Presented

(ADDITIONAL [LAST] PARAGRAPH OF SUCCESSOR ACCOUNTANT'S REPORT)

I. REVIEW REPORT ISSUED IN PRIOR PERIOD (SSARS 2.18)

The 198X financial statements of XYZ Company were reviewed by other accountants whose report dated March 1, 198Y stated that they were not aware of any material modifications that should be made to those statements in order for them to be in conformity with generally accepted accounting principles.

II. COMPILATION REPORT ISSUED IN PRIOR PERIOD (SSARS 2.19)

The 198X financial statements of XYZ Company were compiled by other accountants whose report dated February 1, 198Y, stated that they did not express an opinion or any other form of assurance on those statements.

Comments:
1.   The reporting principles that apply when the predecessor accountant's report is not reissued have been summarized in Figure 8-5.
2.   The additional last paragraph illustrated in SSARS 2.18 for use if a review report was issued by a predecessor accountant in a prior period refers only to the limited assurance. It would seem that to be properly informative, the paragraph should also state that an opinion was not expressed on the financial statements taken as a whole.

Figure 8-28
Review Report

Supplementary Information Accompanying Basic Financial Statements (Review for Both)

(The three paragraphs of the standard review report may remain intact—unless modified for other reasons—to be followed by the additional paragraph recorded below.)

(ADDITIONAL PARAGRAPH)

The other data accompanying the financial statements, captioned as *Supplementary Information*, are also representations of the management of the XYZ Company and are presented only for supplementary analysis purposes. The data have been subjected to the inquiry and analytical procedures applied in the review of the basic financial statements and, similarly, no opinion as to such data is being expressed. Based on my (our) review, I am (we are) not aware of any material modifications that should be made to the supplementary information.

Comments:

1.   The above report would appear to meet the reporting standards of SSARS 1.43.

2.   If the supplementary information is presented in a separate report on such data, that report should include the content of the above paragraph (appropriately rephrased) and also a statement (as in the standard report) on the nature of the review of the basic financial statements.

Figure 8-29
Review Report

Review of Basic Financial Statements; Compilation
of Supplementary Information

(The three paragraphs of the standard review report may remain intact—unless modified for other reasons—to be followed by the additional paragraph recorded below.)

(ADDITIONAL PARAGRAPH)

The other data accompanying the financial statements, captioned as *Supplementary Information,* are presented only for supplementary analysis purposes. The data have not been subjected to the inquiry and analytical procedures applied in the review of the basic financial statements, but were compiled from information that is the representation of management, without audit or review and, accordingly, I (we) do not express an opinion or any other form of assurance on such data.

Comment. The above report would appear to meet the reporting standards of SSARS 1.43 for the given circumstance.

Figure 8-30
Review Report

Comparative Financial Statements: Prior Period Audited

(SEPARATE PARAGRAPH REFERENCE TO AUDIT REPORT) (SSARS 2)

The financial statements for the year ended December 31, 198X were examined by us (other accountants) and we (they) expressed an unqualified opinion on them in our (their) reported dated March 1, 198Y, but we (they) have not performed any auditing procedures since that date.

Comments:

1.   The foregoing is an illustration of a paragraph to be added to a compilation or review report on current-period financial statements when those of the prior period have been audited. Alternatively, the report on the prior period should be reissued.

2.   The added paragraph should state that the prior-period statements had been examined, specify the date of the previous report, the type of opinion expressed, and reasons for an opinion other than unqualified, and note that no auditing procedures were performed subsequent to the date of the previous report. (SSARS 2.28)

Figure 8-31
Review Report

Statements Prepared on Cash Basis

I (we) have reviewed the accompanying statement of assets and liabilities arising from cash transactions of XYZ Company as of December 31, 198Y, and the related statement of revenue collected and expenses paid for the year then ended, in accordance with standards established by the American Institute of Certified Public Accountants. All information included in these financial statements is the representation of the management (owners) of XYZ Company.

A review consists principally of inquiries of company personnel and analytical procedures applied to financial data. It is substantially less in scope than an examination in accordance with generally accepted auditing standards, the objective of which is the expression of an opinion regarding the financial statements taken as a whole. Accordingly, I (we) do not express such an opinion.

As described in Note X, the Company's policy is to prepare its financial statements on the basis of cash receipts and disbursements; consequently, certain revenue and the related assets are recognized when received rather than when earned, and certain expenses are recognized when paid rather than when the obligation is incurred. Accordingly, the accompanying financial statements are not intended to present financial position and results of operations in conformity with generally accepted accounting principles.

Based on my (our) review, I am (we are) not aware of any material modifications that should be made to the accompanying financial statements in order for them to be in conformity with the basis of accounting described in Note X.

Comments:

1.   This report was prepared on an informal and unofficial basis by the AICPA technical information service. Apparently it adapts and combines the report format for audited financial statements prepared on a cash basis, as illustrated in AU 621.08, with the standard review report.

2.   It also merits reiteration that SSARS also applies to a comprehensive basis of accounting other than generally accepted accounting principles, including the cash basis or income tax basis of accounting. (SSARS 1.4 and later paragraphs.)

Figure 8-32
Review Report

Statements Prepared on Income Tax Basis

I (we) have reviewed the accompanying statement of assets, liabilities and capital—income tax basis—of XYZ Company as of December 31, 198Y and the related statements of revenue and expenses—income tax basis—for the year then ended, in accordance with standards established by the American Institute of Certified Public Accountants. All information included in these financial statements is the representation of the management (owners) of XYZ Company.

A review consists principally of inquiries of company personnel and analytical procedure applied to financial data. It is substantially less in scope than an examination in accordance with generally accepted auditing standards, the objective of which is the expression of an opinion regarding the financial statements taken as a whole. Accordingly, I (we) do not express such an opinion.

As described in Note X, the Company's policy is to prepare its financial statements on the accounting basis used for income tax purposes; consequently, certain revenue and the related assets are recognized when received rather than when earned, and certain expenses are recognized when paid rather than when the obligation is incurred. Accordingly, the accompanying financial statements are not intended to present financial position and results of operations in conformity with generally accepted accounting principles.

Based on my (our) review, I am (we are) not aware of any material modifications that should be made to the accompanying financial statements in order for them to be in conformity with the basis of accounting described in Note X.

Comment. The comments appended to the preceding figure on cash basis statements similarly apply to the report presented above.

CHECKLIST REVIEW GUIDE FOR USE IN REVIEW
ENGAGEMENTS FOR NONPUBLIC ENTITIES

A checklist review guide for use by the engagement partner and any other reviewers on review engagements is shown in Figure 8-33. It is made up of three segments covering the accountant's report, the financial statements, and working papers and other matters. They have been combined as a single review guide, but with differentiated sections, to achieve simplicity in presentation. An integral part of the guide, however, is a fourth section covering financial statement disclosures. Such a guide bearing the title, Financial Statement Disclosures Checklist Reminder and Review Guide, has already been provided in Figure 7-5 for use on audit engagements. However, it is also suitable for use with only slight modifications on review engagements for reminder and review purposes as its title suggests. It is not here reproduced in order to avoid needless repetition. Because of its voluminousness, moreover, the accountant on a review engagement may wish in any event to handle it physically as a separate item, although, as stated, it should be viewed as an integral part of the combined review guide.

Figure 8-33
Review of Financial Statements of Nonpublic
Companies: Accountant's Checklist Review Guide

Client

Period of financial statements

Prepared by   Date   Reviewed by   Date

INSTRUCTIONS

1. This guide, whose proper use and completion is the responsibility of the engagement partner, is designed to assist those persons participating in a final review of the accountant's report, the financial statements, and the working papers. All persons so involved—the preparer responsible for the initial completion of the checklist and any other reviewers including the engagement partner—are expected to undertake a careful review adequate in scope to support the responses and conclusions set forth in this guide.

2. A *No* response is presumed to signify an unsatisfactory condition, and all such responses should be fully explained, substantiated, and commented on in the comment section at the end of the guide. The manner in which the matter has been remedied or resolved, the basis for the decision, and partner approval of the action taken, should similarly be recorded in the comment section and keyed to the item in question.

3. The comment section may also be used for any other comments that may be needed or helpful in accomplishing a proper review, but the details and approvals relative to the disposition of any questions and problems must be clearly noted.

4. If a standard or guide relating to a listed item has been provided in the AICPA's Statements on Standards for Accounting and Review Services (SSARS), appropriate parenthetical reference to the statement will be made; for example, the reference SSARS 2.12 would signify Statement No. 2, paragraph 12. Where the accountant using this guide has any doubt about the full range of responsibilities in a particular area, the original reference sources should be consulted.

CHECKLIST

	Yes	No	NA

I. Accountant's Report

1. Cognizance has been taken of the following basic principles applicable to reporting on unaudited financial statements of a nonpublic entity: (SSARS 1.1)

(a) The report can only be based on either a compilation or a review of financial statements.

(b) A report must be issued whenever a compilation or review engagement is completed in accordance with the requirements and provisions of SSARS.

(c) Neither a report nor the financial statements may be submitted unless the compilation or review engagement is completed and in accordance with the requirements and provisions of SSARS.

2. The accountant is independent with respect to the client. In making this judgment, which takes in the accounting firm and its personnel assigned to the engagement, all pertinent facts and circumstances are to be considered, as well as the specific criteria stated in the AICPA Code of Professional Ethics. A review report should not be issued if the accountant is not independent, but a compilation report may be issued despite a lack of independence provided compilation standards are adhered to. (SSARS 1.38)

3. The date of the accountant's report is the same as the date of completion of the accountant's inquiry and analytical procedures. (SSARS 1.33)

4. The report has been addressed to the proper party (e.g., company, board of directors, or stockholders) as indicated by the individual engagement.

5. The report is in the standard form for a review and states that:

(a)   A review was performed in accordance with AICPA standards and identifies the financial statements reviewed. (SSARS 1.32) It is permissible to issue a review report on one financial statement like the balance sheet, and not on other related financial statements, providing the scope of the review has not been restricted. (SSARS 1.37)

(b)   The financial statements and the included information are the representations of the management (owners). (SSARS 1.32)

(c)   A review consists principally of inquiries of company personnel and analytical procedures applied to financial data. (SSARS 1.32)

(d)   A review is substantially less in scope than an audit, the objective of which is the expression of an opinion regarding the financial statements taken as a whole, and therefore an opinion is not expressed. (SSARS 1.32) This constitutes a disclaimer of opinion.

(e)   The accountant is not aware of any material modifications that should be made to the financial statements in order for them to be in conformity with generally accepted accounting principles, other than those modifications, if any, mentioned in the report. (SSARS 1.32) This statement is referred to in SSARS No. 1 as expressing "limited assurance."

6.   Each page of the financial statements contains a reference such as "See Accountant's Review Report." (SSARS 1.34) The reference should be clearly and prominently displayed. If desired, the legend on each page of the financial statements might read: "Unaudited" or "Unaudited—See Accountant's Review Report."

7.   Any words or phrases in the accountant's report, the financial statements, and working papers have been avoided that might indicate or suggest that an audit was performed. Examples of such expressions are: audit, auditing, auditor, examination, auditing procedures, audit fees, accrued auditing expense.

8.   The review of the financial statements:

(a)   Was made in accordance with the standards, requirements, and provisions of SSARS.

(b)   Was not restricted by the client nor were there any other limitations on our ability to conduct a proper review.

(c)   Has been properly completed and included the inquiry and analytical procedures considered necessary to achieve, and to express in the report, the limited assurance identified with a review.

9.   If the accountant was originally engaged to conduct an audit in accordance with generally accepted auditing standards but, before the completion of the examination, has been requested by the client to change the engagement to a review (or compilation) of financial statements, before agreeing to the change consideration has been given to:

(a)   The reason given for the request. A change in circumstances so that an audit is no longer needed, or an honest misunderstanding by the client of the nature of an audit, may be acceptable reasons. (SSARS 1.45, .46)

(b)   The possibility that a change because of restriction(s) in the audit scope by the client or by circumstances may signify that information in question may be incorrect, incomplete, or otherwise unsatisfactory. (SSARS 1.47)

(c)   The fact that a review (or compilation) report should not ordinarily be issued if the client, during the original audit engagement, has prohibited the accountant from corresponding with the entity's legal counsel or refused to sign a representation letter. (SSARS 1.47)

(d)   The propriety of accepting a change in the engagement if the auditing procedures are substantially complete or the cost to complete the audit engagement is relatively insignificant. (SSARS 1.48)

(e)   The requirement that, if the change to a review (or compilation) engagement is justified and the standards applicable to such an engagement are adhered to, the review report should not make reference to the original engagement, the auditing procedures performed, or the scope limitations, if any, that resulted in changing the engagement. (SSARS 1.49)

10.   If the accountant was originally engaged to conduct a review of the financial statements but is unable to perform the inquiry and analytical procedures necessary to achieve the limited assurance that a proper review is intended to provide; and he has been requested by the client or is otherwise planning to submit a compilation report; consideration has been given to:

(a)   Whether the circumstances underlying the incomplete review also preclude the issuance of a compilation report. (SSARS 1.36)

(b)   Any matters similar to those noted in the item above regarding a change from an audit to a compilation or review engagement. (SSARS 1.36 and 1.44–.49)

11.   The report does not describe any procedures the accountant might have performed before or during the review engagement or in connection with a compilation of the financial statements. (SSARS 1.32)

12.   If the financial statements are prepared on a comprehensive basis of accounting other than GAAP, the report so indicates.

13.   The financial statements appear to be in conformity with GAAP including informative disclosures as required by GAAP.

14.   If there is awareness of a material departure from generally accepted accounting principles and the financial statements are not revised:

(a)   The standard review report has been modified to disclose the departure, including the effects on the financial statements if such effects have been determined by management or otherwise known. (SSARS 1.40) If the effects are not known, the accountant is not required to determine what they are, but the report must state that a determination was not made. (SSARS 1.40)

(b)   If such modification of the report is not adequate (perhaps because of the magnitude, quantity or pervasiveness of the deficiencies and the impact upon the financial statements taken as a whole, or for any other reason), the following action is being taken: withdrawal from the engagement and withholding of any further services with respect to the financial statements. (SSARS 1.41)

15. Consideration has been given to introducing a separate paragraph in the report to emphasize a matter of importance (apart from any accounting deficiency) regarding the financial statements. (SSARS 1.40)

16. Material uncertainties affecting the financial statements as well as inconsistencies in the application of accounting principles, if applicable, are disclosed in the financial statements. If so disclosed, there is normally no need to modify the standard report. (SSARS 1.40)

17. If the basic financial statements are accompanied by information presented for supplementary analysis purposes, the degree of responsibility assumed with respect to such data is clearly indicated in the report. (SSARS 1.43)

18. If reference is made to the work of other accountants, the magnitude of the portion of the financial statements audited or reviewed by them is indicated. (SSARS 1.27)

19. Note has been taken of the guidance in AU 561, also relevant to review engagements, to be followed when there is awareness, subsequent to the date of the accountant's report, that facts may have existed at that date which might have led him to believe that information supplied by the entity was incorrect, incomplete, or otherwise unsatisfactory. (SSARS 1.42)

20. If the review report covers comparative financial statements, the reporting standards set forth in SSARS No. 2 have been complied with. (See listing, in Figure 8-5, of reporting principles related to a review in which comparative financial statements are to be reported on.)

21. The working papers contain adequate support, consistent with the review character of the engagement, for all matters mentioned in the accountant's report.

22. The accountant's report has been prepared in accordance with the standards and provisions of SSARS. (Note should be taken of the injunction that if an accountant performs more than one service, for example, compilation and audit or compilation and review, he should issue a report appropriate for the highest level of service. (SSARS 1.5) Starting with the highest level, the order is: audit, review, compilation.)

II. Financial Statements

23. The financial statements reflect:

(a) The precise legal name of the entity.

(b) Clear identification of the several financial statements. (SSARS 1.4)

(c) Correct dates and periods covered.

24.   The financial statements have been read analytically and, based on the reading, the inquiry and analytical procedures performed, and the engagement review procedures undertaken, appear to:

(a)   Conform with generally accepted accounting principles (or, if applicable, other comprehensive basis of accounting).

(b)   Include all necessary informative disclosures of material matters whose disclosure is necessary for the statements to be fair and not misleading.

(c)   Have clearly worded and adequate notes appropriately referenced to the basic financial statements.

(d)   Reflect proper form, classification, content, and terminology.

25.   We are not aware of any accounting principles and methods (required to be disclosed) or of any material uncertainties that have not been disclosed in the financial statements.

26.   The financial statement disclosures checklist reminder and review guide (Figure 7-5, as modified) has been prepared and reviewed; any applicable matters set forth in the guide as requiring disclosure in the financial statements have in fact been disclosed; and all questions and initially unresolved matters commented on in the guide have been satisfactorily resolved.

27.   The financial statements have been checked for intra- and interstatement consistency and for mathematical accuracy.

28.   The financial statement accounts and balances have been traced to and correspond to the adjusted balances per the working trial balance, and to other applicable information contained in the working papers.

29.   An analytical review of the financial statements has been made. Any significant variations in account balances, relationships, trends and other important factors with respect to current and comparable prior periods, budgets, forecasts, and industry data have been satisfactorily explained and written up in the working papers.

III.   Working Papers and Other Matters

30.   All working papers are clearly identified as to client, title and purpose, and financial statement date or period.

31.   Working papers are properly indexed and filed.

32.   Clear explanations are provided for any symbols used.

33.   Initials or signatures of both preparer and reviewer, as well as dates of such prepration and review, appear on all working papers including program and review guides.

34.   Working papers bear clear evidence of review, as appropriate for the individual item in question, by:

(a)   Accountant in charge of the engagement.

(b)   Engagement manager.

(c)   Engagement partner.

35. The basis for, and approval (at the appropriate supervisory level) of, significant modifications of the planning and program guide and the included procedures, are noted and documented in the working papers.

36. The working papers clearly describe:

(a) The inquiry and analytical review procedures undertaken and the matters so reviewed.

(b) Names of client officers and personnel to whom inquiries were directed, the nature of the information so obtained, and the documents or other materials reviewed in connection with such inquiries.

(c) Any unusual matters considered during the review, as well as their disposition.

(d) Discussions with the client and senior officials on troublesome, questionable, complex, or otherwise significant matters.

(e) Information gained or developed regarding the nature of the business and its transactions, industry business and accounting practices, type and condition of the accounting records, and qualifications of accounting personnel.

37. There are no indications in the working papers or otherwise of client restrictions on the conduct of the review engagement.

38. The adjustments to the general ledger accounts appear to be proper, are satisfactorily supported in the working papers, have been accepted by the client, and have been posted to the working trial balance.

39. With respect to any of the following conditions—fraud, defalcations, significant errors, irregularities, illegal acts or related party transactions:

(a) There is no indication in the working papers or otherwise that any have come to our attention.

(b) If any have come to our attention, the circumstances have been satisfactorily reviewed and dealt with, the relevant working paper reference being noted in the comment section of this guide.

40. A properly prepared engagement letter signed by the client is included in the working papers.

41. The terms of the engagement letter have been complied with.

42. Properly prepared representation letters signed by the client are included in the working papers.

43. All "to do" notes, points to be cleared, and matters noted for further consultation and discussion with client or engagement supervisors and engagement partner have been satisfactorily cleared and resolved and so noted in the working papers.

44. Time budgets have been prepared, completed, and reviewed for each phase of the engagement, and significant differences between actual and budgeted data have been satisfactorily explained and clarified.

45. A memorandum containing helpful suggestions for use on the next engagement has been properly prepared, approved, and included in the working papers.

46. The engagement has been satisfactorily completed in conformity

with the standards and requirements of the AICPA's SSARS, and the review report may be processed and issued.

Comments on Items Listed Above

(Record below comments on *No* responses or on any other matters to be clarified or resolved. A clear indication of how the matter was resolved should also be noted. Comments are to be keyed to the pertinent checklist item, dated, and initialed by the person recording the comment; notations as to their disposition are to be initialed and dated by the engagement partner.)

_____

_____

REVIEW OF INTERIM FINANCIAL INFORMATION

SAS 24 (AU 721) provides guidance for the independent accountant in engagements devoted to a review of interim financial information standing alone (including interim financial statements) of a public entity, or a review of interim financial information included in a note to audited financial statements of a public or nonpublic entity.

The procedures for making a review, as prescribed by SAS 24, consist primarily of inquiries and analytical review procedures, and are essentially the same as those that are described in SSARS 1 for conducting a review of the annual or interim financial statements of nonpublic entities. If any difference can be said to exist it would be found mainly with respect to the items noted below. (In this connection, SAS 24, AU 721.06, should be compared with SSARS 1.27.)

1. *Corporate minutes.* According to SAS, the minutes are to be *read*, while SSARS refers to *inquiries* regarding actions taken at such meetings. However, Figure 8-17, which presents an engagement planning and program guide for a review of financial statements of a nonpublic entity, indicates that the accountant will probably wish to have the minutes made available for reading.

2. *Client representation letter.* Obtaining such a letter is an SAS 24 requirement, whereas SSARS 1 (Appendix D) refers to the procedure as being advisable. In Figure 8-17, it is assumed that the accountant will deem it necessary to obtain representation letters from management.

3. *System of internal accounting control.* By SAS 24 standards, the accountant is expected to inquire concerning any significant changes in the system of internal accounting control in order to ascertain the effect on the preparation of interim financial information. The emphasis is upon *change* inasmuch as the accountant presumably became familiar with the system of internal accounting control as it existed during the prior annual engagement. An SSARS 1 review, however (see para. 29), does not encompass a study and evaluation of internal accounting control. Inquiry with respect to the system of internal accounting control, however, is included as a procedure in Figure 8-17, but only for the limited objective—similar to that stated in SAS 24—of gaining a better understanding of the impact of the controls on the quality and reliability of the records and, hence, on the preparation of financial statements—interim as well as year-end.

It would make for needless repetition to provide program and review guides in this book for SAS 24 engagements when the accountant can utilize for that purpose, the following guides that have already been provided for SSARS review engagements: Figure 8-17, Engagement Planning and Program Guide, and Figure 8-33, Checklist Review Guide. In fact, as previously explained, the guides have been constructed to provide for the two types of engagements, and any additional adaptation of the guides would be quite minimal. A reporting standards guide for review of interim financial information, however, is provided in Figure 8-34, based on the guidance contained in SAS 24, and this is followed by illustrative reports for use on such engagements.

Figure 8-34
Reporting Standards Guide for
Review of Interim Financial Information

This guide should be used in conjunction with careful reference to, and a close reading of, provisions of Statement on Auditing Standards (SAS) No. 24 (AU 721). SAS 24 applies to reviews of interim financial information, standing alone, of public entities, and to reviews of interim financial information included in a note to audited financial statements of a public or nonpublic entity. While the guide reflects both the letter and spirit of the statement, it does not purport to provide a complete summary of the reporting standards contained therein.

Information Presented Other Than in a Note to
Audited Financial Statements

1.   An accountant may consent to the use of his name and the inclusion of his report in a written communication by the client setting forth interim financial information if he has reviewed the interim financial information in accordance with the requirements of SAS No. 24. (AU 721.16) The accountant may not consent to the use of his name unless his report is also included in the communication. (AU 721.23) An accountant may, however, undertake a review engagement by arrangement with the client in which a review is made but no report is to be issued.

2.   The accountant should not consent to the use of his name if restrictions on the scope of a review prevent him from completing a review. Such restrictions may be the result of client restrictions or such circumstances as timing of the review procedures, inadequate accounting records, or material weaknesses in internal accounting control affecting the records and/or the preparation of the interim financial information in conformity with GAAP. (AU 721.16) The circumstances relating to material weaknesses in internal accounting control should be discussed with senior management and the board of directors or its audit committee. (AU 721.10)

3.   The report should be dated as of the date of completion of the review. (AU 721.17)

4.   The report should be addressed, as appropriate in the circumstances, to the company, the board of directors, or the stockholders. (AU 721.17)

5.   The spirit and essence of the fourth reporting standard of the generally accepted auditing standards also applies to reporting on interim financial information. The standard requires that the accountant indicate clearly in his report the character of the work done by him and the

degree of responsibility he is assuming. A disclaimer of opinion must therefore be expressed in a review engagement. (AU 721.17)

6. In addition to the disclaimer, limited assurance is expressed that the accountant is not aware of any material modifications that should be made to the financial information for it to conform with GAAP. (AU 721.17)

7. Each page of the interim financial information should be marked as "*Unaudited.*"

8. In addition to expressing the disclaimer and limited assurance, the review report should (AU 721.17):

(a) State that a review was made in accordance with AICPA standards.

(b) Identify the financial information reviewed.

(c) Explain what is meant by a review and that it is not an audit.

9. If the accountant is aware that the interim financial information reflects a material departure from GAAP (including inadequate disclosure) and the presentation is not revised, the standard review report must be modified to disclose and describe the departure and, if practicable, the effects on the financial information. (AU 721.21, .22)

10. In determining whether adequate disclosures have been made, the accountant should be aware that the minimum disclosure requirements of APB Opinion No. 28 for interim financial information are considerably less than for annual financial statements. Moreover, as stated in APB 28, there is a presumption that users of summarized interim financial information will have read the latest published annual report including the disclosures required by GAAP. (AU 721.22)

11. The standard report need not normally be modified to disclose a material uncertainty or an inconsistency in the application of accounting principles if such disclosures have been made in the interim financial information or statements. However, a change to an accounting principle that does not conform with GAAP must be disclosed in the accountant's report. (AU 721.20)

Information Presented in a Note to Audited Financial Statements

Regulation S-X of the SEC requires certain companies to include in audited financial statements a note that may be designated as "unaudited," containing selected interim financial information. Other companies too may choose to include such a note in their audited financial statements. (AU 721.24)

12. When interim financial information is presented in a note to audited financial statements and the note is marked as "unaudited", the accountant's report on review of such interim information need not accompany the report on the audited financial statements. Moreover, the

audit report need not be modified to make reference to the note, inasmuch as the note is not required for the fairness of the financial statements. (AU 721.26)

13. However, the accountant's report on the audited financial statements should be expanded if, with respect to the interim financial information (AU 721.27, .28):

(a) Scope of review was restricted.

(b) The information is not in conformity with GAAP.

(c) The information was not reviewed, unless that is revealed in the note.

(d) The note is not marked as "unaudited."

(e) The note states that a review was made but does not explain that a review is different from an audit, and does not express a disclaimer with respect to the interim financial information. But, as stated above, if the note is simply designated as "unaudited" and does not refer to a review, the audit report need not be expanded.

Figure 8-35
Report on Interim Financial Information

Standard Report (AU 721)

We have made a review of (describe the information or statements reviewed) ABC Company and consolidated subsidiaries as of September 30, 198Y, and for the three-month and nine-month periods then ended, in accordance with standards established by the American Institute of Certified Public Accountants.

A review of interim financial information consists principally of obtaining an understanding of the system for the preparation of interim financial information, applying analytical review procedures to financial data, and making inquiries of persons responsible for financial and accounting matters. It is substantially less in scope than an examination in accordance with generally accepted auditing standards, the objective of which is the expression of an opinion regarding the financial statements taken as a whole. Accordingly, we do not express such an opinion.

Based on our review, we are not aware of any material modifications that should be made to the accompanying financial (information or statements) for them to be in conformity with generally accepted accounting principles.

Comment. If the review also covers a prior period included in the report, the first sentence might read:

"We have made . . . subsidiaries as of September 30, 198X and 198Y, and for the three-month and nine-month periods then ended . . . "

Figure 8-36
Report on Interim Financial Information

Divided Responsibility with Another Accountant (AU 721)

We have made a review of (describe the information or statements reviewed) of ABC Company and consolidated subsidiaries as of September 30, 198Y, and for the three-month and nine-month periods then ended, in accordance with standards established by the American Institute of Certified Public Accountants. We were furnished with the report of other accountants on their review of the interim financial information of the ADE subsidiary, whose total assets and revenues constitute 20 percent and 22 percent, respectively, of the related consolidated totals.

A review of interim financial information consists principally of obtaining an understanding of the system for the preparation of interim financial information, applying analytical review procedures to financial data, and making inquiries of persons responsible for financial and accounting matters. It is substantially less in scope than an examination in accordance with generally accepted auditing standards, the objective of which is the expression of an opinion regarding the financial statements taken as a whole. Accordingly, we do not express such an opinion.

Based on our review and the report of other accountants, we are not aware of any material modifications that should be made to the accompanying financial (information or statements) for them to be in conformity with generally accepted accounting principles.

Figure 8-37
Report on Interim Financial Information

Departure from GAAP Disclosed (AU 721)

(EXPLANATORY THIRD PARAGRAPH)

Based on information furnished us by management, we believe that the Company has excluded from property and debt in the accompanying balance sheet certain lease obligations that should be capitalized in order to conform with generally accepted accounting principles. This information indicates that if these lease obligations were capitalized at September 30, 198Y, property would be increased by $ . . . , and long-term debt by $ . . . , and net income and earnings per share would be increased (decreased) by $ . . . , $ . . . , $ . . . , and $ . . . , respectively, for the three-month and nine-month periods then ended.

(CONCLUDING PARAGRAPH)

Based on our review, with the exception of the matter(s) described in the preceding paragraph(s), we are not aware of any material modifications that should be made to the accompanying financial (information or statements) for them to be in conformity with generally accepted accounting principles.

Comment. For form of first two paragraphs, see standard report for review of interim financial information.

Figure 8-38
Report on Interim Financial Information

Inadequate Disclosure Reported (AU 721)

(EXPLANATORY THIRD PARAGRAPH)

Management has informed us that the Company is presently contesting deficiencies in federal income taxes proposed by the Internal Revenue Service for the years 19XX through 19XX in the aggregate amount of approximately $ . . . , and that the extent of the Company's liability, if any, and the effect on the accompanying (information or statements) are not determinable at this time. The (information or statements) fail to disclose these matters, which we believe are required to be disclosed in conformity with generally accepted accounting principles.

(CONCLUDING PARAGRAPH)

Based on our review, with the exception of the matter(s) described in the preceding paragraph(s), we are not aware of any material modifications that should be made to the accompanying financial (information or statements) for them to be in conformity with generally accepted accounting principles.

Comment.   As noted in SAS No. 24, the minimum disclosure requirements of APB No. 28 relating to interim financial reporting are considerably less exacting than for annual reports, and this should be considered by the accountant in making a judgment regarding the adequacy of disclosures in interim financial information reviewed by him.

Figure 8-39
Comment in Audited Annual Report on Note Relating
to Interim Financial Information (AU 721)

(ADDITIONAL PARAGRAPH)

Note X, "Unaudited Interim Financial Information," contains information that we did not audit and, accordingly, we do not express an opinion on the information. We attempted but were unable to make a review of such interim information in accordance with standards established by the American Institute of Certified Public Accountants because we believe that the Company's system for preparing interim financial information does not provide an adequate basis to enable us to complete such a review.

Comment. Ordinarily, the auditor need make no reference in his report on audited annual financial statements to the note that has been marked as "Unaudited Interim Financial Information." However, comment is required if the review scope has been restricted, as in the above paragraph, or if the interim financial information departs from GAAP.

UNAUDITED FINANCIAL STATEMENTS OF PUBLIC ENTITIES

The standards to be followed by an accountant who is associated with unaudited financial statements of a public entity are provided in SAS No. 26, except that the requirements governing the accountant's review of unaudited interim financial information presented by a public company, as discussed previously in this chapter, are covered in SAS No. 24. SAS No. 26 supersedes those sections of SAS No. 1 and SAS No. 15 corresponding to AU 516, 517, 518 and 505.13-.15.

An accountant who is associated with unaudited financial statements of a public entity (see definitions of "association" and of "unaudited financial statements" in Figure 8-40) is not precluded thereby from undertaking some procedures that may be similar to those undertaken in either a review or an audit engagement. Since engagements in which the financial statements for a public entity are neither reviewed nor audited may vary considerably in the amount of work undertaken—ranging from no procedures whatsoever (except for reading the financial statements for obvious errors) to a scope falling short of either a review or an audit—it would be meaningless to include in this book a suggested engagement planning and program guide for use on "unaudited" engagements for public companies. However, a reporting standards guide for such engagements would be useful, and one is presented as Figure 8-40. Following the guide, illustrative reports on unaudited financial statements of public entities are presented.

Figure 8-40
Reporting Standards Guide for
Unaudited Financial Statements of Public Entities

(Note: This is an interpretive guide and does not purport to present a complete summary of the applicable reporting standards. It should be used in conjunction with a careful reference to and reading of the relevant AICPA pronouncements. Paragraph numbers cited refer to corresponding paragraphs of SAS No. 26.)

1.   Underlying the standards that follow is the fourth reporting standard of the generally accepted auditing standards which states, in effect, that whenever an accountant is associated with financial statements, his report should indicate clearly the character of the work done by him, if any, and the degree of responsibility he is assuming (i.e., either the expression of an opinion or a disclaimer). (para. 1)

2.   An accountant may be associated with audited or unaudited financial statements. An association exists when:

(a)   The accountant has allowed his name to be used in a report, document, or written communication containing the financial statements; or

(b)   Has submitted to the client or others financial statements that he has prepared or assisted in preparing even though his name is not appended. (para. 3)

3.   Financial statements are audited if the auditing procedures undertaken by the auditor were sufficient to permit him to report on them in the manner described in SAS No. 2 (AU 509), *Reports on Audited Financial Statements.* The failure to conform with this definition would cause financial statements to be characterized as unaudited; a *review* of unaudited interim financial statements of a public company must meet the standards of SAS No. 24, except that when a public entity (in a rare circumstance) does not have its annual financial statements audited, a review of either its annual or interim financial statements must conform with the requirements of SSARS Nos. 1 and 2. An accountant associated with the unaudited financial statements of a nonpublic company must comply with the standards of SSARS Nos. 1 and 2 which limit reports on such statements to either a *compilation* or a *review*. (para. 4)

4.   The line of demarcation between audited financial statements on which a disclaimer of opinion should be expressed because of a significant scope limitation (AU 509.45–.47), and unaudited financial statements, is sometimes not clear. Considerable judgment must be exercised by the accountant in deciding whether his disclaimer is to apply to financial statements identified as unaudited. The following considerations are relevant:

(a) The original purpose of the engagement and whether it was agreed upon or understood that the examination was to be conducted in accordance with generally accepted auditing standards and was to include all auditing procedures considered necessary in the circumstances.

(b) Whether the examination was in fact conducted in accordance with generally accepted auditing standards.

(c) A reasonable and acceptable change in circumstances and an understanding reached with the client that the original purpose of the engagement is to be changed (e.g., from audited to unaudited financial statements).

(d) Audit restrictions deliberately imposed by the client or acquiesced in by the auditor.

5. If the accountant is associated with unaudited financial statements that he has not audited or reviewed he must (para. 5):

(a) Issue a disclaimer of opinion stating that the financial statements are unaudited and accordingly he does not express an opinion on them. This disclaimer may accompany the statements or be placed on them.

(b) In addition, mark each page of the financial statements clearly and conspicuously as *unaudited*.

(c) Not describe any procedures he may actually have employed; to do so could mislead the user, causing him to believe that the statements have been audited or reviewed. In any event, when a disclaimer of the type described is issued, the accountant has no responsibility to apply any procedures beyond reading the financial statements for obvious errors, although he is not precluded from doing so.

6. If the accountant is aware that his name is included in a written communication of a public entity prepared by the client which contains financial statements that have not been audited or reviewed, he should request that the client: (a) remove his name; or (b) mark the financial statements as unaudited and note that an accountant's opinion is not being expressed. (para. 6)

7. If an accountant is not independent, the financial statements are, for that very reason, unaudited inasmuch as the auditing standards require that the auditor conducting an examination in accordance with AU 509 be independent. His report must, therefore, include, in addition to the disclaimer, a statement that he is not independent. (para. 8–10) The procedures performed must not be described nor may the reason be given for lack of independence.

8. In the event the unaudited financial statements are not in conformity with generally accepted accounting principles including disclosure of material matters required to be disclosed by GAAP (para. 11–13):

(a) The accountant should encourage the client to revise the financial statements. It should be noted, however, that when SAS 26 refers to

GAAP, the term also includes another comprehensive basis of accounting (such as the cash basis), but the basis should be identified in the disclaimer report and described in a note to financial statements. (para. 7)

(b) But if the financial statements are not revised, the disclaimer should include a description of the departure from GAAP and, if practicable, the effect on the financial statements or a statement to the effect that the impact of the departure on the financial statements was not determinable.

(c) Necessary disclosures that have not been made in the financial statements should be included in the accountant's disclaimer report. But if it is not feasible to include all such disclosures—especially if substantially all required disclosures have been omitted by the client—that should be indicated in the report.

(d) If the client refuses to accept the disclaimer report with disclosures of departure from GAAP and also refuses to revise the financial statements, the accountant should refuse to be associated with the statements and consider withdrawing from the engagement.

(e) If the accountant believes that the financial statements are false and misleading even though appropriate disclosures were to be made in the report regarding departures from GAAP, he should refuse to be associated with the financial statements and take other appropriate action.

9. When financial statements presented in comparative form are audited and unaudited;

(a) The unaudited financial statements should be clearly marked as *unaudited*. (para. 15)

(b) The report on the prior period should be reissued or, equally acceptable, the report on the current period should describe in a separate paragraph the responsibility (type of opinion, etc.) assumed in the prior-period report. (para. 15)

(c) The separate paragraph of the current report (if that alternative is used) should provide the following information when the prior period has been audited: that an examination was performed in the prior period; date of previous report, type of opinion previously expressed and reasons for an opinion that was other than unqualified; and that no auditing procedures were performed after the prior-period report. (para. 16)

(d) The separate paragraph of the current report (if that alternative is used) should provide the following information when the prior-period statements have not been audited: description of service performed; date of prior-period report; material modifications noted in that report; if a public company, a disclaimer of opinion in the required form for unaudited statements; if a nonpublic company, a disclaimer of opinion and other data similar to the form required for reports on compilation or review of financial statements. (para. 17)

10. If unaudited financial statements are presented with audited

financial statements in comparative form in documents filed with the SEC, the unaudited statements should be clearly marked as *unaudited* and should not be referred to in the auditor's report. (para. 14)

11. Even though the accountant may in fact not be aware of any departures from GAAP, a disclaimer of opinion should not be contradicted by giving "negative assurance" (that is, by the assertion that he is not aware of departures from GAAP) except where such negative assurance is permitted by AICPA standards (para. 18). Such negative assurance is permitted, subject to specified limitations, in letters to underwriters (para. 19) and in connection with acquisition agreements (para. 20). A form of negative assurance is permitted in reviews of interim financial information of public entities (SAS 24) and in reviews of financial statements of nonpublic entities (SSARS 1).

Figure 8-41
Reporting on Unaudited Financial
Statements of Public Entities

Disclaimer of Opinion in Standard Form (SAS 26)

The accompanying balance sheet of X Company as of December 31, 198Y, and the related statements of income, retained earnings, and changes in financial position for the year then ended were not audited by us and, accordingly, we do not express an opinion on them.

Comments.

1. In a report containing a disclaimer on unaudited financial statements, the disclaimer may accompany the statements or can be recorded on their face.

2. Each page of those statements should be clearly and conspicuously marked as unaudited.

3. No mention should be made of any procedures performed (SAS 26, para. 5).

Figure 8-42
Reporting on Unaudited Financial
Statements of Public Entities

Disclaimer of Opinion: Accountant
Not Independent (SAS 26)

We are not independent with respect to XYZ Company, and the accompanying balance sheet as of December 31, 198Y, and the related statements of income, retained earnings, and changes in financial position for the year then ended were not audited by us and, accordingly, we do not express an opinion on them.

Comment. Neither the reasons for lack of independence nor any procedures performed should be described (SAS 26, para. 10).

Figure 8-43
Reporting on Unaudited Financial
Statements of Public Entities

Disclaimer of Opinion: Financial
Statements Prepared on Cash Basis (SAS 26)

The accompanying statement of assets and liabilities resulting from cash transactions of XYZ Corporation as of December 31, 198Y, and the related statement of revenues collected and expenses paid during the year then ended were not audited by us and, accordingly, we do not express an opinion on them.

Figure 8-44
Reporting on Unaudited Financial
Statements of Public Entities

Comparative Financial Statements:
Prior Period Audited (SAS 26)

(SEPARATE PARAGRAPH IN REPORT ON CURRENT PERIOD)

The financial statements for the year ended December 31, 198X were examined by us (other accountants) and we (they) expressed an unqualified opinion on them in our (their) report dated March 1, 198Y, but we (they) have not performed any auditing procedures since that date.

Comment.   This added paragraph in the report on the current period includes the information required by SAS 26, para. 16.

Figure 8-45
Reporting on Comparative Audited and Unaudited
Financial Statements

Current Period Audited; Prior Period Unaudited (SAS 26)

Note: Applicable to nonpublic entities; for public entities, see comment below.

SEPARATE PARAGRAPH IN REPORT ON CURRENT PERIOD

PRIOR PERIOD REVIEWED

The 198X financial statements were reviewed by us (other accountants) and our (their) report thereon, dated March 1, 198Y, stated we (they) were not aware of any material modifications that should be made to those statements for them to be in conformity with generally accepted accounting principles. However, a review is substantially less in scope than an audit and does not provide a basis for the expression of an opinion on the financial statements taken as a whole.

PRIOR PERIOD COMPILED

The 198X financial statements were compiled by us (other accountants) and our (their) report thereon, dated March 1, 198Y, stated we (they) did not audit or review those financial statements and, accordingly, express no opinion or other form of assurance on them.

Comments:
1. In the case of a public company, the separate paragraph should include a disclaimer in the standard form (SAS 26, para. 17)
2. See SSARS 2, paragraph 28, on reporting on comparative financial statements of nonpublic entities when the prior period has been audited but the current period has been compiled or reviewed.

Index